✉ In Volume 4 you wrote that you wanted to doodle on a dog. Please feel free to doodle on our dog (actually, a photo of him) to your heart's content! His name is Chaamii (but we call him "Tome.")

Monkey Lover ♡,
Shizuoka Prefecture

⊕ Thank you very much. I've taken it upon myself to make Tome very handsome. Animals in nature evolve all sorts of protective coloring. For example, a dog that lives in a field of sunflowers might evolve these markings to conceal it from its enemies. The ways of nature are indeed mysterious. Do you like it, Monkey Lover ♡?

Eiichiro Oda began his manga career at the age of 17, when his one-shot cowboy manga **Wanted!** won second place in the coveted Tezuka manga awards. Oda went on to work as an assistant to some of the biggest manga artists in the industry, including Nobuhiro Watsuki, before winning the Hop Step Award for new artists. His pirate adventure **One Piece**, which debuted in **Weekly Shonen Jump** in 1997, quickly became one of the most popular manga in Japan.

ONE PIECE VOL. 5
EAST BLUE PART 5

SHONEN JUMP Manga Edition

This volume contains material that was originally published in
English in **SHONEN JUMP** #18–22.

STORY AND ART BY EIICHIRO ODA

English Adaptation/Lance Caselman
Translation/Naoko Amemiya
Touch-up Art & Lettering/Mark McMurray, Wayne Truman
Graphics & Cover Design/Sean Lee
Editors/Megan Bates, Shaenon K. Garrity

Printed in the U.S.A.

Published by VIZ Media, LLC
P.O. Box 77010
San Francisco, CA 94107

11
First printing, October 2004
Eleventh printing, September 2014

www.viz.com

THE WORLD'S
MOST POPULAR MANGA
SHONEN JUMP
www.shonenjump.com

SHONEN JUMP MANGA

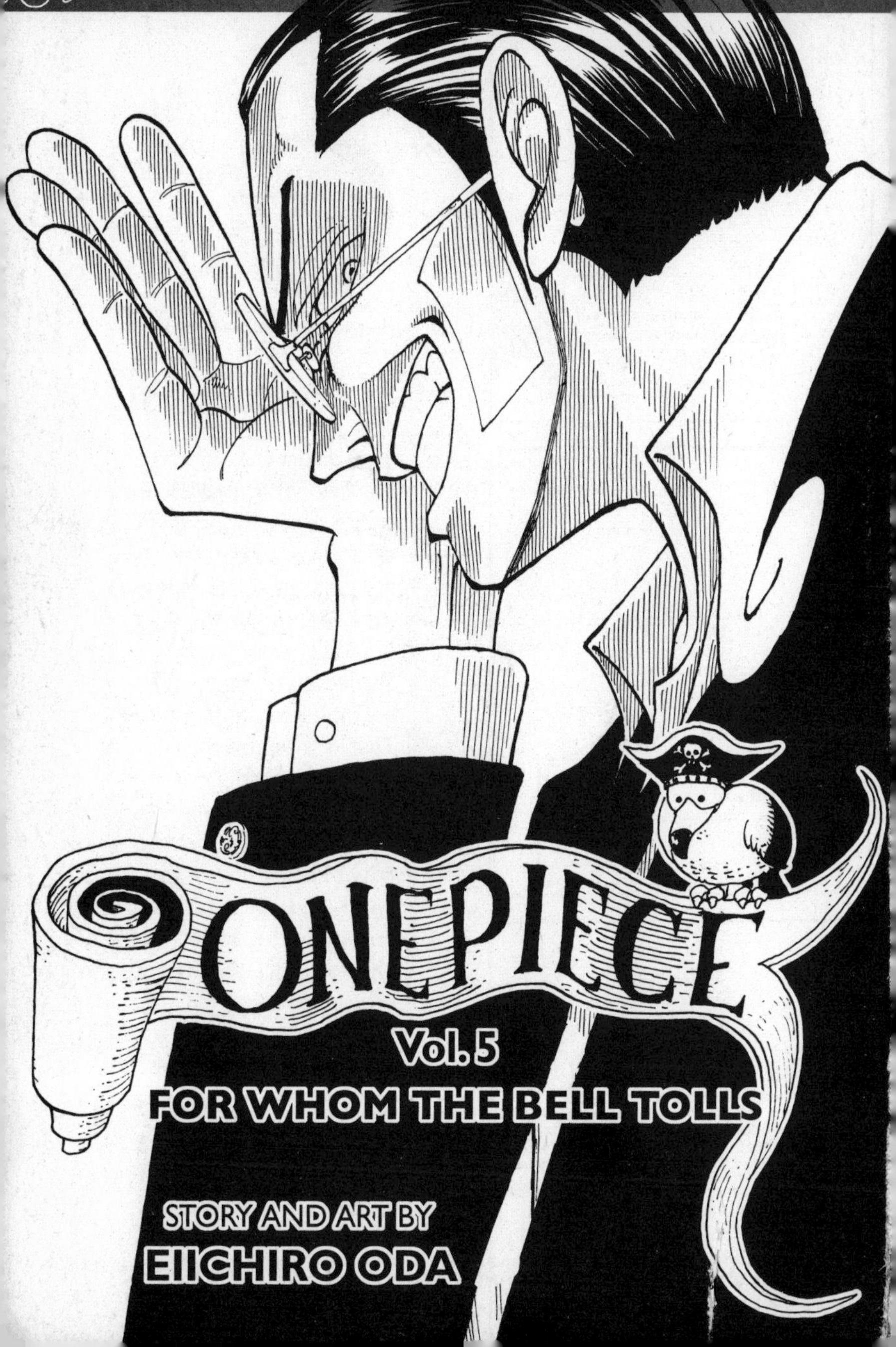

ONE PIECE

Vol. 5

FOR WHOM THE BELL TOLLS

STORY AND ART BY

EIICHIRO ODA

THE STORY OF ONE PIECE

Volume 5

Monkey D. Luffy started out as just a kid with a dream – and that dream was to become the greatest pirate in history! Stirred by the tales of pirate "Red-Haired" Shanks, Luffy vowed to become a pirate himself. That was before the enchanted Devil Fruit gave Luffy the power to stretch like rubber, at the cost of being unable to swim – a serious handicap for an aspiring sea dog. Undeterred, Luffy set out to sea and recruited a couple of crewmates: master swordsman Zolo and treasure-hunting thief Nami.

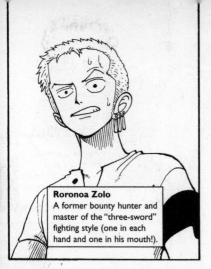

Roronoa Zolo
A former bounty hunter and master of the "three-sword" fighting style (one in each hand and one in his mouth!).

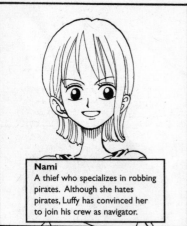

Nami
A thief who specializes in robbing pirates. Although she hates pirates, Luffy has convinced her to join his crew as navigator.

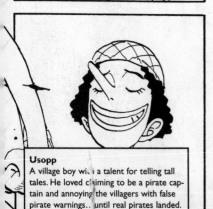

Usopp
A village boy with a talent for telling tall tales. He loved claiming to be a pirate captain and annoying the villagers with false pirate warnings.. until real pirates landed.

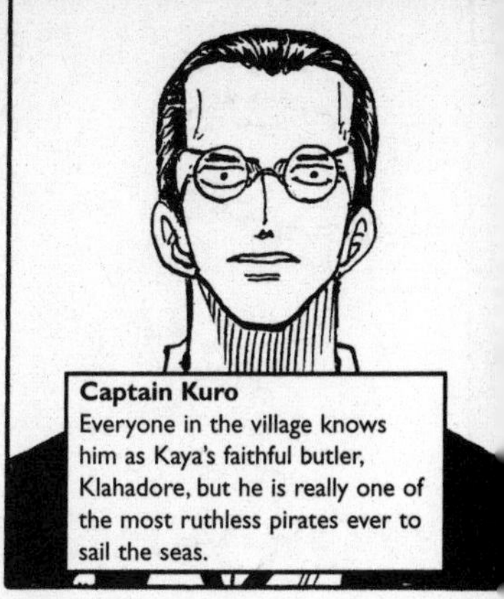
Captain Kuro
Everyone in the village knows him as Kaya's faithful butler, Klahadore, but he is really one of the most ruthless pirates ever to sail the seas.

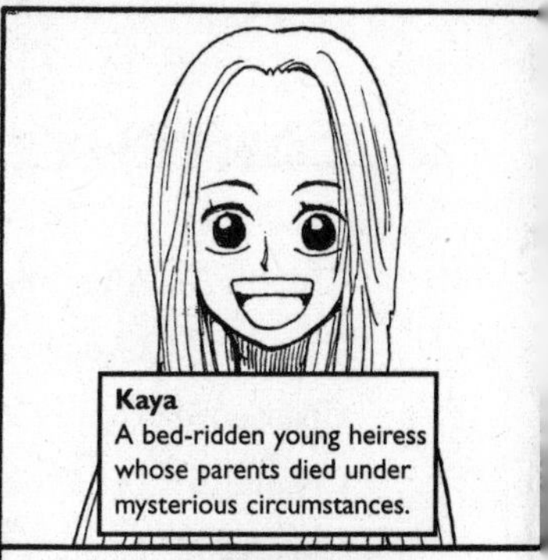
Kaya
A bed-ridden young heiress whose parents died under mysterious circumstances.

The battle with the Black Cat pirates rages on, as Luffy and company try to help Usopp defend his village against the plunder-hungry raiders. But despite the team's heroic efforts, the supply of deadly enemies seems inexhaustible. Though Luffy mows down some with the ship's feline stempost, and Usopp's pint-sized "pirates" and Nami join the fray, victory is still far from certain. But even as Zolo fights for his life against the strange, catlike Meowban brothers, Siam and Butchie, a still more terrible menace emerges. Captain Kuro has arrived on the battlefield, and Luffy's little coalition is about to discover the hard way why he was once the terror of the seas…

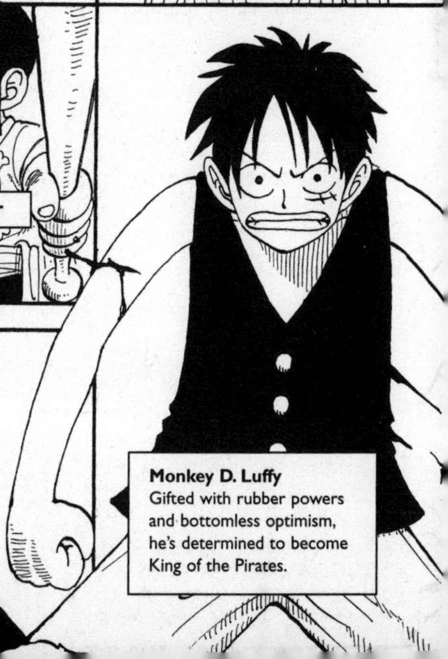
Monkey D. Luffy
Gifted with rubber powers and bottomless optimism, he's determined to become King of the Pirates.

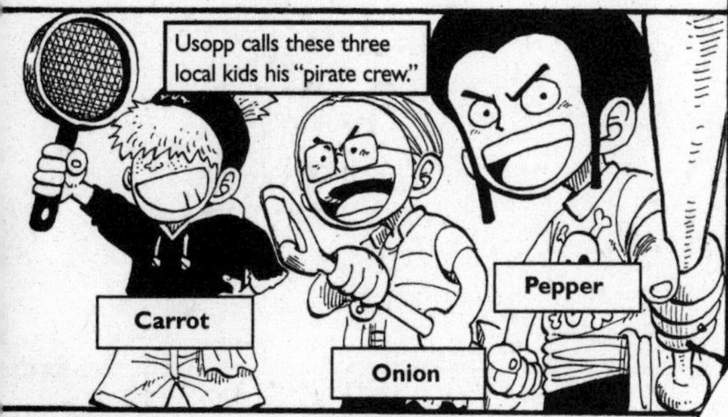
Usopp calls these three local kids his "pirate crew."
Pepper
Onion
Carrot

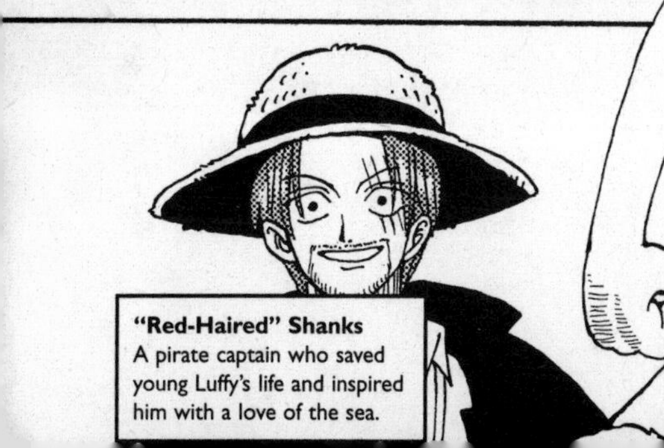
"Red-Haired" Shanks
A pirate captain who saved young Luffy's life and inspired him with a love of the sea.

Vol. 5
FOR WHOM THE BELL TOLLS

CONTENTS

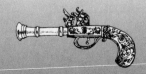

Chapter 36:

AFTER THEM!!

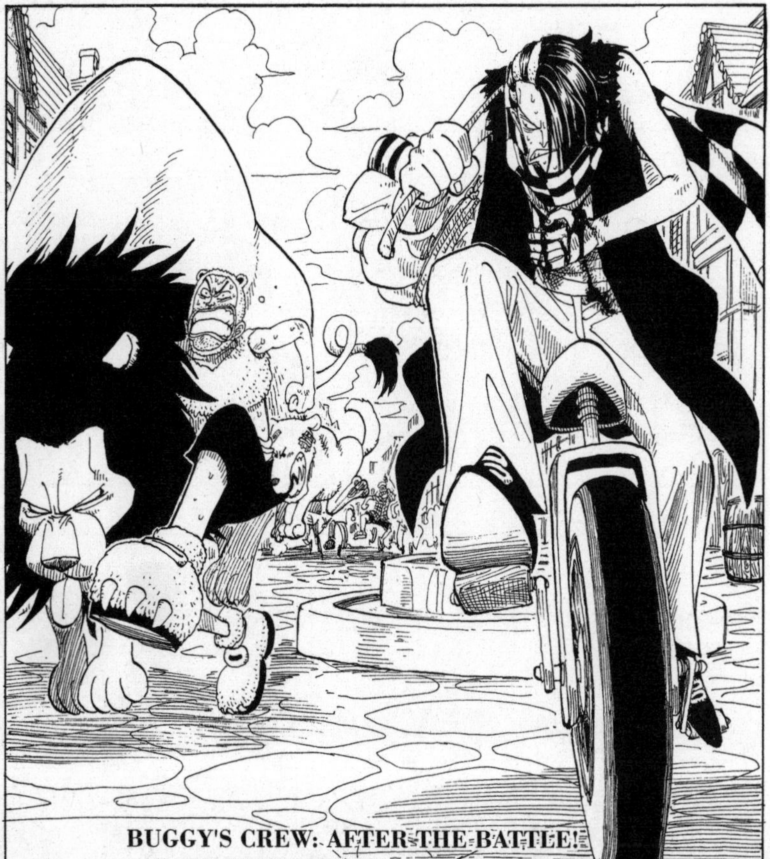
BUGGY'S CREW: AFTER THE BATTLE!
PART TWO: "MOHJI AND CABAJI"

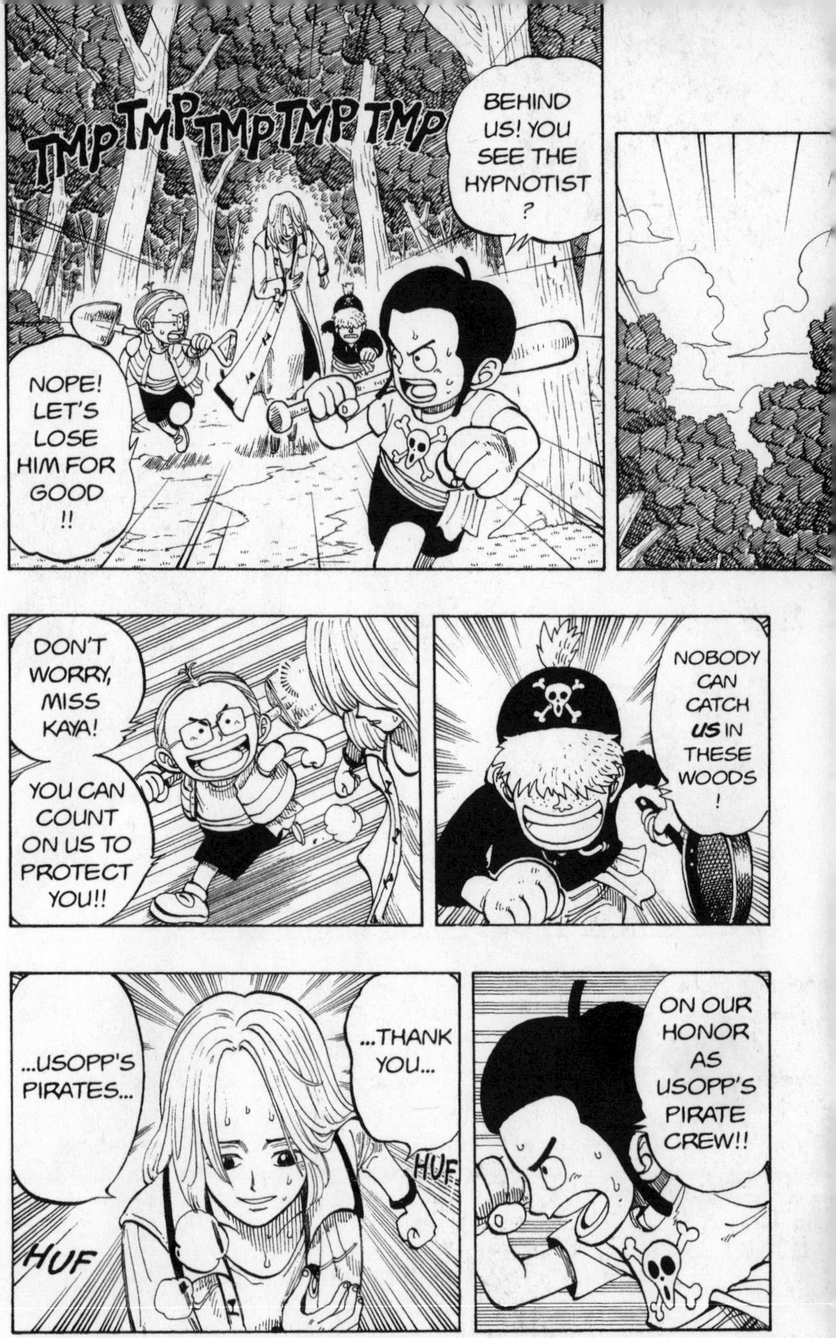

BEHIND US! YOU SEE THE HYPNOTIST?
TMP TMP TMP TMP TMP
NOPE! LET'S LOSE HIM FOR GOOD!!
NOBODY CAN CATCH **US** IN THESE WOODS!
DON'T WORRY, MISS KAYA!
YOU CAN COUNT ON US TO PROTECT YOU!!
ON OUR HONOR AS USOPP'S PIRATE CREW!!
...THANK YOU...
HUF
...USOPP'S PIRATES...
HUF

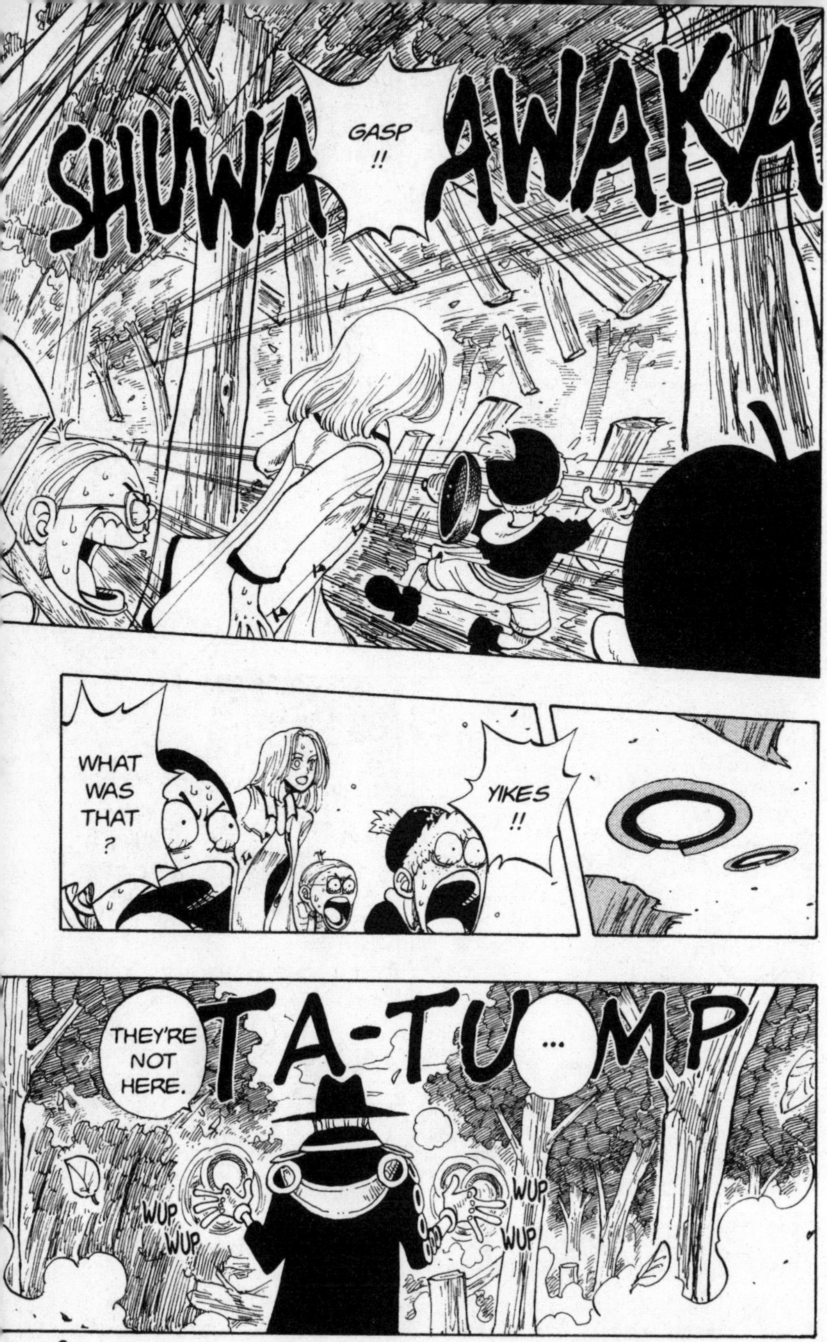
SHUWA AWAKA
GASP !!
YIKES !!
WHAT WAS THAT ?
TA-TUMP
...
THEY'RE NOT HERE.
WUP WUP
WUP WUP

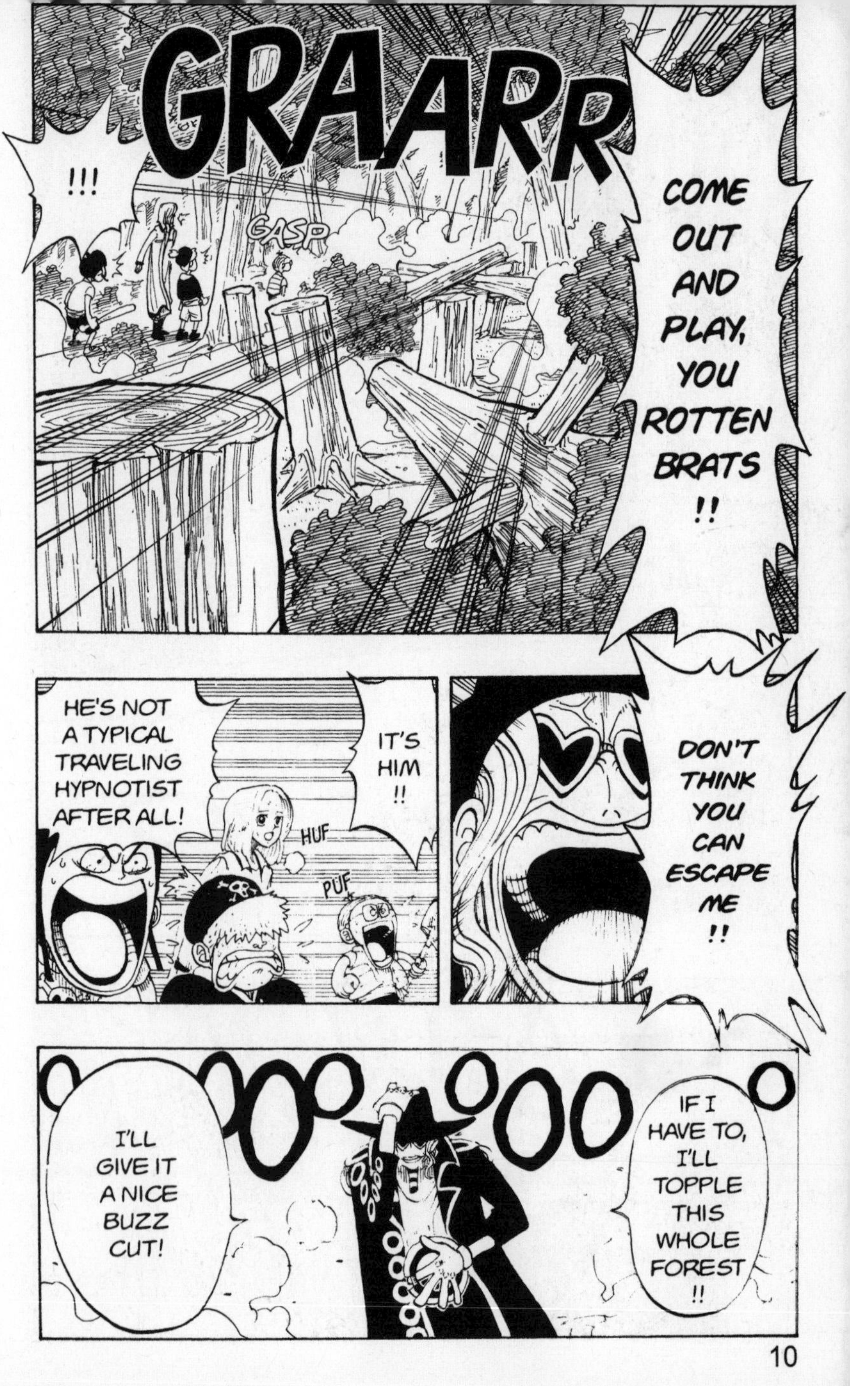
GRAARR
COME OUT AND PLAY, YOU ROTTEN BRATS !!
GASP
!!!
DON'T THINK YOU CAN ESCAPE ME !!
IT'S HIM !!
HE'S NOT A TYPICAL TRAVELING HYPNOTIST AFTER ALL!
HUF
PUF
IF I HAVE TO, I'LL TOPPLE THIS WHOLE FOREST !!
OOOOOOOOO
I'LL GIVE IT A NICE BUZZ CUT!

READ THIS WAY

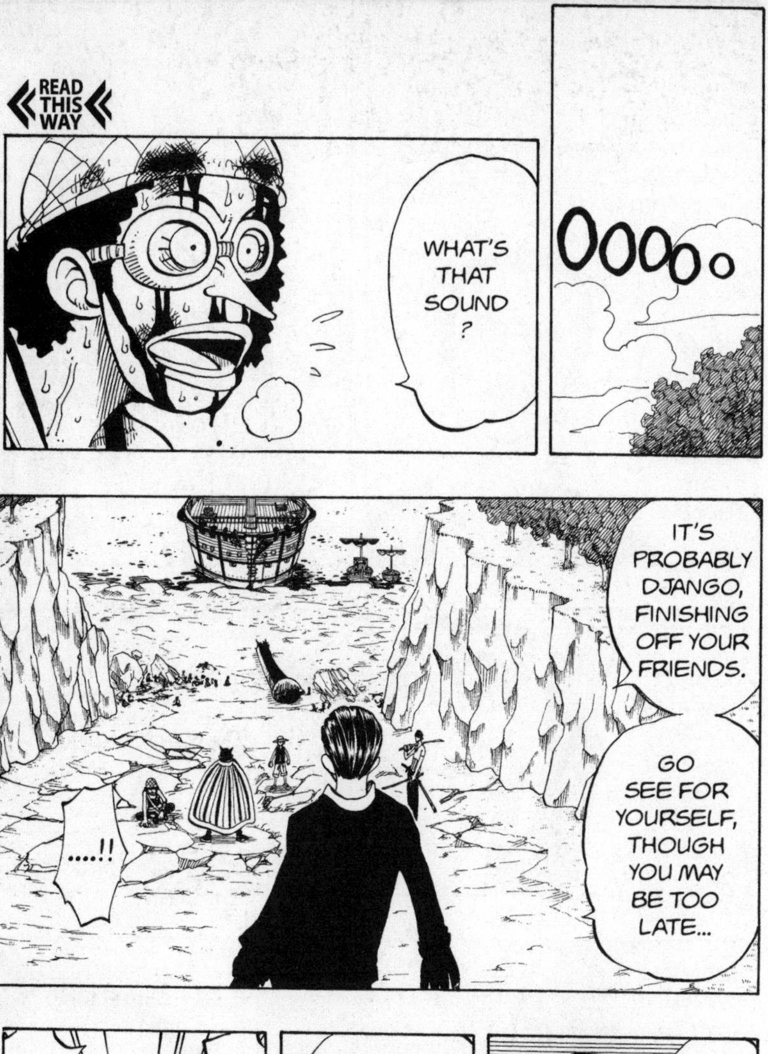

OOOOo
WHAT'S THAT SOUND ?
IT'S PROBABLY DJANGO, FINISHING OFF YOUR FRIENDS.
GO SEE FOR YOURSELF, THOUGH YOU MAY BE TOO LATE...
....!!
YOU'D BETTER HURRY TO THEIR AID.
IF YOU CAN...
...!!
WHY, YOU...

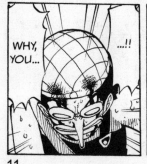

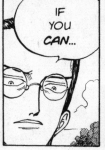

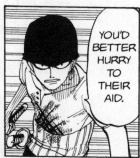

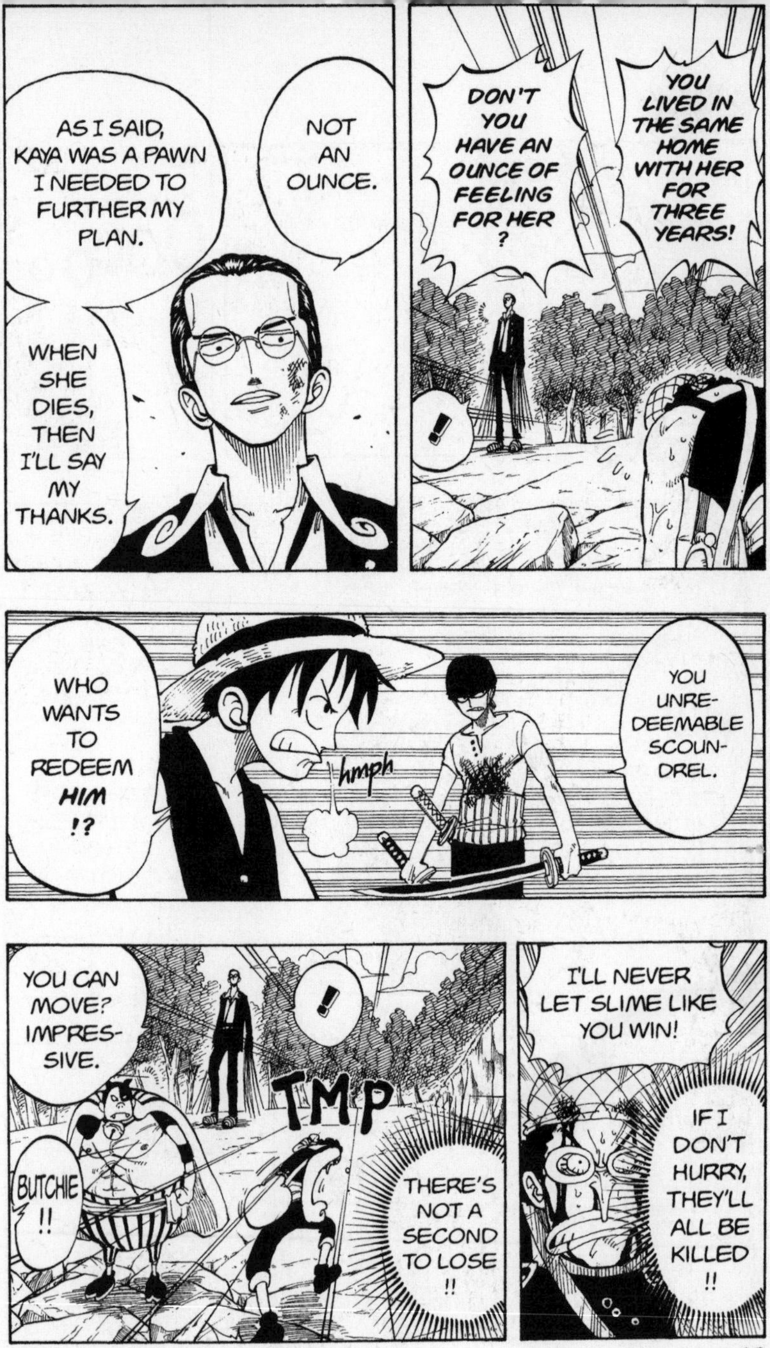
YOU LIVED IN THE SAME HOME WITH HER FOR THREE YEARS!
DON'T YOU HAVE AN OUNCE OF FEELING FOR HER ?
!
NOT AN OUNCE.
AS I SAID, KAYA WAS A PAWN I NEEDED TO FURTHER MY PLAN.
WHEN SHE DIES, THEN I'LL SAY MY THANKS.
YOU UNRE-DEEMABLE SCOUN-DREL.
hmph
WHO WANTS TO REDEEM HIM !?
I'LL NEVER LET SLIME LIKE YOU WIN!
IF I DON'T HURRY, THEY'LL ALL BE KILLED !!
!
YOU CAN MOVE? IMPRES-SIVE.
TMP
THERE'S NOT A SECOND TO LOSE !!
BUTCHIE !!

READ THIS WAY

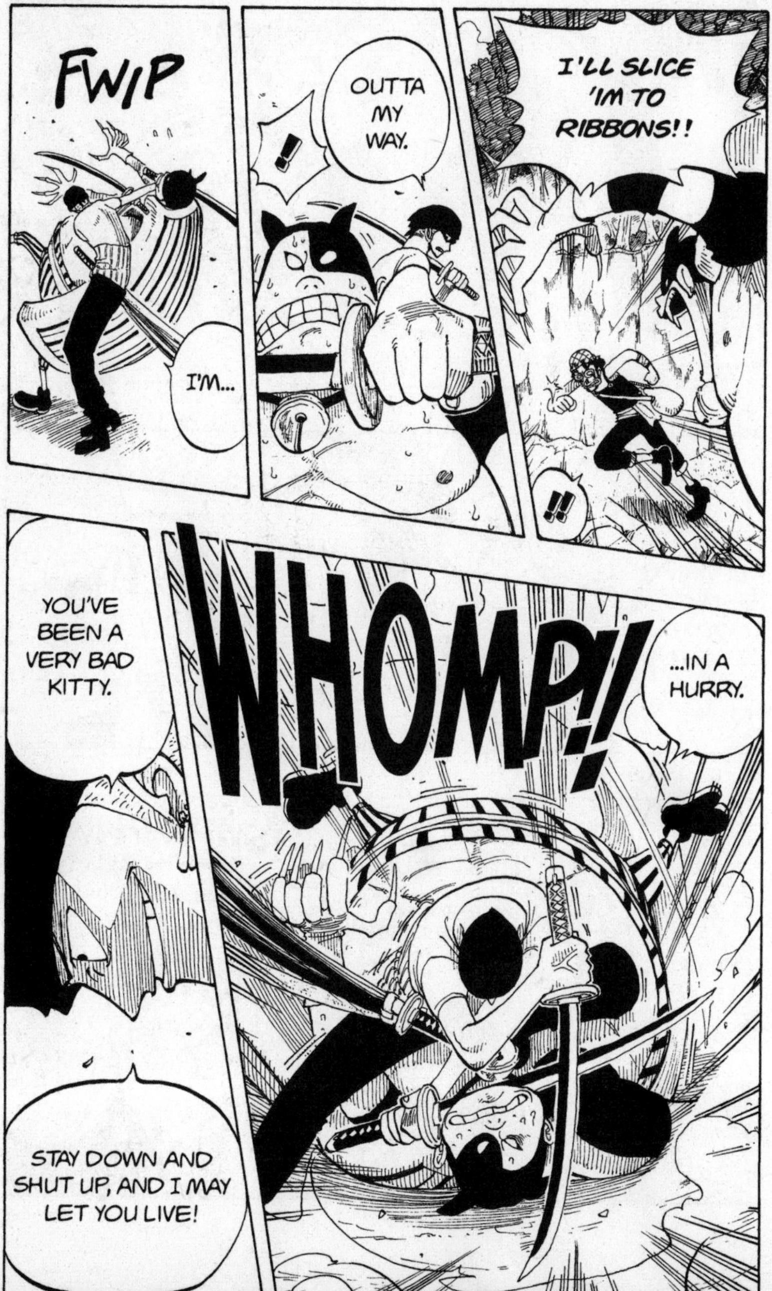
I'LL SLICE 'IM TO RIBBONS!!
!!
OUTTA MY WAY.
!
FWIP
I'M...
...IN A HURRY.
WHOMP!!
YOU'VE BEEN A VERY BAD KITTY.
STAY DOWN AND SHUT UP, AND I MAY LET YOU LIVE!

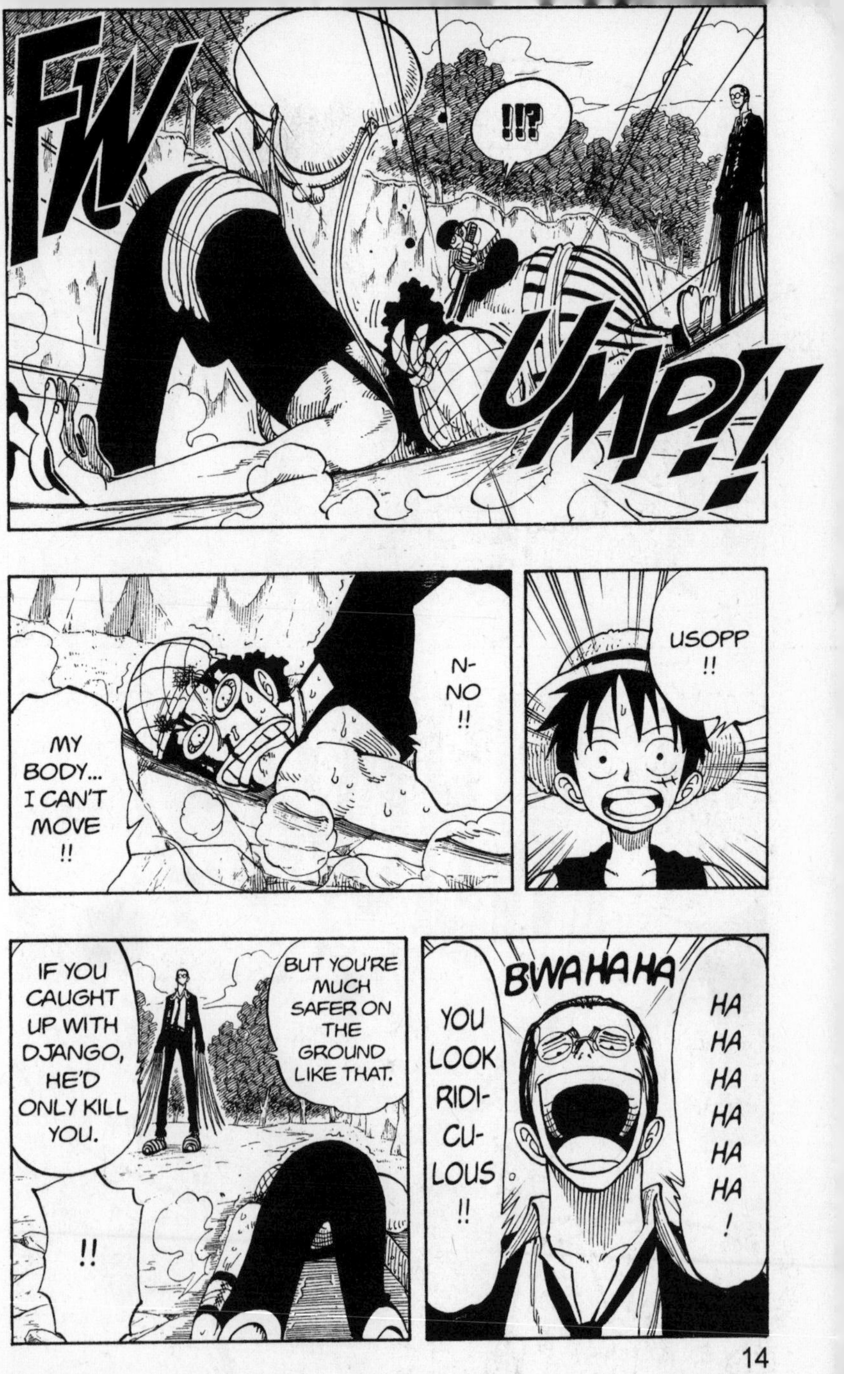
FWUMP!!
!!?
USOPP!!
N-NO!!
MY BODY... I CAN'T MOVE!!
BWAHAHA
HA HA HA HA HA HA!
YOU LOOK RIDICULOUS!!
BUT YOU'RE MUCH SAFER ON THE GROUND LIKE THAT.
IF YOU CAUGHT UP WITH DJANGO, HE'D ONLY KILL YOU.
!!

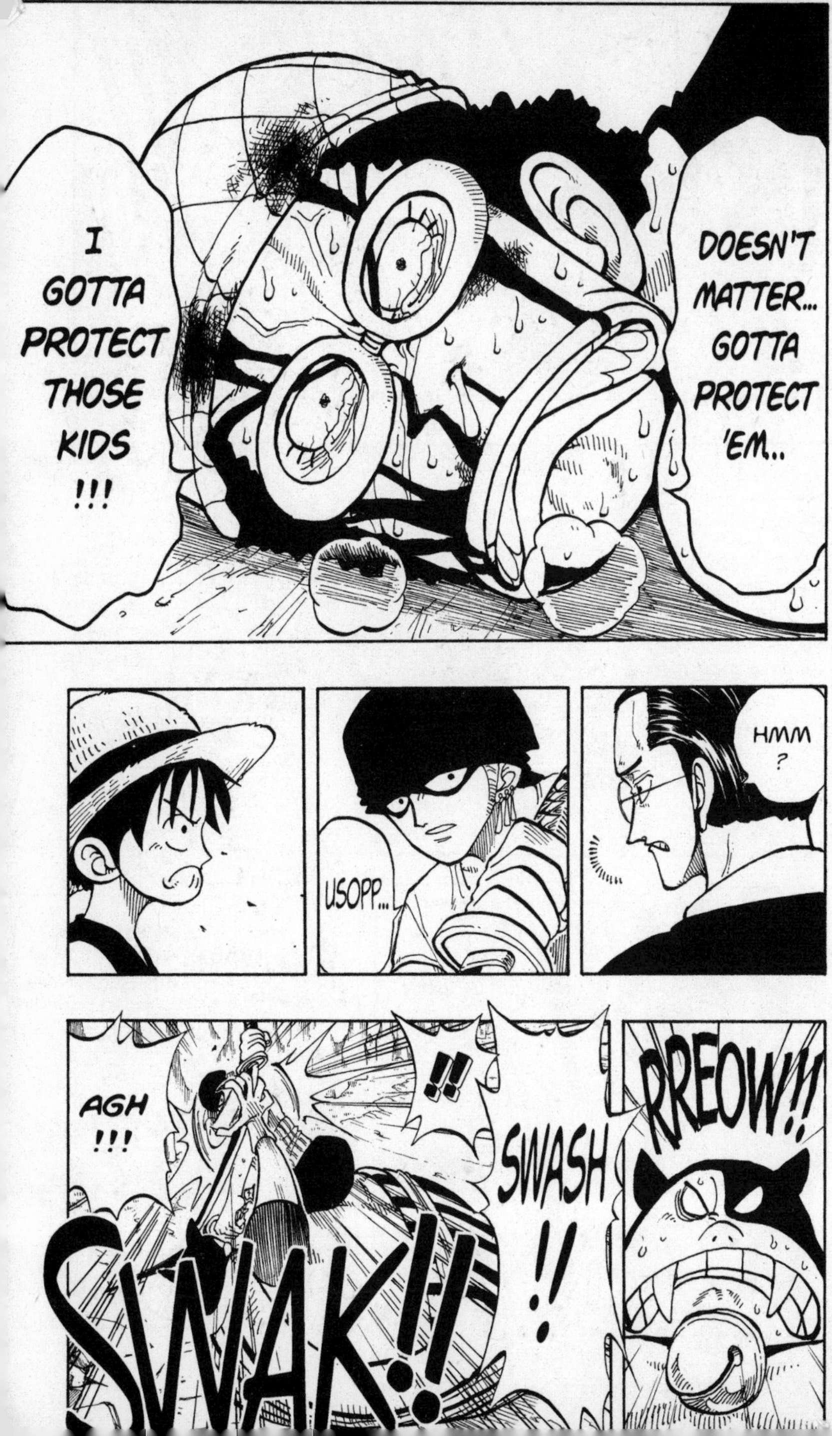
DOESN'T MATTER... GOTTA PROTECT 'EM...
I GOTTA PROTECT THOSE KIDS !!!
HMM ?
USOPP...
RREOW!!
!!
SWASH !!
AGH !!!
SWAK!!

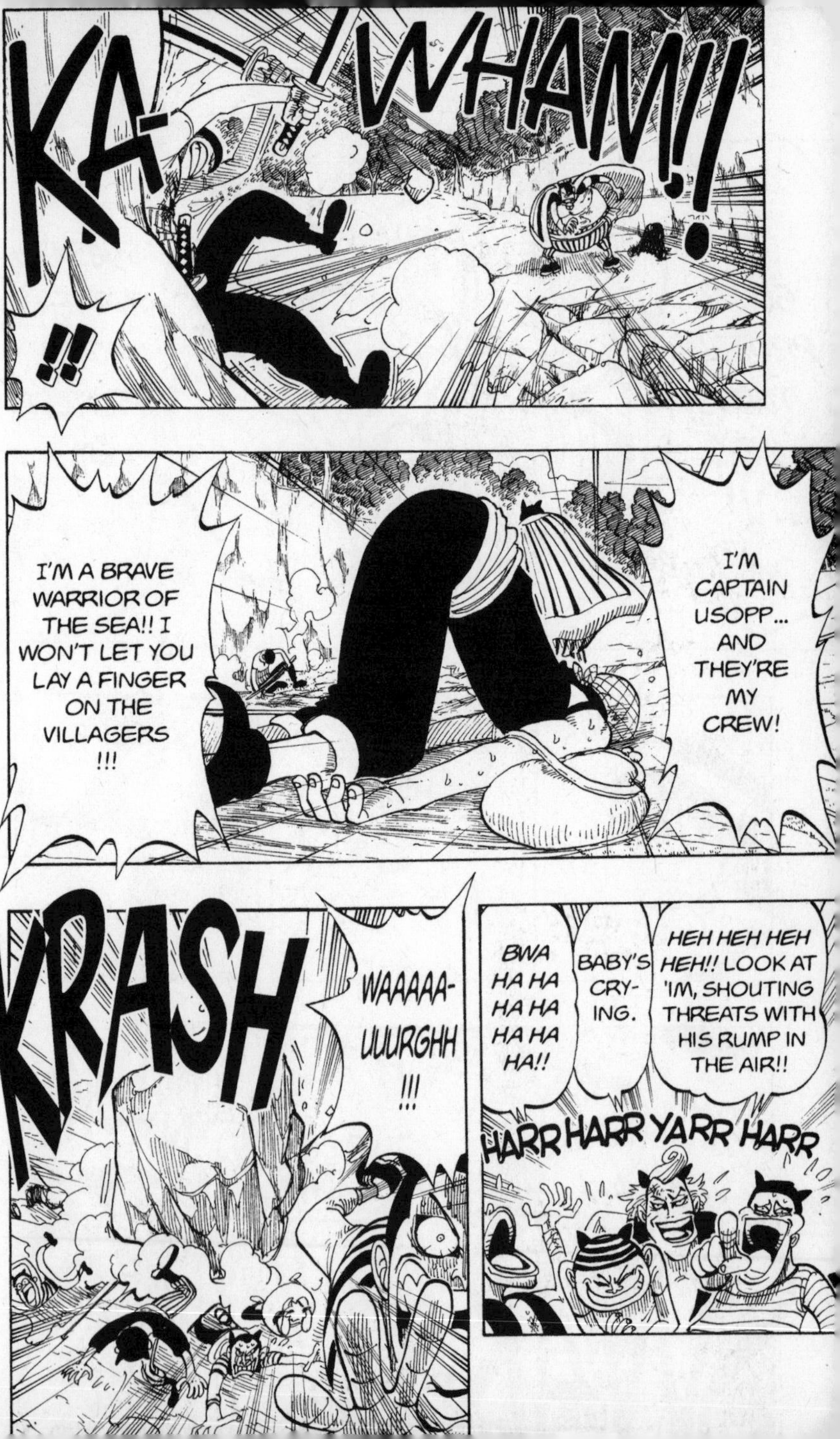
KA-WHAM!!
!!
I'M CAPTAIN USOPP... AND THEY'RE MY CREW!
I'M A BRAVE WARRIOR OF THE SEA!! I WON'T LET YOU LAY A FINGER ON THE VILLAGERS !!!
HEH HEH HEH HEH!! LOOK AT 'IM, SHOUTING THREATS WITH HIS RUMP IN THE AIR!!
BABY'S CRY-ING.
BWA HA HA HA HA HA HA HA!!
HARR HARR YARR HARR
WAAAAA-UUURGHH !!!
KRASH

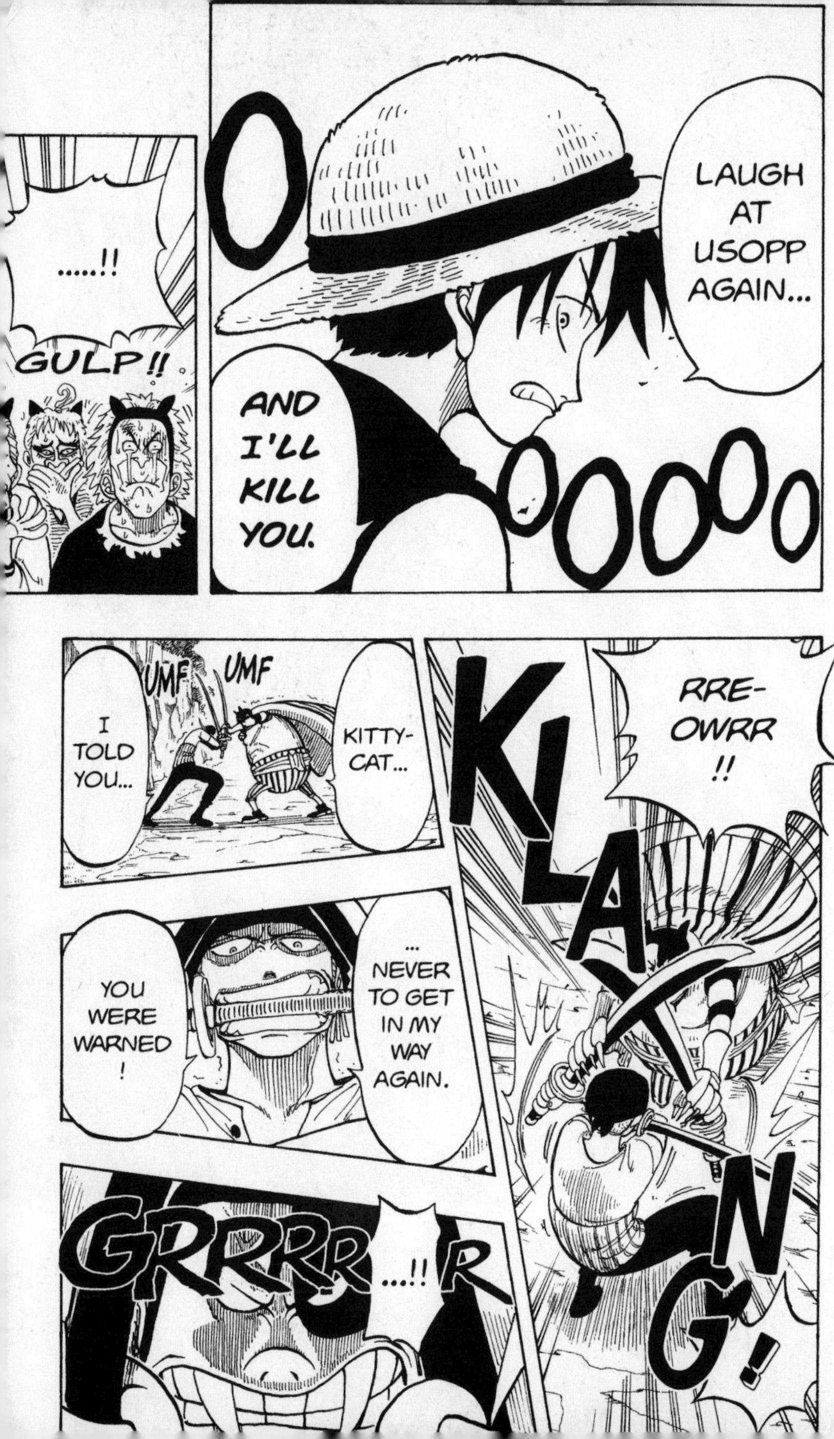
LAUGH AT USOPP AGAIN...
AND I'LL KILL YOU.
OOOOOO
.....!!
GULP!!
RRE-OWRR!!
KLANG!
KITTY-CAT...
UMF UMF
I TOLD YOU...
...NEVER TO GET IN MY WAY AGAIN.
YOU WERE WARNED!
GRRRRR ...!!

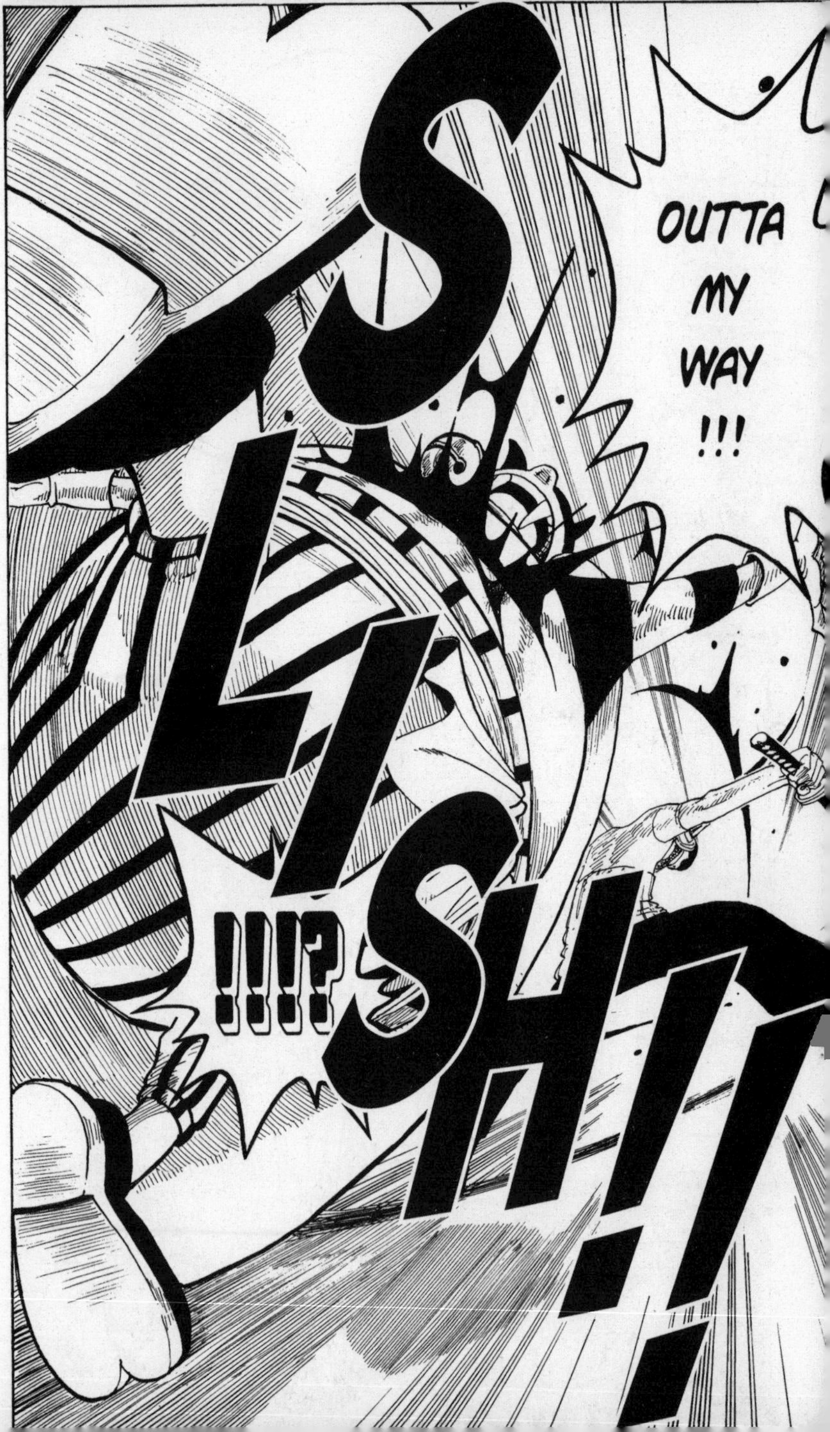
OUTTA MY WAY !!!
SLISH!!
!!!?

READ THIS WAY

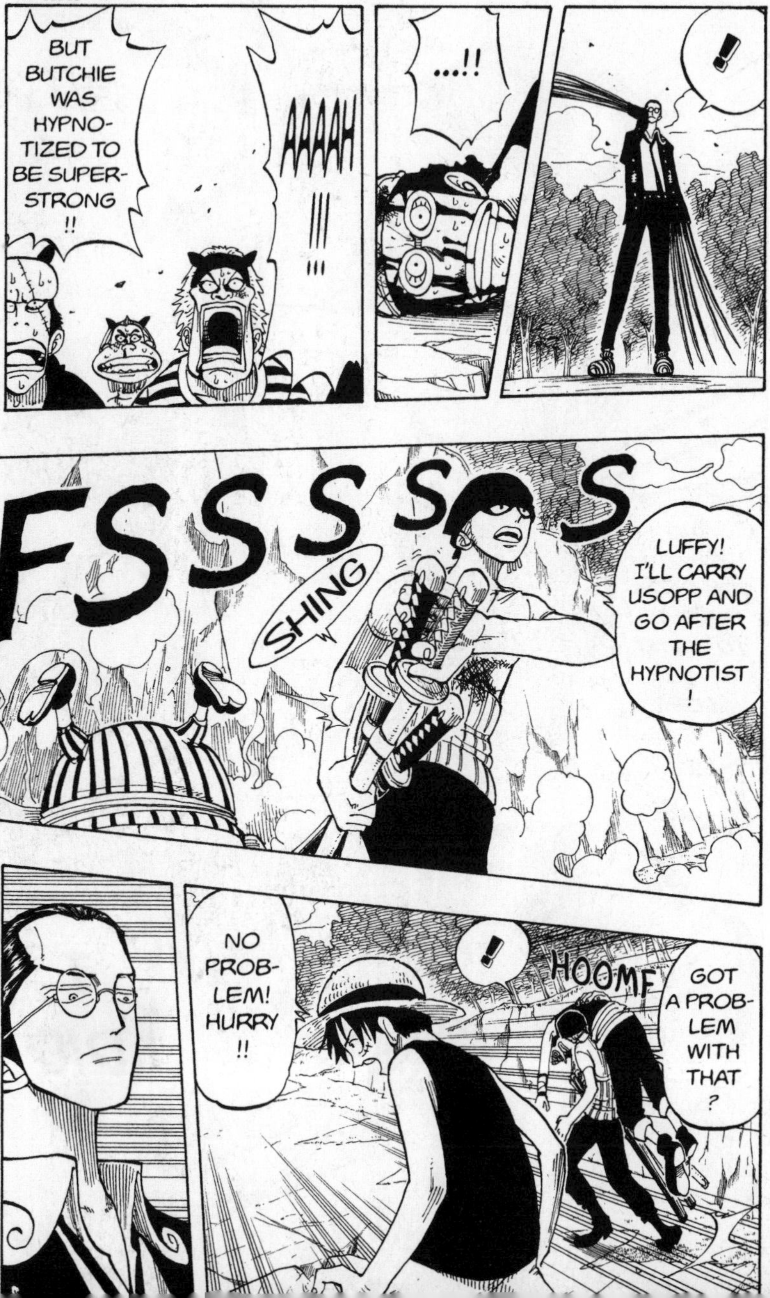
!
...!!
AAAAH !!! !!!
BUT BUTCHIE WAS HYPNOTIZED TO BE SUPER-STRONG !!
LUFFY! I'LL CARRY USOPP AND GO AFTER THE HYPNOTIST !
FSSSSSS
SHING
GOT A PROBLEM WITH THAT ?
HOOMF
!
NO PROBLEM! HURRY !!

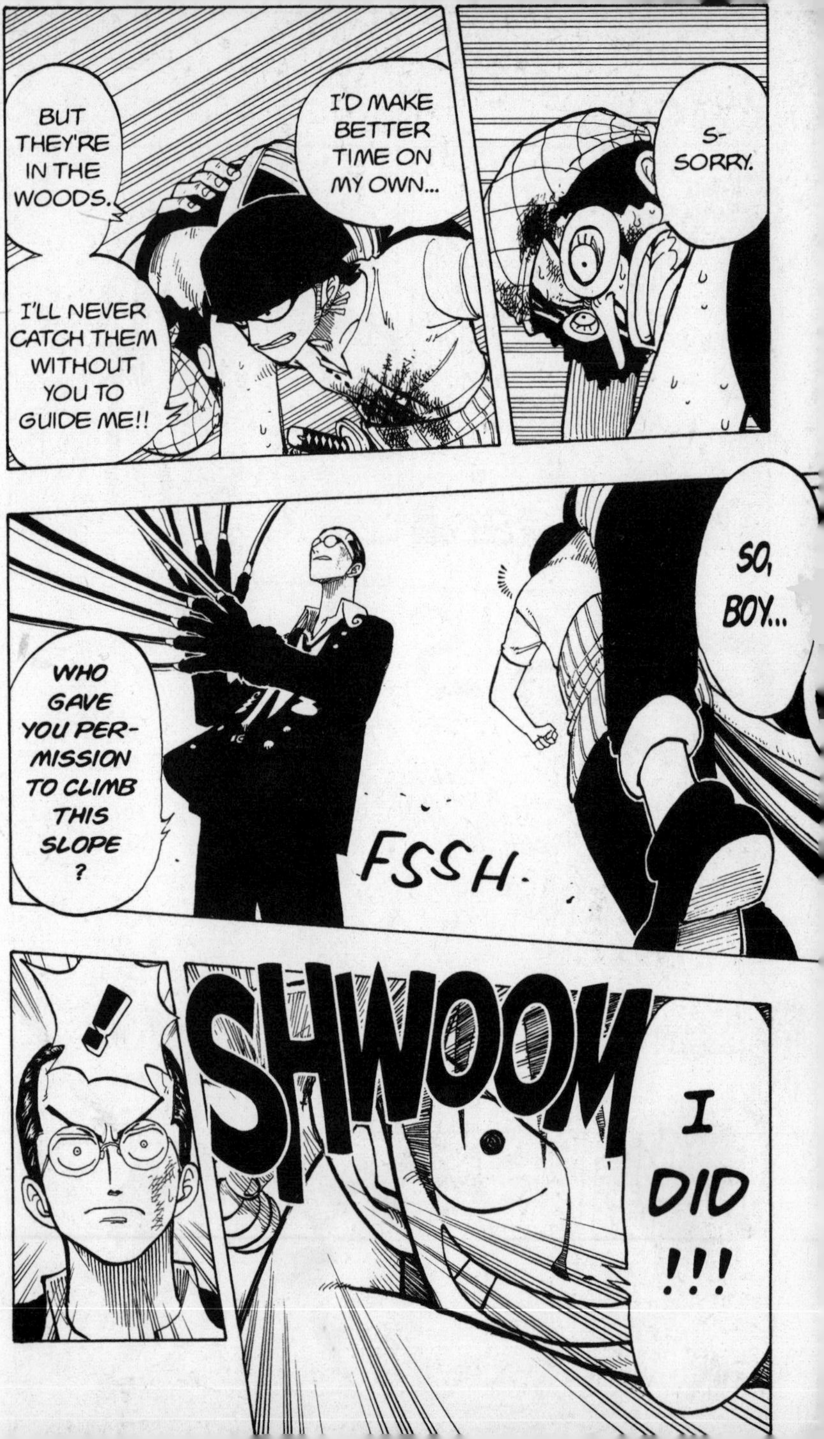
S-SORRY.
I'D MAKE BETTER TIME ON MY OWN...
BUT THEY'RE IN THE WOODS.
I'LL NEVER CATCH THEM WITHOUT YOU TO GUIDE ME!!
SO, BOY...
FSSH
WHO GAVE YOU PERMISSION TO CLIMB THIS SLOPE?
I DID!!!
SHWOOM
!

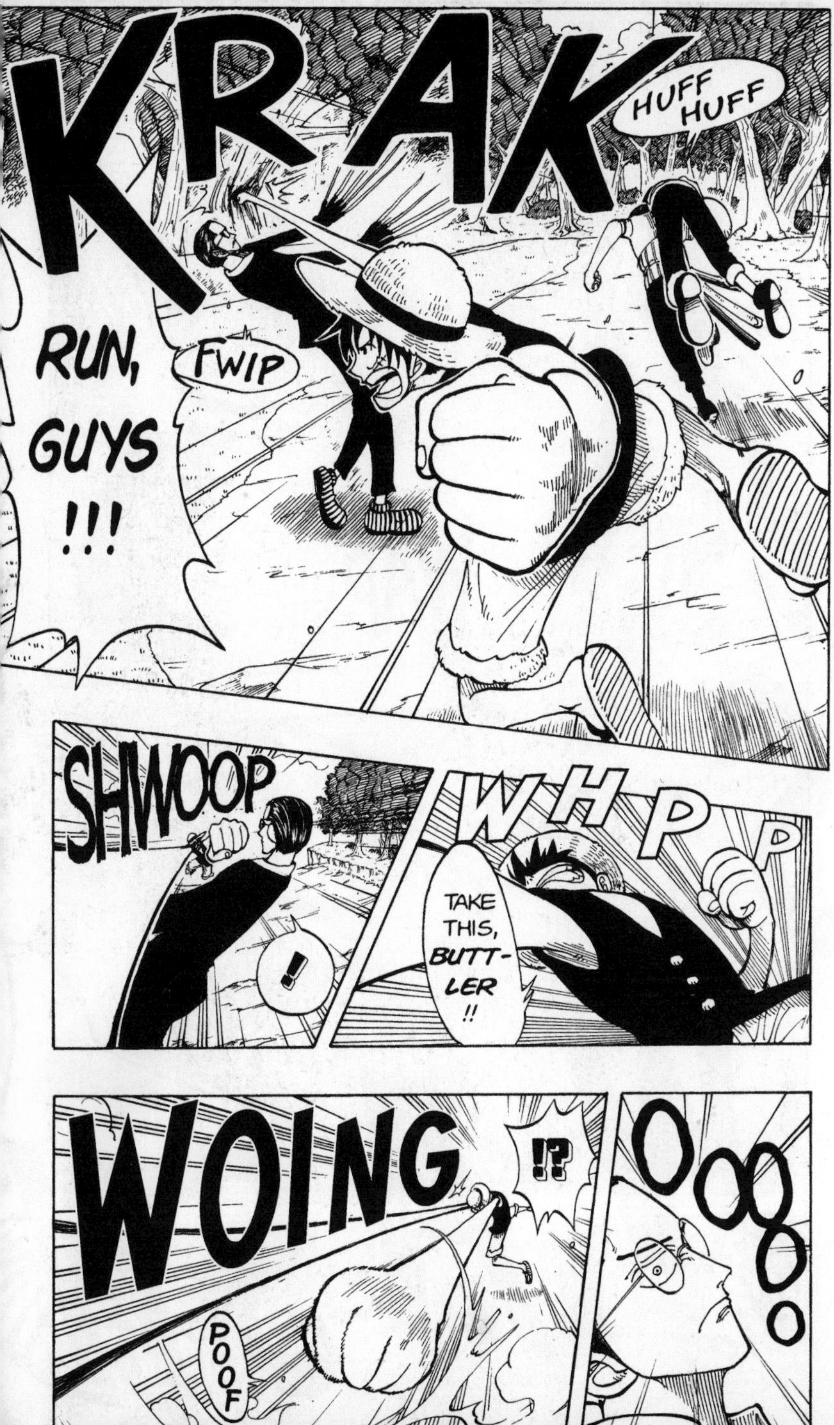
KRAK
HUFF HUFF
FWIP
RUN, GUYS!!!
WHPP
TAKE THIS, BUTT-LER!!
SHWOOP
!
OOOOOO
WOING
!?
POOF

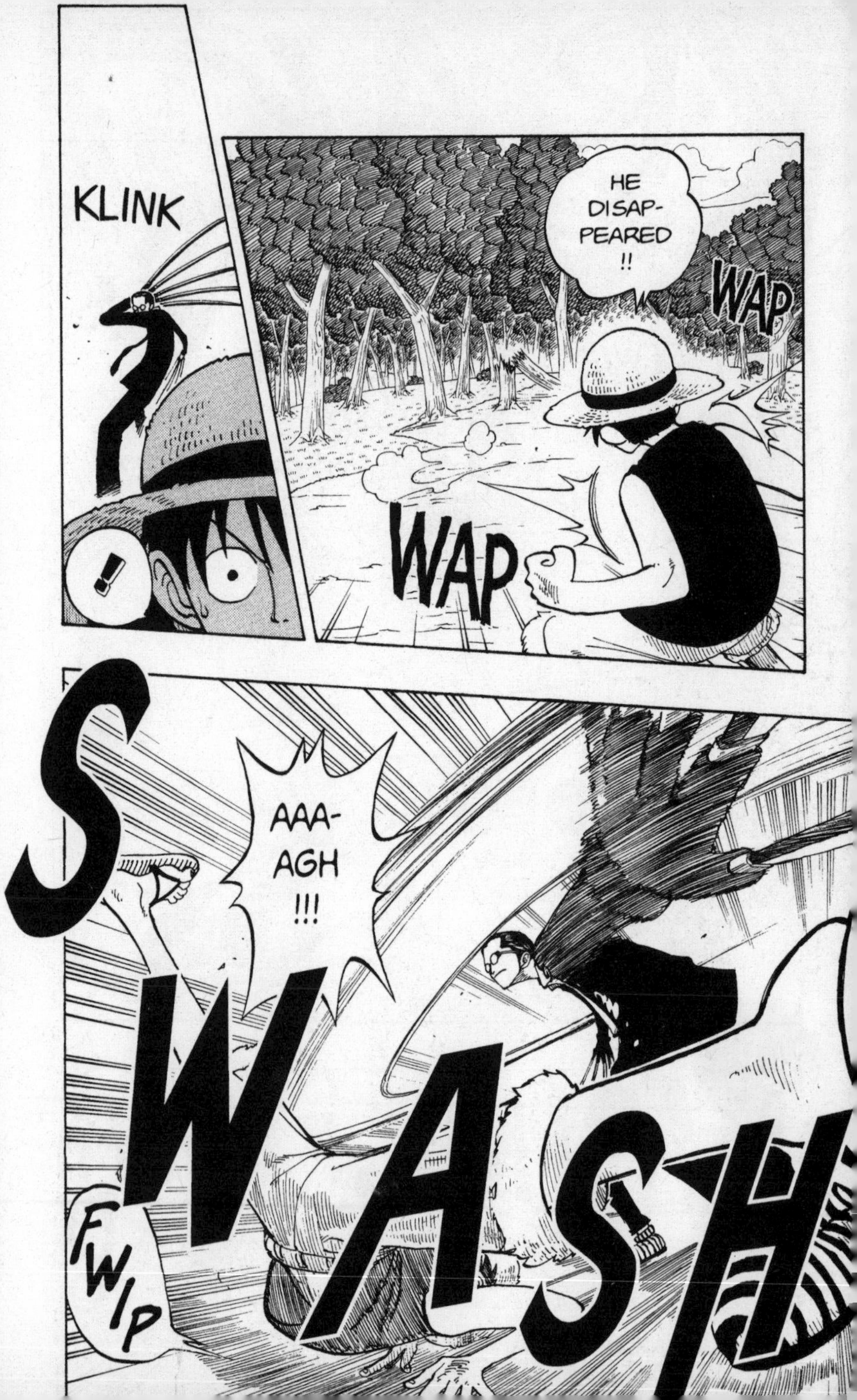

HE DISAP-PEARED !!
WAP
WAP
KLINK
!
AAA-AGH !!!
SWASH
FWIP

READ THIS WAY

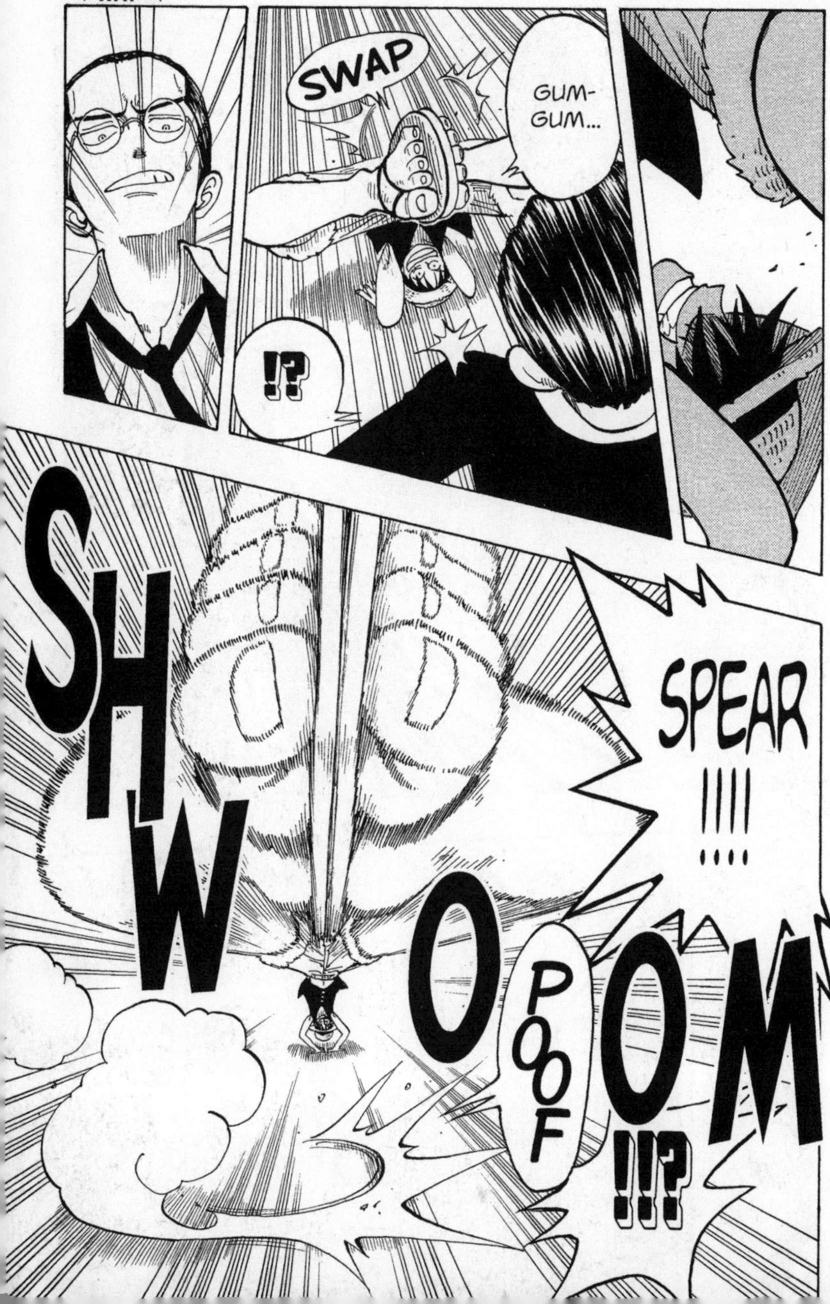
GUM-GUM...
SWAP
!?
SPEAR!!!!
SHWOOM
POOF
!!?

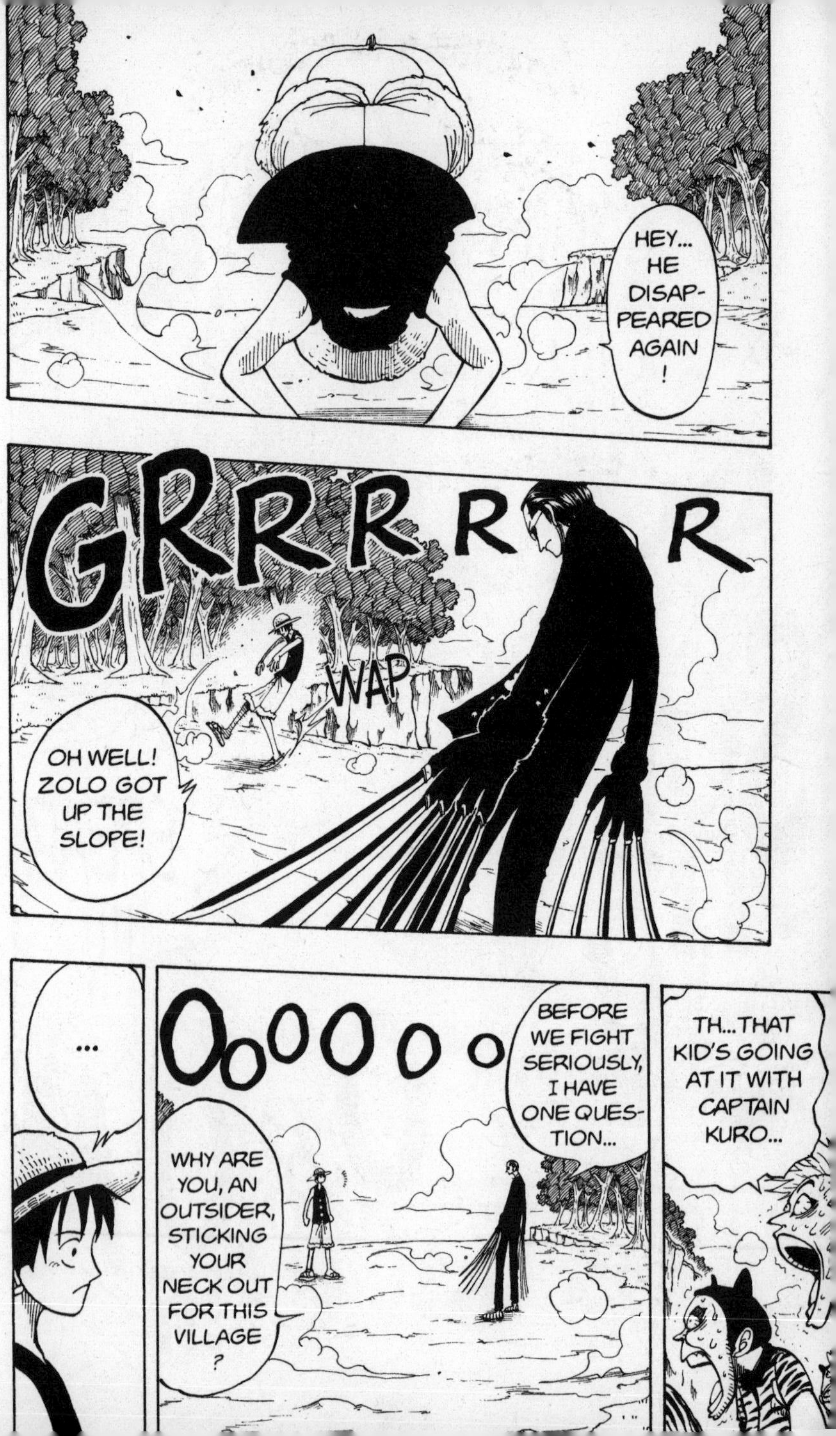
HEY... HE DISAPPEARED AGAIN!
GRRRRRR
WAP
OH WELL! ZOLO GOT UP THE SLOPE!
TH...THAT KID'S GOING AT IT WITH CAPTAIN KURO...
OOOOOO
BEFORE WE FIGHT SERIOUSLY, I HAVE ONE QUESTION...
WHY ARE YOU, AN OUTSIDER, STICKING YOUR NECK OUT FOR THIS VILLAGE?
...

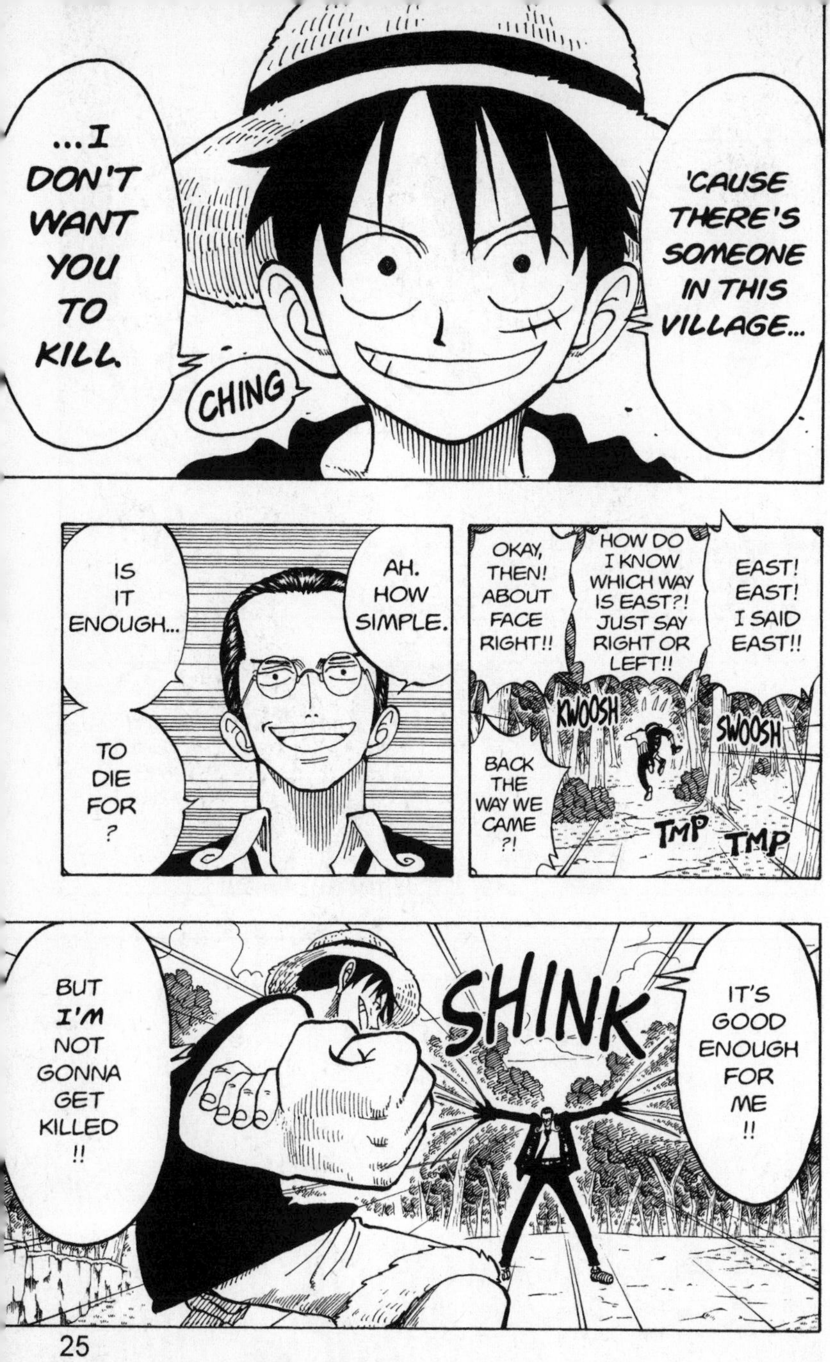
'CAUSE THERE'S SOMEONE IN THIS VILLAGE...
CHING
...I DON'T WANT YOU TO KILL.
EAST! EAST! I SAID EAST!!
HOW DO I KNOW WHICH WAY IS EAST?! JUST SAY RIGHT OR LEFT!!
OKAY, THEN! ABOUT FACE RIGHT!!
SWOOSH
KWOOSH
BACK THE WAY WE CAME?!
TMP
TMP
AH. HOW SIMPLE.
IS IT ENOUGH...
TO DIE FOR?
IT'S GOOD ENOUGH FOR ME!!
SHINK
BUT I'M NOT GONNA GET KILLED!!

KRASH

KRAK

KRAK

KRA'K

KRAK

KRAK

...

NOW WHERE'D THEY RUN TO?

WHAT!? BUT IT'S OUR DUTY TO PROTECT YOU!!

...HUFF... I'M SORRY... YOU BOYS GO ON.

UNH...

WUMP

MISS KAYA!!

HUFF...

HUFF...

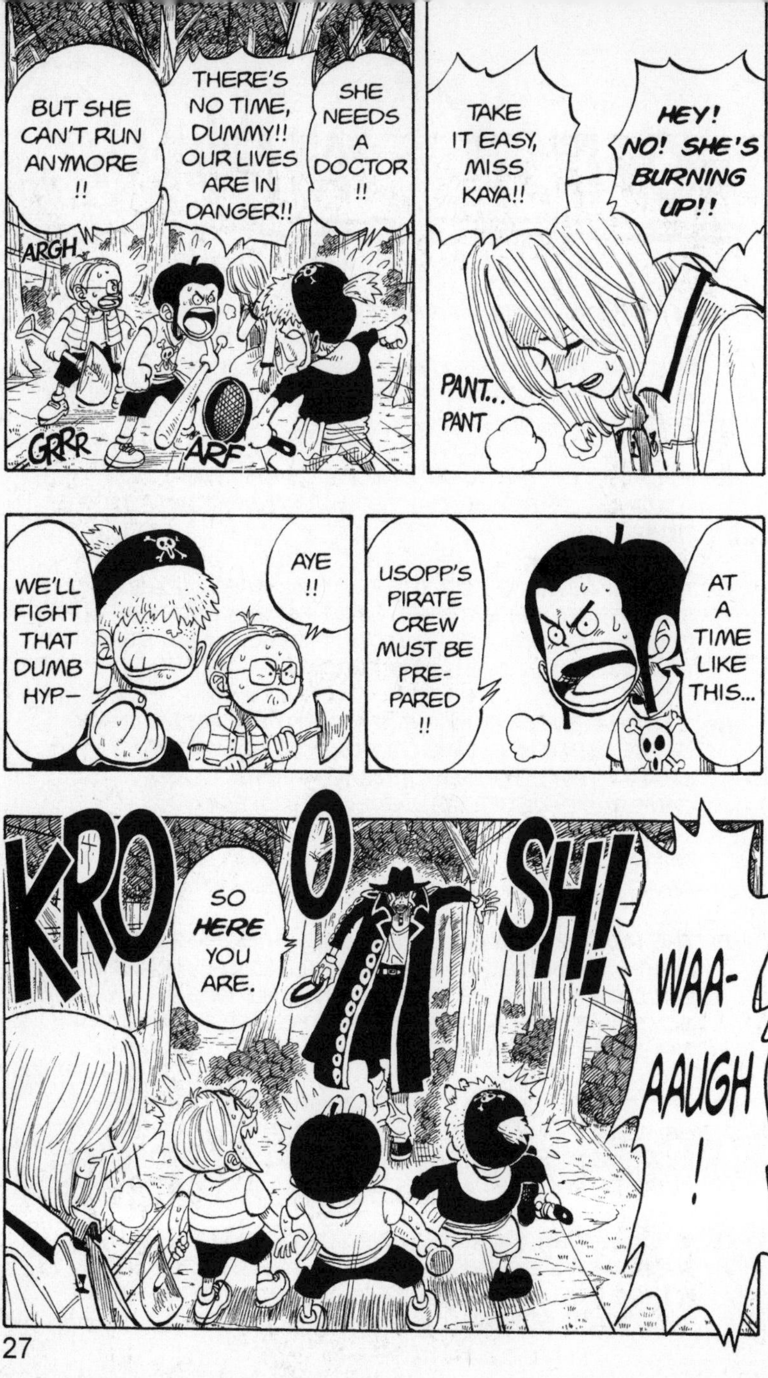
HEY! NO! SHE'S BURNING UP!!
TAKE IT EASY, MISS KAYA!!
PANT... PANT
SHE NEEDS A DOCTOR!!
THERE'S NO TIME, DUMMY!! OUR LIVES ARE IN DANGER!!
BUT SHE CAN'T RUN ANYMORE!!
ARGH
ARF
GRRR
AT A TIME LIKE THIS...
USOPP'S PIRATE CREW MUST BE PRE-PARED!!
AYE!!
WE'LL FIGHT THAT DUMB HYP—
WAA-AAUGH!
KRO O SH!
SO HERE YOU ARE.

NOW IT'S AN ANIME!

- IN 1998, *ONE PIECE* WAS PART OF SOMETHING CALLED "JUMP SUPER ANIME TOUR '98." IT WAS A FUN FILM FESTIVAL FEATURING THREE *SHONEN JUMP* COMICS ADAPTED INTO SHORT ANIMATED FILMS. IT PLAYED IN THEATERS ACROSS JAPAN.

- BECAUSE OF THE TOUR, *ONE PIECE* HAD THE GOOD FORTUNE OF BEING ADAPTED INTO ANIMATION FOR THE FIRST TIME.

- THE ANIME MADE FOR THE FESTIVAL WAS CALLED "ONE PIECE: DEFEAT THEM! THE GANZAK PIRATES." LUFFY, ZOLO, AND NAMI WERE IN IT, BUT IT WAS A NEW STORY THAT WASN'T IN THE COMIC BOOK.

- TO CREATE ANIME, MANY DIFFERENT PROFESSIONALS COME TOGETHER: DIRECTORS, SCREENWRITERS, CHARACTER DESIGNERS, ILLUSTRATORS, COLORISTS, CAMERAMEN, EDITORS, DEVELOPERS, SOUND TECHNICIANS, COMPOSERS, ENGINEERS, PRODUCERS, ANIMATORS, VOICE ACTORS, AND ON AND ON. IT'S AMAZING. BRINGS TEARS TO MY EYES.

- THE REASON IT BRINGS TEARS TO MY EYES IS THAT EVERYONE INVOLVED HAS SUCH PASSION FOR PROVIDING ENJOYMENT FOR PEOPLE. SEEING THIS WAS A GOOD INFLUENCE ON ME. IT LIT THE FIRES OF MY WRITER SOUL. *OW*, HOT!

- AND ON TOP OF THAT, THE FINISHED PRODUCT WAS SO WELL DONE! LUFFY'S AND THE OTHERS' VOICES AND MOVEMENTS WERE AMAZING, TOTALLY BEYOND WHAT I'D IMAGINED!

- IF YOU WEREN'T ABLE TO CATCH IT DURING THE ANIME TOUR, I HOPE SOMEDAY YOU WILL HAVE THE OPPORTUNITY TO SEE IT: LUFFY'S STRETCHING, THE CRY OF GANZAK THE PIRATE GENERAL, AND THE FUN SONGS.

Chapter 37:

CAPTAIN KURO, OF THE THOUSAND PLANS

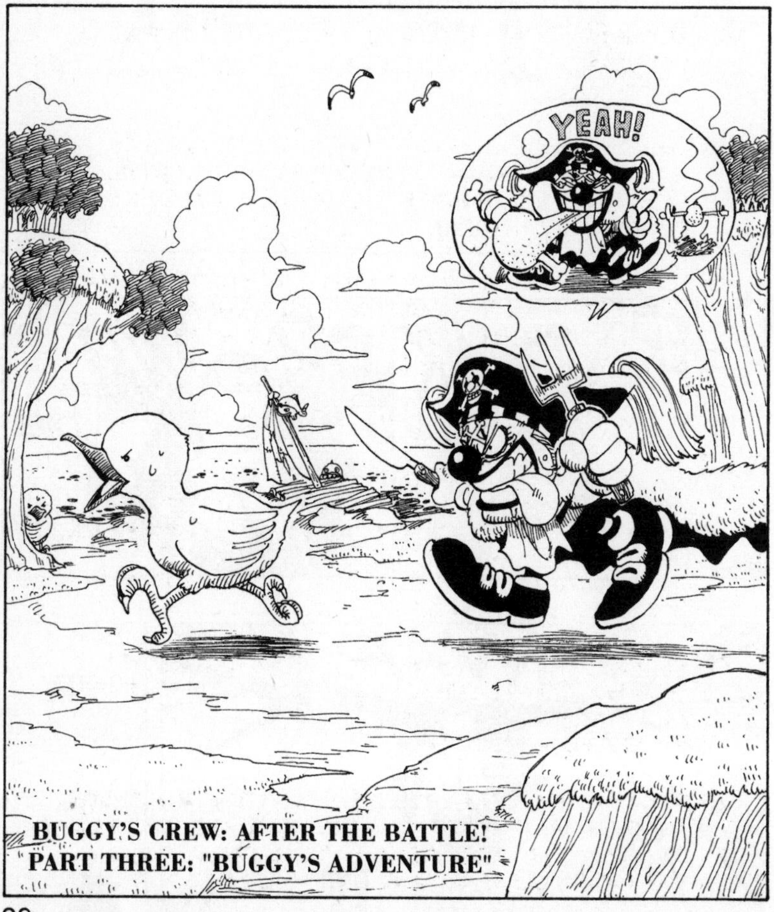
YEAH!
BUGGY'S CREW: AFTER THE BATTLE!
PART THREE: "BUGGY'S ADVENTURE"

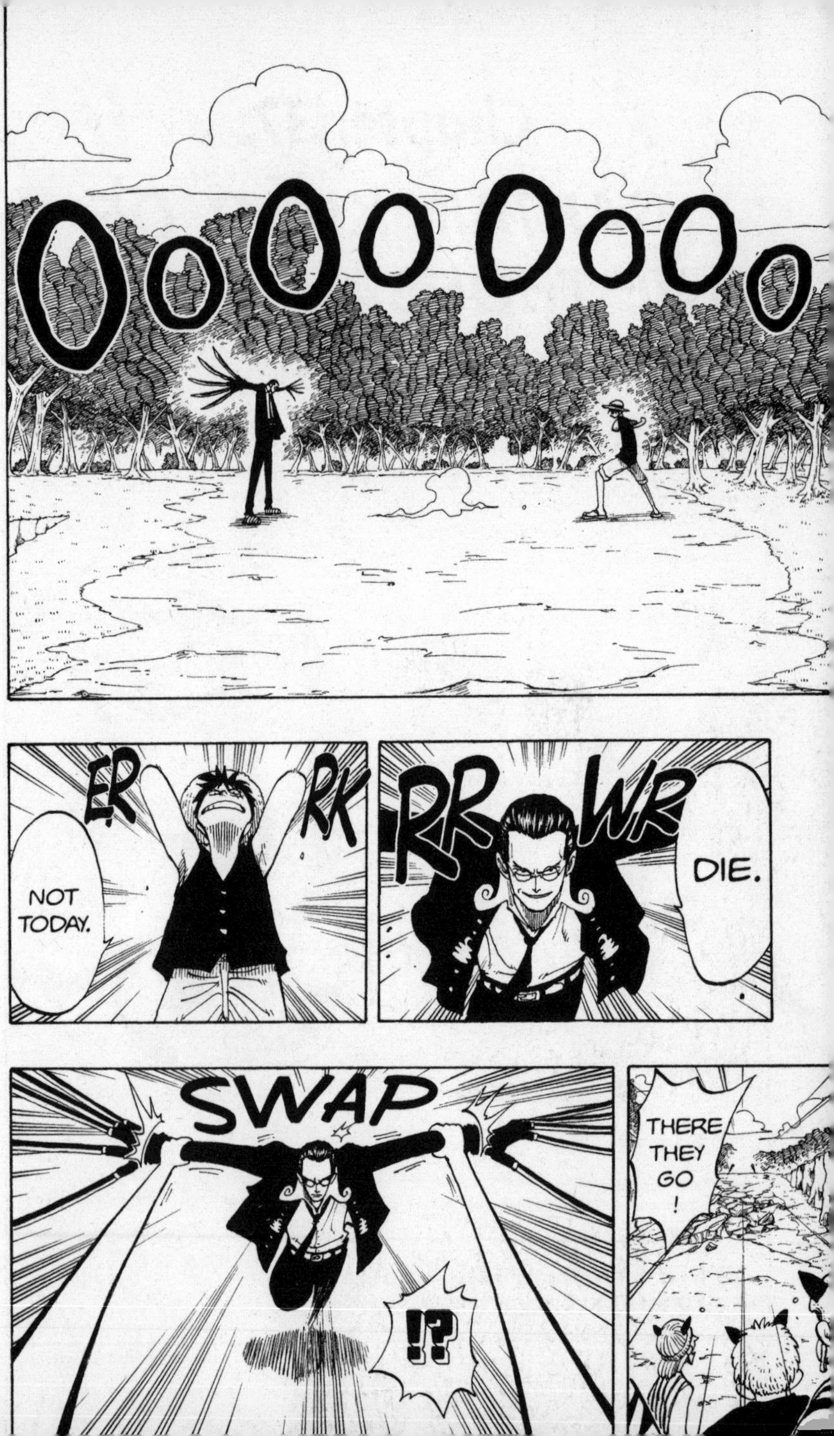
OOOOOOOOO
RRWR
DIE.
ERRK
NOT TODAY.
THERE THEY GO!
SWAP
!?

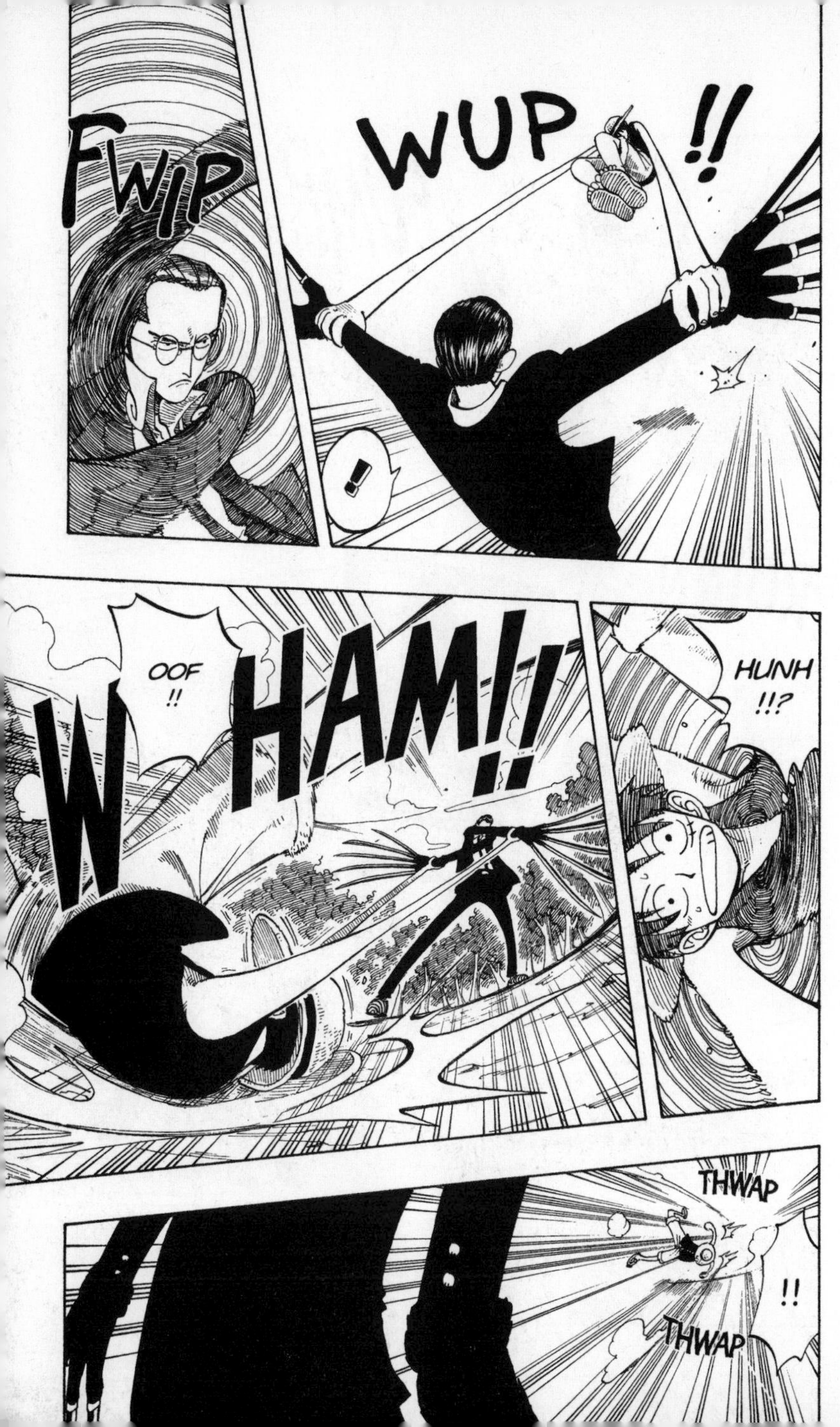
WUP !!
!
FWIP
HUNH !!?
OOF !!
WHAM!!
THWAP
!!
THWAP

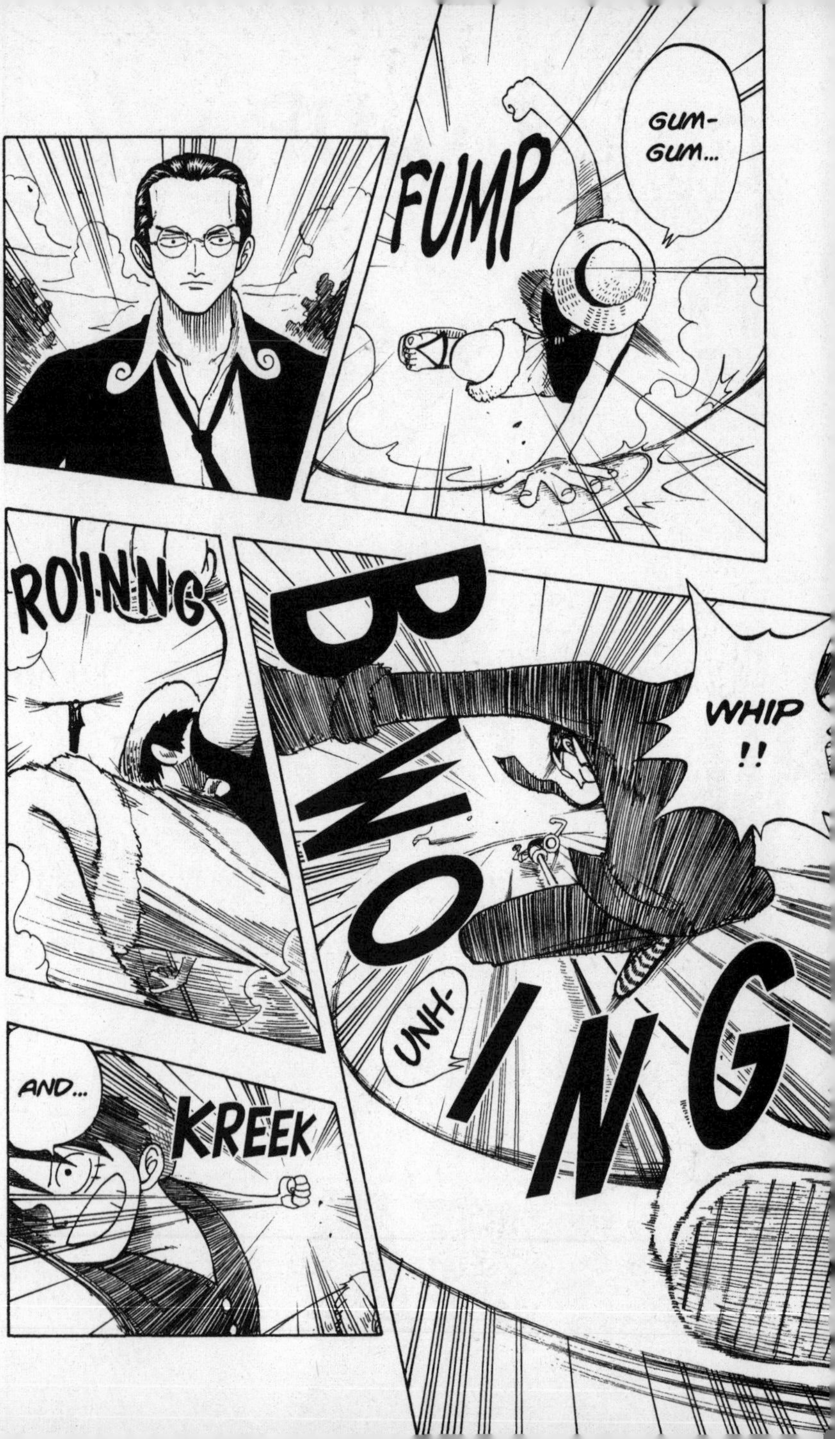
GUM-GUM...
FUMP
WHIP !!
BOING
UNH-
ROINNG
AND...
KREEK

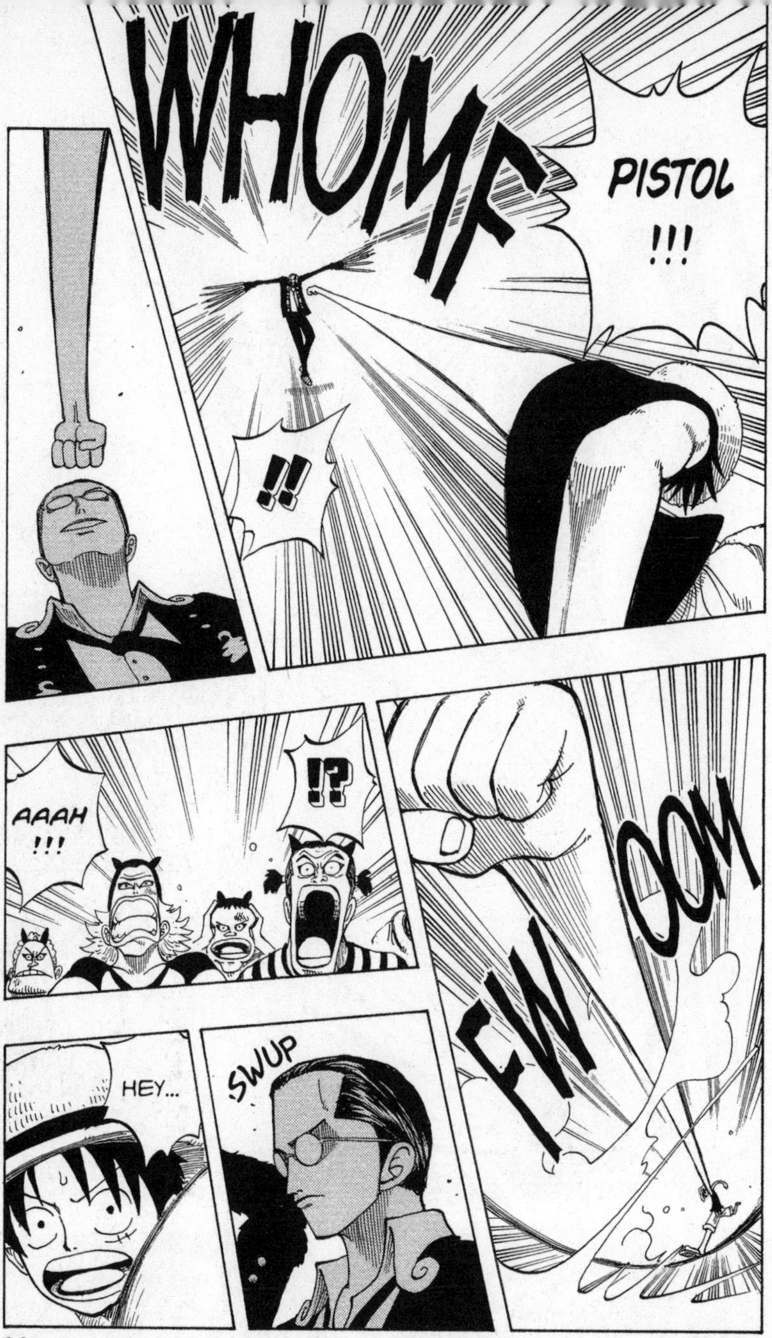
WHOMP
PISTOL !!!
!!
FWOOM
!?
AAAH !!!
SWUP
HEY...

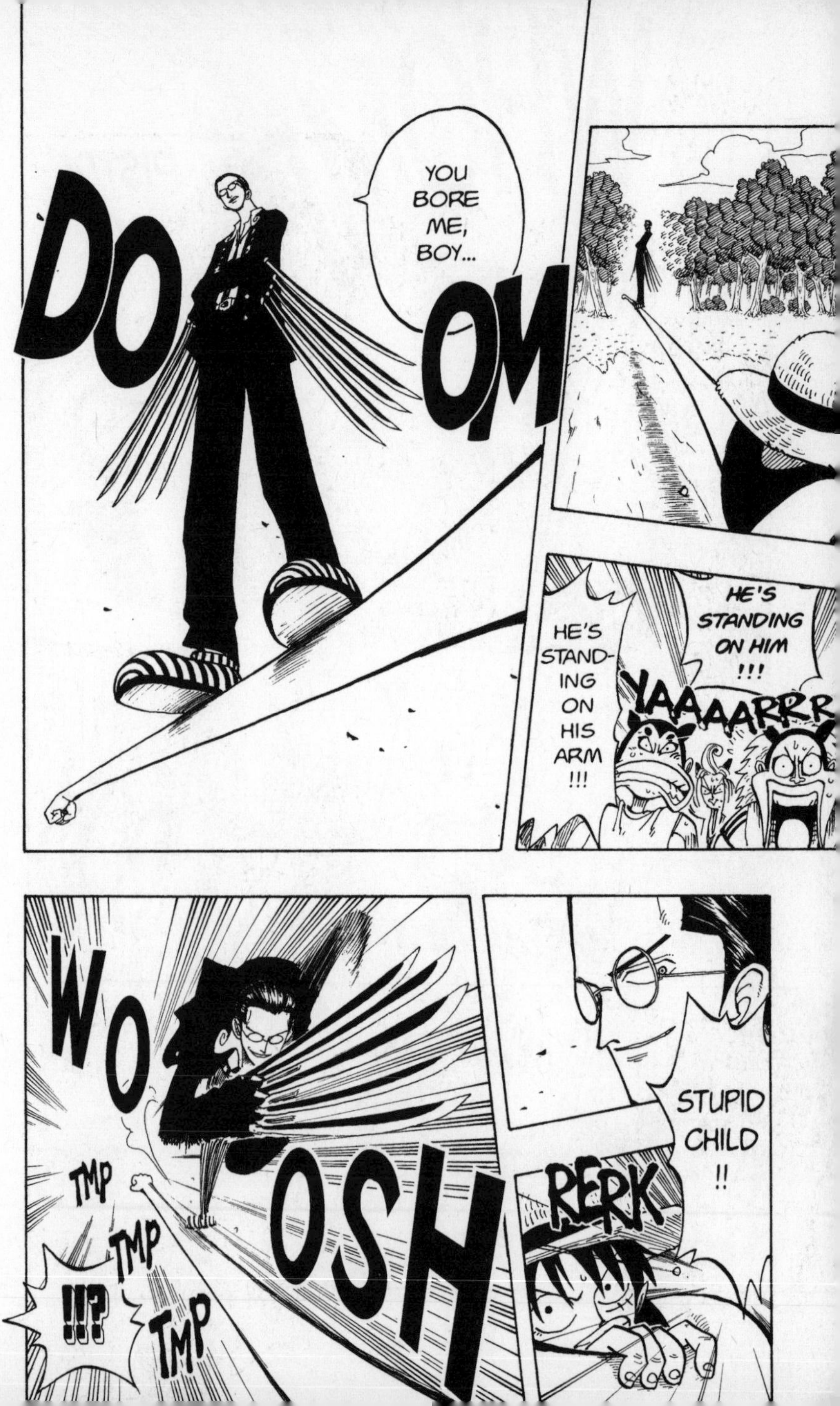
HE'S STANDING ON HIM!!!
HE'S STAND-ING ON HIS ARM!!!
YAAAARRR
YOU BORE ME, BOY...
DOOM
STUPID CHILD!!
RERK
WOOSH
TMP
TMP
TMP
!!?

READ THIS WAY

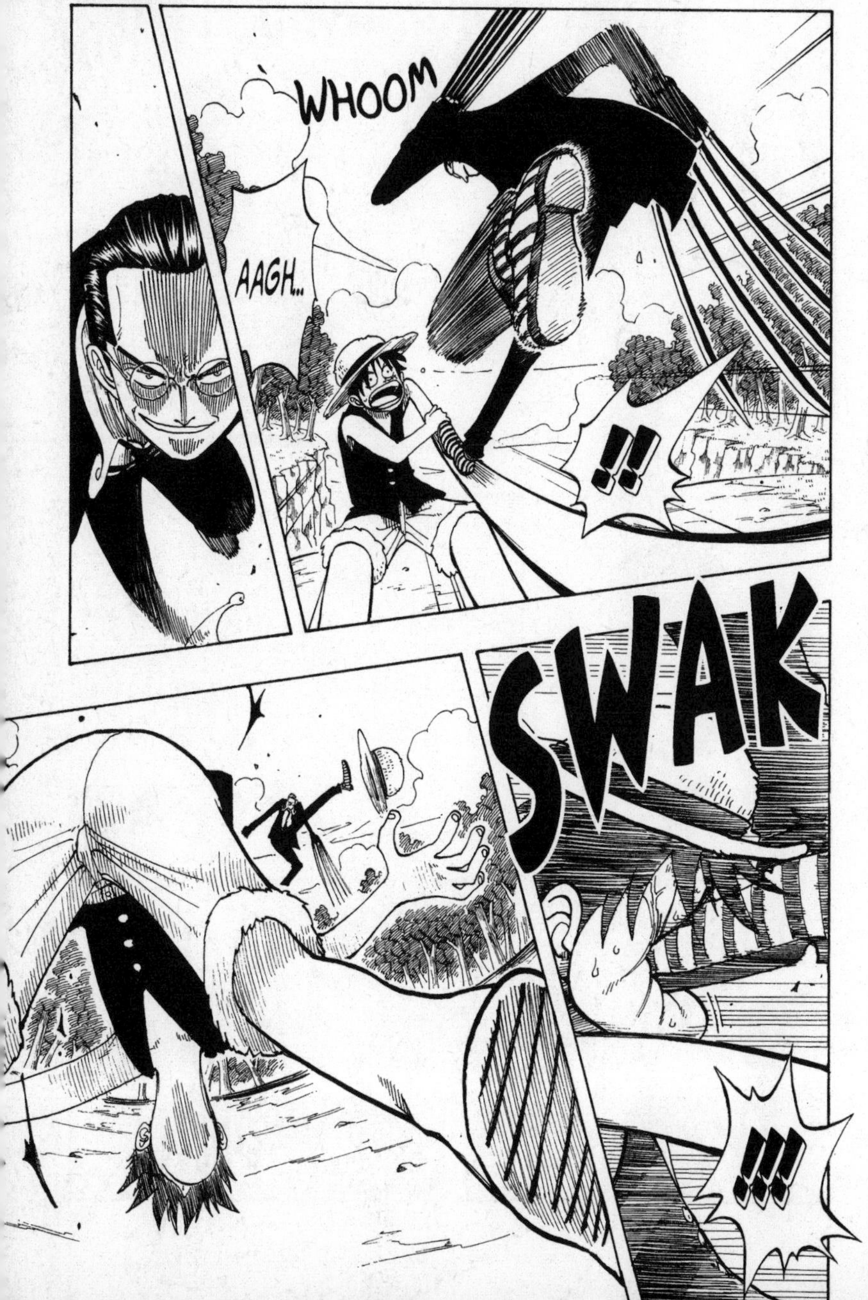
WHOOM
AAGH...
!!
SWAK
!!!

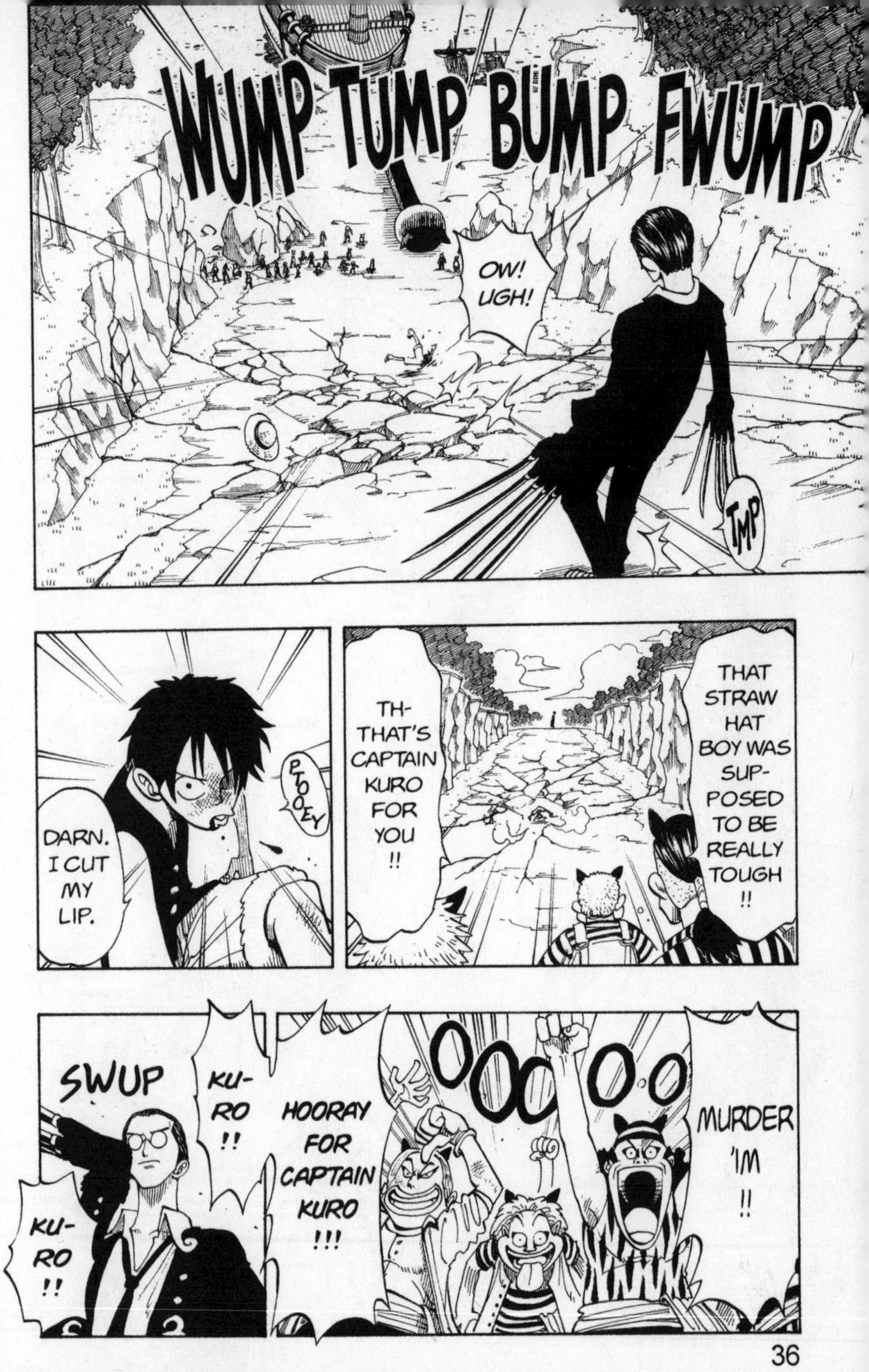
WUMP TUMP BUMP FWUMP
OW! UGH!
TMP
THAT STRAW HAT BOY WAS SUP-POSED TO BE REALLY TOUGH!!
TH-THAT'S CAPTAIN KURO FOR YOU!!
PTOOEY
DARN. I CUT MY LIP.
MURDER 'IM!!
OOOOOO
HOORAY FOR CAPTAIN KURO!!!
KU-RO!!
SWUP
KU-RO!!

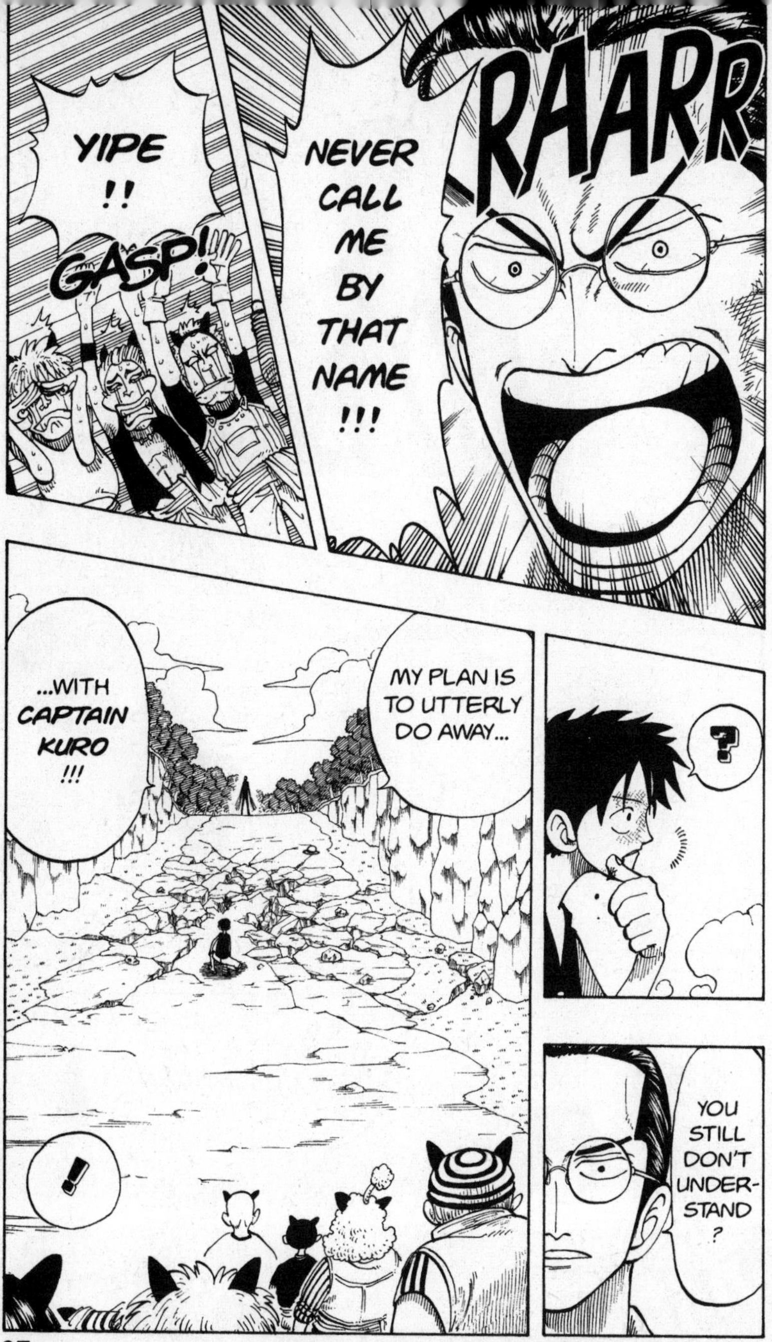
RAARR
NEVER CALL ME BY THAT NAME!!!
YIPE!!
GASP!
?
YOU STILL DON'T UNDER-STAND?
MY PLAN IS TO UTTERLY DO AWAY...
...WITH CAPTAIN KURO!!!
!

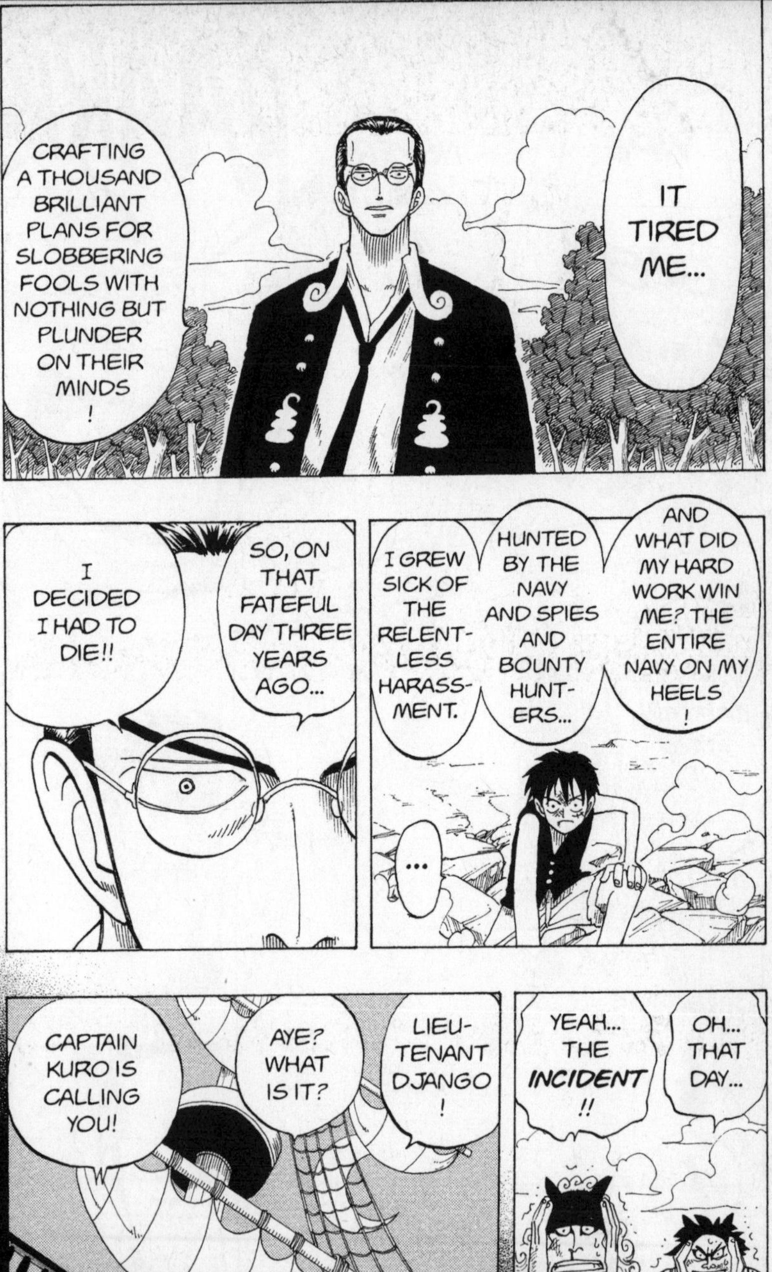
IT TIRED ME...
CRAFTING A THOUSAND BRILLIANT PLANS FOR SLOBBERING FOOLS WITH NOTHING BUT PLUNDER ON THEIR MINDS!
AND WHAT DID MY HARD WORK WIN ME? THE ENTIRE NAVY ON MY HEELS!
HUNTED BY THE NAVY AND SPIES AND BOUNTY HUNTERS...
I GREW SICK OF THE RELENTLESS HARASSMENT.
...
SO, ON THAT FATEFUL DAY THREE YEARS AGO...
I DECIDED I HAD TO DIE!!
OH... THAT DAY...
YEAH... THE *INCIDENT*!!
LIEUTENANT DJANGO!
AYE? WHAT IS IT?
CAPTAIN KURO IS CALLING YOU!

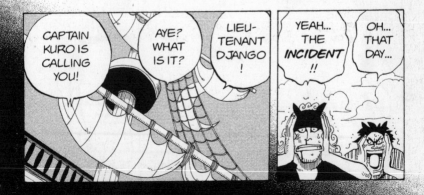

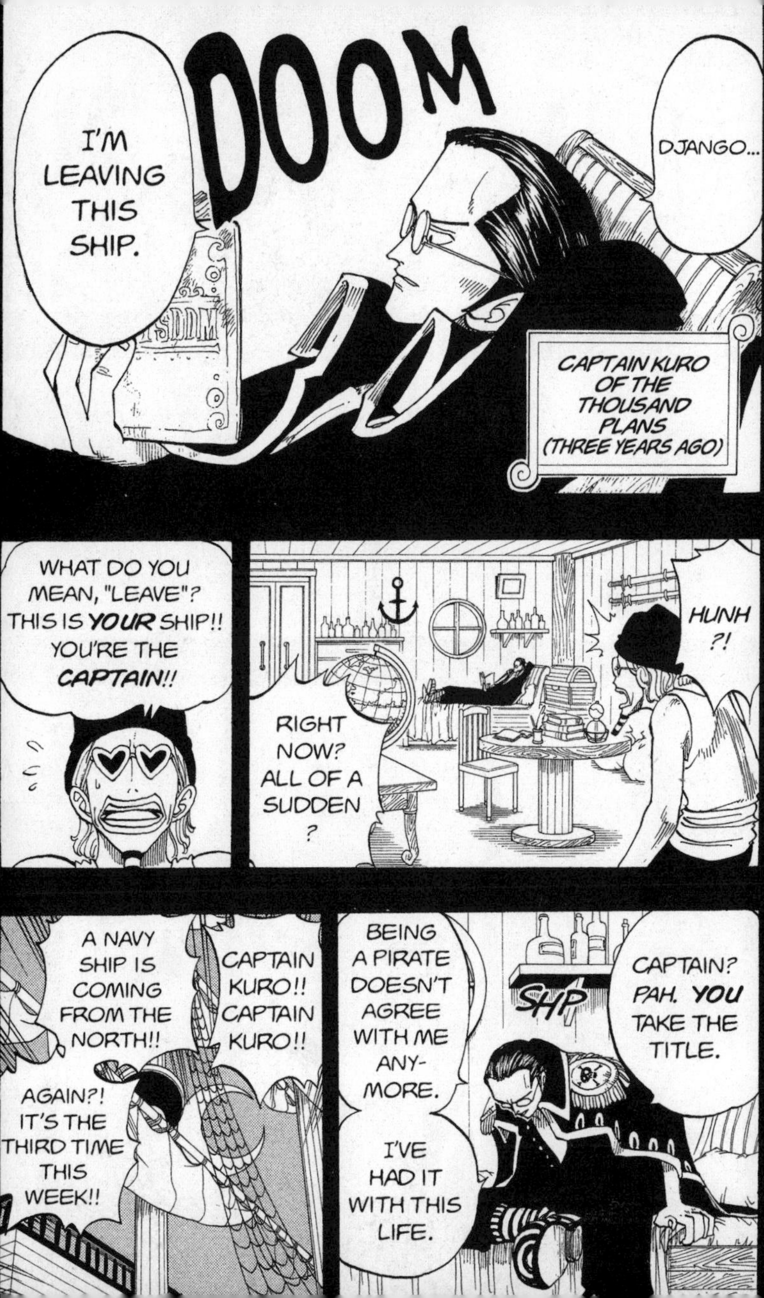
DJANGO...
DOOM
I'M LEAVING THIS SHIP.
CAPTAIN KURO OF THE THOUSAND PLANS (THREE YEARS AGO)
HUNH ?!
RIGHT NOW? ALL OF A SUDDEN ?
WHAT DO YOU MEAN, "LEAVE"? THIS IS YOUR SHIP!! YOU'RE THE CAPTAIN!!
CAPTAIN? PAH. YOU TAKE THE TITLE.
SHIP
BEING A PIRATE DOESN'T AGREE WITH ME ANY-MORE.
I'VE HAD IT WITH THIS LIFE.
CAPTAIN KURO!! CAPTAIN KURO!!
A NAVY SHIP IS COMING FROM THE NORTH!!
AGAIN?! IT'S THE THIRD TIME THIS WEEK!!

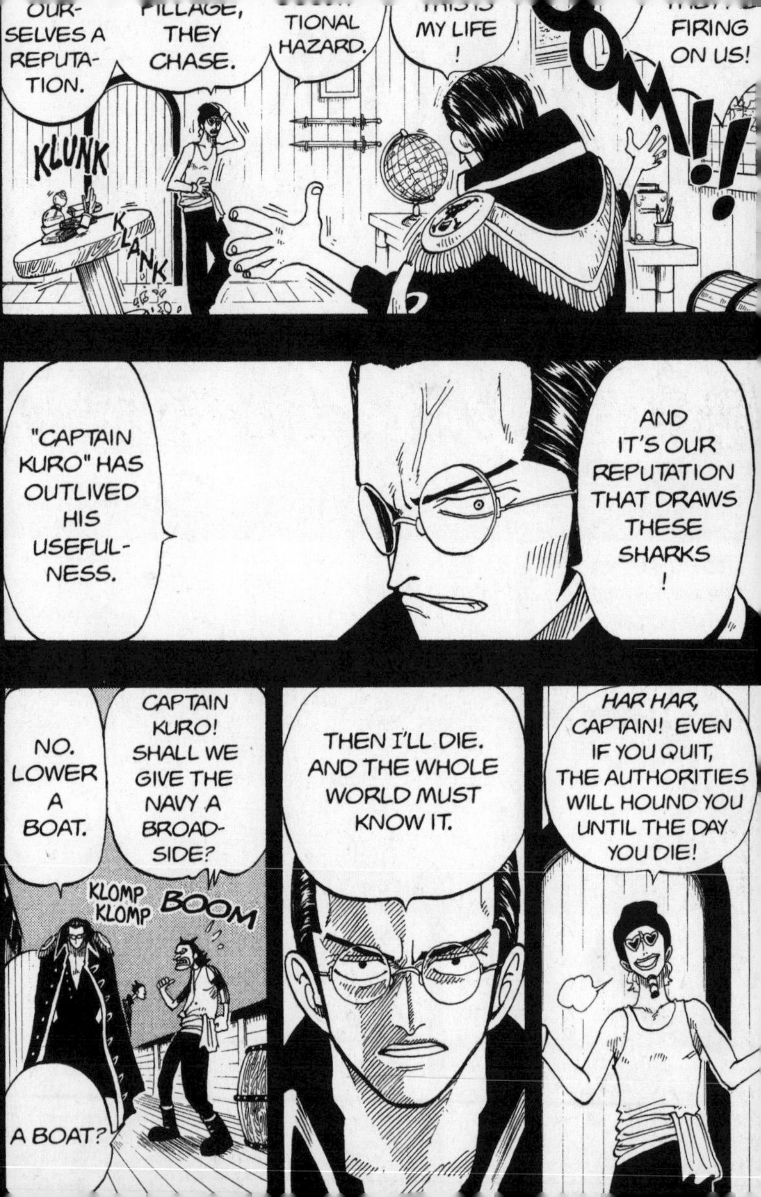
FIRING ON US!
OOM!!
MY LIFE !
TIONAL HAZARD.
PILLAGE, THEY CHASE.
OUR- SELVES A REPUTA- TION.
KLUNK
KLANK
AND IT'S OUR REPUTATION THAT DRAWS THESE SHARKS !
"CAPTAIN KURO" HAS OUTLIVED HIS USEFUL- NESS.
HAR HAR, CAPTAIN! EVEN IF YOU QUIT, THE AUTHORITIES WILL HOUND YOU UNTIL THE DAY YOU DIE!
THEN I'LL DIE. AND THE WHOLE WORLD MUST KNOW IT.
CAPTAIN KURO! SHALL WE GIVE THE NAVY A BROAD- SIDE?
NO. LOWER A BOAT.
BOOM
KLOMP KLOMP
A BOAT?

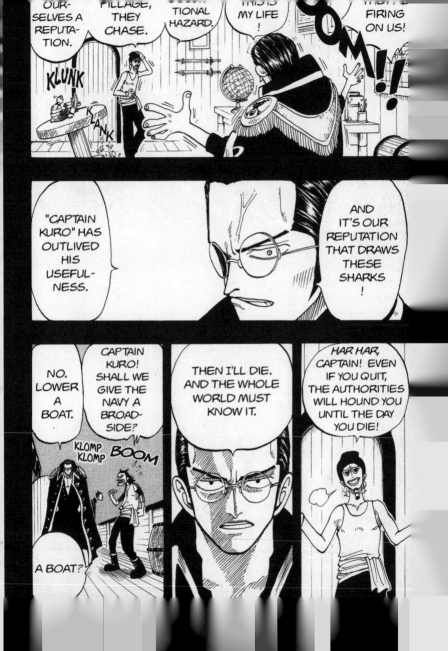

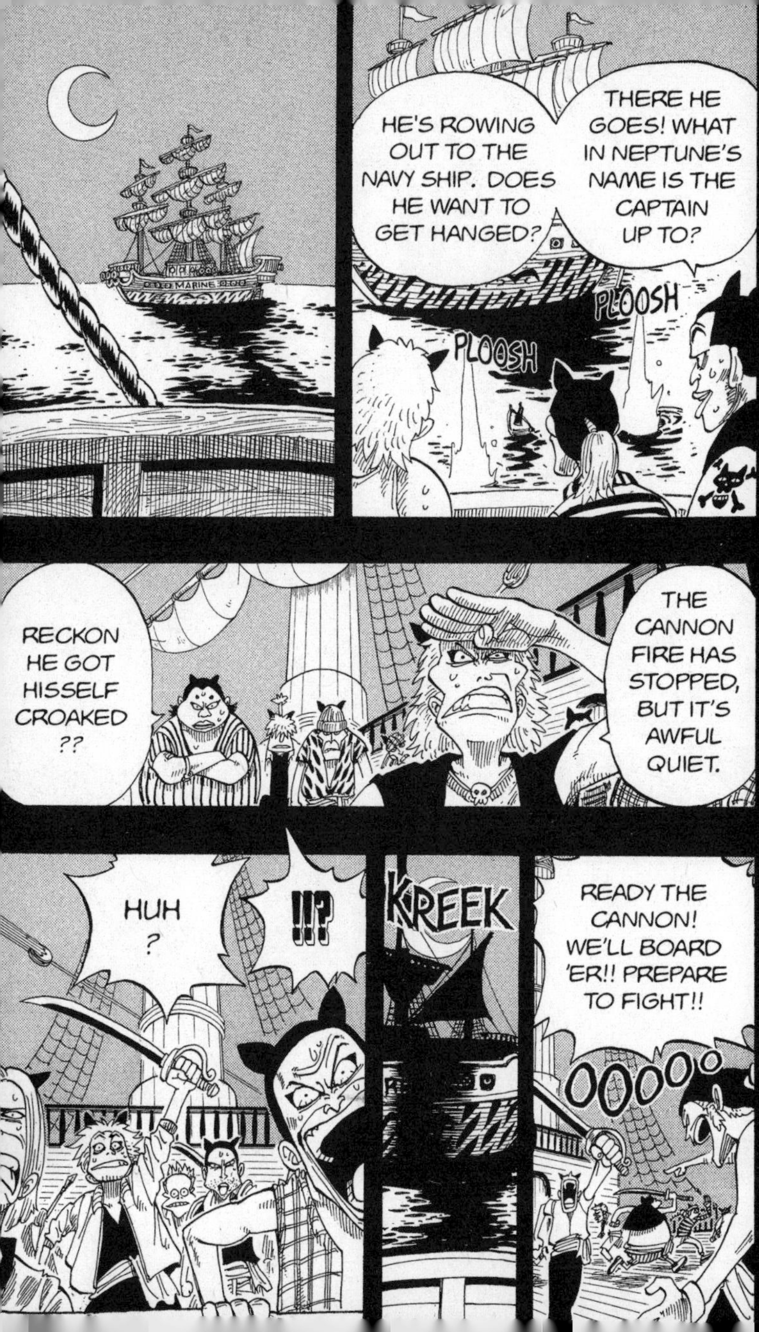
THERE HE GOES! WHAT IN NEPTUNE'S NAME IS THE CAPTAIN UP TO?
HE'S ROWING OUT TO THE NAVY SHIP. DOES HE WANT TO GET HANGED?
PLOOSH
PLOOSH
MARINE
THE CANNON FIRE HAS STOPPED, BUT IT'S AWFUL QUIET.
RECKON HE GOT HISSELF CROAKED ??
READY THE CANNON! WE'LL BOARD 'ER!! PREPARE TO FIGHT!!
OOOOO
KREEK
!!?
HUH ?

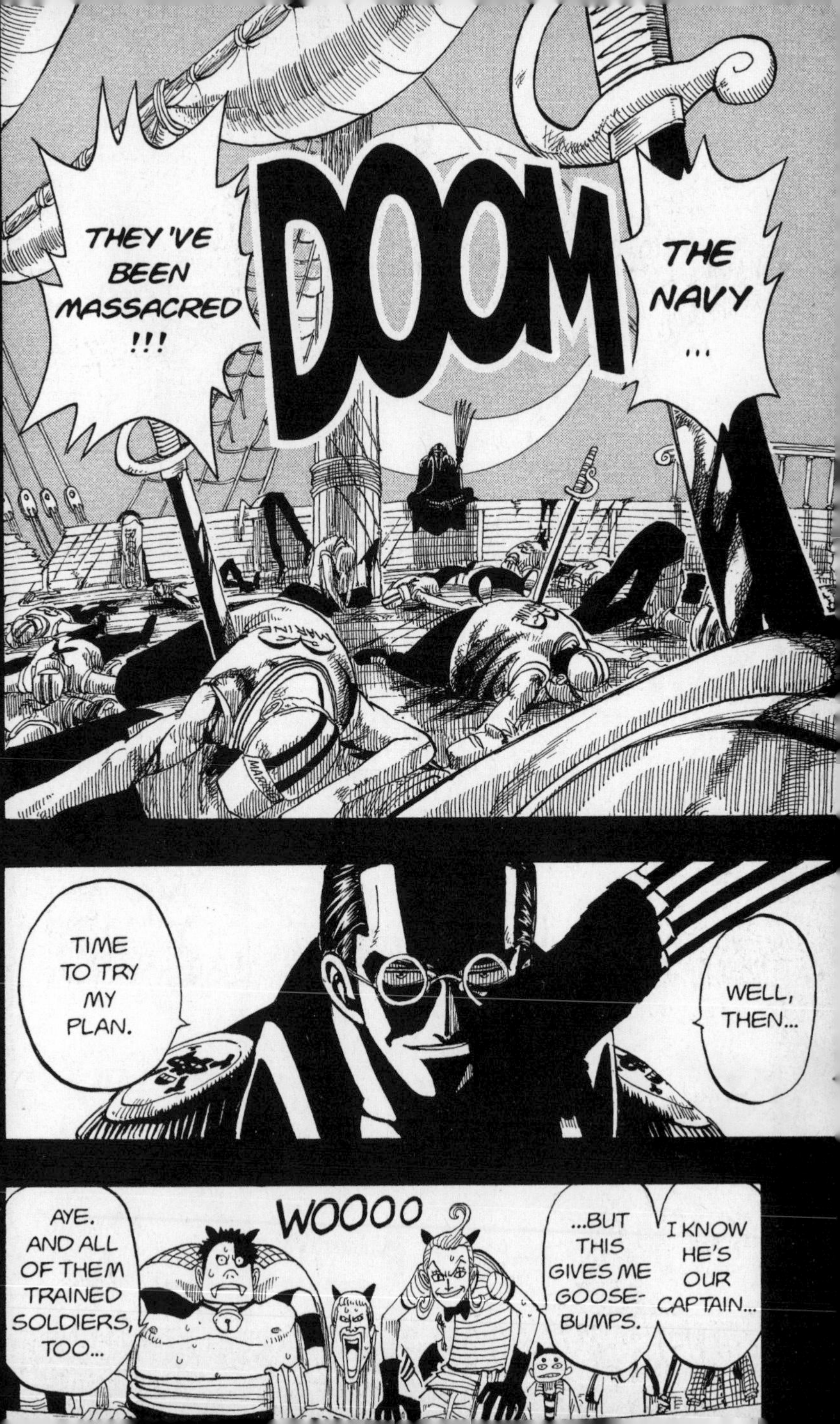
THE NAVY ...
DOOM
THEY'VE BEEN MASSACRED !!!
WELL, THEN...
TIME TO TRY MY PLAN.
I KNOW HE'S OUR CAPTAIN...
...BUT THIS GIVES ME GOOSE-BUMPS.
WOOOO
AYE. AND ALL OF THEM TRAINED SOLDIERS, TOO...

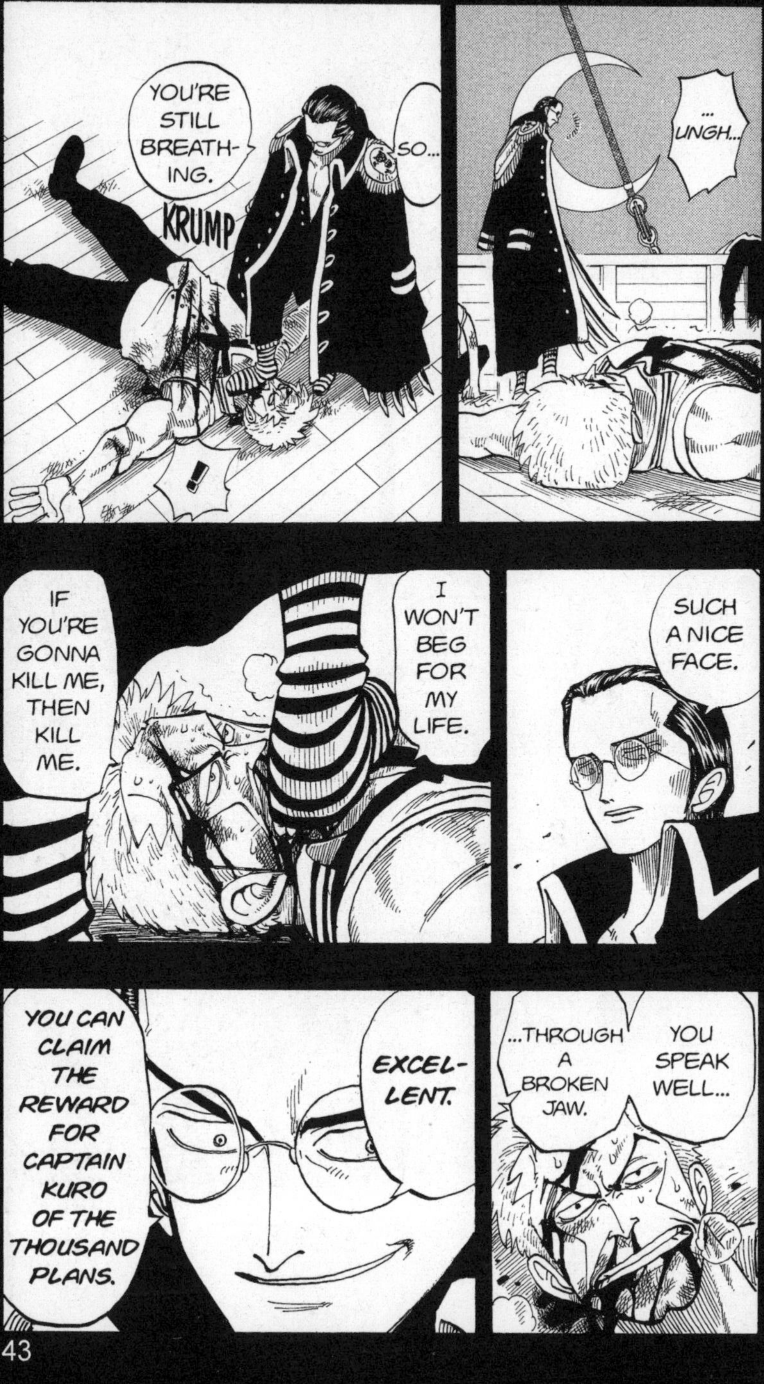
... UNGH...
SO...
YOU'RE STILL BREATH-ING.
KRUMP
!
SUCH A NICE FACE.
I WON'T BEG FOR MY LIFE.
IF YOU'RE GONNA KILL ME, THEN KILL ME.
YOU SPEAK WELL...
...THROUGH A BROKEN JAW.
EXCEL-LENT.
YOU CAN CLAIM THE REWARD FOR CAPTAIN KURO OF THE THOUSAND PLANS.

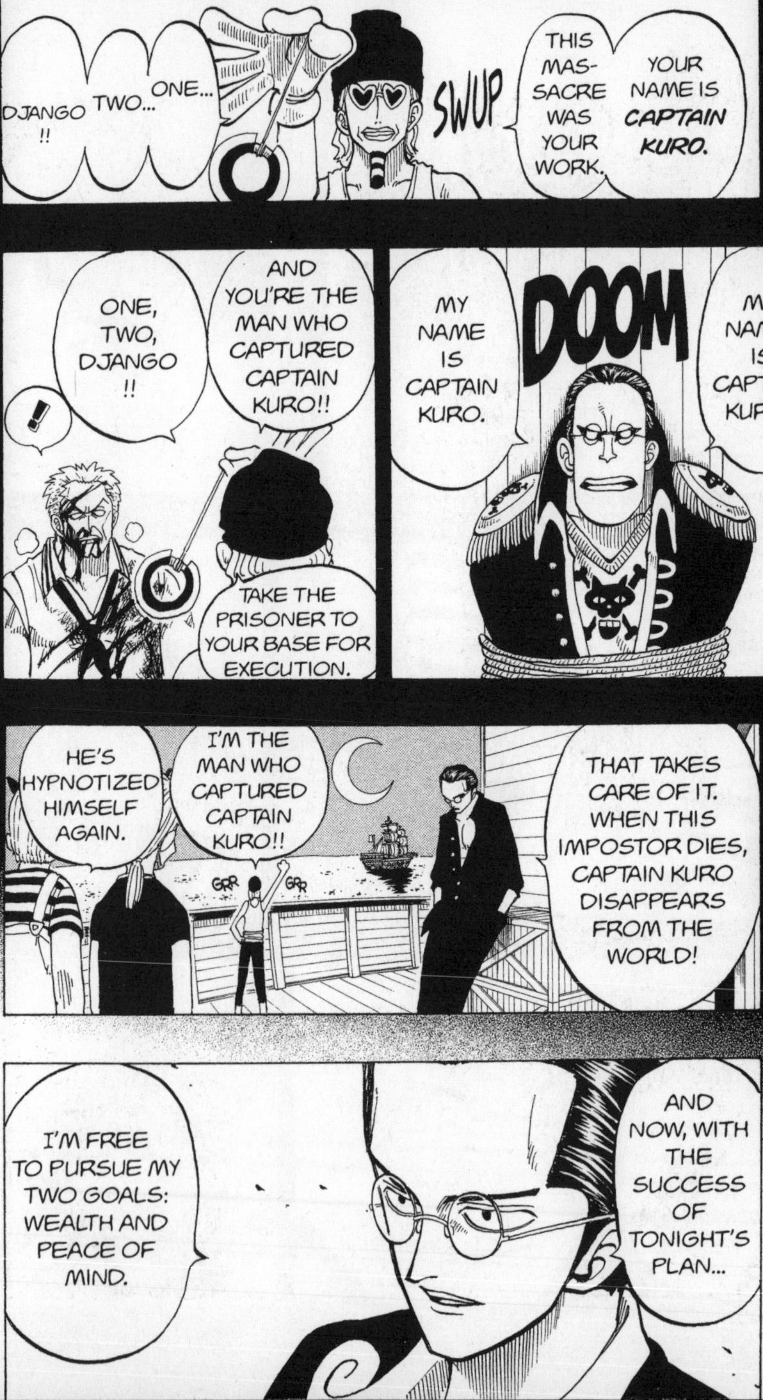
YOUR NAME IS CAPTAIN KURO.
THIS MAS-SACRE WAS YOUR WORK.
SWUP
ONE... TWO... DJANGO !!
MY NAME IS CAPTAIN KURO.
DOOM
MY NAME IS CAPTAIN KURO.
AND YOU'RE THE MAN WHO CAPTURED CAPTAIN KURO!!
ONE, TWO, DJANGO !!
!
TAKE THE PRISONER TO YOUR BASE FOR EXECUTION.
THAT TAKES CARE OF IT. WHEN THIS IMPOSTOR DIES, CAPTAIN KURO DISAPPEARS FROM THE WORLD!
I'M THE MAN WHO CAPTURED CAPTAIN KURO!!
GRR
GRR
HE'S HYPNOTIZED HIMSELF AGAIN.
AND NOW, WITH THE SUCCESS OF TONIGHT'S PLAN...
I'M FREE TO PURSUE MY TWO GOALS: WEALTH AND PEACE OF MIND.

READ THIS WAY

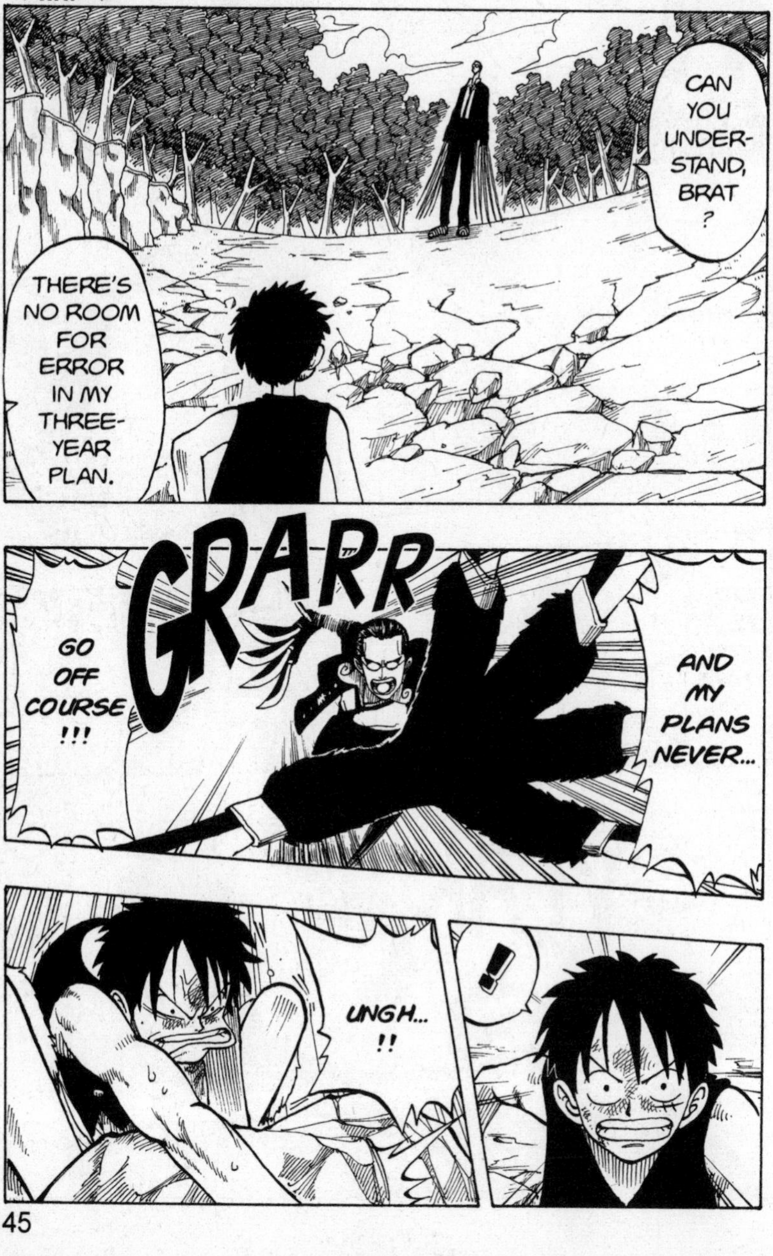
CAN YOU UNDER-STAND, BRAT?
THERE'S NO ROOM FOR ERROR IN MY THREE-YEAR PLAN.
AND MY PLANS NEVER...
GRARR
GO OFF COURSE!!!
!
UNGH...!!

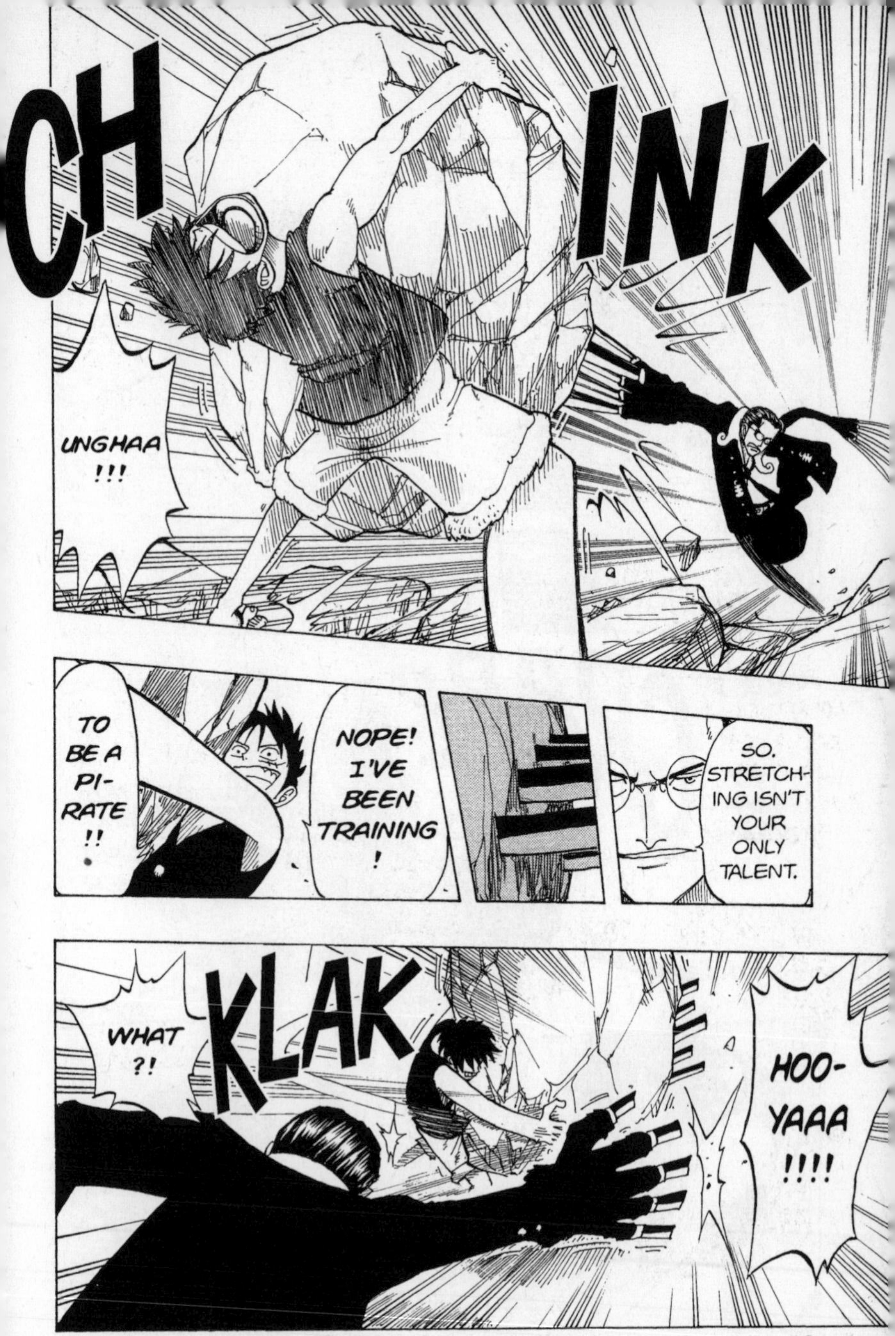
CHINK
UNGHAA!!!
SO. STRETCHING ISN'T YOUR ONLY TALENT.
NOPE! I'VE BEEN TRAINING!
TO BE A PIRATE!!
HOO-YAAA!!!!
KLAK
WHAT?!

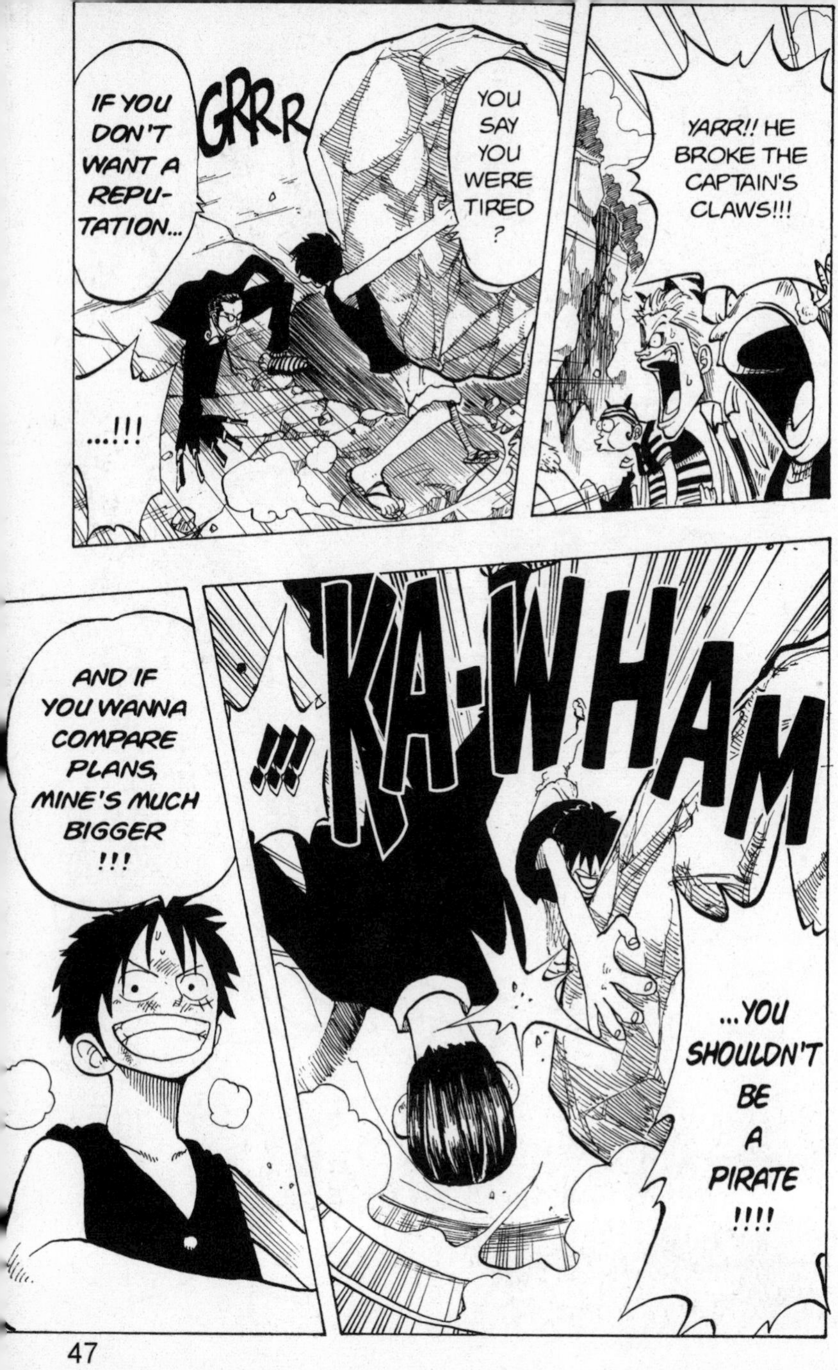
YARR!! HE BROKE THE CAPTAIN'S CLAWS!!!
YOU SAY YOU WERE TIRED?
GRRR
IF YOU DON'T WANT A REPUTATION...
...!!!
KA-WHAM
!!!
...YOU SHOULDN'T BE A PIRATE!!!!
AND IF YOU WANNA COMPARE PLANS, MINE'S MUCH BIGGER!!!

One Piece Character Sketches!

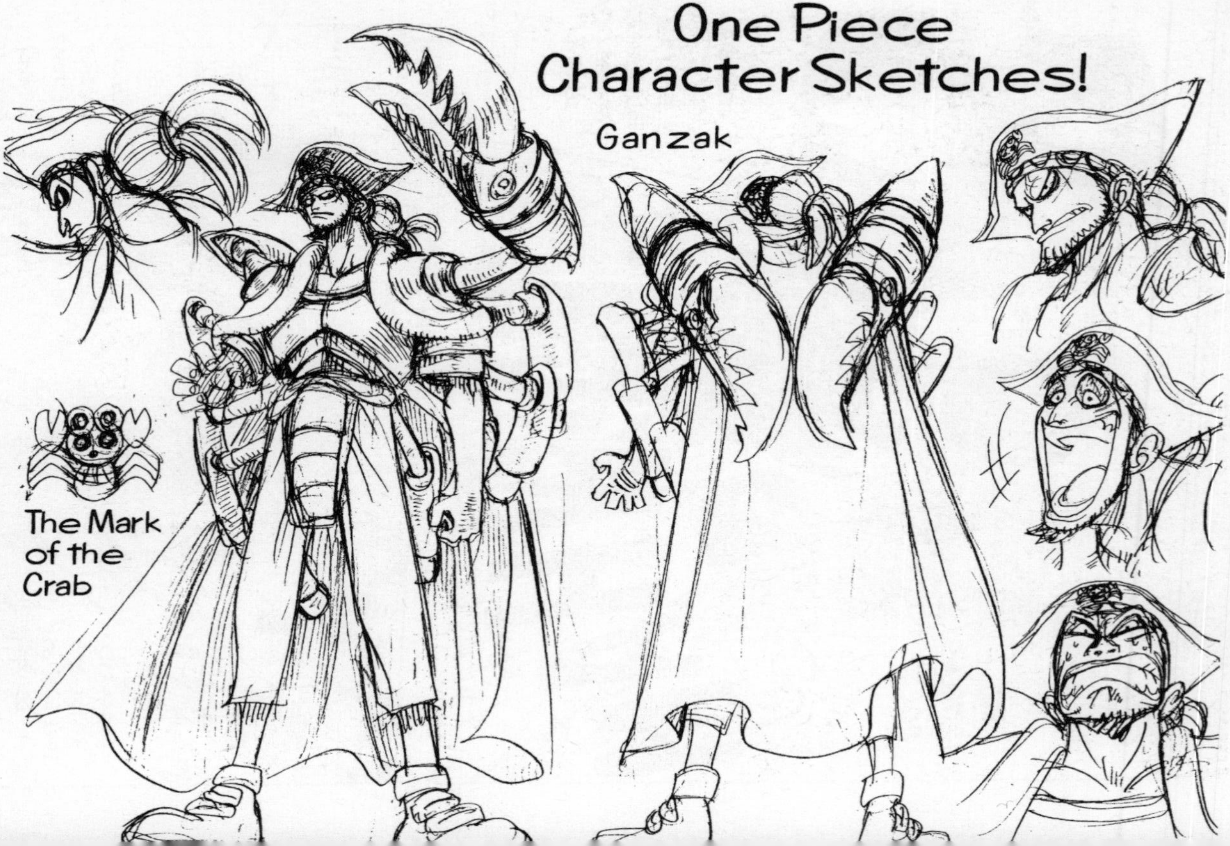
Ganzak
The Mark of the Crab

Chapter 38:
PIRATE CREW

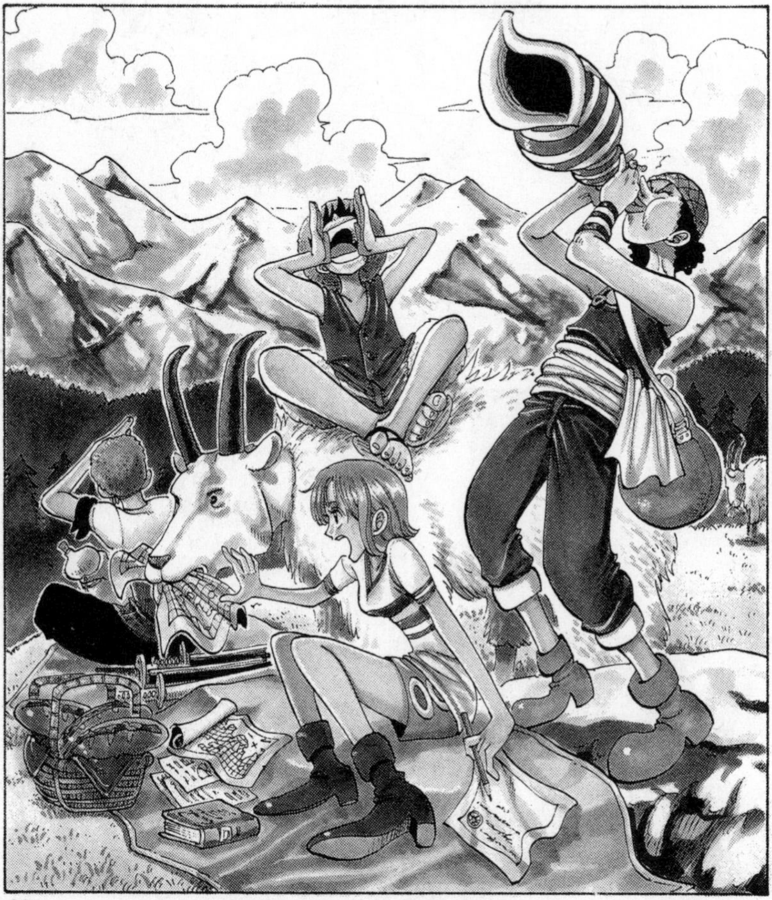

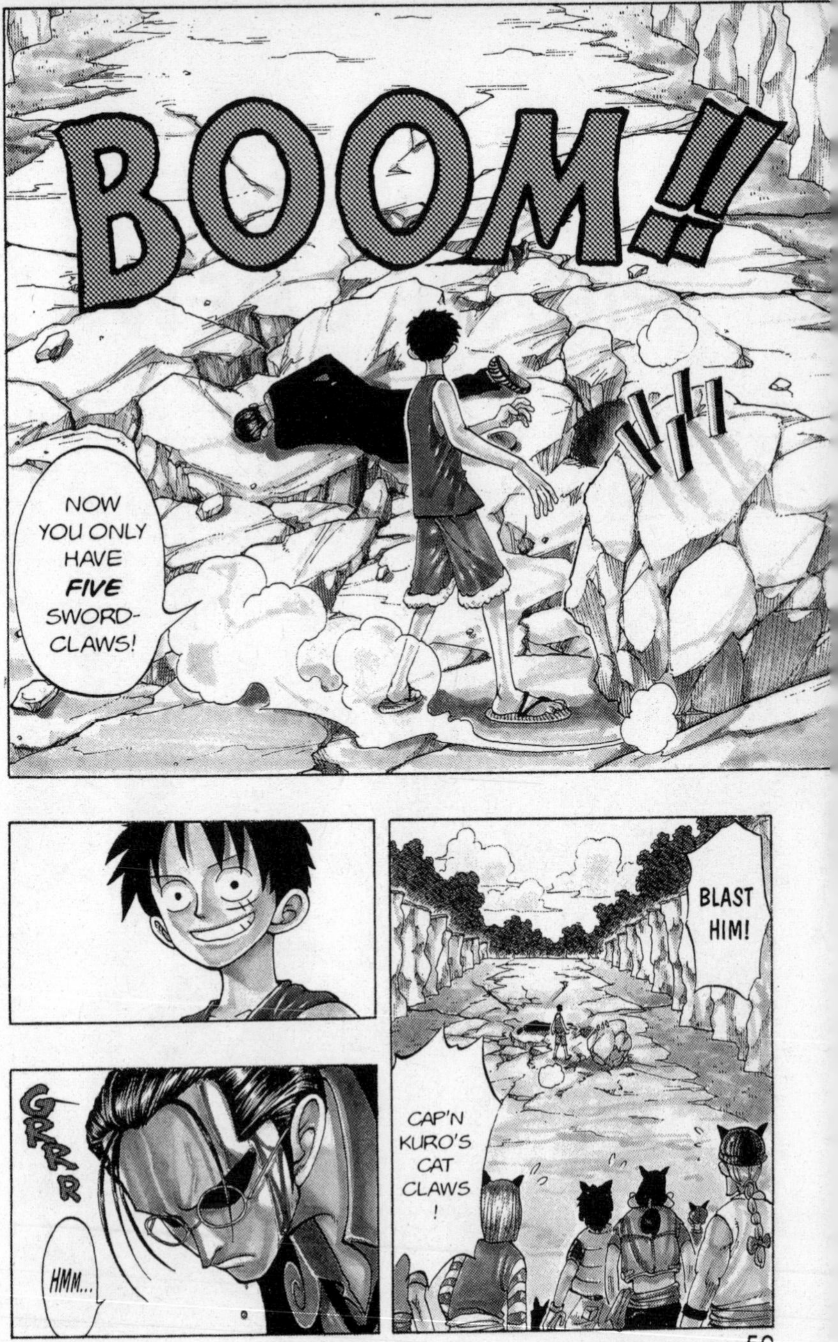
BOOM!!
NOW YOU ONLY HAVE *FIVE* SWORD-CLAWS!
BLAST HIM!
CAP'N KURO'S CAT CLAWS!
GRRR
HMM...

READ THIS WAY

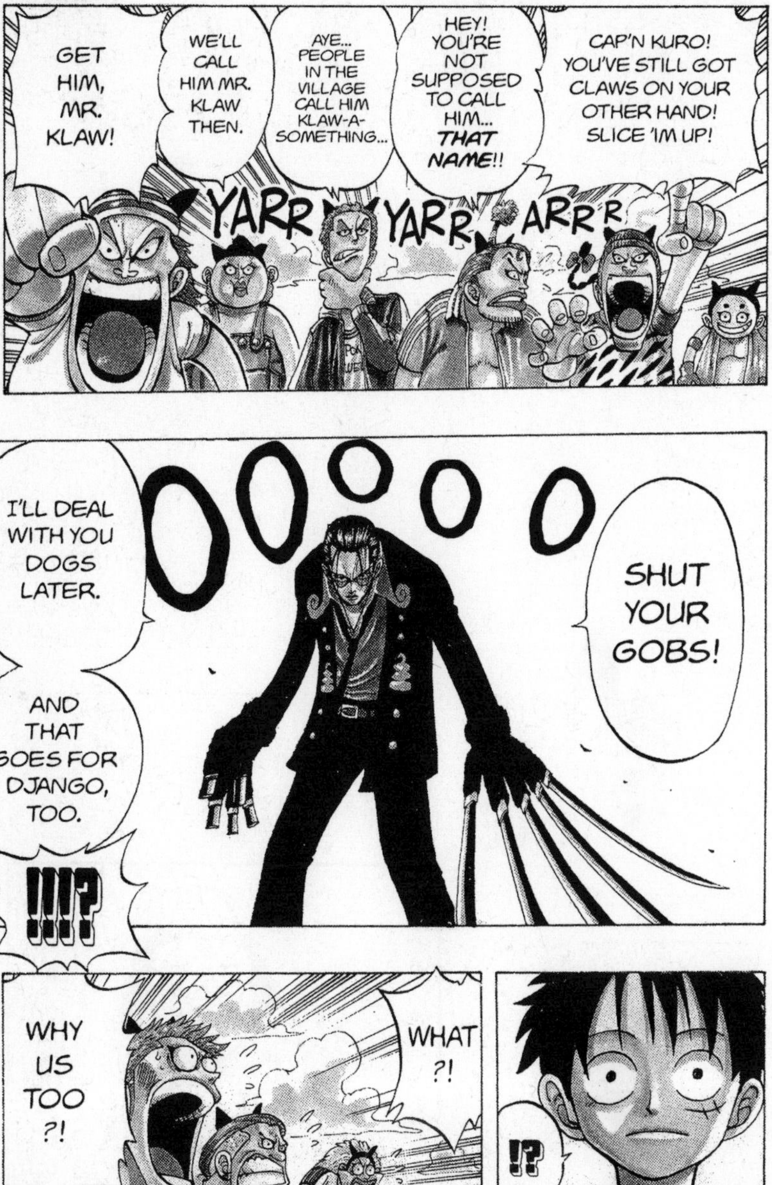

CAP'N KURO! YOU'VE STILL GOT CLAWS ON YOUR OTHER HAND! SLICE 'IM UP!
HEY! YOU'RE NOT SUPPOSED TO CALL HIM... THAT NAME!!
AYE... PEOPLE IN THE VILLAGE CALL HIM KLAW-A-SOMETHING...
WE'LL CALL HIM MR. KLAW THEN.
GET HIM, MR. KLAW!
ARRR
YARR
YARR
SHUT YOUR GOBS!
OOOOO
I'LL DEAL WITH YOU DOGS LATER.
AND THAT GOES FOR DJANGO, TOO.
!!!?
!?
WHAT ?!
WHY US TOO ?!

READ THIS WAY

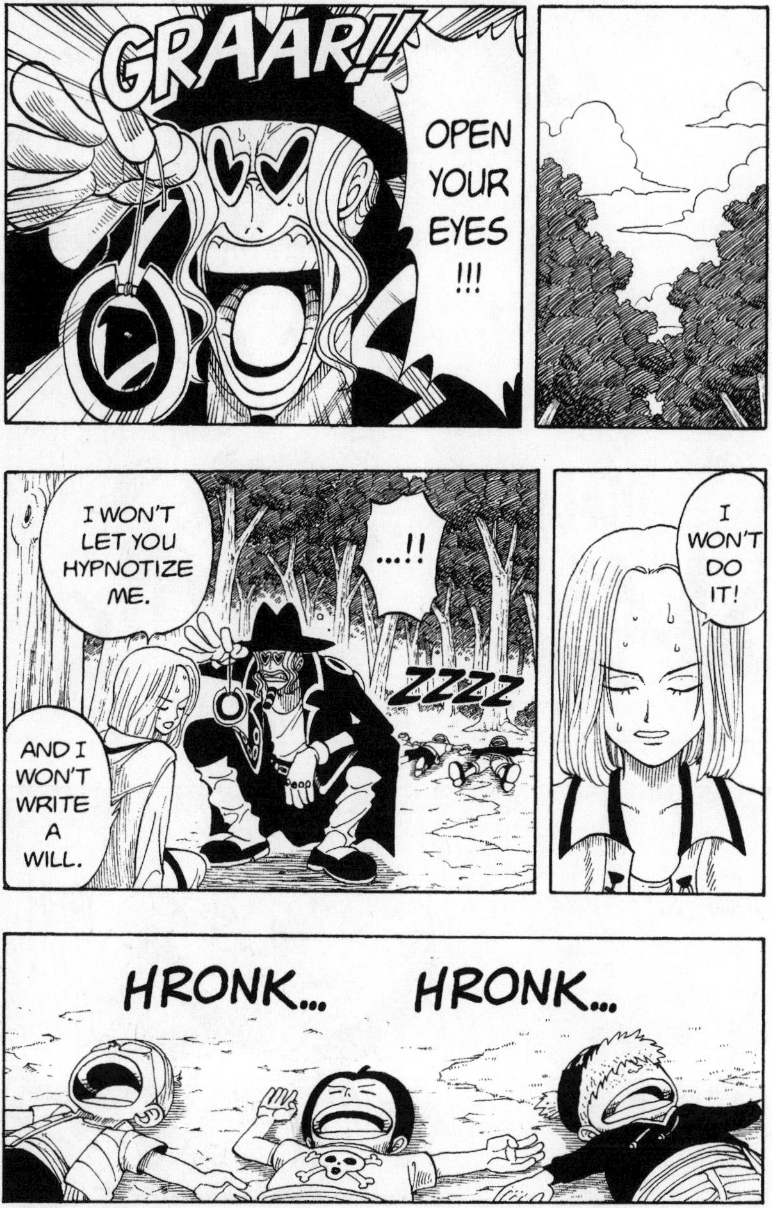
GRAAR!!
OPEN YOUR EYES!!!
I WON'T DO IT!
...!!
I WON'T LET YOU HYPNOTIZE ME.
ZZZZ
AND I WON'T WRITE A WILL.
HRONK...
HRONK...

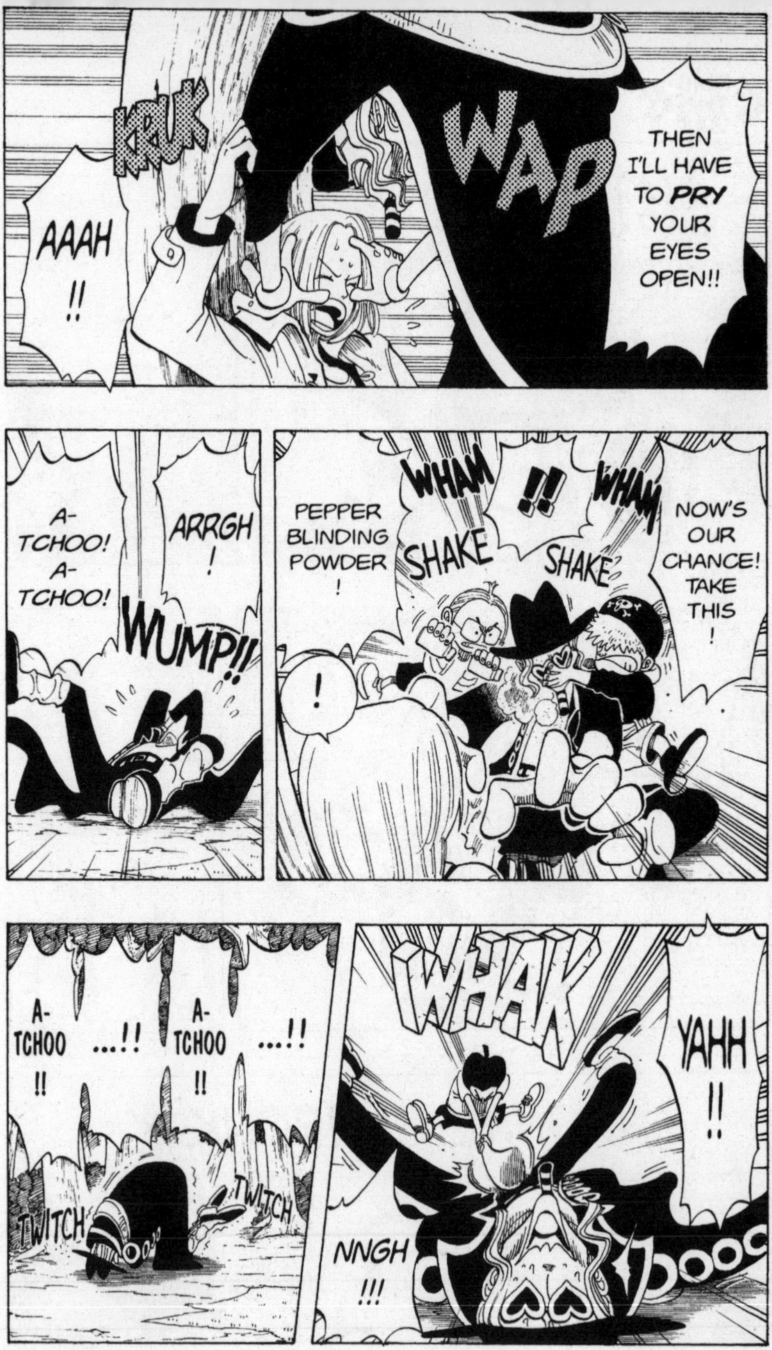

THEN I'LL HAVE TO PRY YOUR EYES OPEN!!
WAP
KRUK
AAAH !!
NOW'S OUR CHANCE! TAKE THIS!
WHAM
!!
WHAM
SHAKE
SHAKE
PEPPER BLINDING POWDER!
!
ARRGH!
A-TCHOO! A-TCHOO!
WUMP!!
YAHH!!
WHAK
NNGH!!!
...!!
A-TCHOO!!
...!!
A-TCHOO!!
TWITCH
TWITCH

READ THIS WAY

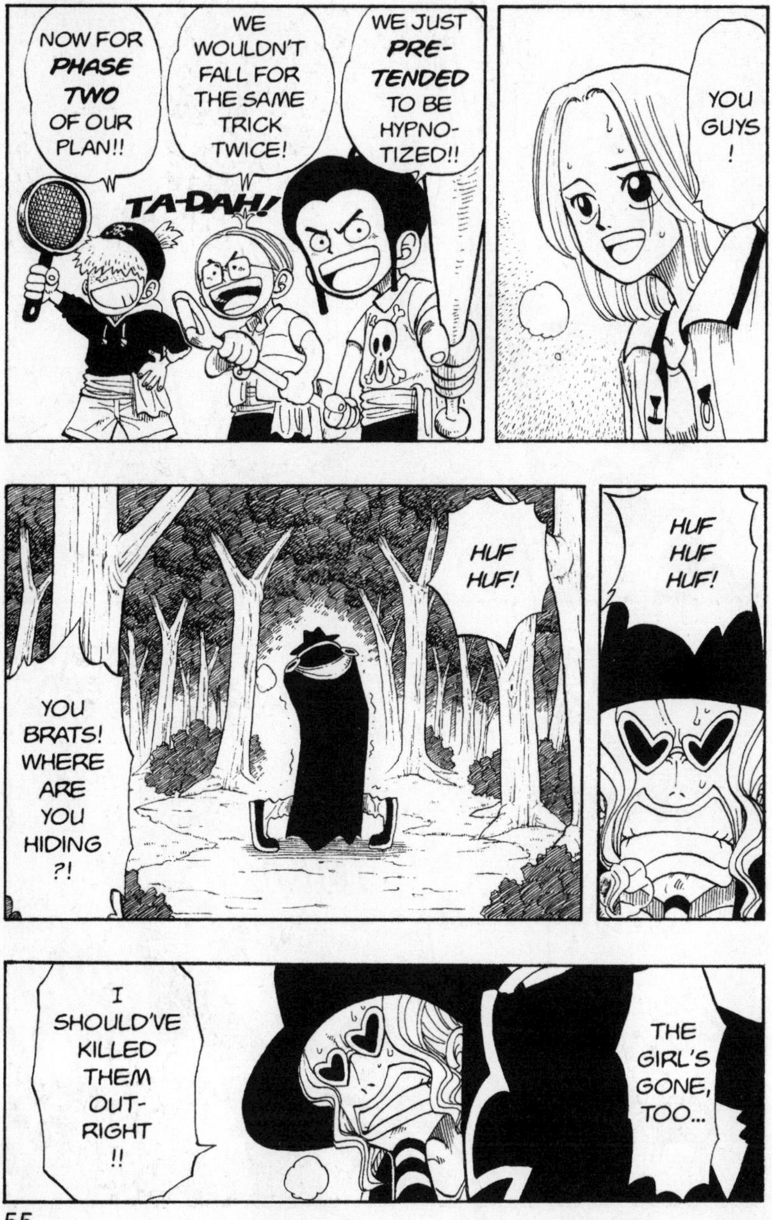
YOU GUYS!
WE JUST PRETENDED TO BE HYPNOTIZED!!
WE WOULDN'T FALL FOR THE SAME TRICK TWICE!
NOW FOR PHASE TWO OF OUR PLAN!!
TA-DAH!
HUF HUF HUF!
HUF HUF!
YOU BRATS! WHERE ARE YOU HIDING?!
THE GIRL'S GONE, TOO...
I SHOULD'VE KILLED THEM OUTRIGHT!!

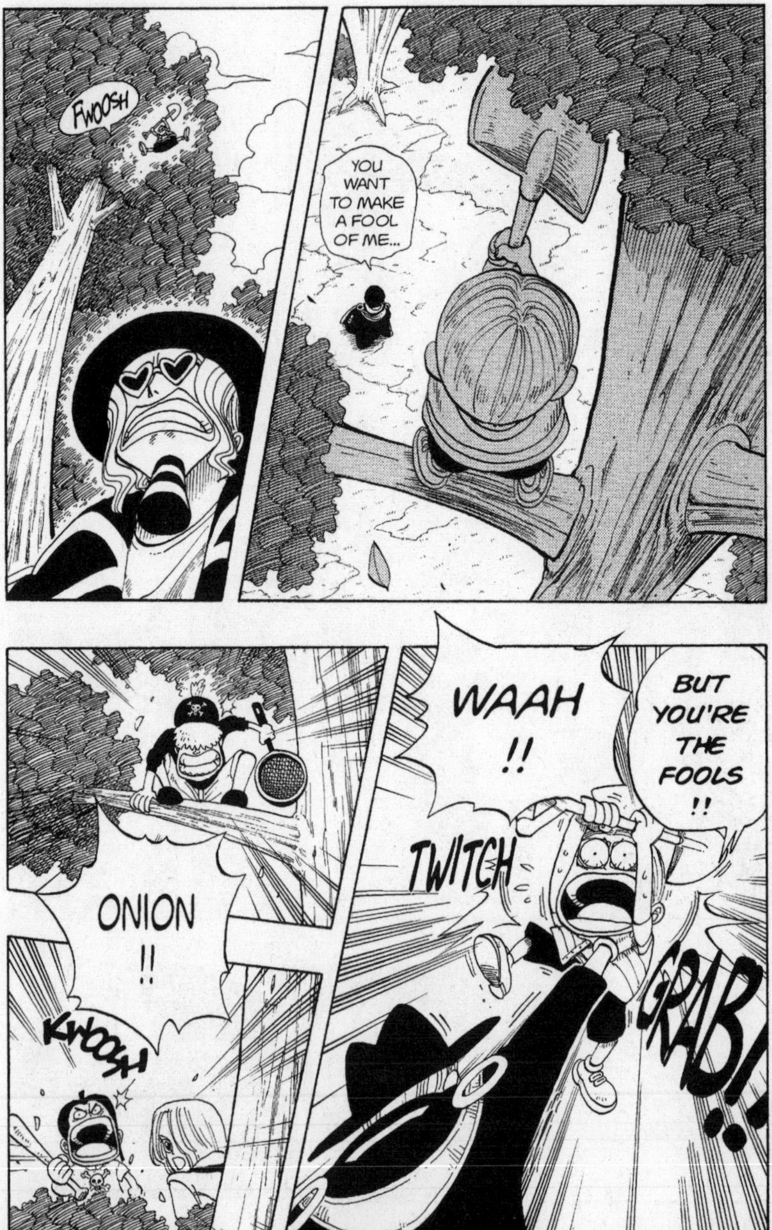
YOU WANT TO MAKE A FOOL OF ME...
FWOOSH
BUT YOU'RE THE FOOLS !!
WAAH !!
TWITCH
GRAB!!
ONION !!
KWOOSH

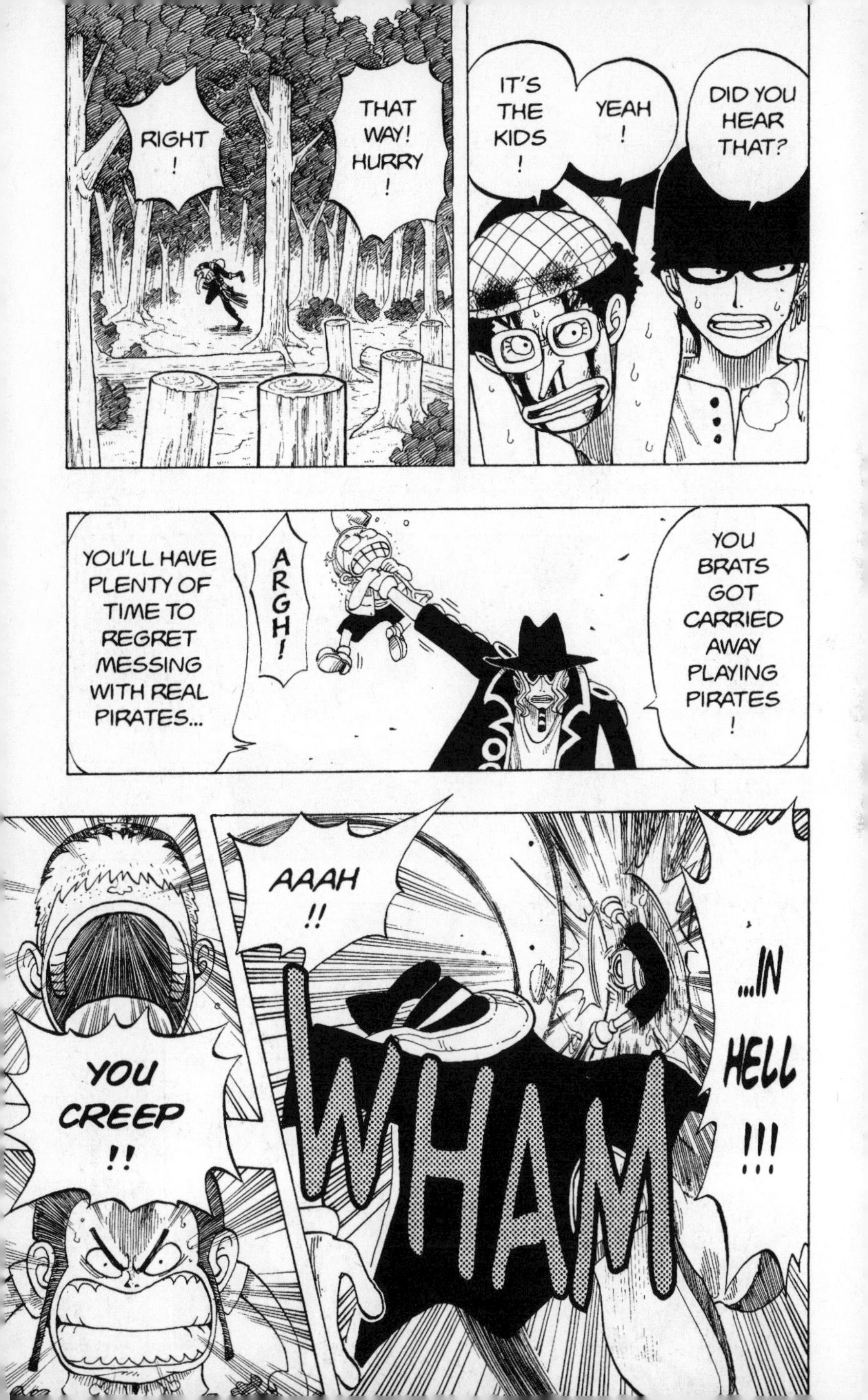
DID YOU HEAR THAT?
YEAH!
IT'S THE KIDS!
THAT WAY! HURRY!
RIGHT!
YOU BRATS GOT CARRIED AWAY PLAYING PIRATES!
ARGH!
YOU'LL HAVE PLENTY OF TIME TO REGRET MESSING WITH REAL PIRATES...
...IN HELL!!!
AAAH!!
WHAM
YOU CREEP!!

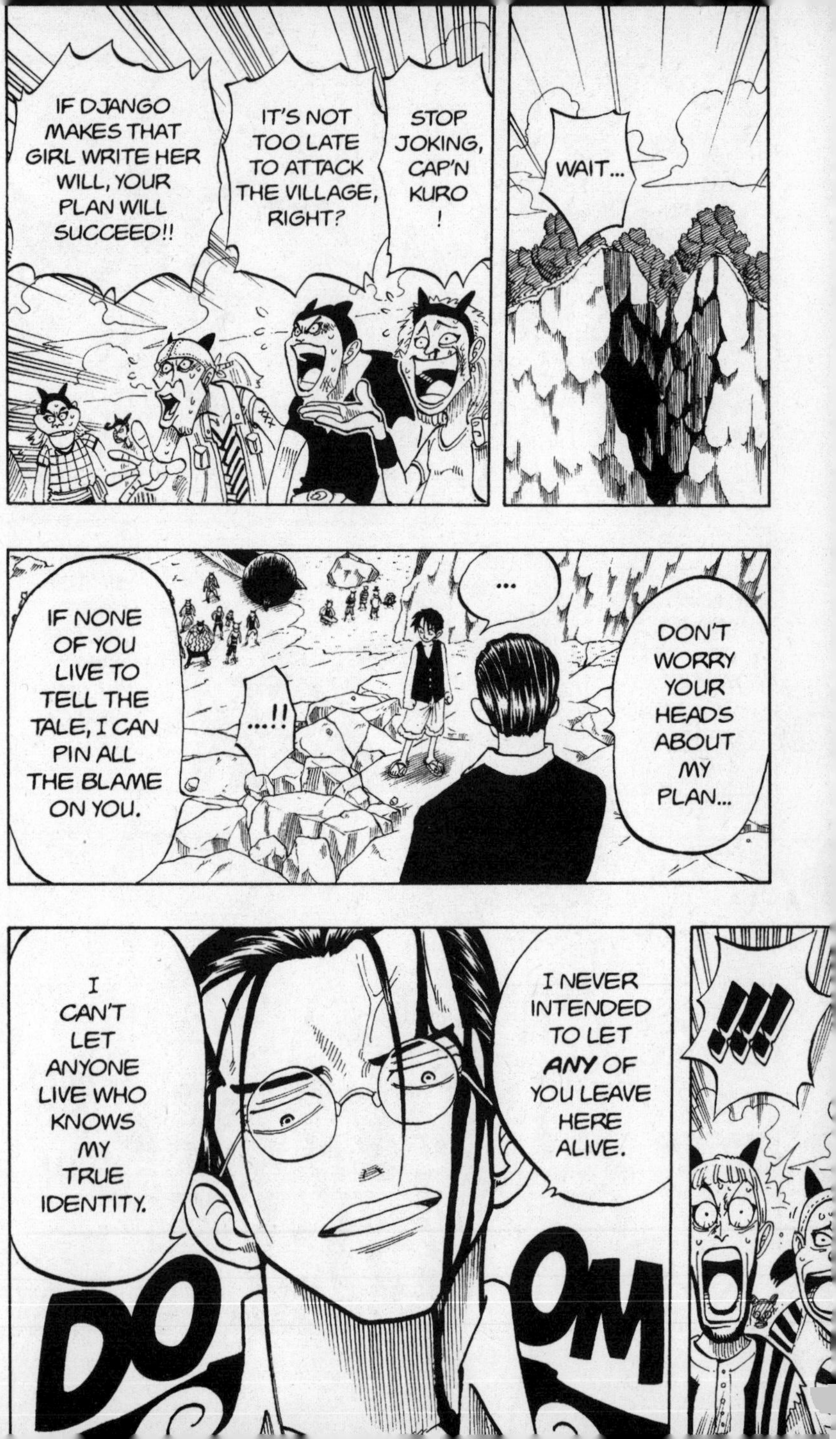
WAIT...
STOP JOKING, CAP'N KURO!
IT'S NOT TOO LATE TO ATTACK THE VILLAGE, RIGHT?
IF DJANGO MAKES THAT GIRL WRITE HER WILL, YOUR PLAN WILL SUCCEED!!
DON'T WORRY YOUR HEADS ABOUT MY PLAN...
...
...!!
IF NONE OF YOU LIVE TO TELL THE TALE, I CAN PIN ALL THE BLAME ON YOU.
!!!
I NEVER INTENDED TO LET ANY OF YOU LEAVE HERE ALIVE.
I CAN'T LET ANYONE LIVE WHO KNOWS MY TRUE IDENTITY.
DO OM

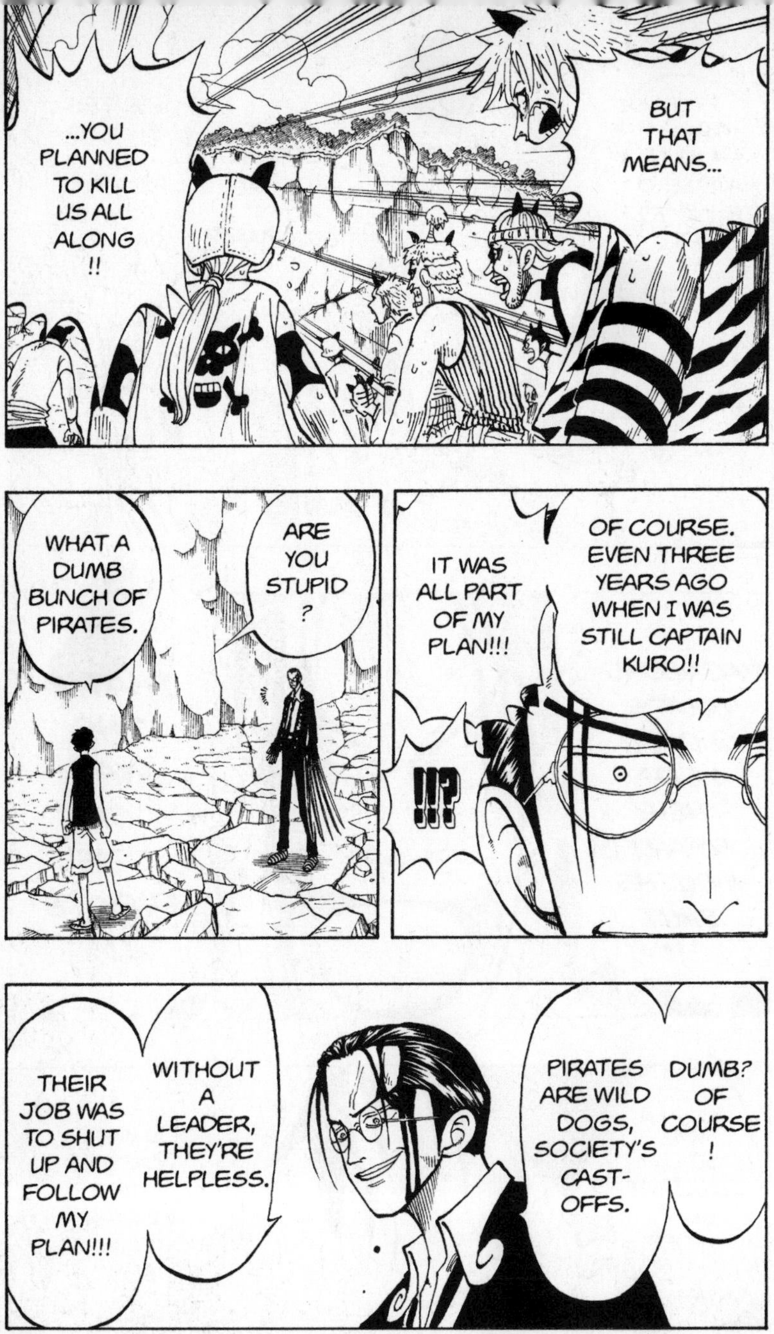
BUT THAT MEANS...
...YOU PLANNED TO KILL US ALL ALONG !!
OF COURSE. EVEN THREE YEARS AGO WHEN I WAS STILL CAPTAIN KURO!!
IT WAS ALL PART OF MY PLAN!!!
!!?
ARE YOU STUPID ?
WHAT A DUMB BUNCH OF PIRATES.
DUMB? OF COURSE !
PIRATES ARE WILD DOGS, SOCIETY'S CAST-OFFS.
WITHOUT A LEADER, THEY'RE HELPLESS.
THEIR JOB WAS TO SHUT UP AND FOLLOW MY PLAN!!!

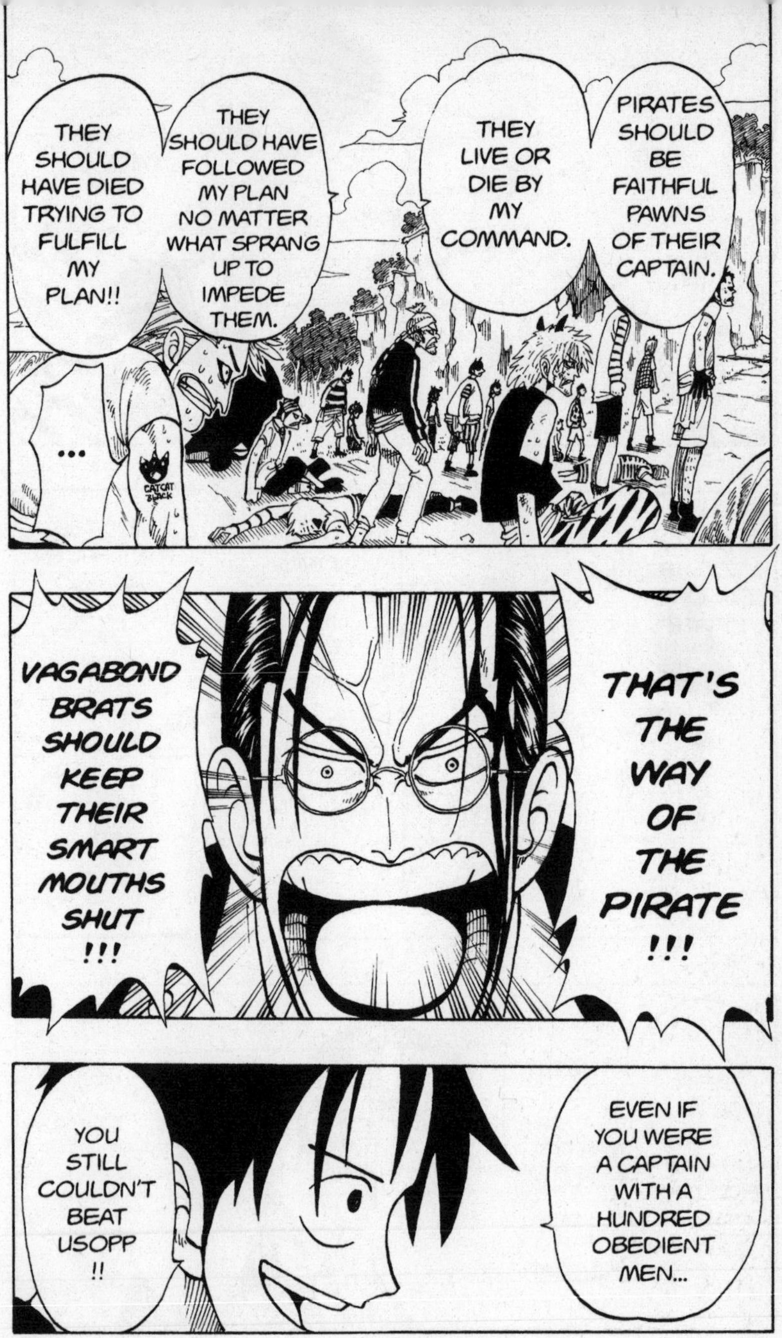
PIRATES SHOULD BE FAITHFUL PAWNS OF THEIR CAPTAIN.
THEY LIVE OR DIE BY MY COMMAND.
THEY SHOULD HAVE FOLLOWED MY PLAN NO MATTER WHAT SPRANG UP TO IMPEDE THEM.
THEY SHOULD HAVE DIED TRYING TO FULFILL MY PLAN!!
...
CATCAT BLACK
THAT'S THE WAY OF THE PIRATE!!!
VAGABOND BRATS SHOULD KEEP THEIR SMART MOUTHS SHUT!!!
EVEN IF YOU WERE A CAPTAIN WITH A HUNDRED OBEDIENT MEN...
YOU STILL COULDN'T BEAT USOPP!!

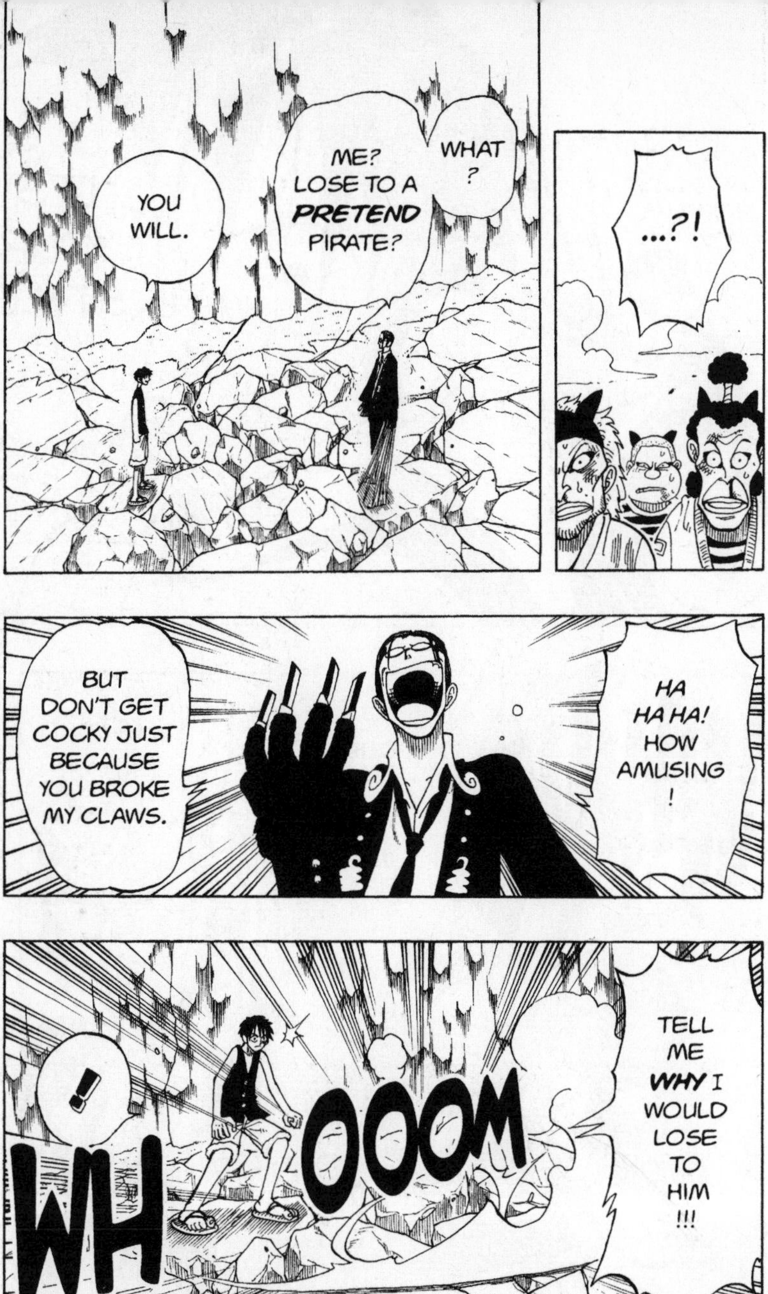
...?!
WHAT ?
ME? LOSE TO A PRETEND PIRATE?
YOU WILL.
HA HA HA! HOW AMUSING !
BUT DON'T GET COCKY JUST BECAUSE YOU BROKE MY CLAWS.
TELL ME WHY I WOULD LOSE TO HIM !!!
!
WHOOOM

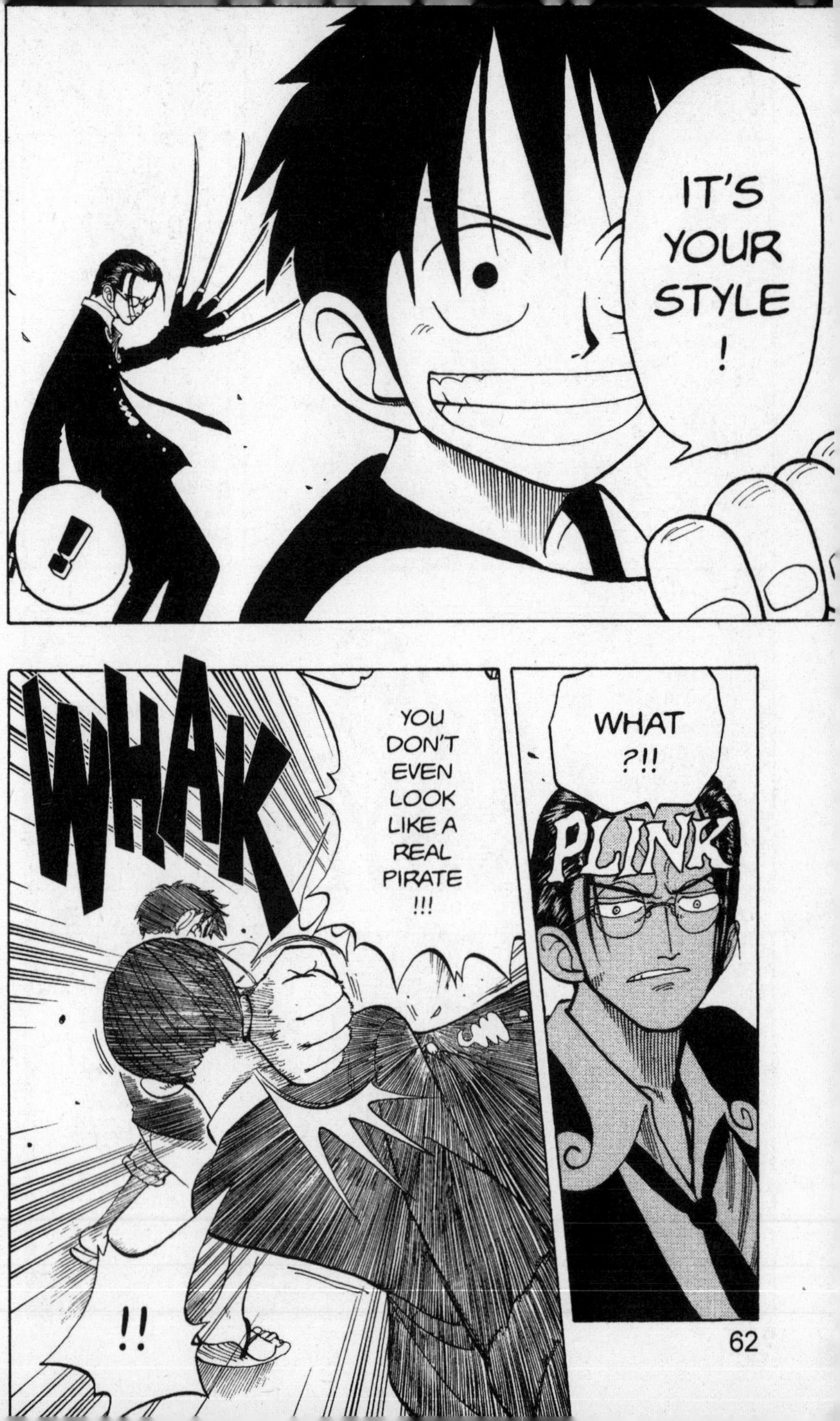
IT'S YOUR STYLE!
!
WHAT?!!
PLINK
YOU DON'T EVEN LOOK LIKE A REAL PIRATE!!!
WHAK
!!

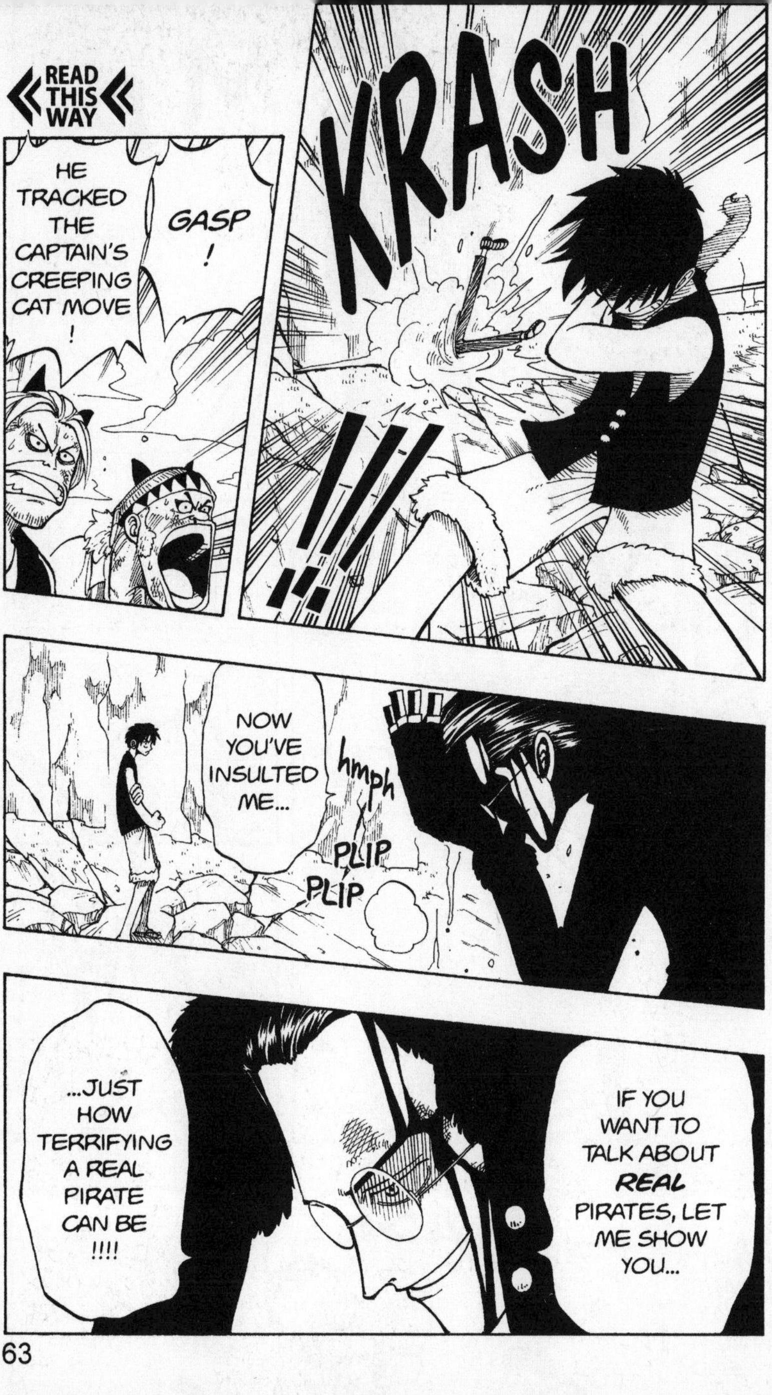
READ THIS WAY
KRASH
!!!
GASP!
HE TRACKED THE CAPTAIN'S CREEPING CAT MOVE!
hmph
PLIP PLIP
NOW YOU'VE INSULTED ME...
IF YOU WANT TO TALK ABOUT **REAL** PIRATES, LET ME SHOW YOU...
...JUST HOW TERRIFYING A REAL PIRATE CAN BE!!!!

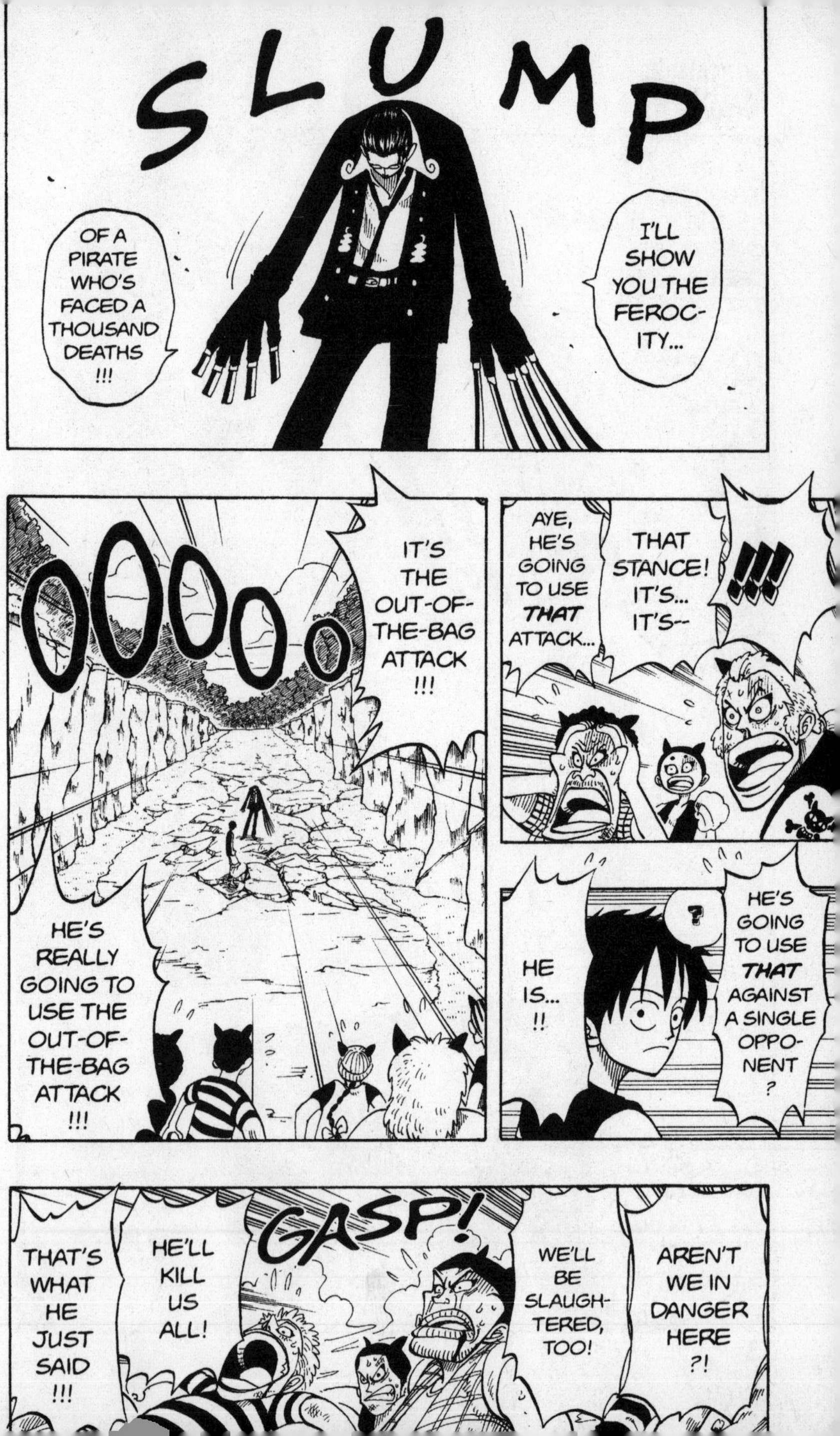
SLUMP
I'LL SHOW YOU THE FEROC-ITY...
OF A PIRATE WHO'S FACED A THOUSAND DEATHS !!!
!!!
THAT STANCE! IT'S... IT'S--
AYE, HE'S GOING TO USE THAT ATTACK...
HE'S GOING TO USE THAT AGAINST A SINGLE OPPO-NENT ?
?
HE IS... !!
IT'S THE OUT-OF-THE-BAG ATTACK !!!
OOOOO
HE'S REALLY GOING TO USE THE OUT-OF-THE-BAG ATTACK !!!
AREN'T WE IN DANGER HERE ?!
WE'LL BE SLAUGH-TERED, TOO!
GASP!
HE'LL KILL US ALL!
THAT'S WHAT HE JUST SAID !!!

READ THIS WAY

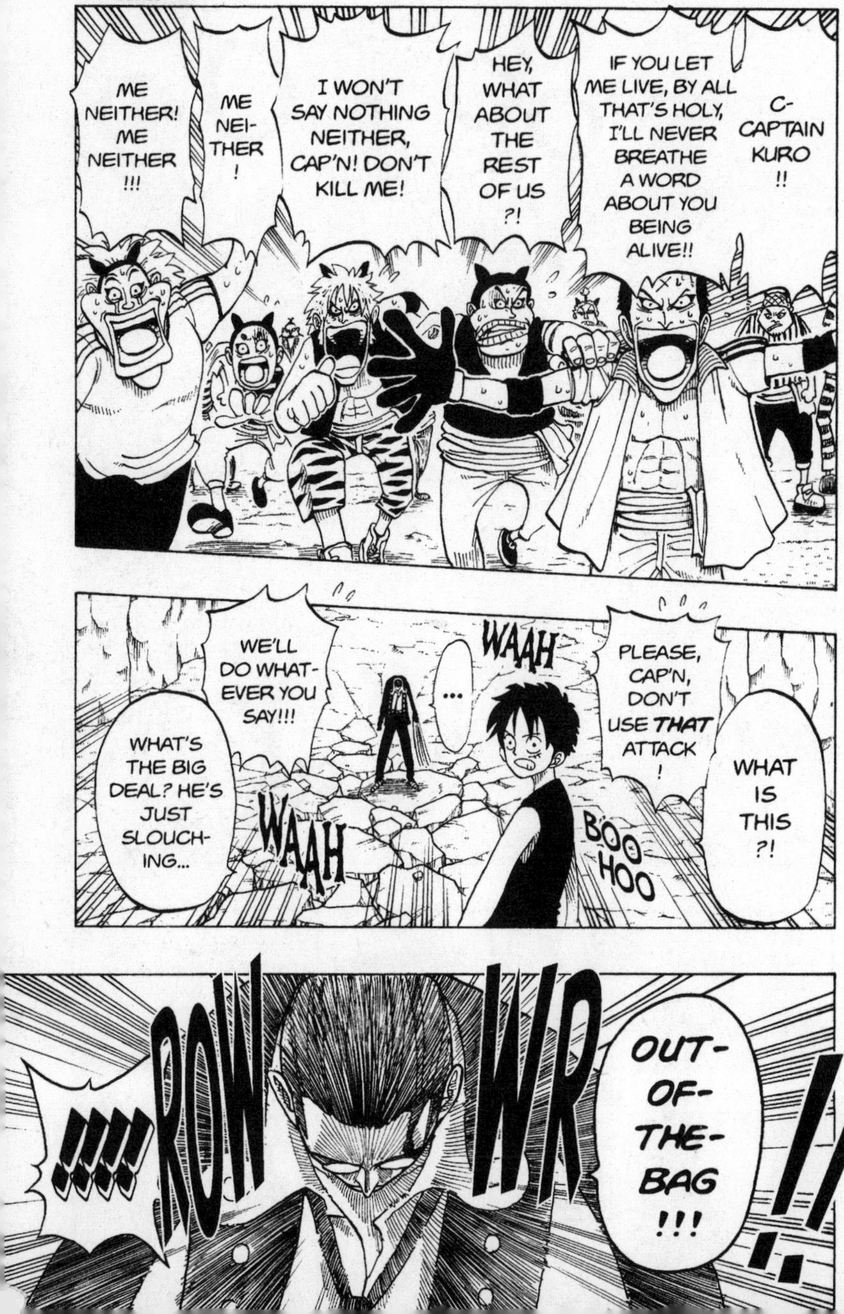
C-CAPTAIN KURO!!
IF YOU LET ME LIVE, BY ALL THAT'S HOLY, I'LL NEVER BREATHE A WORD ABOUT YOU BEING ALIVE!!
HEY, WHAT ABOUT THE REST OF US?!
I WON'T SAY NOTHING NEITHER, CAP'N! DON'T KILL ME!
ME NEI-THER!
ME NEITHER! ME NEITHER!!!
WHAT IS THIS?!
PLEASE, CAP'N, DON'T USE *THAT* ATTACK!
WAAH
...
WE'LL DO WHAT-EVER YOU SAY!!!
BOO HOO
WAAH
WHAT'S THE BIG DEAL? HE'S JUST SLOUCH-ING...
OUT-OF-THE-BAG!!!
WR
ROW

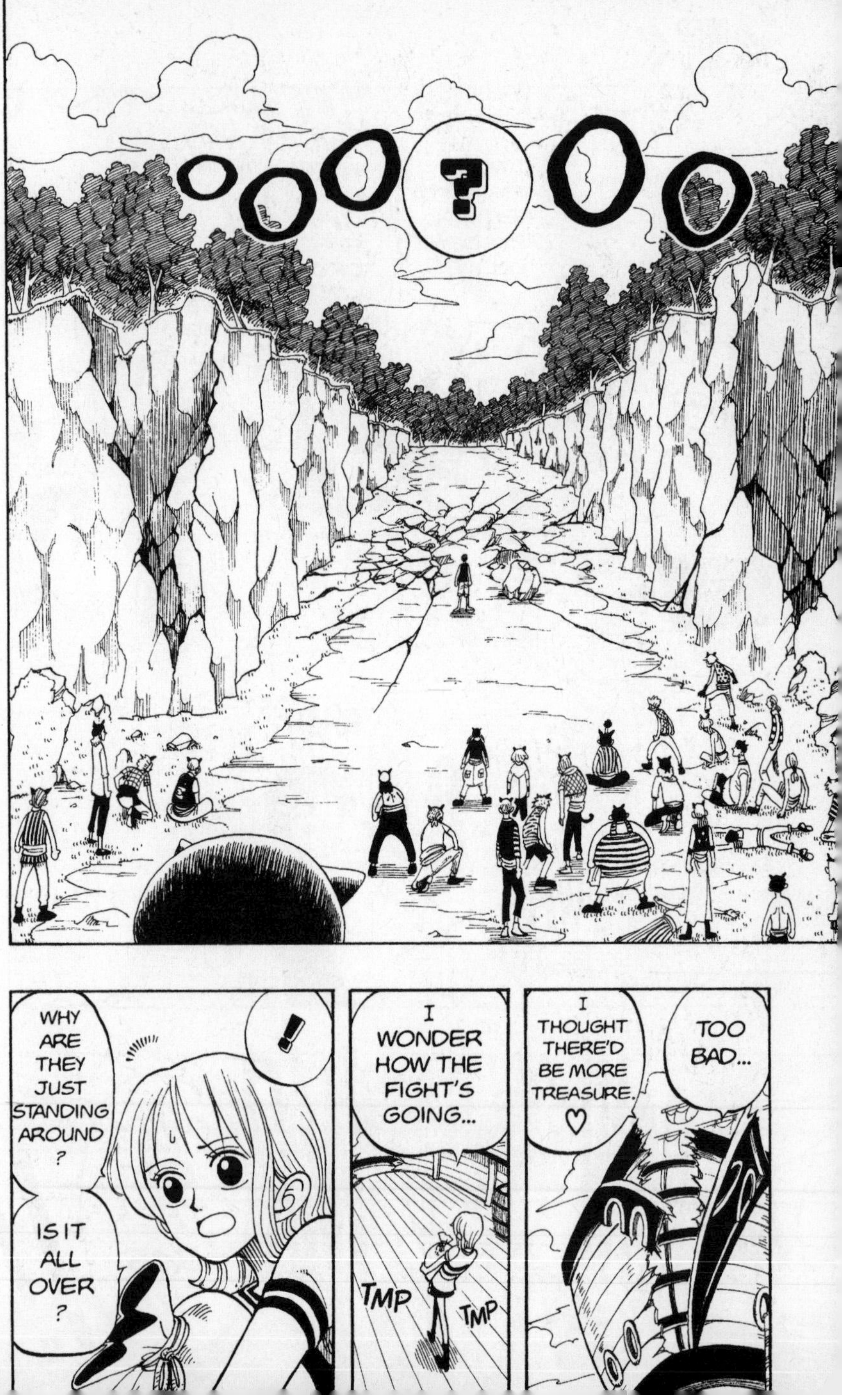
OOO?OO
TOO BAD...
I THOUGHT THERE'D BE MORE TREASURE. ♥
I WONDER HOW THE FIGHT'S GOING...
TMP
TMP
!
WHY ARE THEY JUST STANDING AROUND?
IS IT ALL OVER?

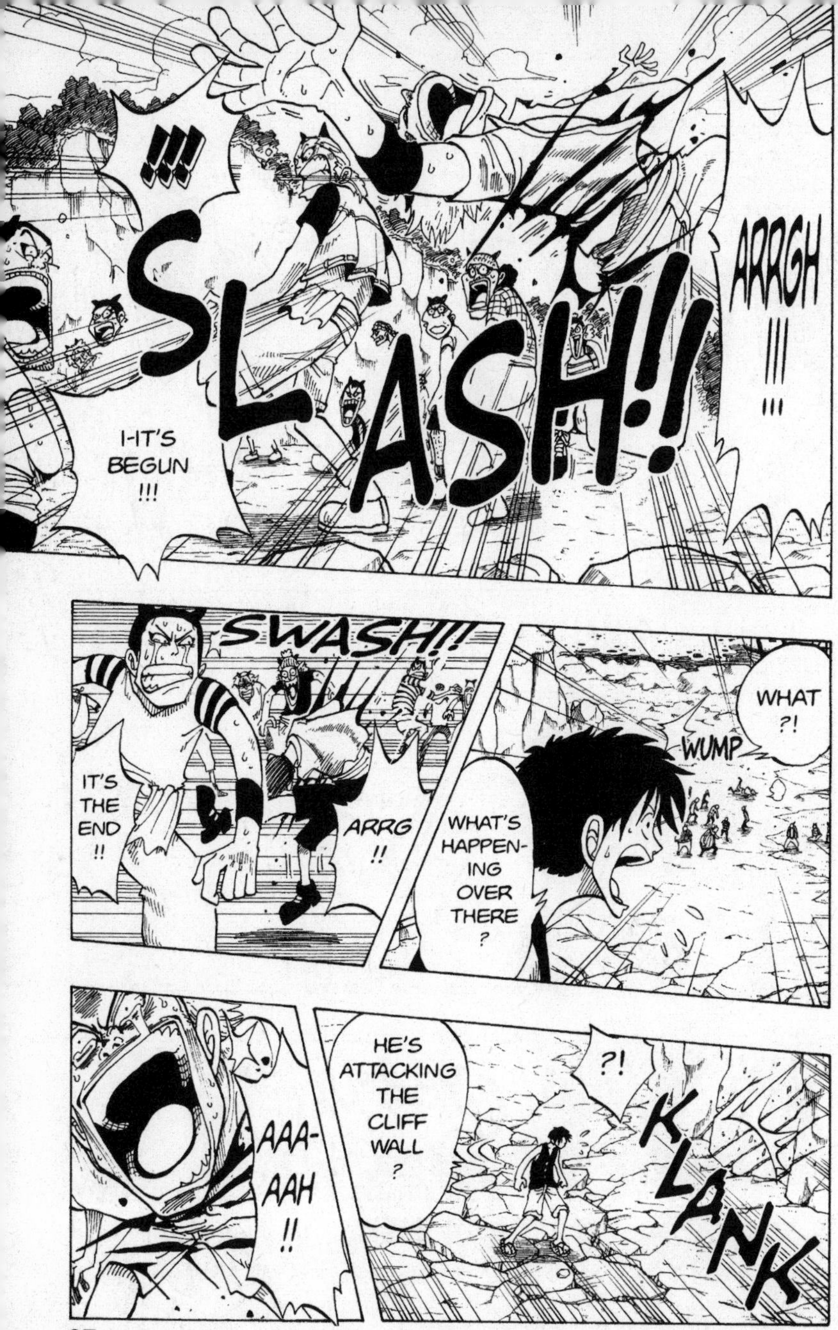
ARRGH!!!!!!
!!!!
SLASH!!
I-IT'S BEGUN!!!
WHAT?!
WUMP
WHAT'S HAPPENING OVER THERE?
SWASH!!
ARRG!!
IT'S THE END!!
?!
KLANK
HE'S ATTACKING THE CLIFF WALL?
AAA-AAH!!

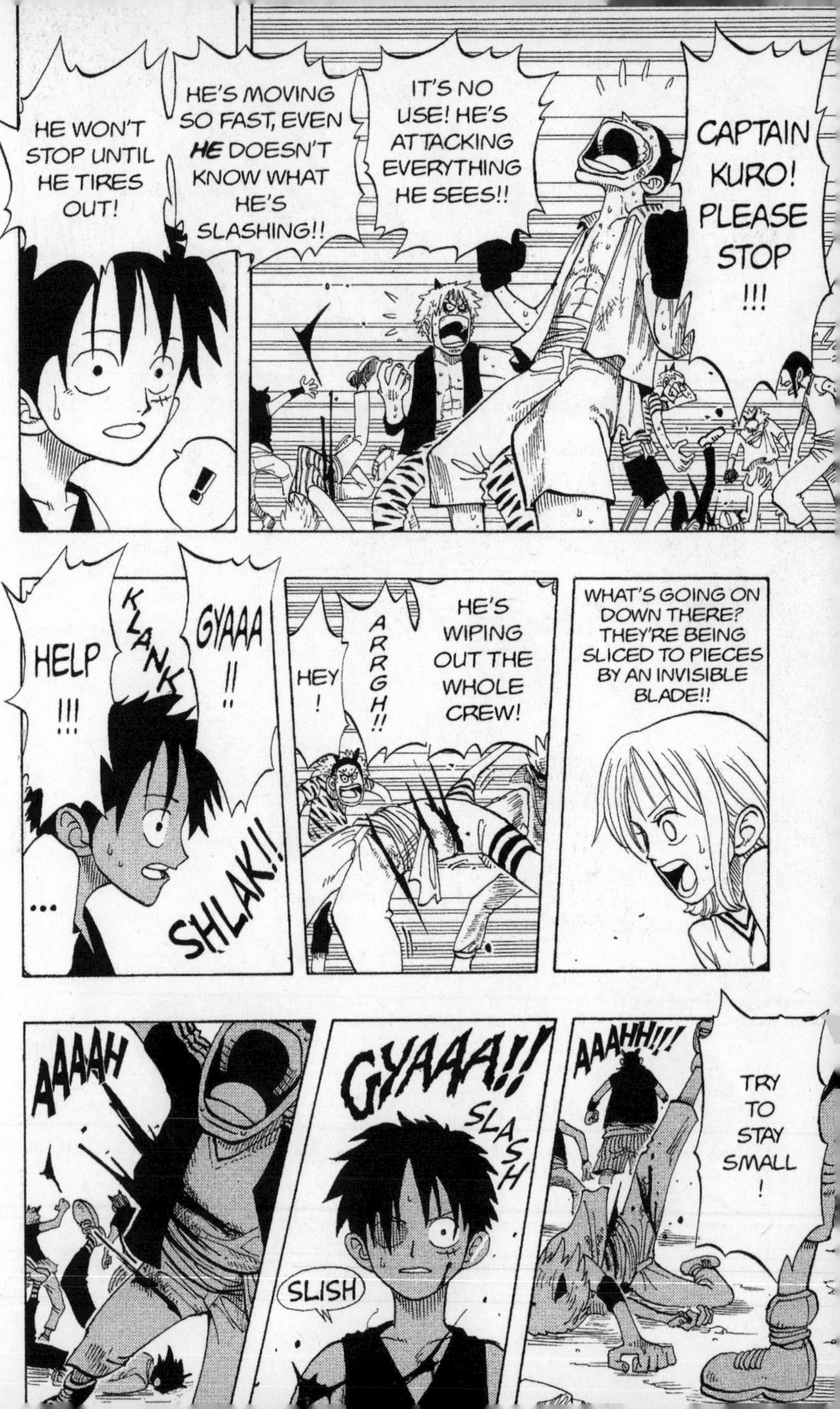
CAPTAIN KURO! PLEASE STOP !!!
IT'S NO USE! HE'S ATTACKING EVERYTHING HE SEES!!
HE'S MOVING SO FAST, EVEN HE DOESN'T KNOW WHAT HE'S SLASHING!!
HE WON'T STOP UNTIL HE TIRES OUT!
!
WHAT'S GOING ON DOWN THERE? THEY'RE BEING SLICED TO PIECES BY AN INVISIBLE BLADE!!
HE'S WIPING OUT THE WHOLE CREW!
ARRGH!!
HEY!
GYAAA !!
KLANK
HELP !!!
SHLAK!!
...
TRY TO STAY SMALL!
AAAHH!!!
GYAAA!!
SLASH
SLISH
AAAAH

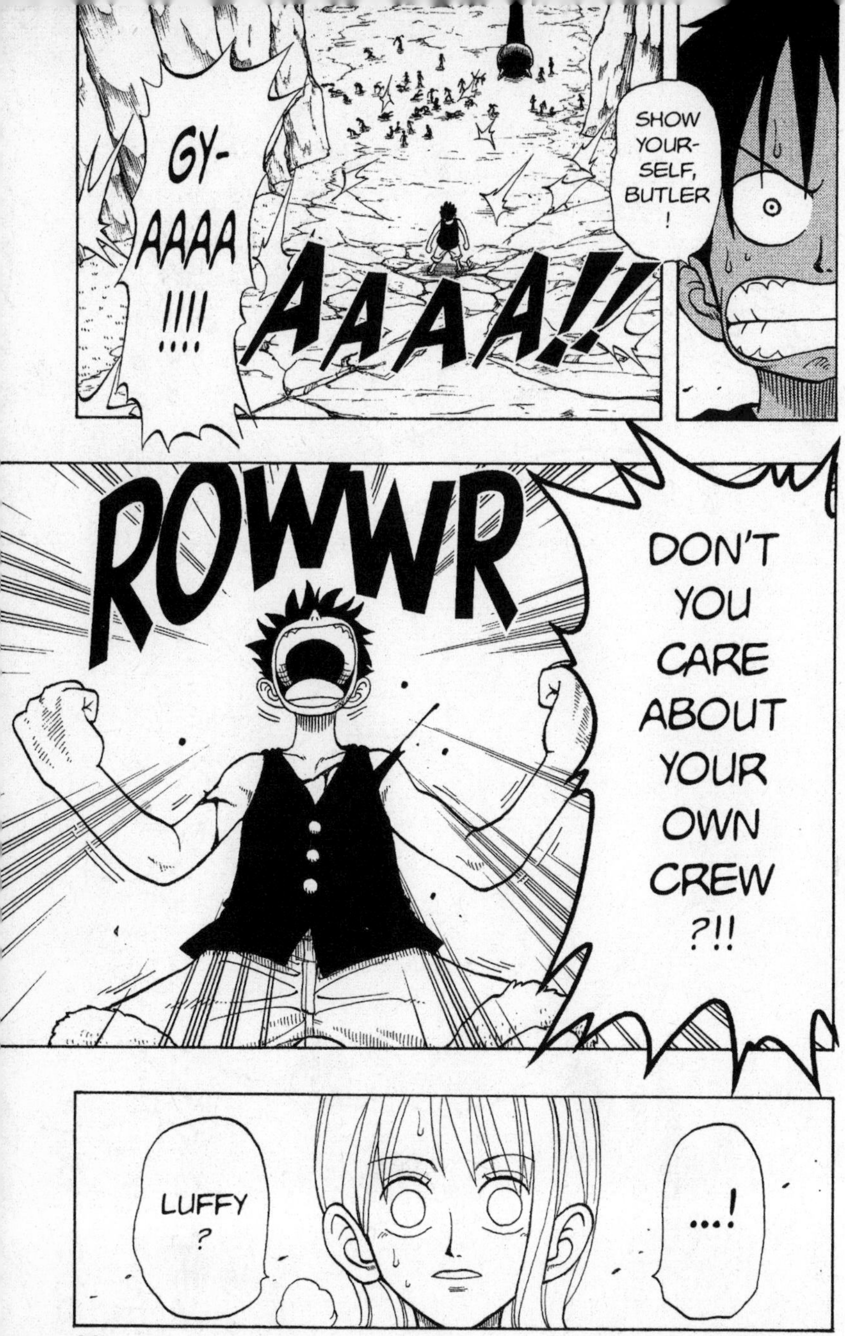
SHOW YOUR-SELF, BUTLER!
GY-AAAA!!!!
AAAA!!
ROWWR
DON'T YOU CARE ABOUT YOUR OWN CREW?!!
...!
LUFFY?

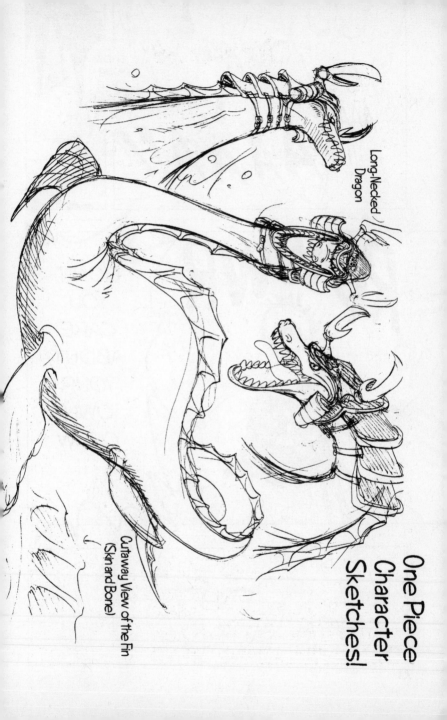

One Piece Character Sketches!

Long-Necked Dragon

Cutaway View of the Fin (Skin and Bone)

Chapter 39:

FOR WHOM THE BELL TOLLS

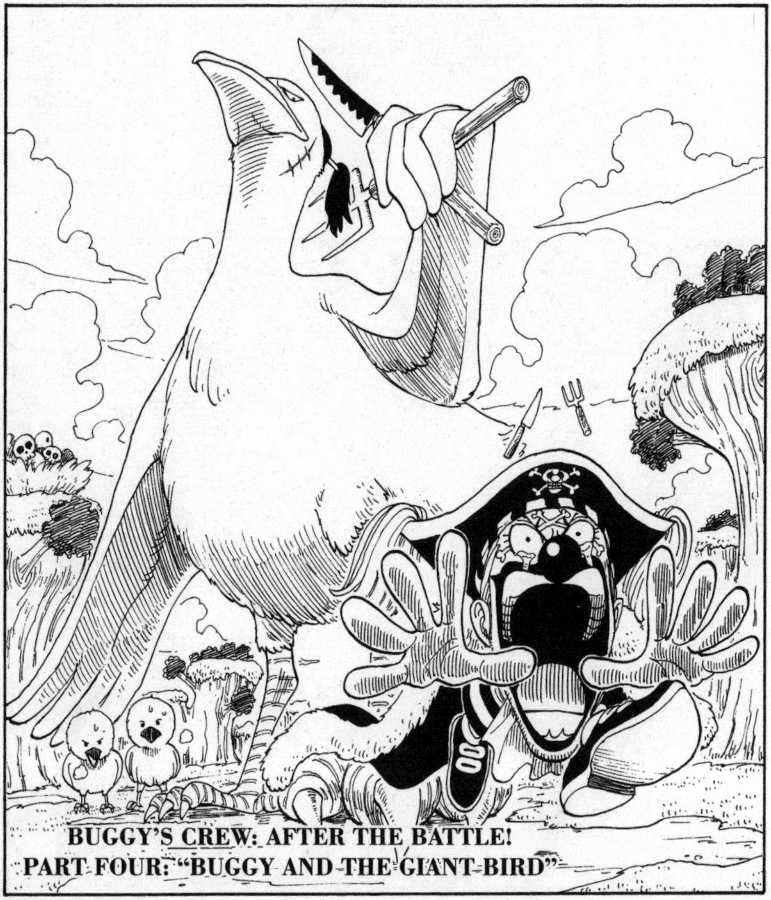
BUGGY'S CREW: AFTER THE BATTLE!
PART FOUR: "BUGGY AND THE GIANT BIRD"

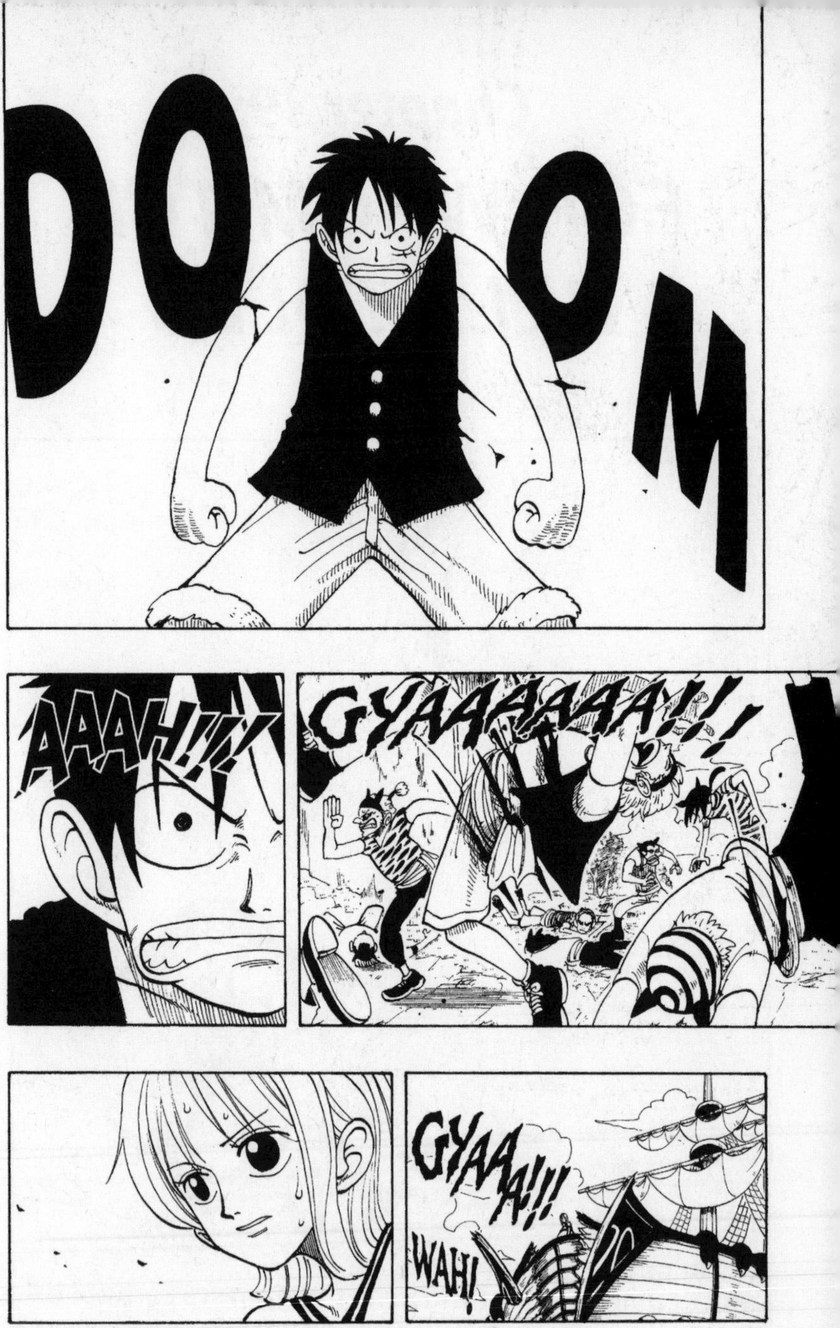
DOOM
GYAAAAAAA!!!
AAAH!!!!
GYAAA!!!
WAH!

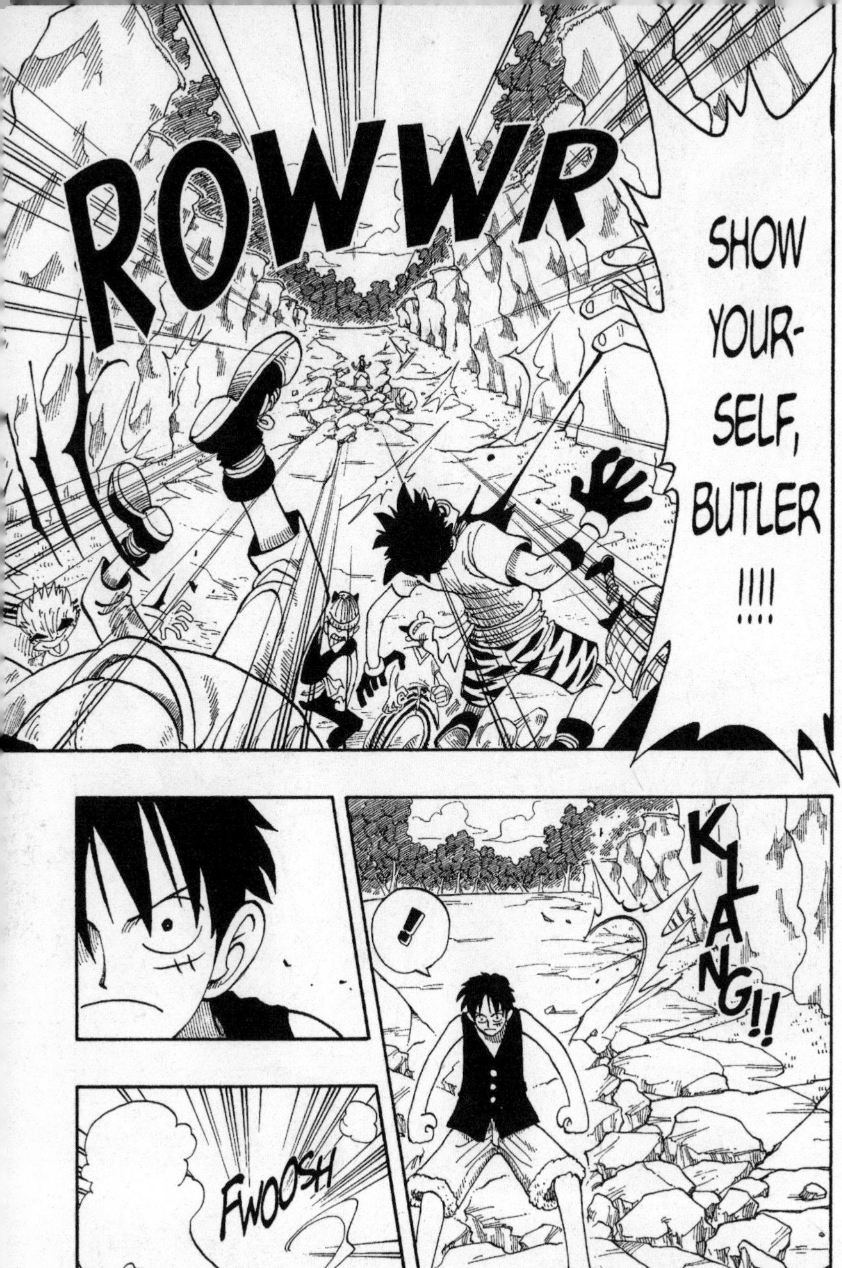
SHOW YOUR-SELF, BUTLER !!!!
ROWWR
KLANG!!
!
FWOOSH

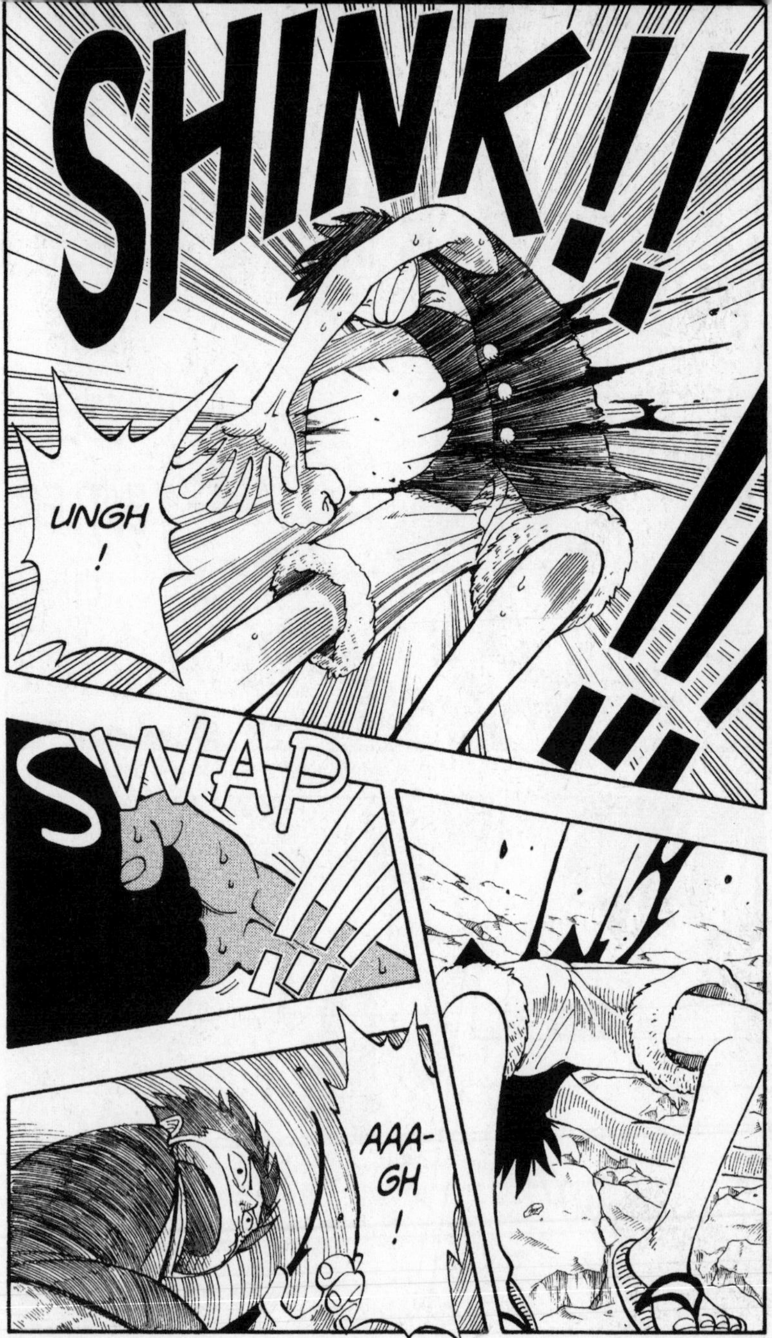
SHINK!!
UNGH!
SWAP
AAA-GH!

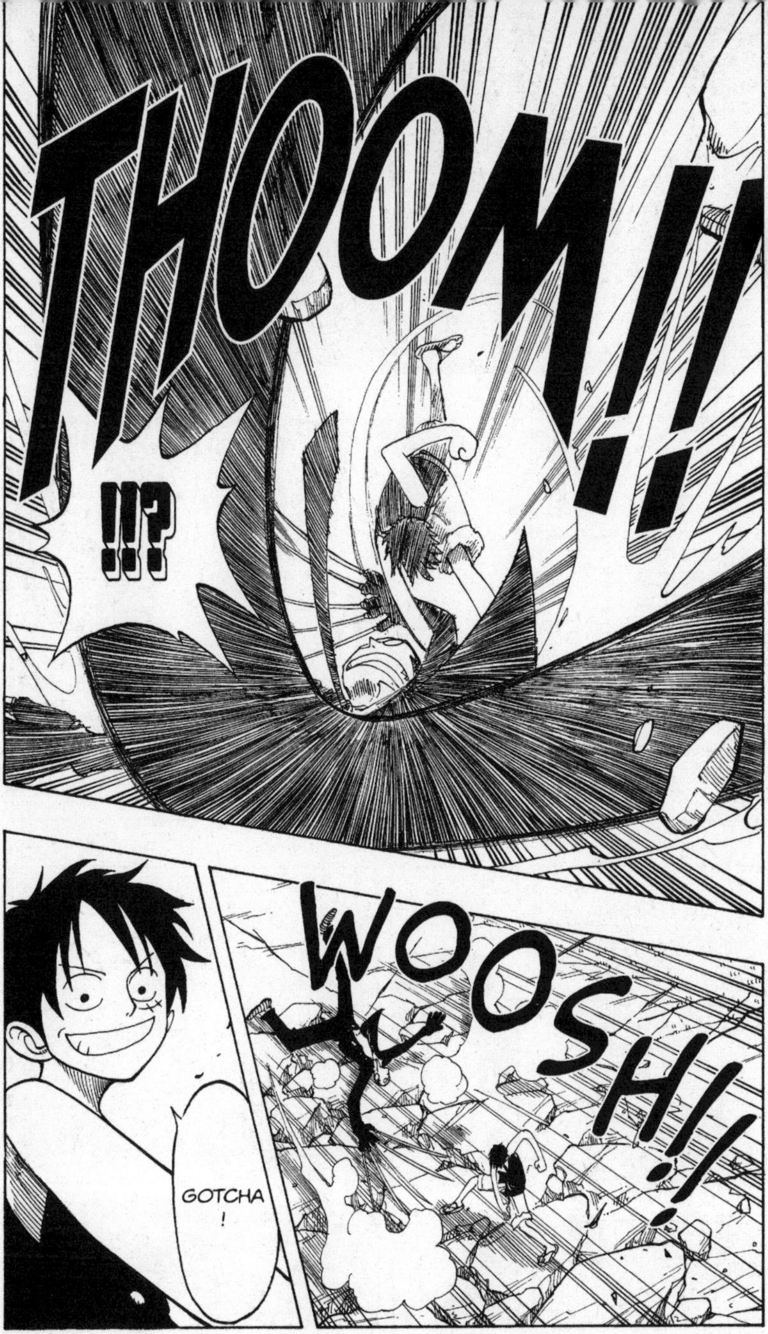
THOOM!!
!!?
WOOSH!!
GOTCHA!

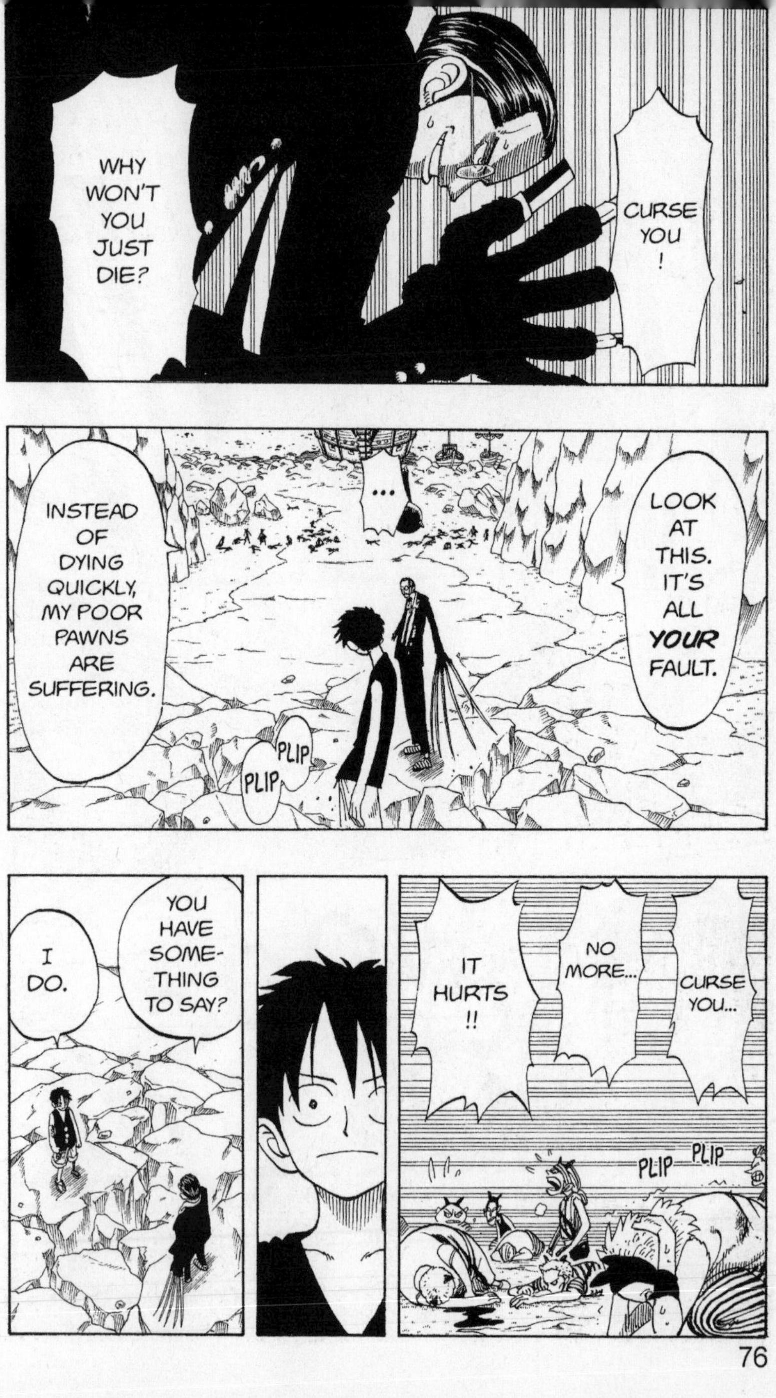
CURSE YOU !
WHY WON'T YOU JUST DIE?
LOOK AT THIS. IT'S ALL **YOUR** FAULT.
...
INSTEAD OF DYING QUICKLY, MY POOR PAWNS ARE SUFFERING.
PLIP
PLIP
CURSE YOU...
NO MORE...
IT HURTS !!
PLIP
PLIP
YOU HAVE SOME-THING TO SAY?
I DO.

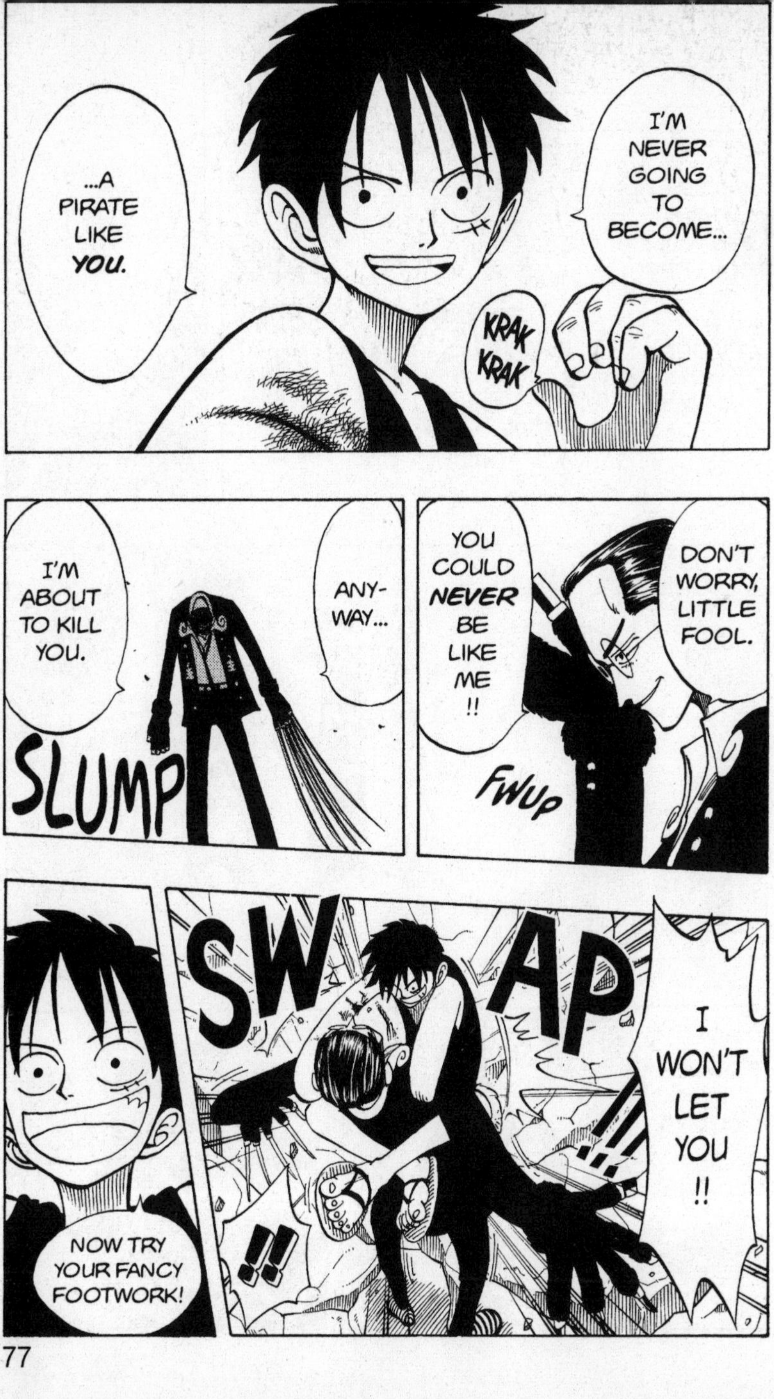
I'M NEVER GOING TO BECOME...
KRAK KRAK
...A PIRATE LIKE YOU.
DON'T WORRY, LITTLE FOOL.
YOU COULD NEVER BE LIKE ME !!
FWUP
ANY-WAY...
I'M ABOUT TO KILL YOU.
SLUMP
I WON'T LET YOU !!
SWAP
NOW TRY YOUR FANCY FOOTWORK!

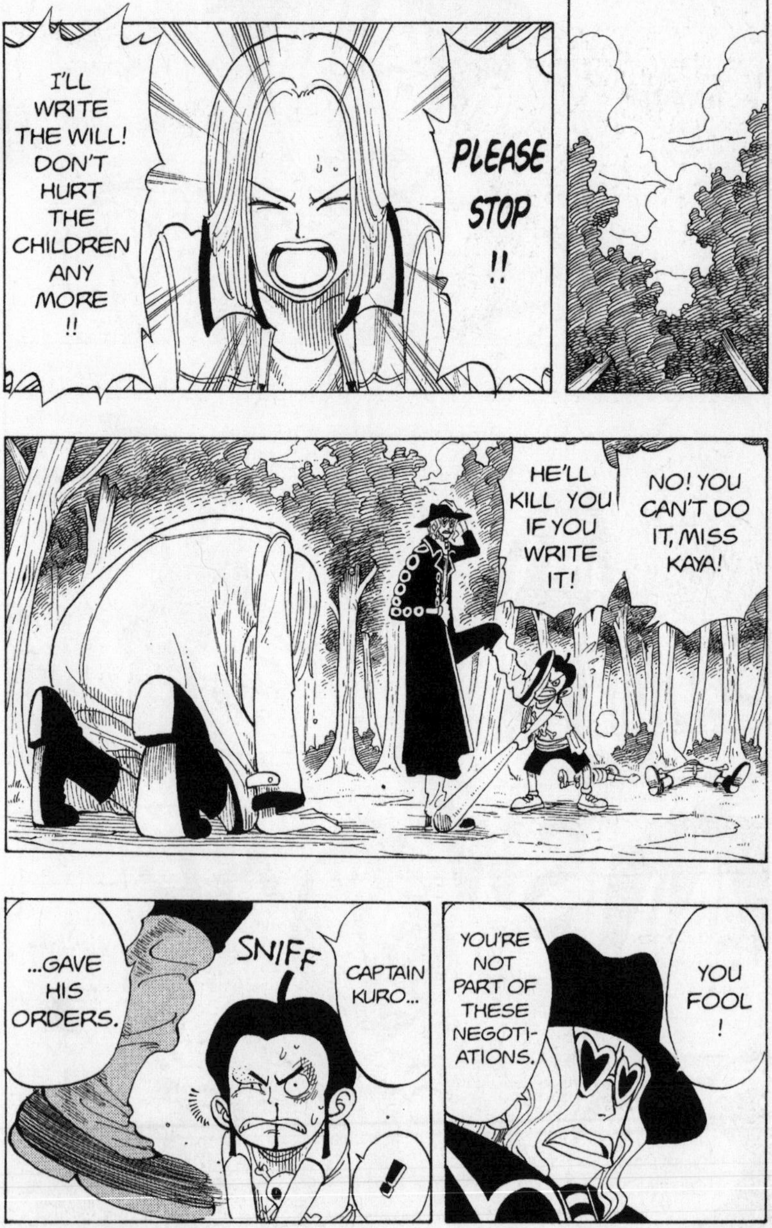
PLEASE STOP !!
I'LL WRITE THE WILL! DON'T HURT THE CHILDREN ANY MORE !!
NO! YOU CAN'T DO IT, MISS KAYA!
HE'LL KILL YOU IF YOU WRITE IT!
YOU FOOL !
YOU'RE NOT PART OF THESE NEGOTI-ATIONS.
CAPTAIN KURO...
SNIFF
!
...GAVE HIS ORDERS.

READ THIS WAY

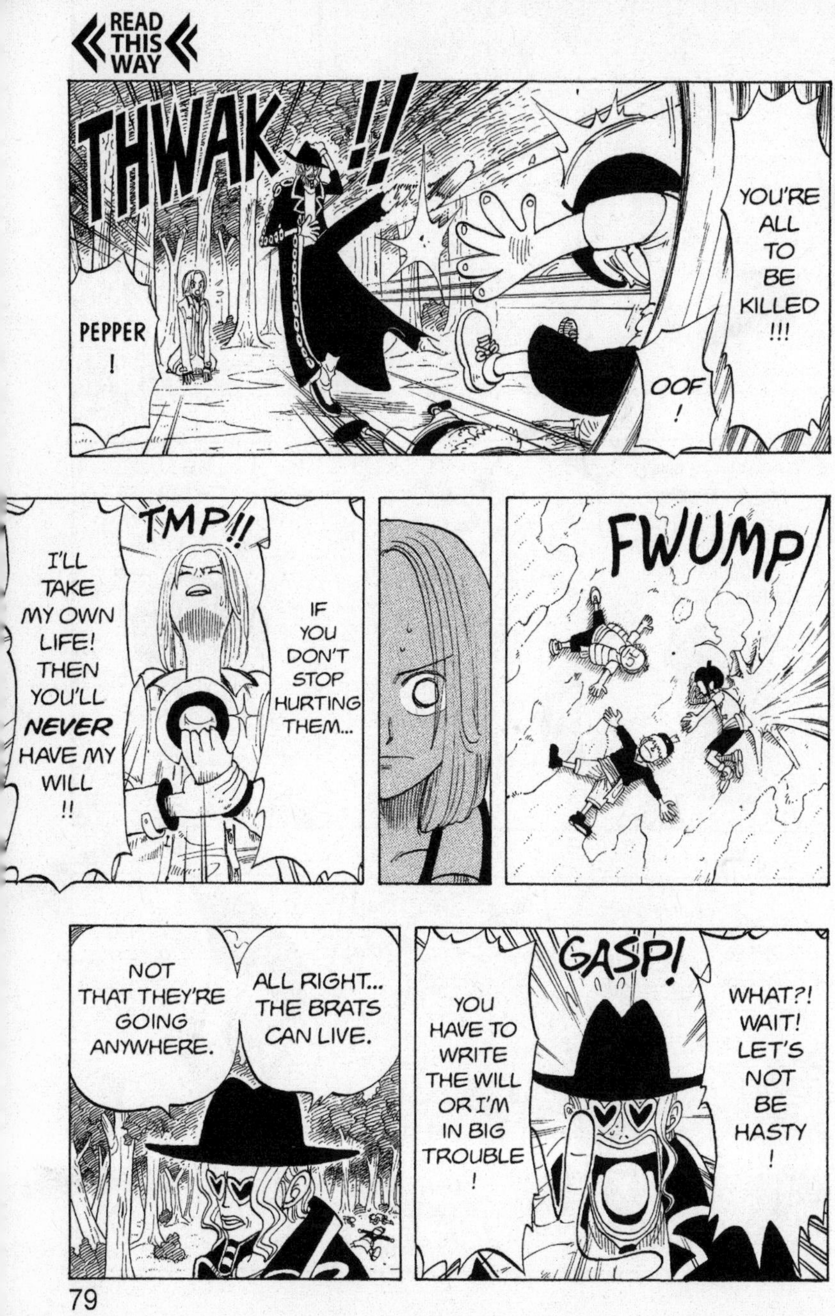
YOU'RE ALL TO BE KILLED!!!
THWAK!!
OOF!
PEPPER!
FWUMP
IF YOU DON'T STOP HURTING THEM...
TMP!!
I'LL TAKE MY OWN LIFE! THEN YOU'LL *NEVER* HAVE MY WILL!!
GASP!
WHAT?! WAIT! LET'S NOT BE HASTY!
YOU HAVE TO WRITE THE WILL OR I'M IN BIG TROUBLE!
ALL RIGHT... THE BRATS CAN LIVE.
NOT THAT THEY'RE GOING ANYWHERE.

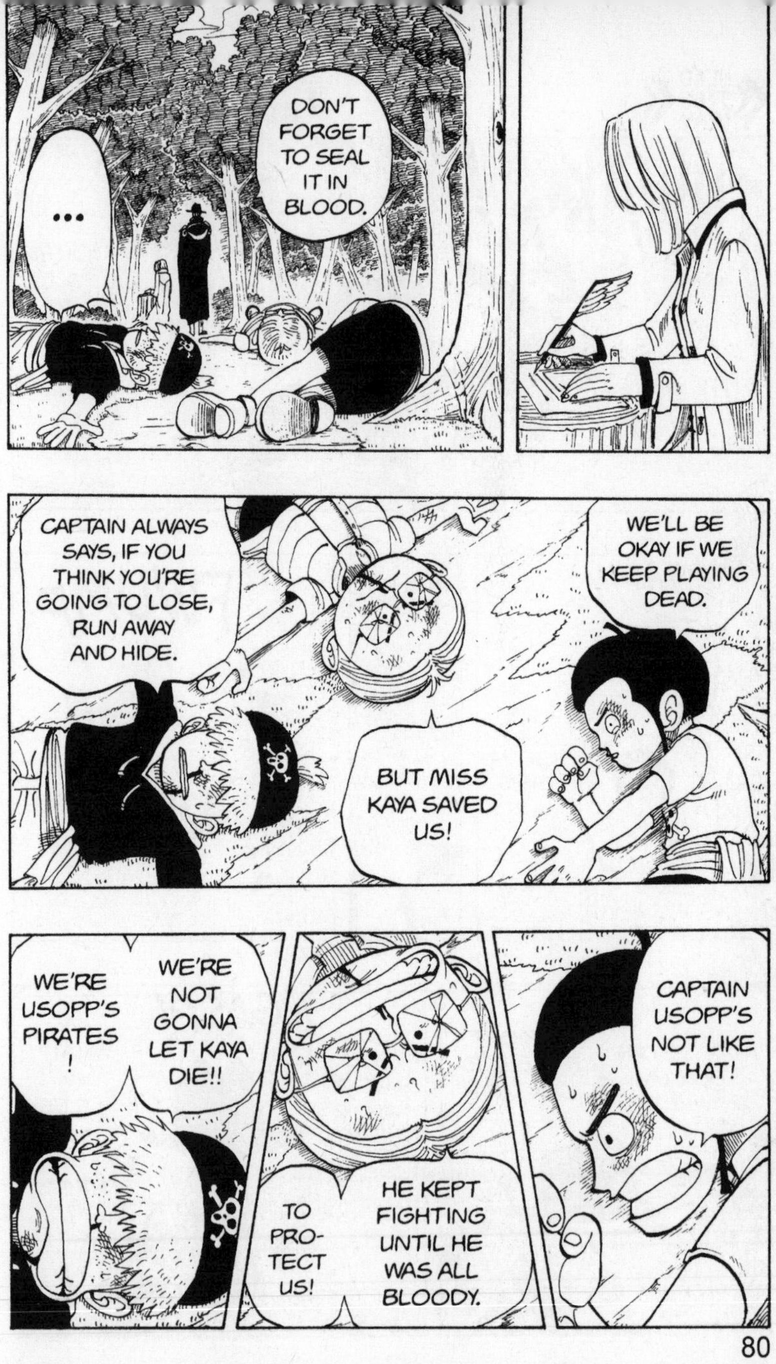
DON'T FORGET TO SEAL IT IN BLOOD.
...
WE'LL BE OKAY IF WE KEEP PLAYING DEAD.
CAPTAIN ALWAYS SAYS, IF YOU THINK YOU'RE GOING TO LOSE, RUN AWAY AND HIDE.
BUT MISS KAYA SAVED US!
CAPTAIN USOPP'S NOT LIKE THAT!
HE KEPT FIGHTING UNTIL HE WAS ALL BLOODY.
TO PRO-TECT US!
WE'RE NOT GONNA LET KAYA DIE!!
WE'RE USOPP'S PIRATES!

READ THIS WAY

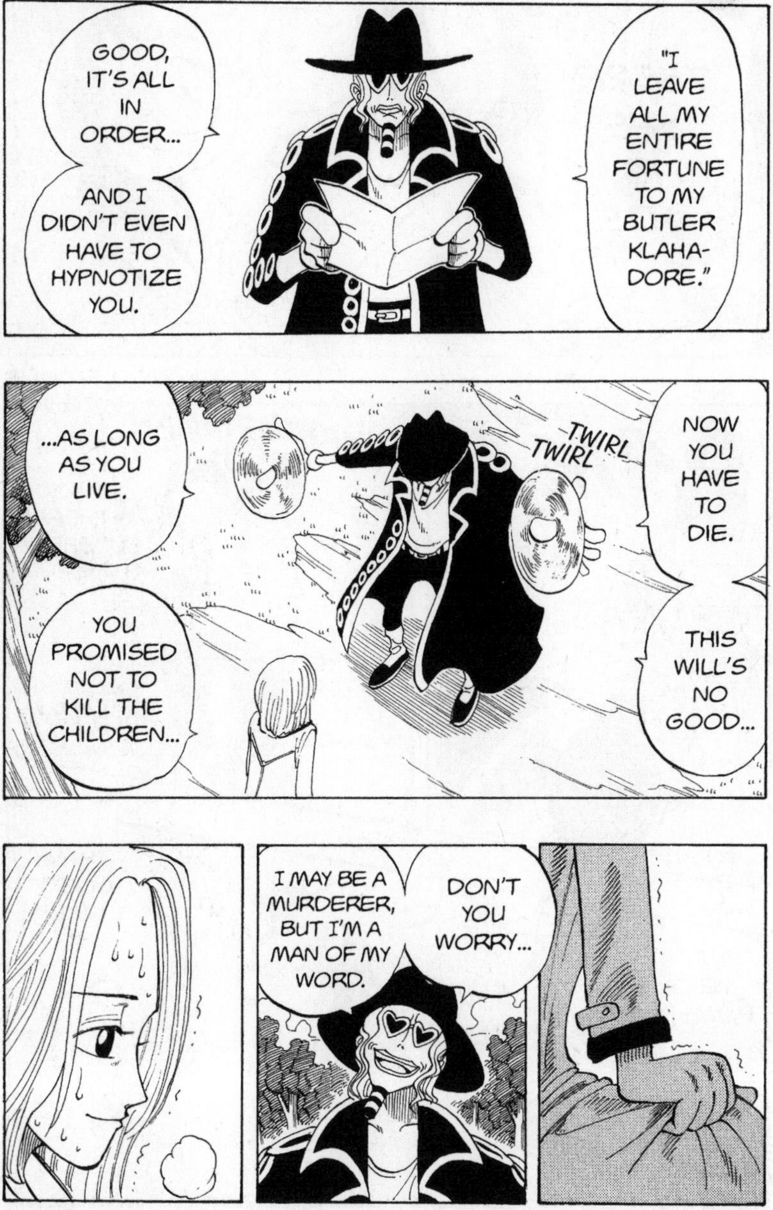
"I LEAVE ALL MY ENTIRE FORTUNE TO MY BUTLER KLAHA-DORE."
GOOD, IT'S ALL IN ORDER...
AND I DIDN'T EVEN HAVE TO HYPNOTIZE YOU.
NOW YOU HAVE TO DIE.
THIS WILL'S NO GOOD...
TWIRL TWIRL
...AS LONG AS YOU LIVE.
YOU PROMISED NOT TO KILL THE CHILDREN...
DON'T YOU WORRY...
I MAY BE A MURDERER, BUT I'M A MAN OF MY WORD.

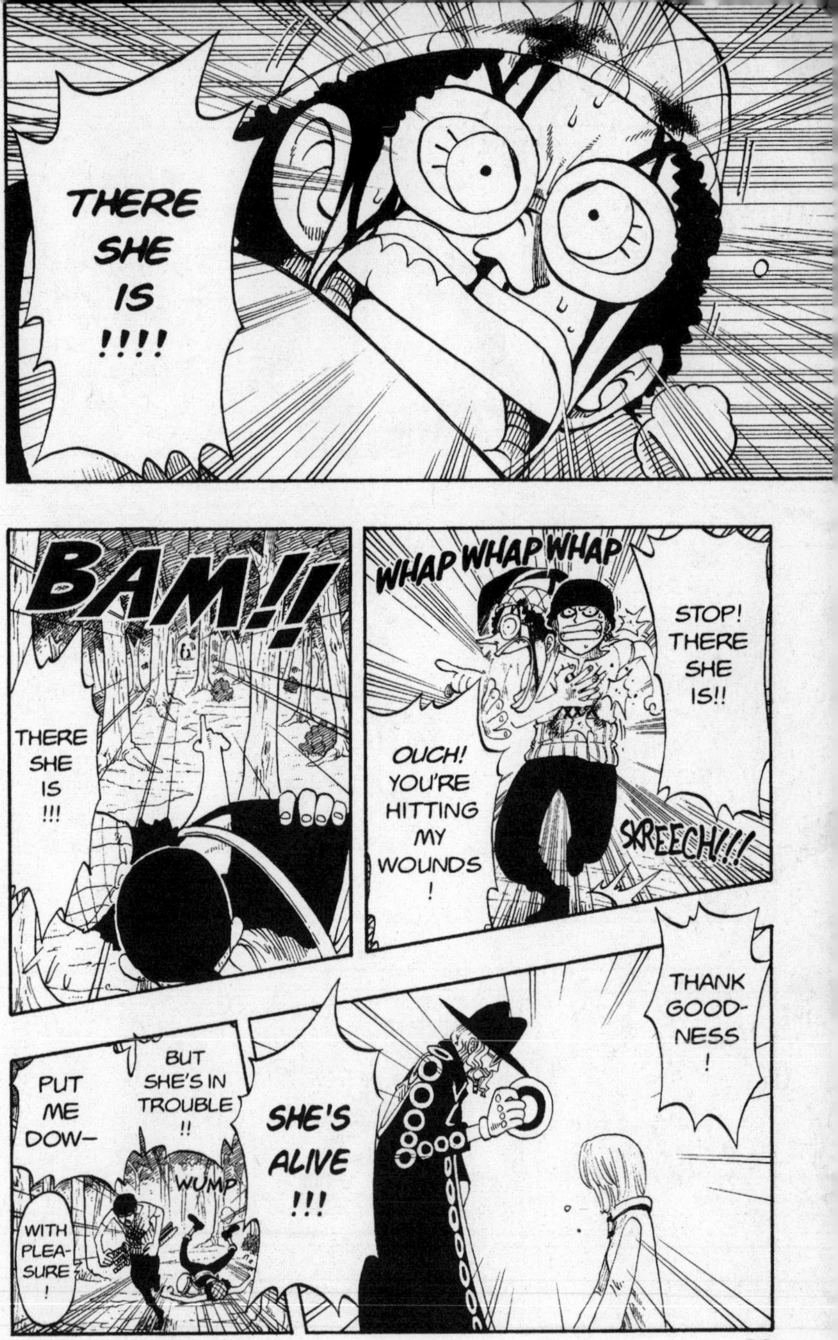
THERE SHE IS !!!!
WHAP WHAP WHAP
STOP! THERE SHE IS!!
OUCH! YOU'RE HITTING MY WOUNDS !
SKREECH!!!
BAM!!
THERE SHE IS !!!
THANK GOODNESS !
SHE'S ALIVE !!!
BUT SHE'S IN TROUBLE !!
PUT ME DOW—
WUMP
WITH PLEASURE !

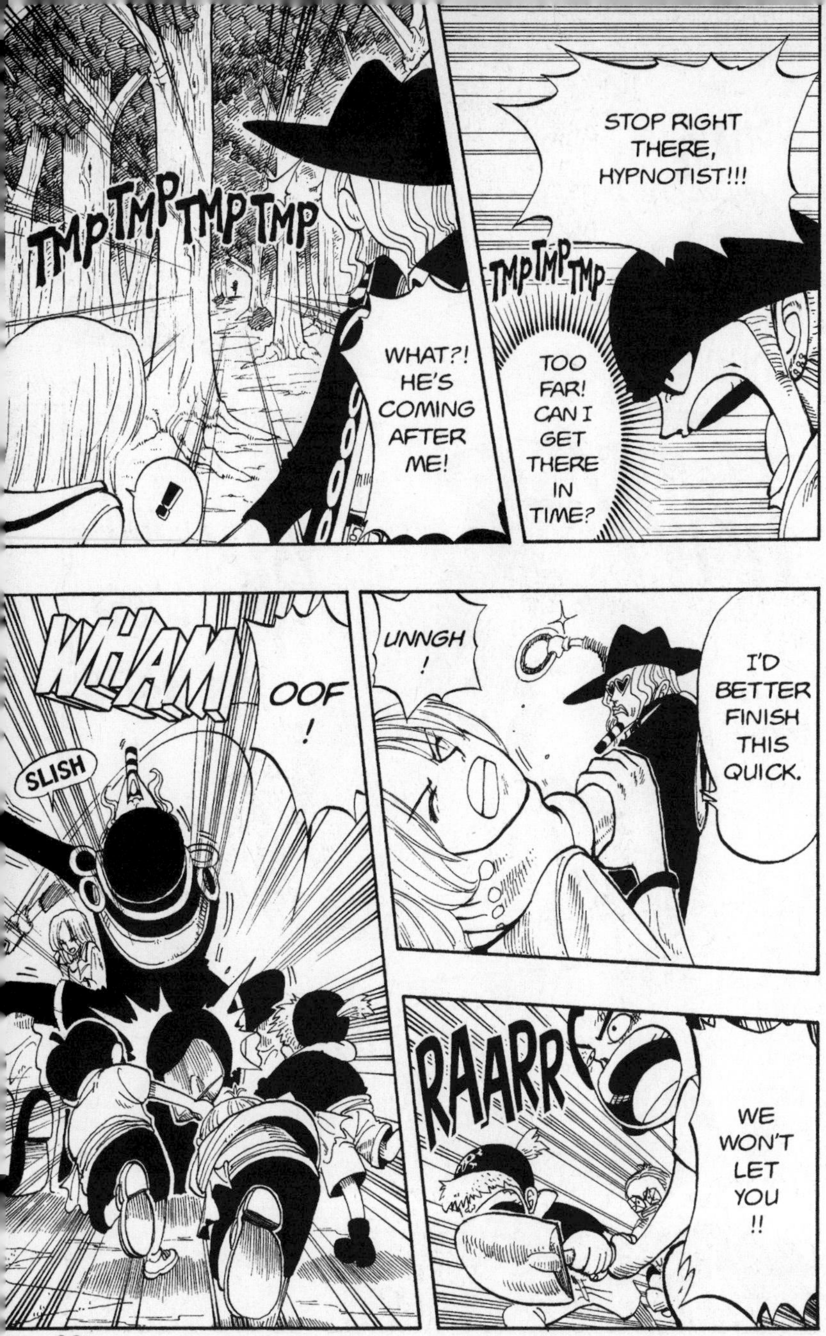
STOP RIGHT THERE, HYPNOTIST!!!
TMP TMP TMP
TOO FAR! CAN I GET THERE IN TIME?
TMP TMP TMP TMP
WHAT?! HE'S COMING AFTER ME!
!
I'D BETTER FINISH THIS QUICK.
UNNGH!
WHAM
OOF!
SLISH
WE WON'T LET YOU!!
RAARR

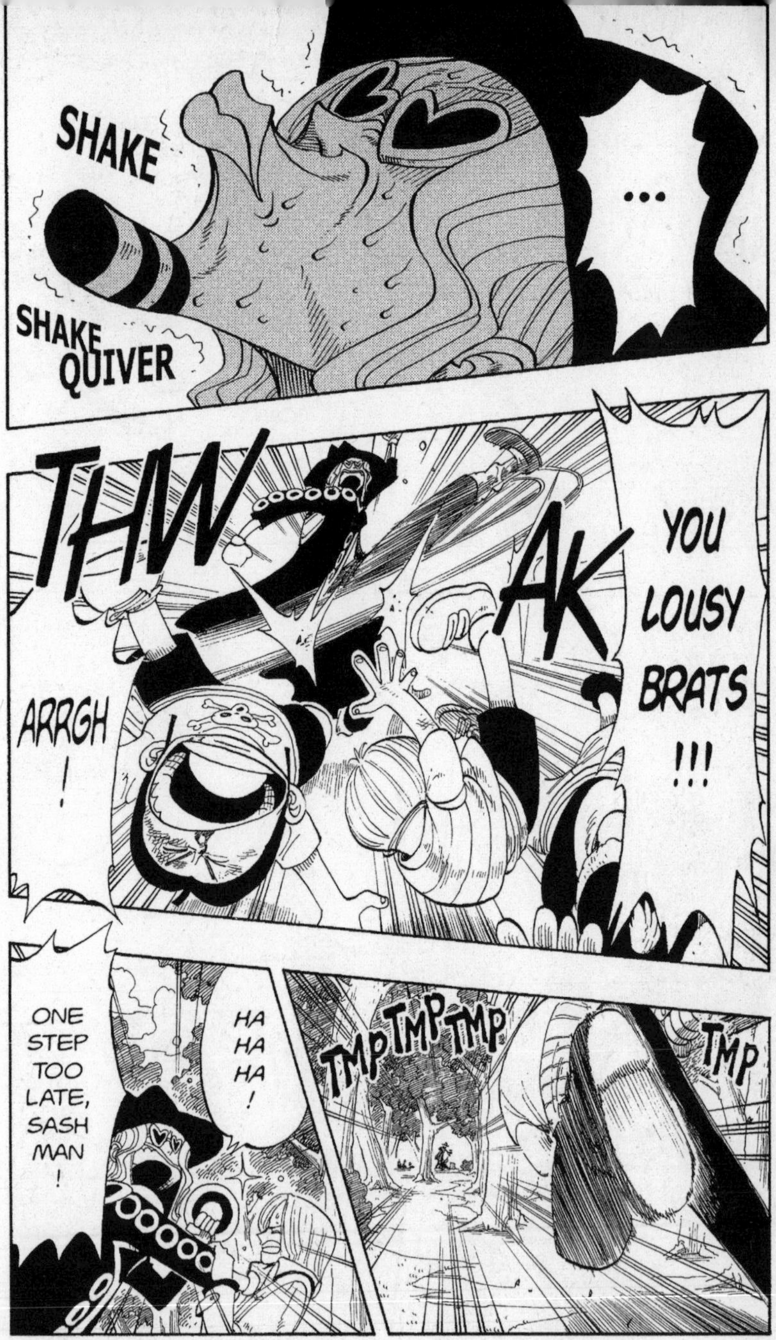
...
SHAKE
SHAKE
QUIVER
YOU LOUSY BRATS!!!
THWAK
ARRGH!
TMP
TMP TMP TMP
HA HA HA!
ONE STEP TOO LATE, SASH MAN!

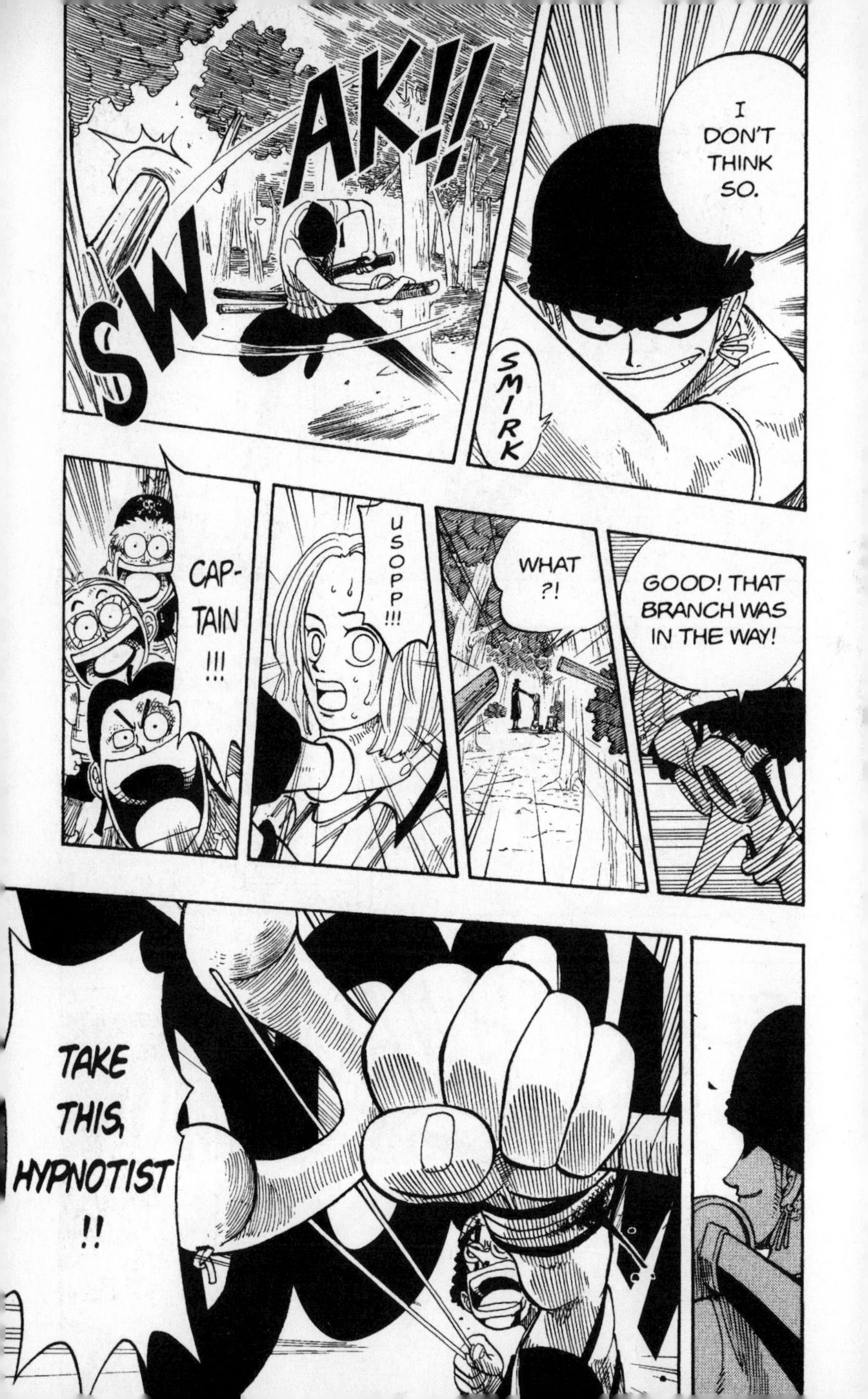
I DON'T THINK SO.
SMIRK
SW
AK!!
GOOD! THAT BRANCH WAS IN THE WAY!
WHAT?!
USOPP!!!
CAP-TAIN!!!
TAKE THIS, HYPNOTIST!!

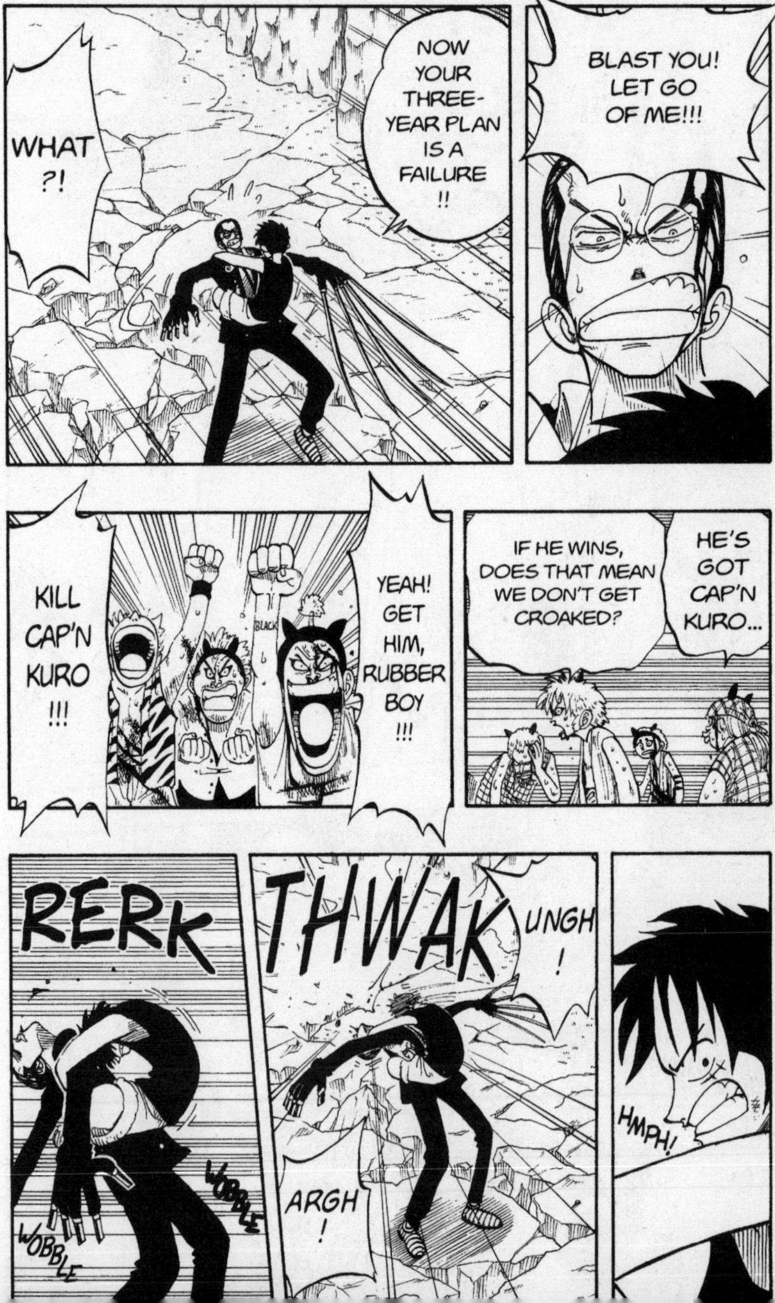
BLAST YOU! LET GO OF ME!!!
NOW YOUR THREE-YEAR PLAN IS A FAILURE !!
WHAT ?!
HE'S GOT CAP'N KURO...
IF HE WINS, DOES THAT MEAN WE DON'T GET CROAKED?
YEAH! GET HIM, RUBBER BOY !!!
KILL CAP'N KURO !!!
HMPH!
UNGH !
THWAK
ARGH !
RERK
WOBBLE
WOBBLE

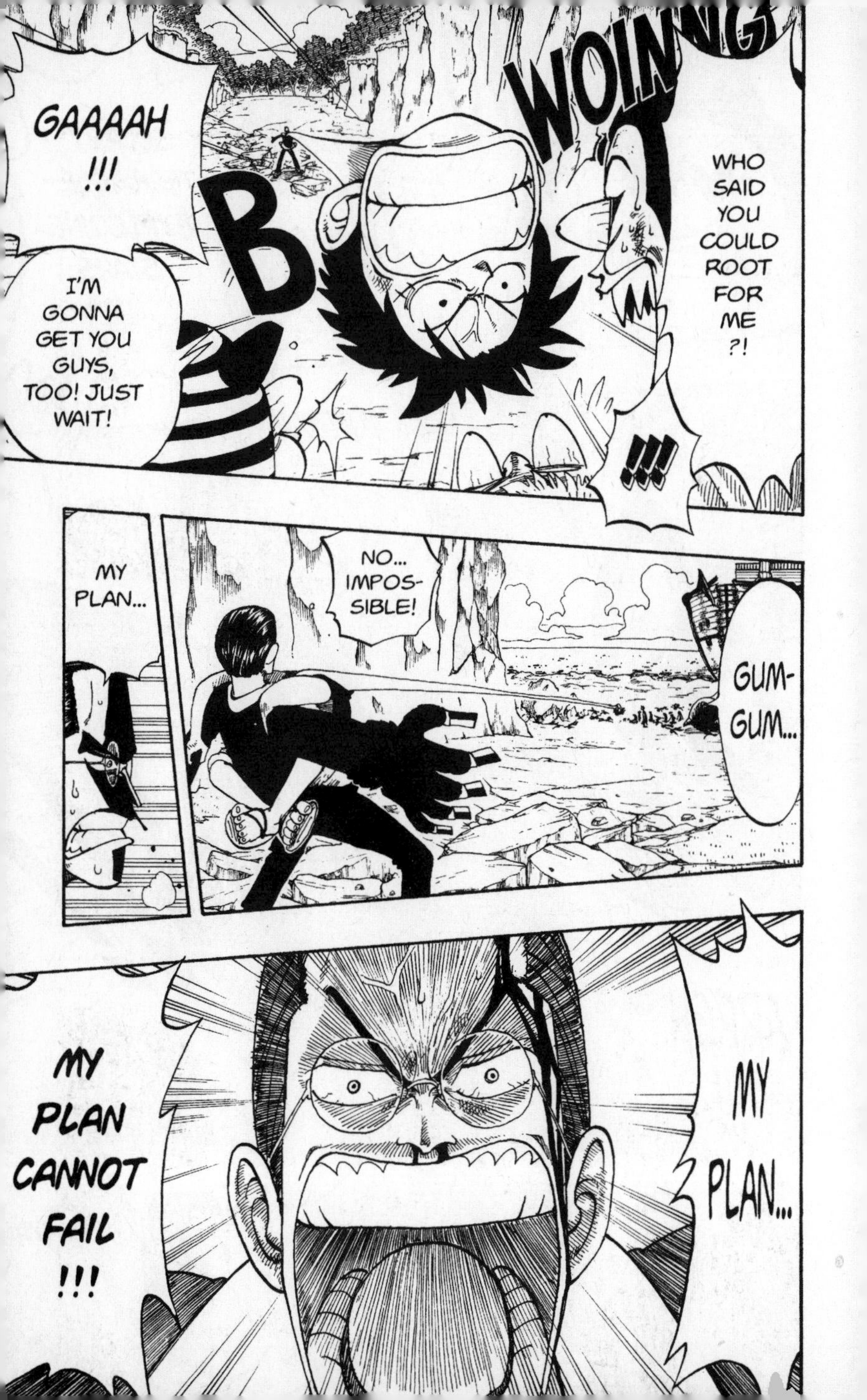
WOINNG
WHO SAID YOU COULD ROOT FOR ME?!
!!!
B
GAAAAH!!!
I'M GONNA GET YOU GUYS, TOO! JUST WAIT!
GUM-GUM...
NO... IMPOS-SIBLE!
MY PLAN...
MY PLAN...
MY PLAN CANNOT FAIL!!!

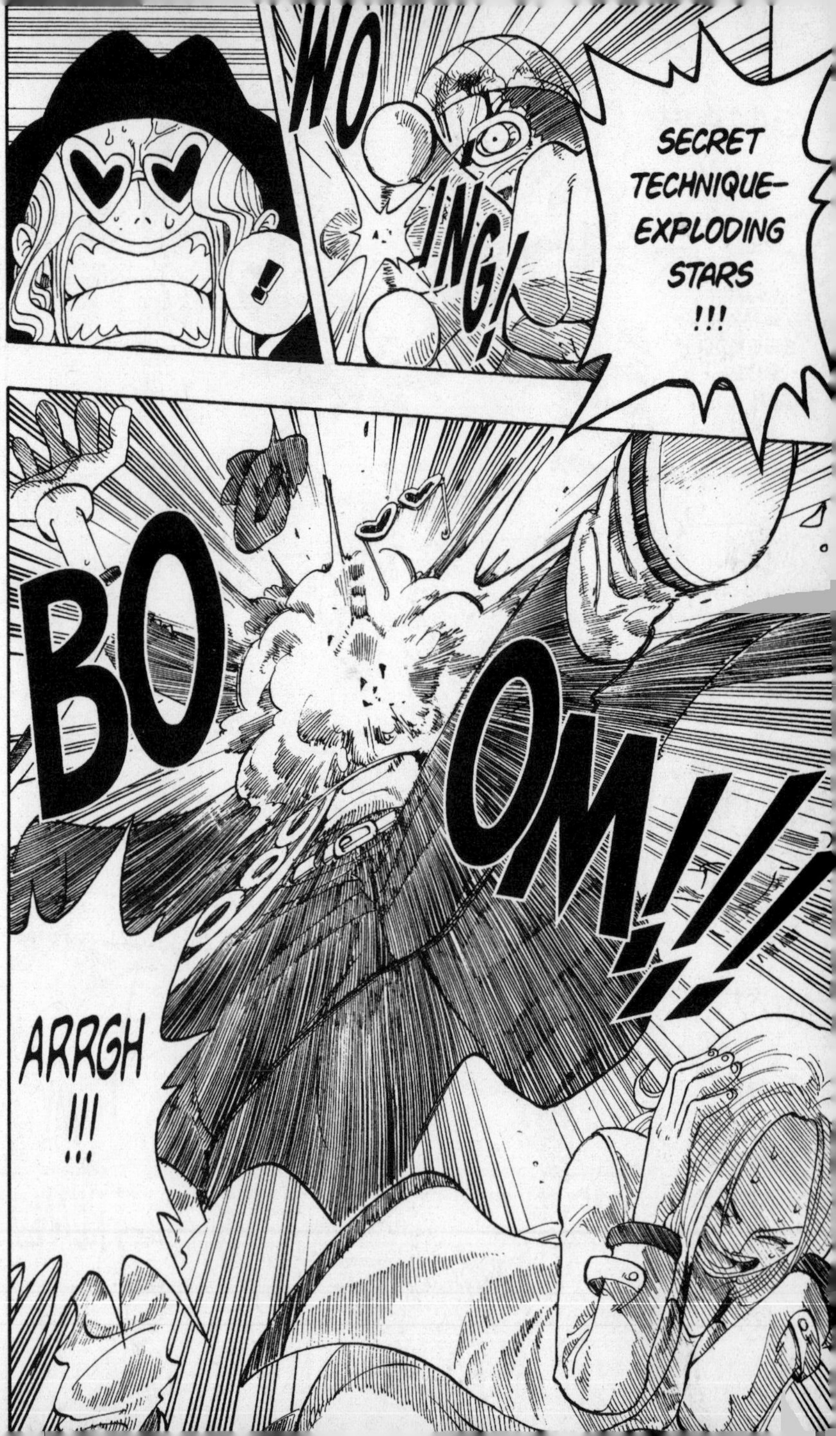
SECRET TECHNIQUE- EXPLODING STARS !!!
WO ING!
!
BO OM!!
ARRGH !!!

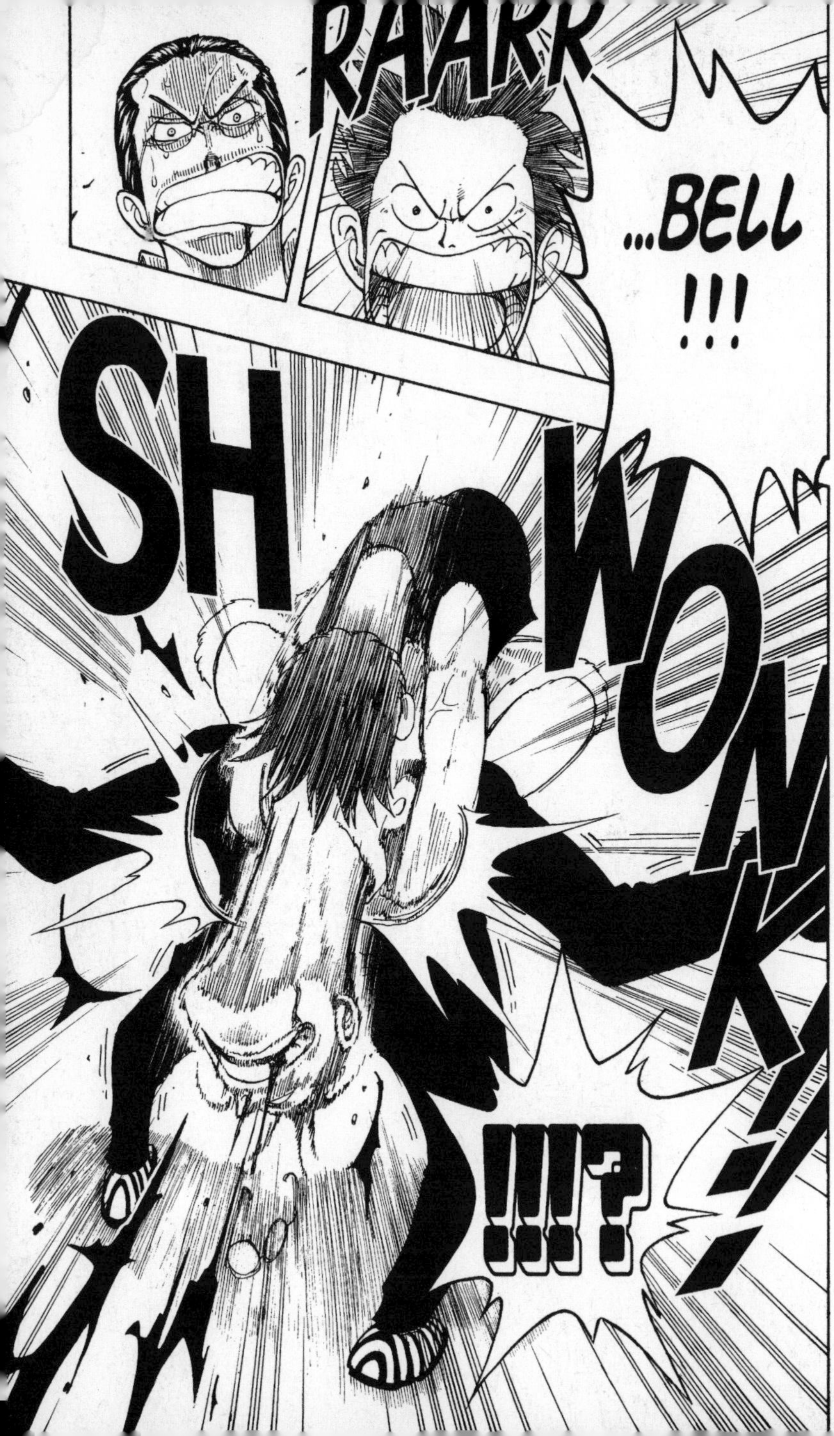
RAARR
...BELL !!!
SHWONK
!!!?

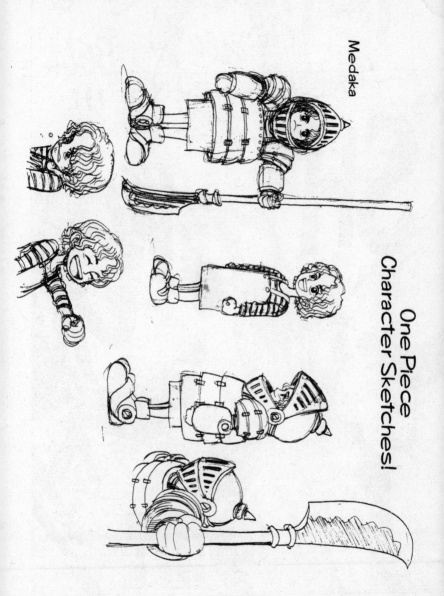

Medaka

One Piece
Character Sketches!

Chapter 40:
USOPP'S PIRATE CREW

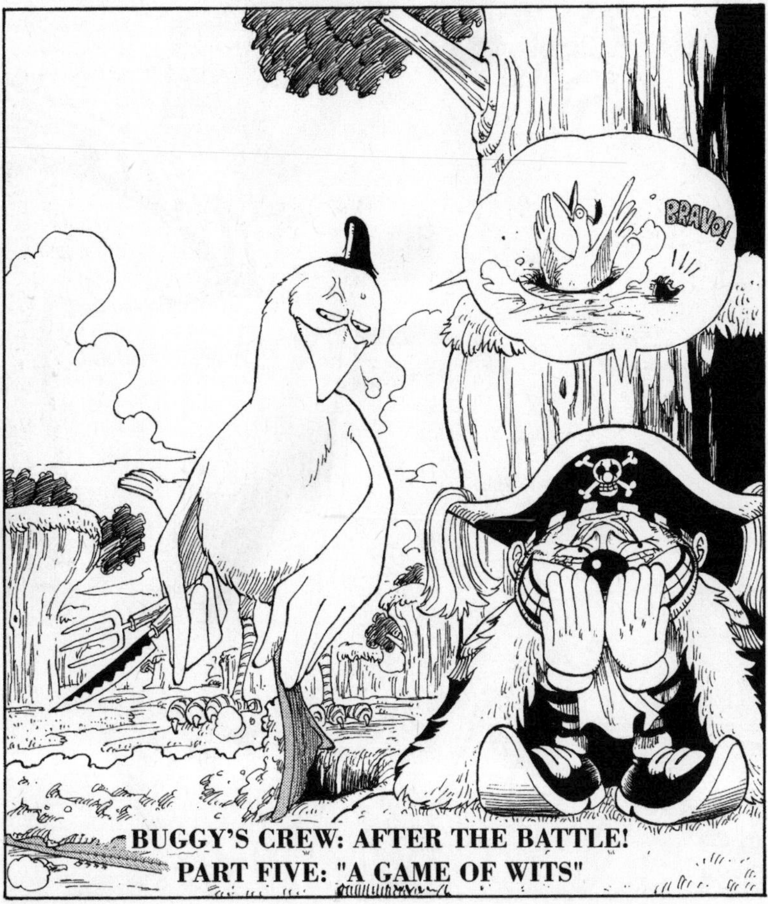
BRAVO!
BUGGY'S CREW: AFTER THE BATTLE!
PART FIVE: "A GAME OF WITS"

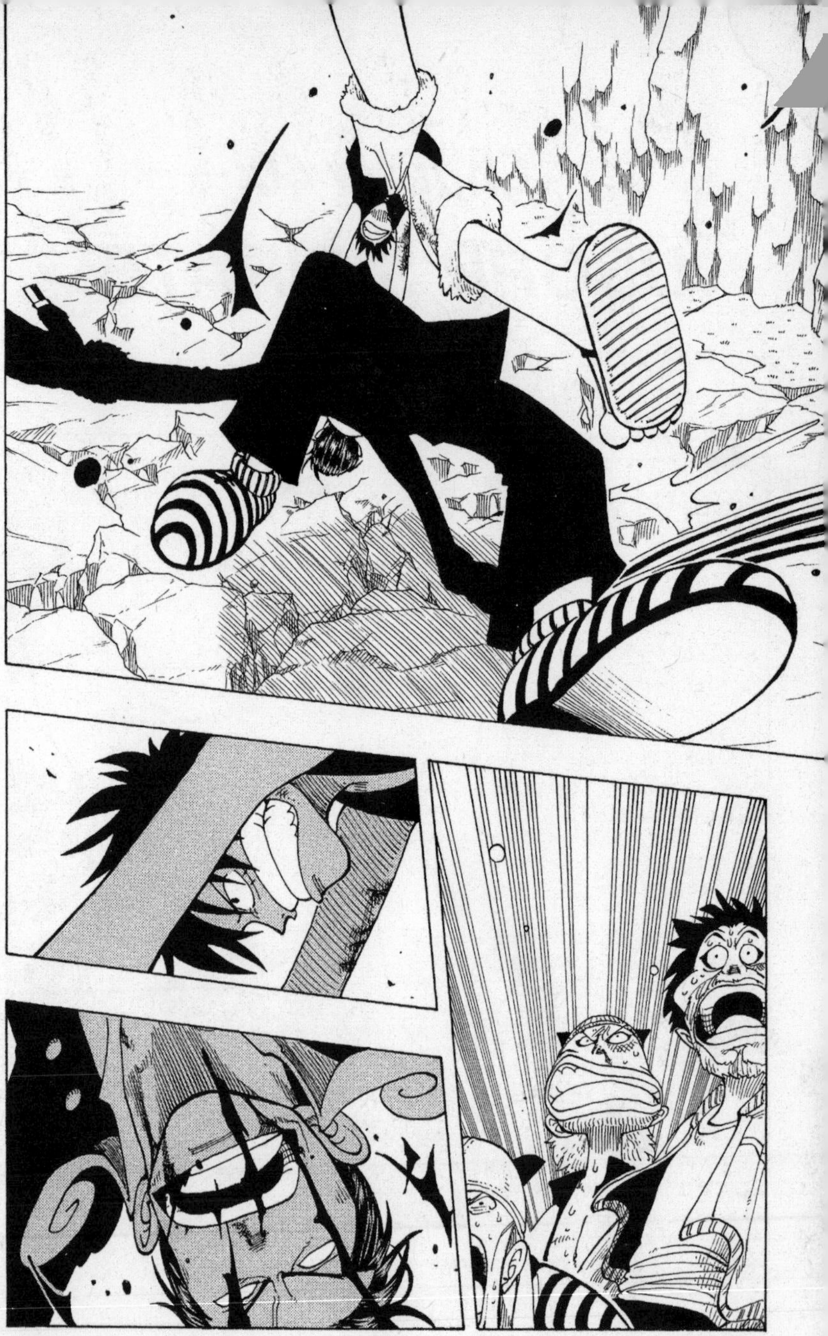

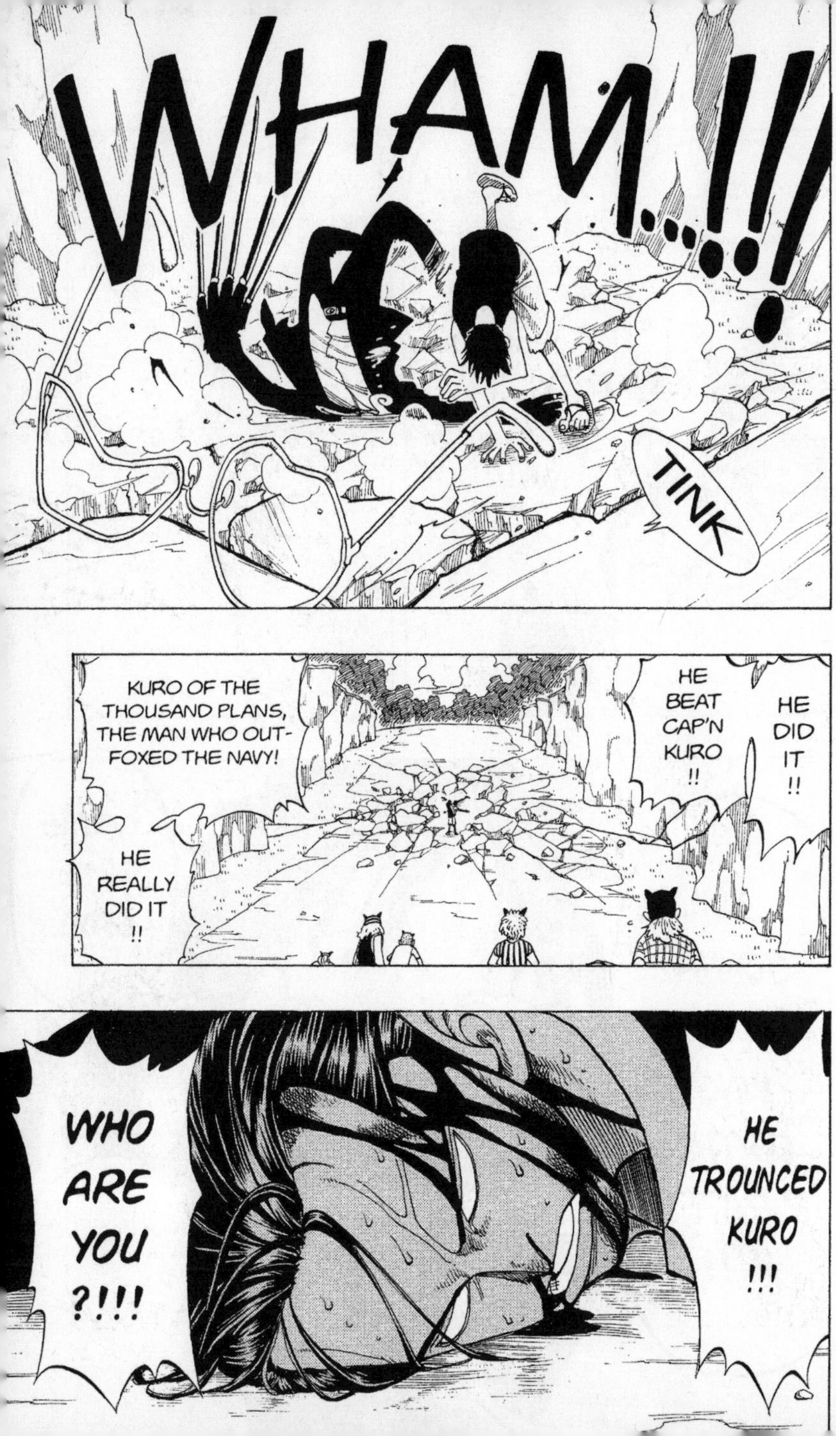
WHAM...!!!
TINK
HE DID IT !!
HE BEAT CAP'N KURO !!
KURO OF THE THOUSAND PLANS, THE MAN WHO OUT-FOXED THE NAVY!
HE REALLY DID IT !!
HE TROUNCED KURO !!!
WHO ARE YOU ?!!!

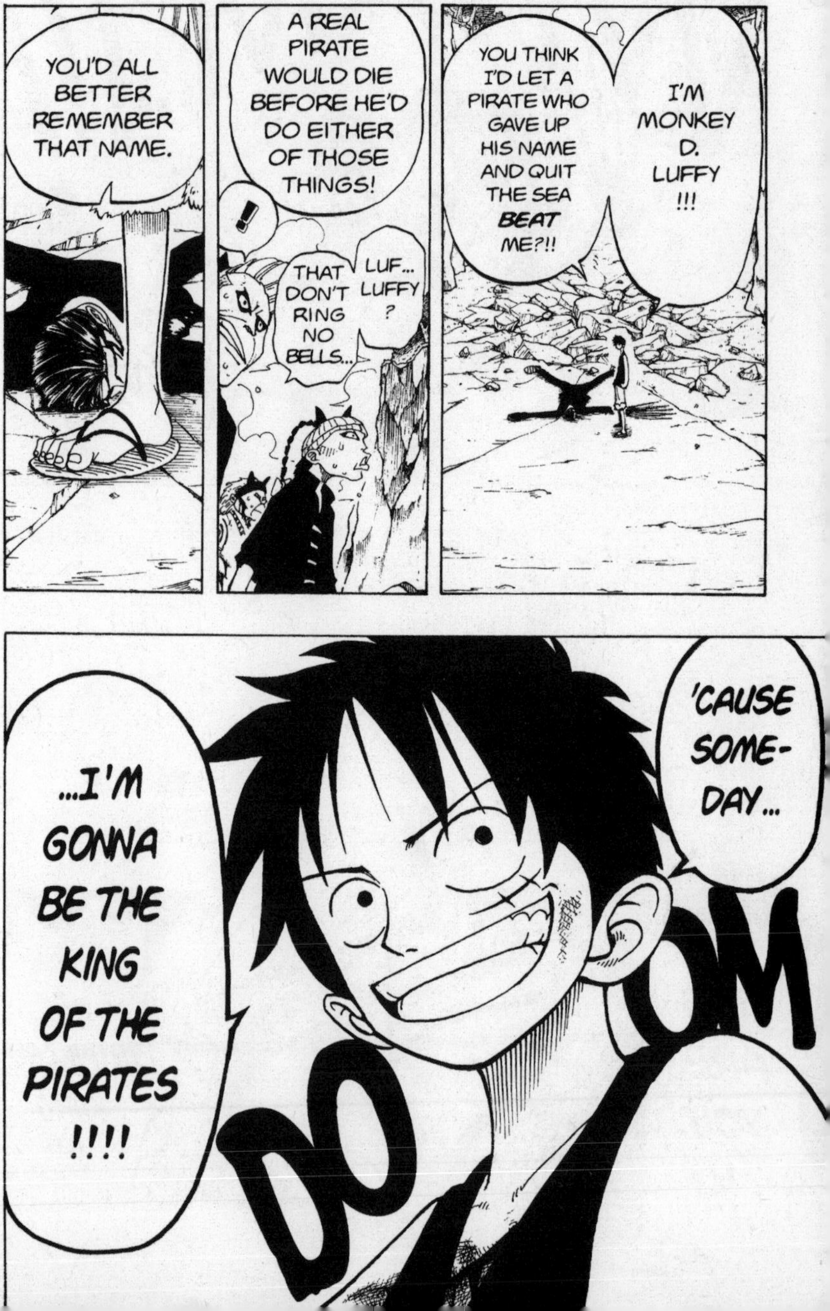
I'M MONKEY D. LUFFY !!!
YOU THINK I'D LET A PIRATE WHO GAVE UP HIS NAME AND QUIT THE SEA *BEAT* ME?!!
A REAL PIRATE WOULD DIE BEFORE HE'D DO EITHER OF THOSE THINGS!
!
LUF... LUFFY ?
THAT DON'T RING NO BELLS...
YOU'D ALL BETTER REMEMBER THAT NAME.
'CAUSE SOME-DAY...
...I'M GONNA BE THE KING OF THE PIRATES !!!!
DO
OM

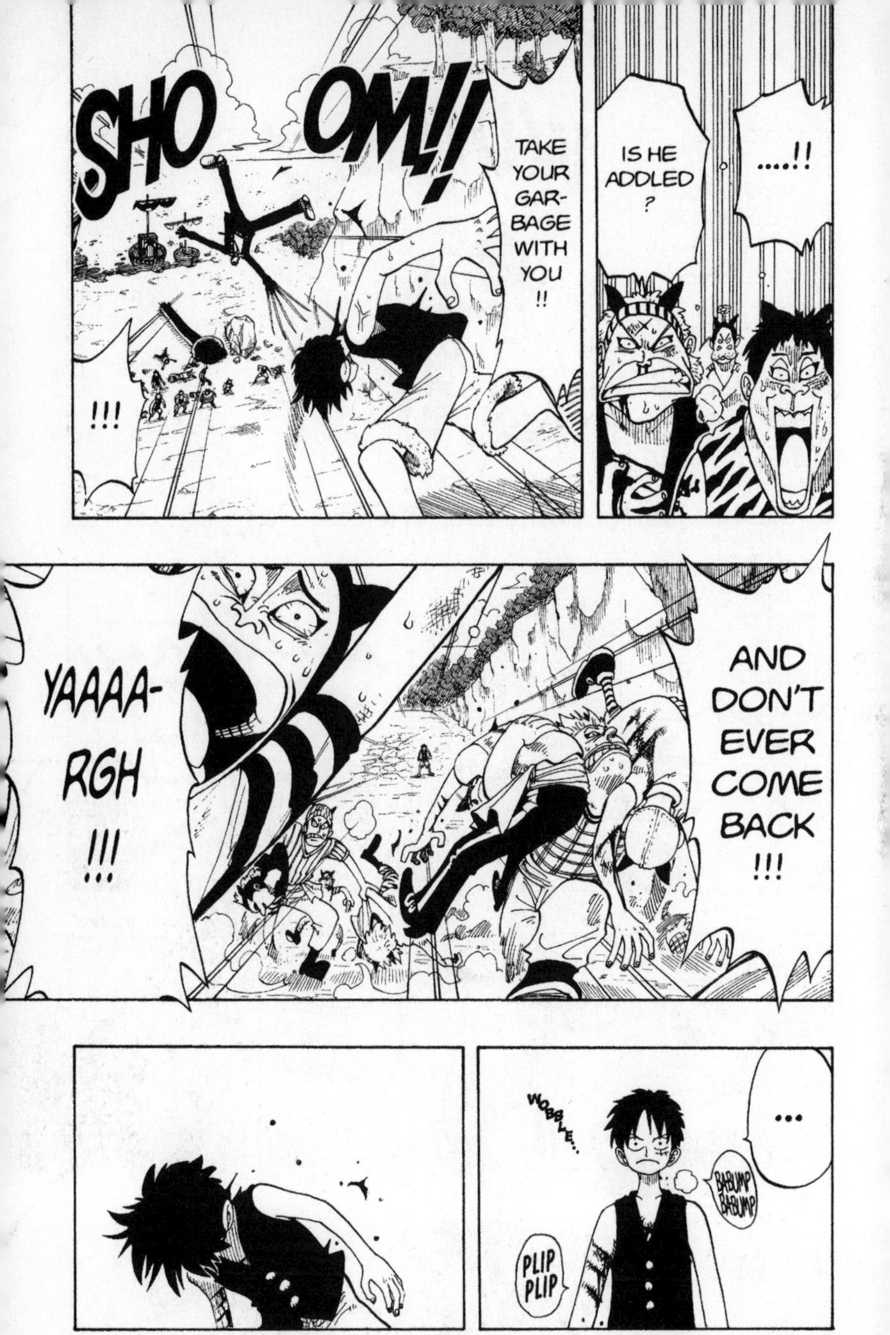
....!!
IS HE ADDLED?
TAKE YOUR GARBAGE WITH YOU!!
SHO OM!!
!!!
AND DON'T EVER COME BACK!!!
YAAAA-RGH!!!
...
BABUMP BABUMP
WOBBLE...
PLIP PLIP

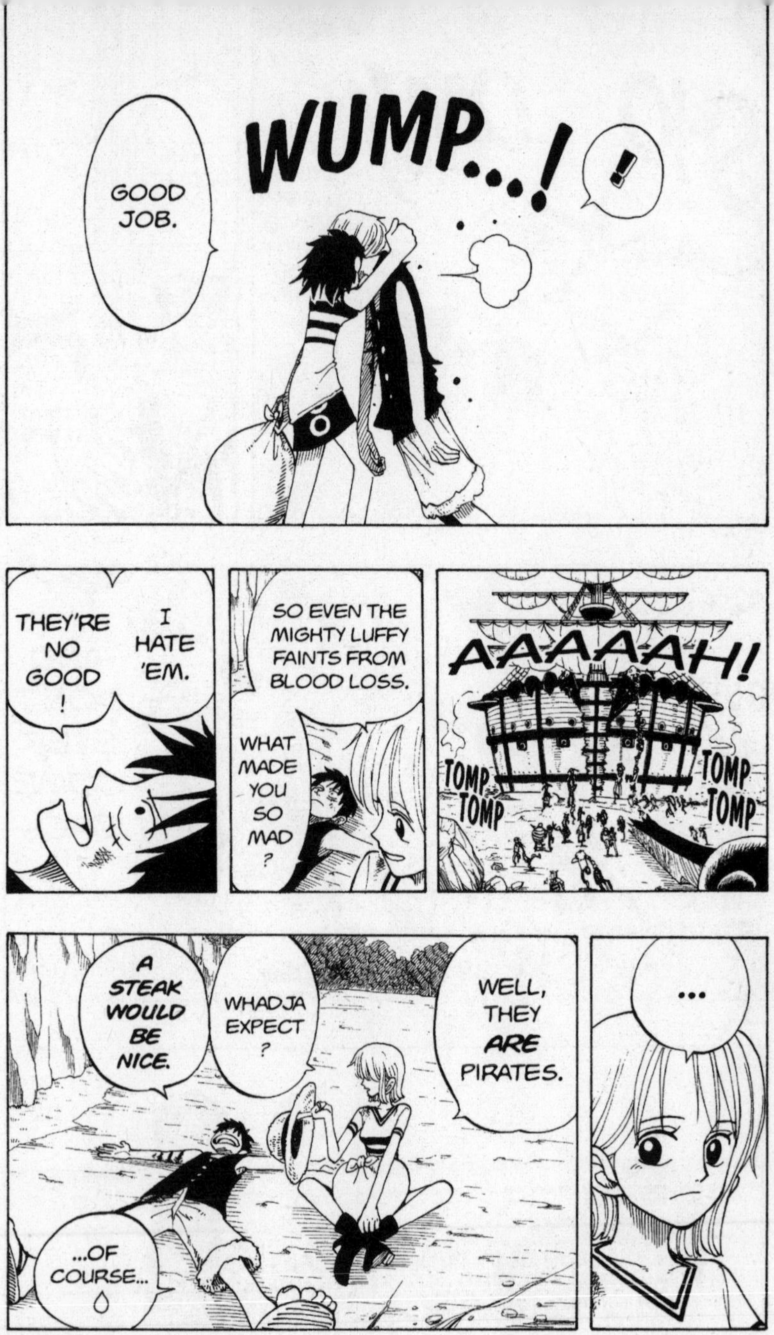
WUMP...!
!
GOOD JOB.
AAAAAH!
TOMP TOMP
TOMP TOMP
SO EVEN THE MIGHTY LUFFY FAINTS FROM BLOOD LOSS.
WHAT MADE YOU SO MAD?
I HATE 'EM.
THEY'RE NO GOOD!
...
WELL, THEY ARE PIRATES.
WHADJA EXPECT?
A STEAK WOULD BE NICE.
...OF COURSE...

READ THIS WAY

TUNK
SWIK
TMP
TMP
TMP

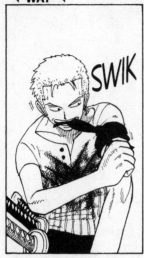

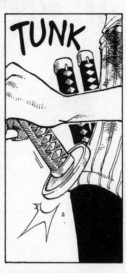

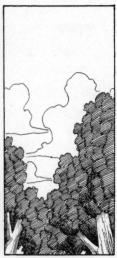

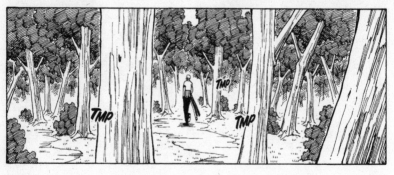

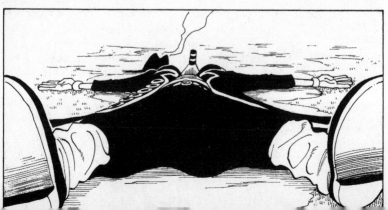

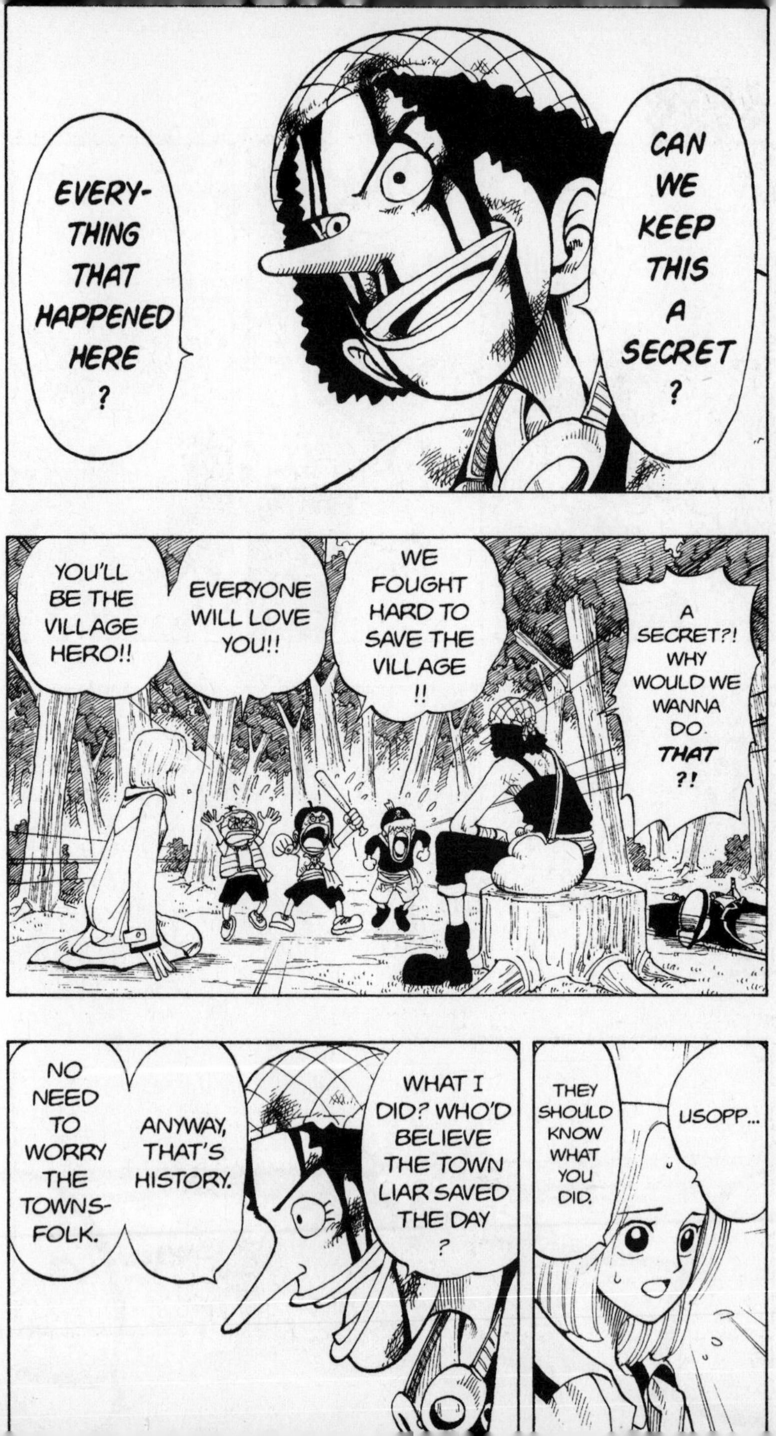

CAN WE KEEP THIS A SECRET?
EVERYTHING THAT HAPPENED HERE?
A SECRET?! WHY WOULD WE WANNA DO. *THAT*?!
WE FOUGHT HARD TO SAVE THE VILLAGE!!
EVERYONE WILL LOVE YOU!!
YOU'LL BE THE VILLAGE HERO!!
USOPP...
THEY SHOULD KNOW WHAT YOU DID.
WHAT I DID? WHO'D BELIEVE THE TOWN LIAR SAVED THE DAY?
ANYWAY, THAT'S HISTORY.
NO NEED TO WORRY THE TOWNSFOLK.

READ THIS WAY

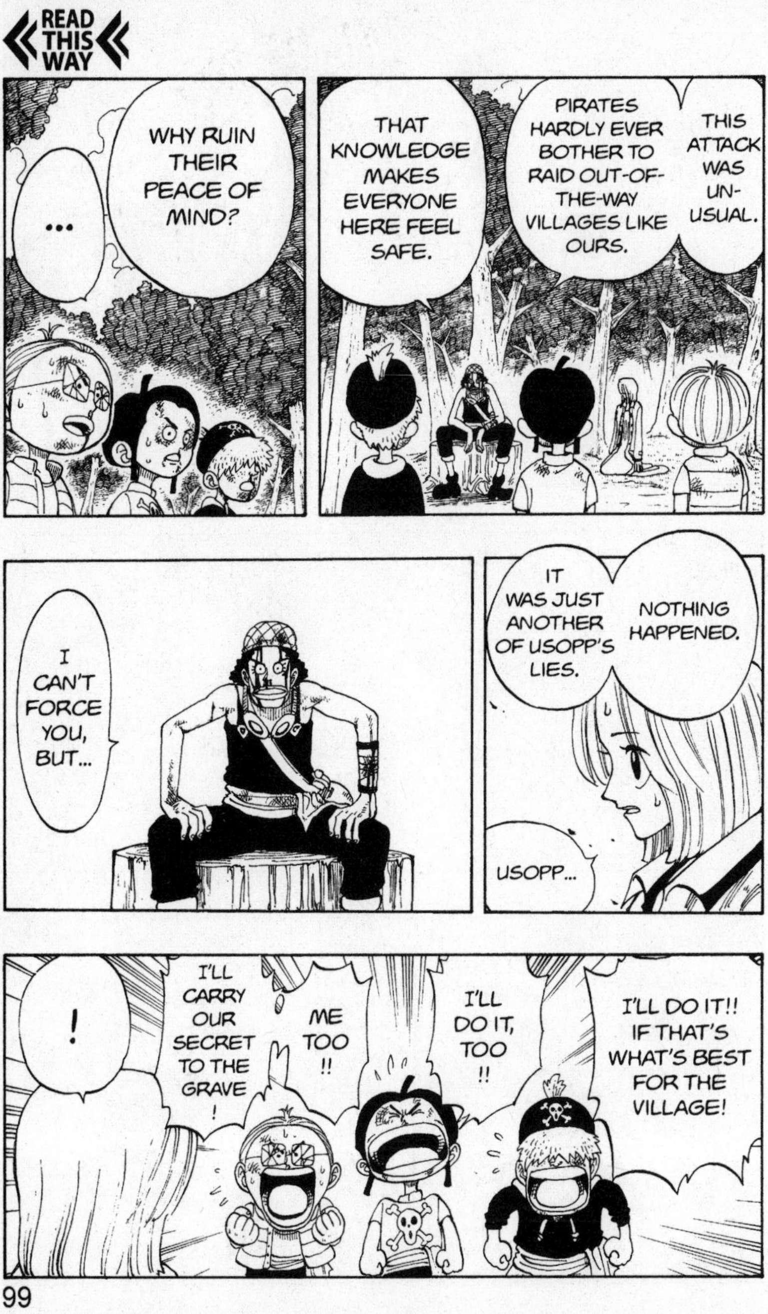

THIS ATTACK WAS UN-USUAL.
PIRATES HARDLY EVER BOTHER TO RAID OUT-OF-THE-WAY VILLAGES LIKE OURS.
THAT KNOWLEDGE MAKES EVERYONE HERE FEEL SAFE.
WHY RUIN THEIR PEACE OF MIND?
...
NOTHING HAPPENED.
IT WAS JUST ANOTHER OF USOPP'S LIES.
USOPP...
I CAN'T FORCE YOU, BUT...
I'LL DO IT!! IF THAT'S WHAT'S BEST FOR THE VILLAGE!
I'LL DO IT, TOO!!
ME TOO!!
I'LL CARRY OUR SECRET TO THE GRAVE!
!

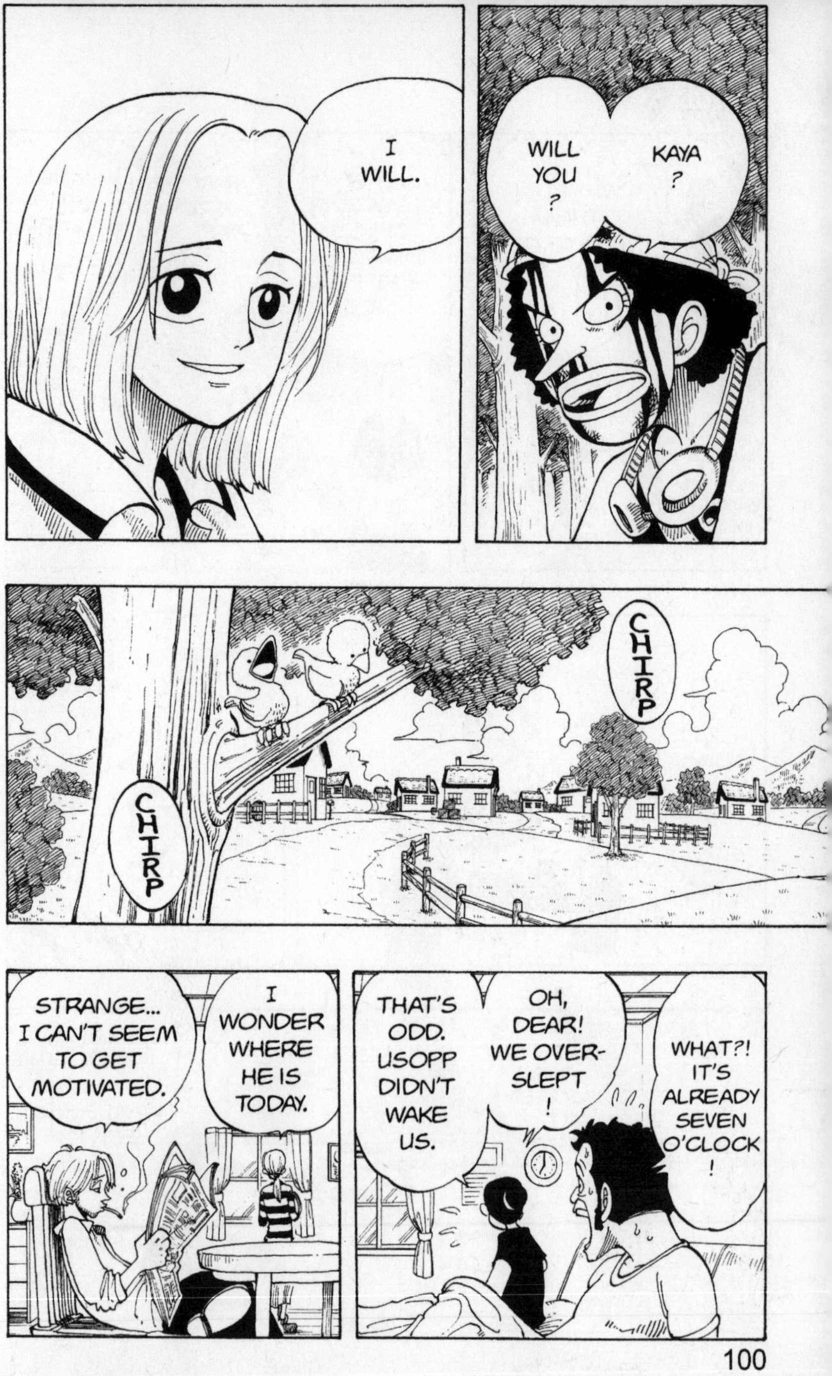
WILL YOU? KAYA?
I WILL.
CHIRP
CHIRP
WHAT?! IT'S ALREADY SEVEN O'CLOCK!
OH, DEAR! WE OVERSLEPT!
THAT'S ODD. USOPP DIDN'T WAKE US.
I WONDER WHERE HE IS TODAY.
STRANGE... I CAN'T SEEM TO GET MOTIVATED.

READ THIS WAY

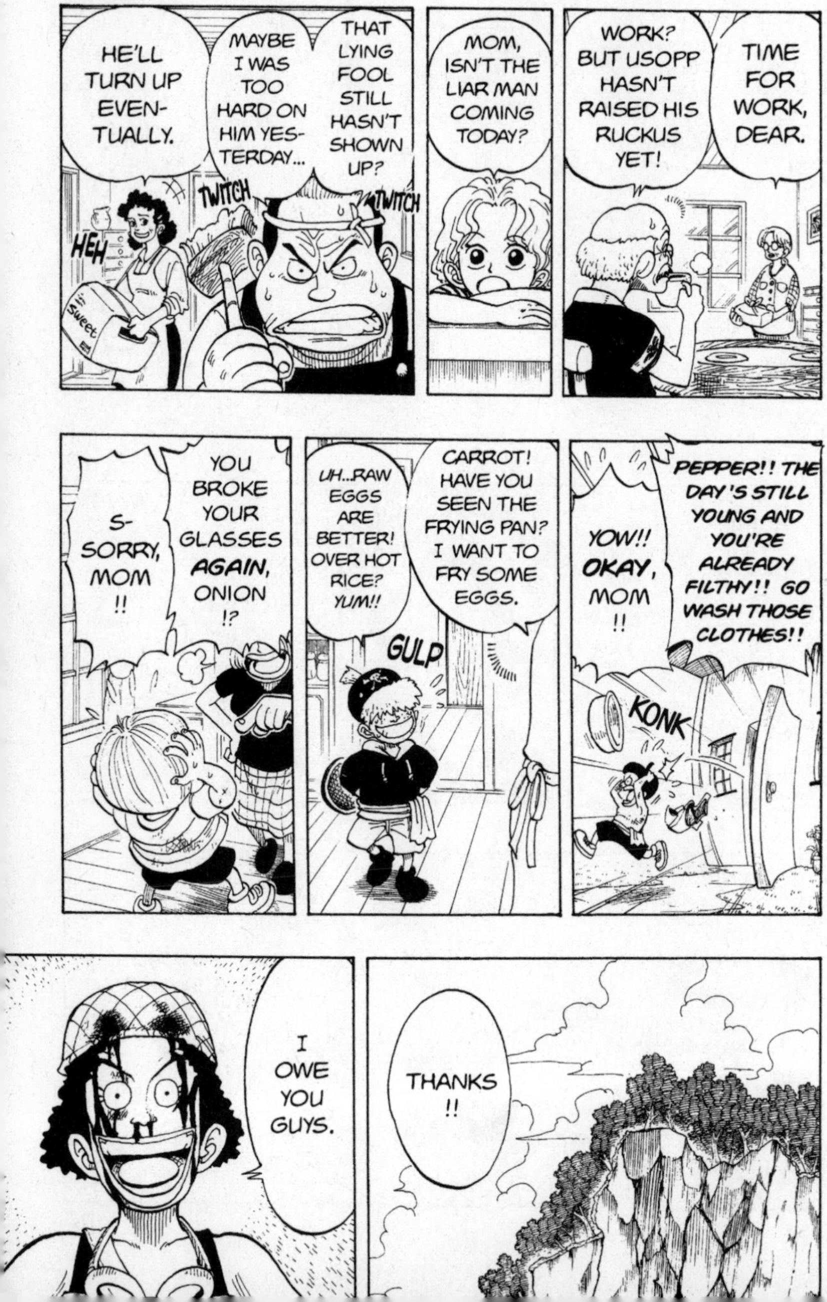
TIME FOR WORK, DEAR.
WORK? BUT USOPP HASN'T RAISED HIS RUCKUS YET!
MOM, ISN'T THE LIAR MAN COMING TODAY?
THAT LYING FOOL STILL HASN'T SHOWN UP?
TWITCH
MAYBE I WAS TOO HARD ON HIM YESTERDAY...
TWITCH
HE'LL TURN UP EVEN-TUALLY.
HEH
Sweet
PEPPER!! THE DAY'S STILL YOUNG AND YOU'RE ALREADY FILTHY!! GO WASH THOSE CLOTHES!!
YOW!! OKAY, MOM!!
KONK
CARROT! HAVE YOU SEEN THE FRYING PAN? I WANT TO FRY SOME EGGS.
UH...RAW EGGS ARE BETTER! OVER HOT RICE? YUM!!
GULP
YOU BROKE YOUR GLASSES AGAIN, ONION!?
S-SORRY, MOM!!
THANKS!!
I OWE YOU GUYS.

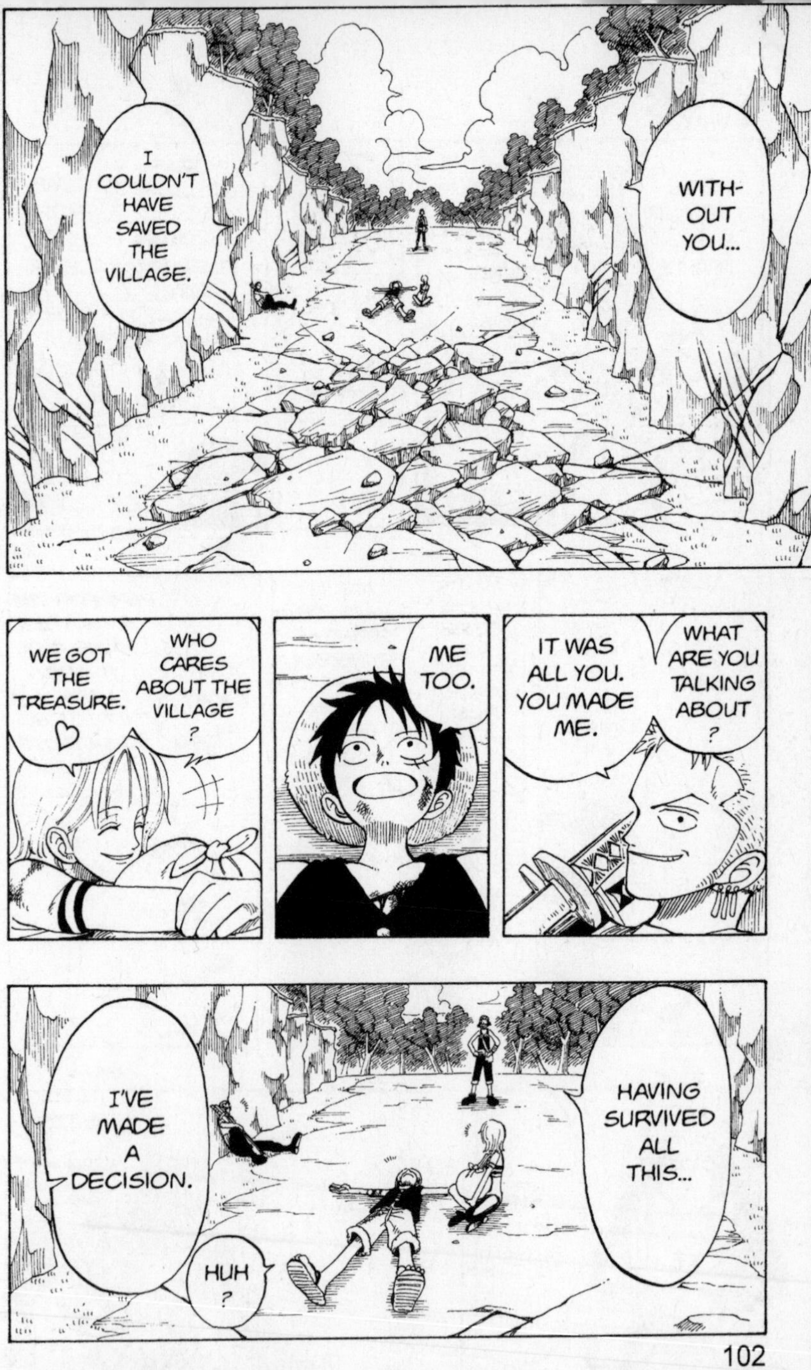
WITH-OUT YOU...
I COULDN'T HAVE SAVED THE VILLAGE.
WHAT ARE YOU TALKING ABOUT?
IT WAS ALL YOU. YOU MADE ME.
ME TOO.
WHO CARES ABOUT THE VILLAGE?
WE GOT THE TREASURE. ♡
HAVING SURVIVED ALL THIS...
I'VE MADE A DECISION.
HUH?

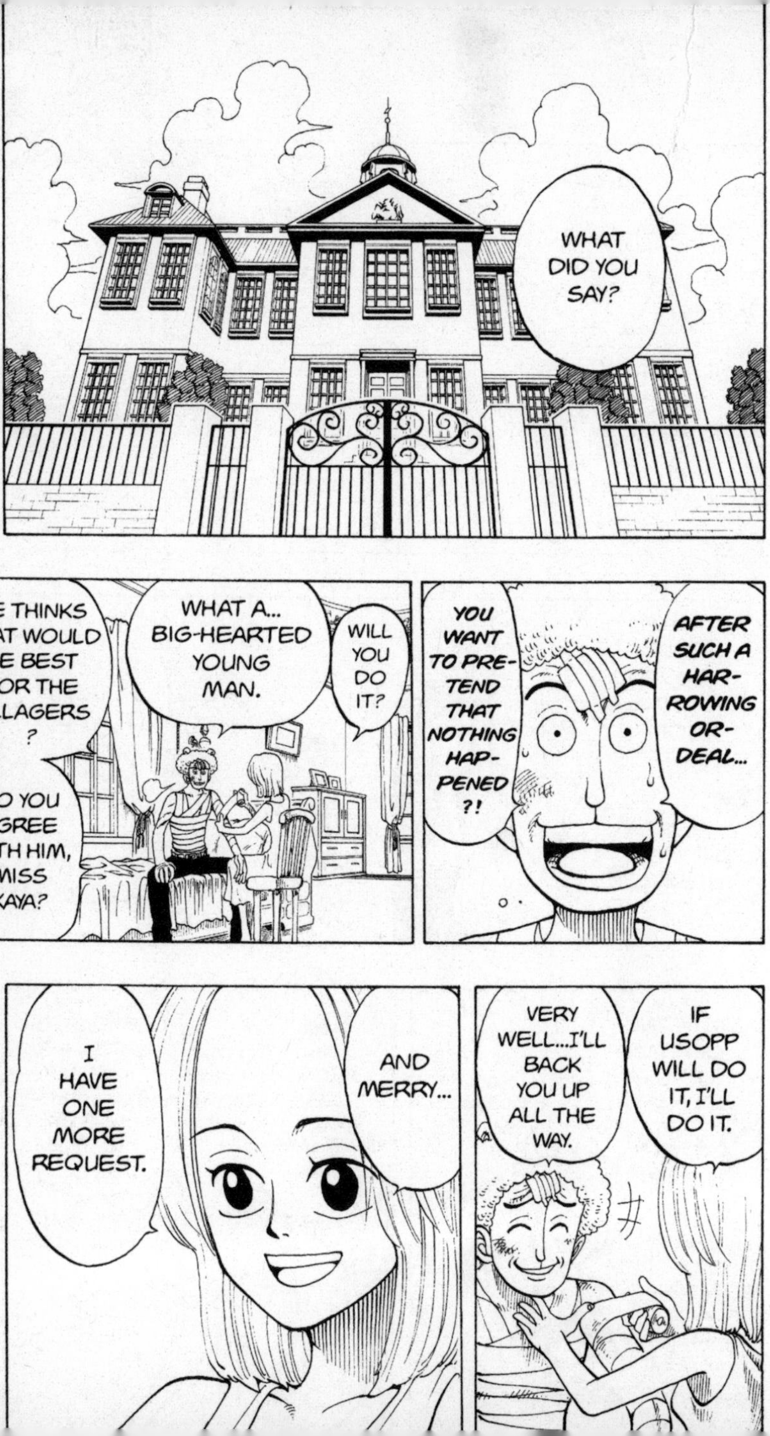
WHAT DID YOU SAY?
AFTER SUCH A HARROWING ORDEAL...
YOU WANT TO PRETEND THAT NOTHING HAPPENED?!
WILL YOU DO IT?
WHAT A... BIG-HEARTED YOUNG MAN.
HE THINKS THAT WOULD BE BEST FOR THE VILLAGERS?
DO YOU AGREE WITH HIM, MISS KAYA?
IF USOPP WILL DO IT, I'LL DO IT.
VERY WELL...I'LL BACK YOU UP ALL THE WAY.
AND MERRY...
I HAVE ONE MORE REQUEST.

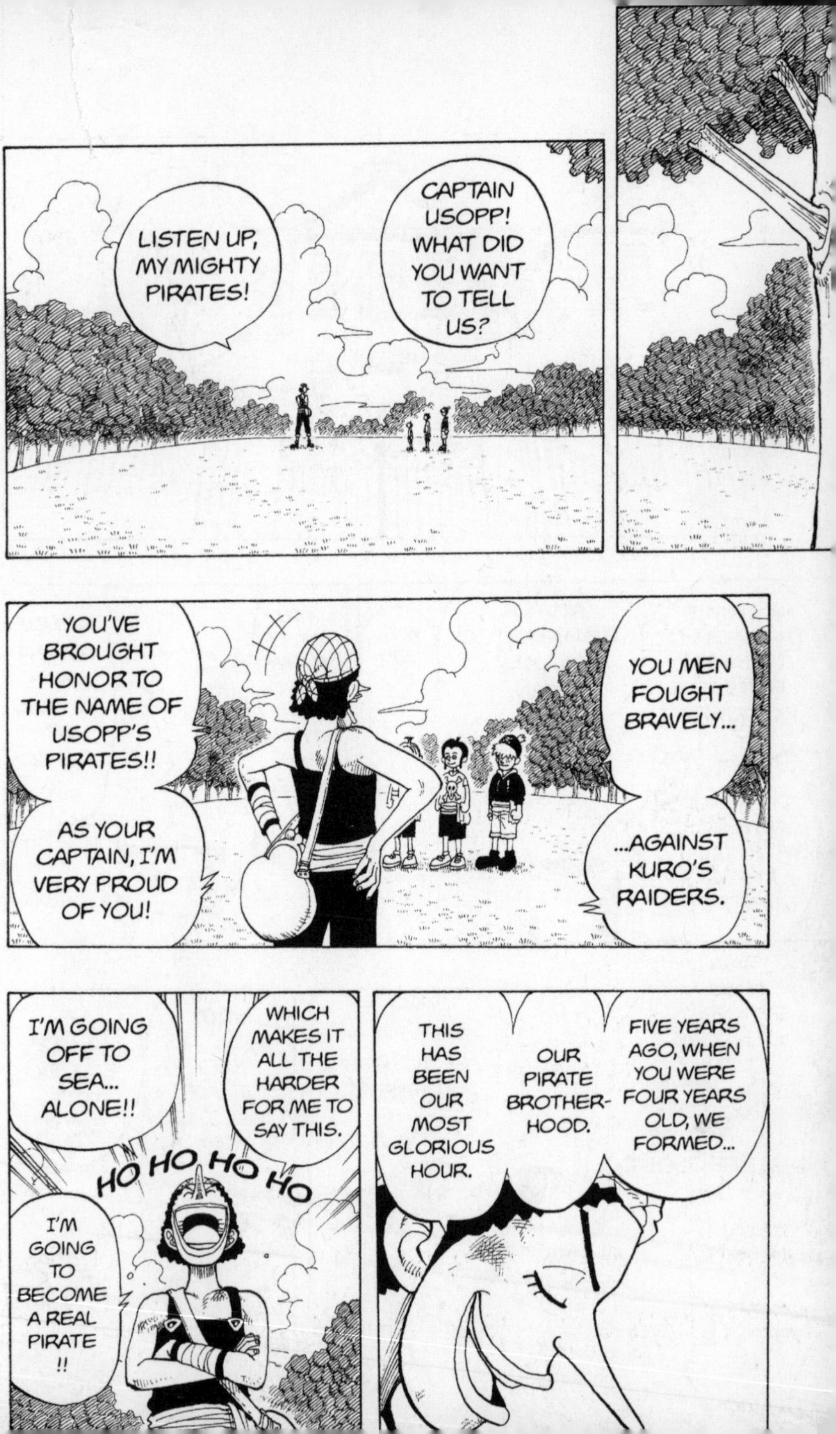
CAPTAIN USOPP! WHAT DID YOU WANT TO TELL US?
LISTEN UP, MY MIGHTY PIRATES!
YOU MEN FOUGHT BRAVELY...
...AGAINST KURO'S RAIDERS.
YOU'VE BROUGHT HONOR TO THE NAME OF USOPP'S PIRATES!!
AS YOUR CAPTAIN, I'M VERY PROUD OF YOU!
FIVE YEARS AGO, WHEN YOU WERE FOUR YEARS OLD, WE FORMED...
OUR PIRATE BROTHER-HOOD.
THIS HAS BEEN OUR MOST GLORIOUS HOUR.
WHICH MAKES IT ALL THE HARDER FOR ME TO SAY THIS.
I'M GOING OFF TO SEA... ALONE!!
HO HO HO HO
I'M GOING TO BECOME A REAL PIRATE !!

READ THIS WAY

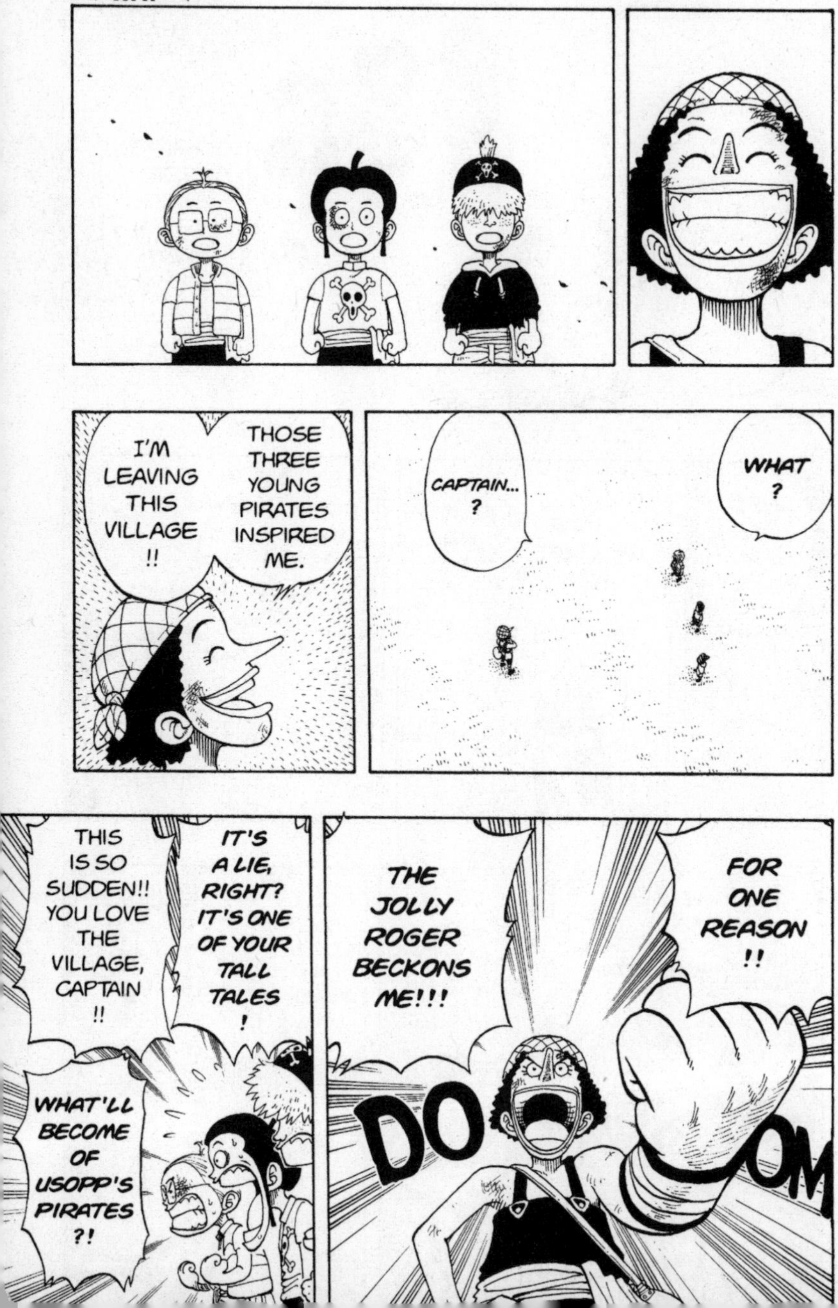
WHAT ?
CAPTAIN... ?
THOSE THREE YOUNG PIRATES INSPIRED ME.
I'M LEAVING THIS VILLAGE !!
FOR ONE REASON !!
THE JOLLY ROGER BECKONS ME!!!
DO
OM
IT'S A LIE, RIGHT? IT'S ONE OF YOUR TALL TALES !
THIS IS SO SUDDEN!! YOU LOVE THE VILLAGE, CAPTAIN !!
WHAT'LL BECOME OF USOPP'S PIRATES ?!

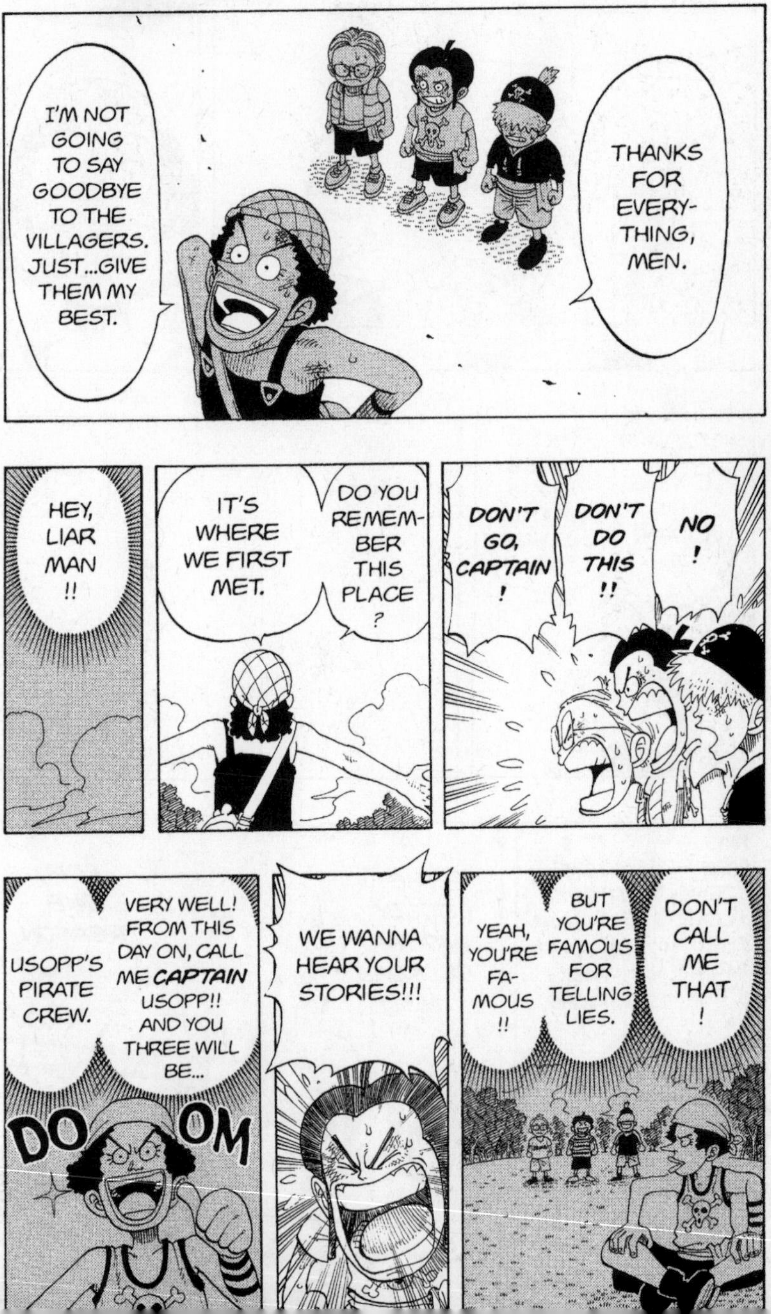
THANKS FOR EVERYTHING, MEN.
I'M NOT GOING TO SAY GOODBYE TO THE VILLAGERS. JUST...GIVE THEM MY BEST.
NO!
DON'T DO THIS!!
DON'T GO, CAPTAIN!
DO YOU REMEMBER THIS PLACE?
IT'S WHERE WE FIRST MET.
HEY, LIAR MAN!!
DON'T CALL ME THAT!
BUT YOU'RE FAMOUS FOR TELLING LIES.
YEAH, YOU'RE FAMOUS!!
WE WANNA HEAR YOUR STORIES!!!
VERY WELL! FROM THIS DAY ON, CALL ME CAPTAIN USOPP!! AND YOU THREE WILL BE...
USOPP'S PIRATE CREW.
DOOM

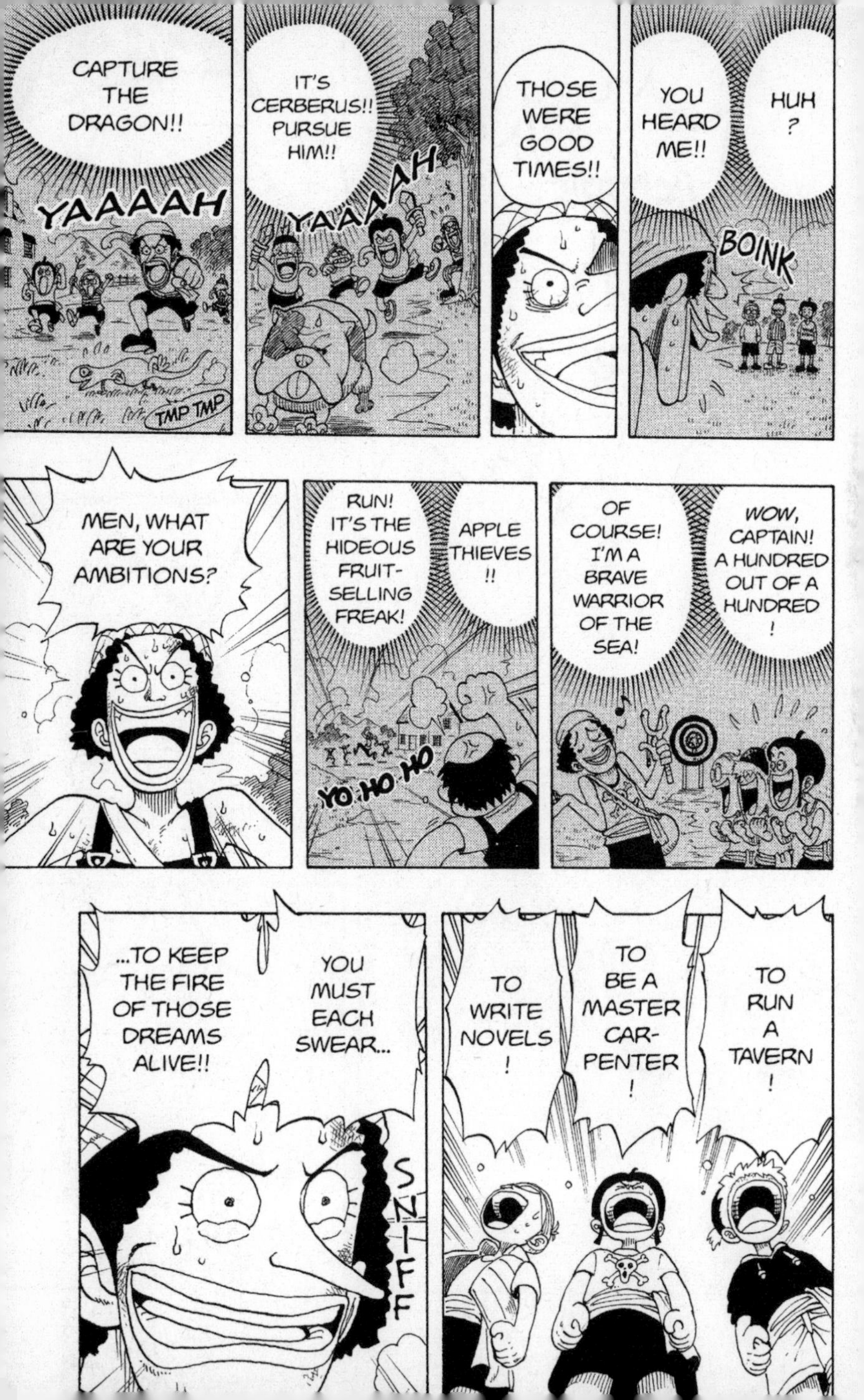
HUH ?
YOU HEARD ME!!
BOINK
THOSE WERE GOOD TIMES!!
IT'S CERBERUS!! PURSUE HIM!!
YAAAAAH
CAPTURE THE DRAGON!!
YAAAAAH
TMP TMP
WOW, CAPTAIN! A HUNDRED OUT OF A HUNDRED!
OF COURSE! I'M A BRAVE WARRIOR OF THE SEA!
APPLE THIEVES!!
RUN! IT'S THE HIDEOUS FRUIT-SELLING FREAK!
YO HO HO
MEN, WHAT ARE YOUR AMBITIONS?
TO RUN A TAVERN!
TO BE A MASTER CAR-PENTER!
TO WRITE NOVELS!
YOU MUST EACH SWEAR...
...TO KEEP THE FIRE OF THOSE DREAMS ALIVE!!
SNIFF

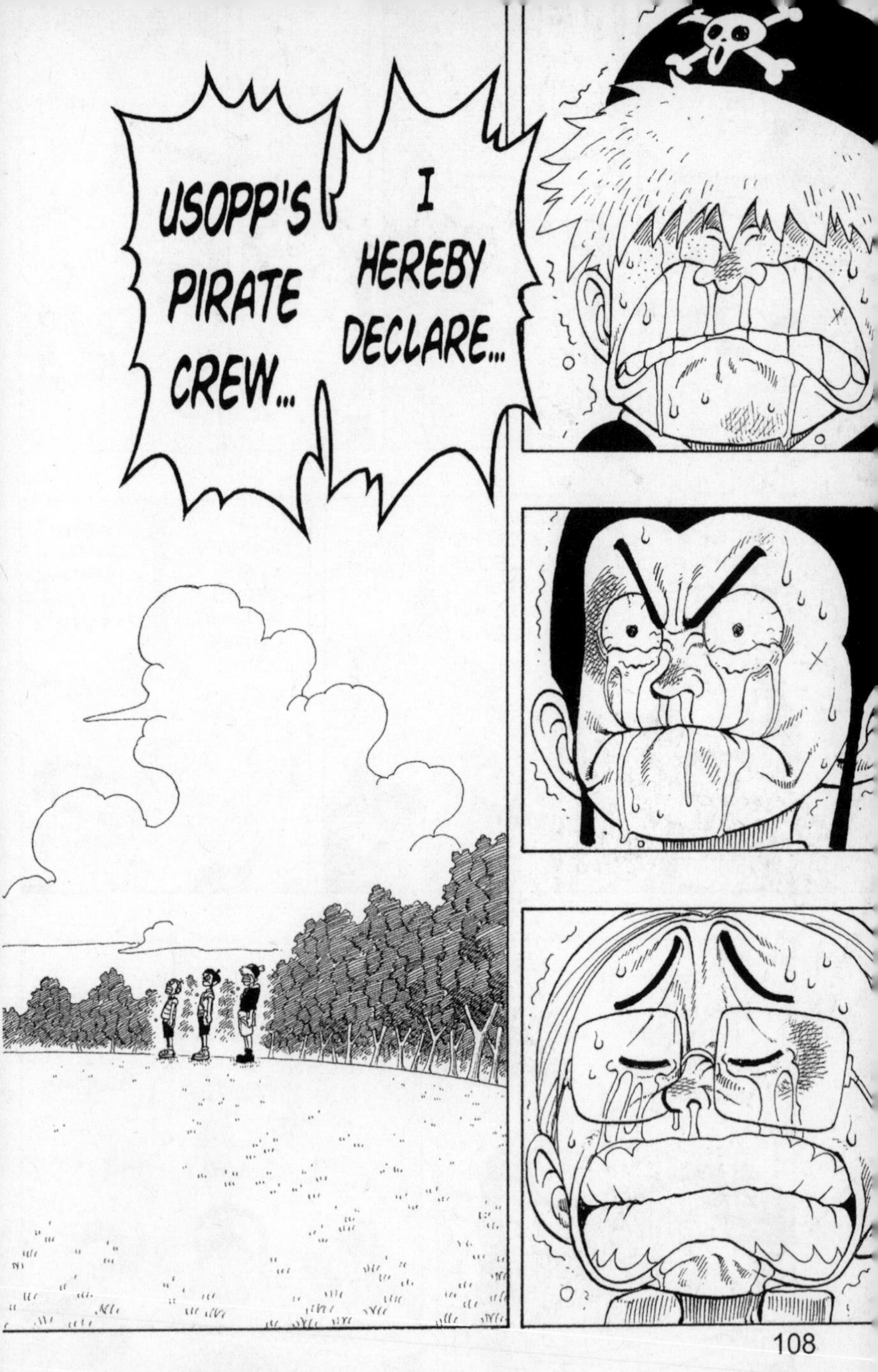
I HEREBY DECLARE...
USOPP'S PIRATE CREW...

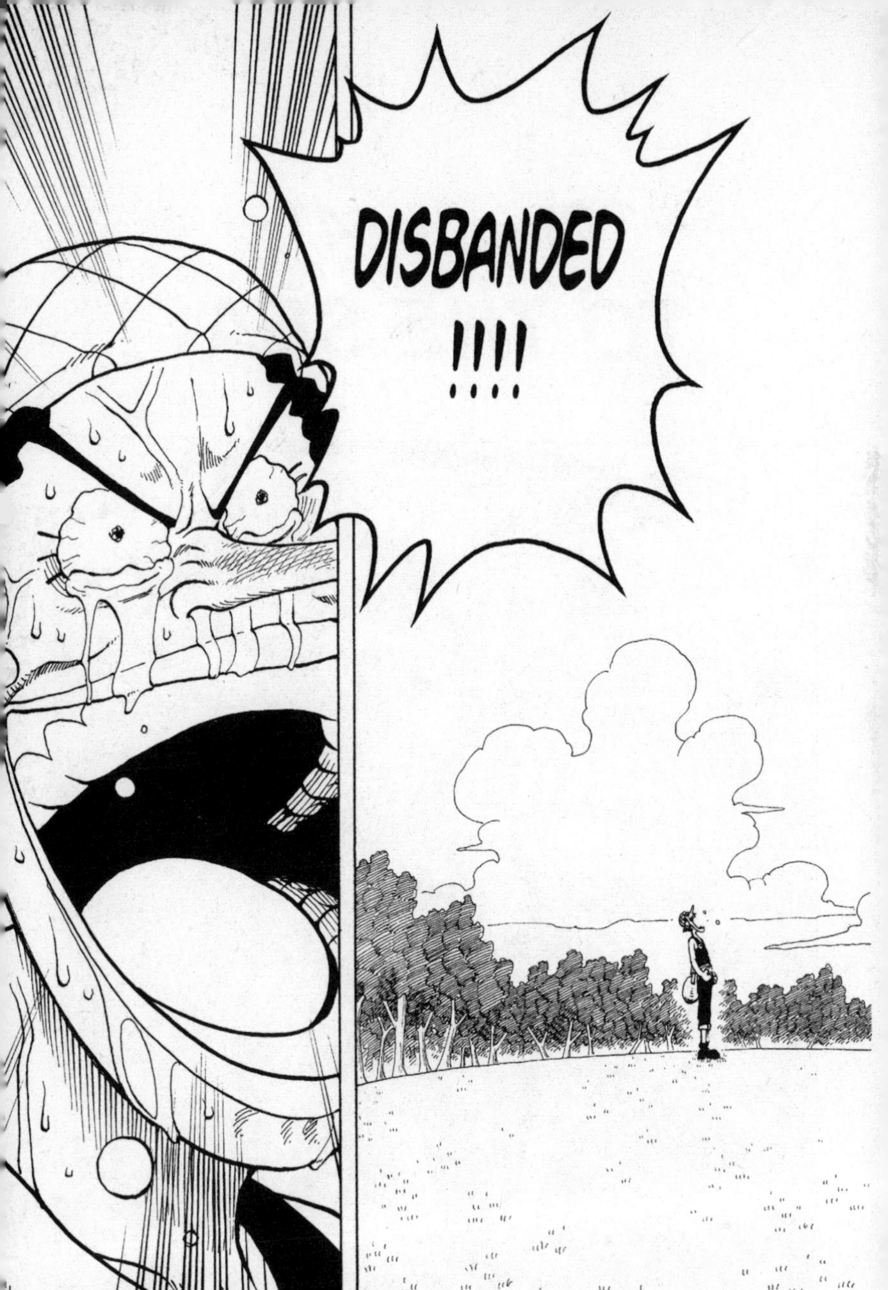
DISBANDED
!!!!

Chapter 41:
TO THE SEA

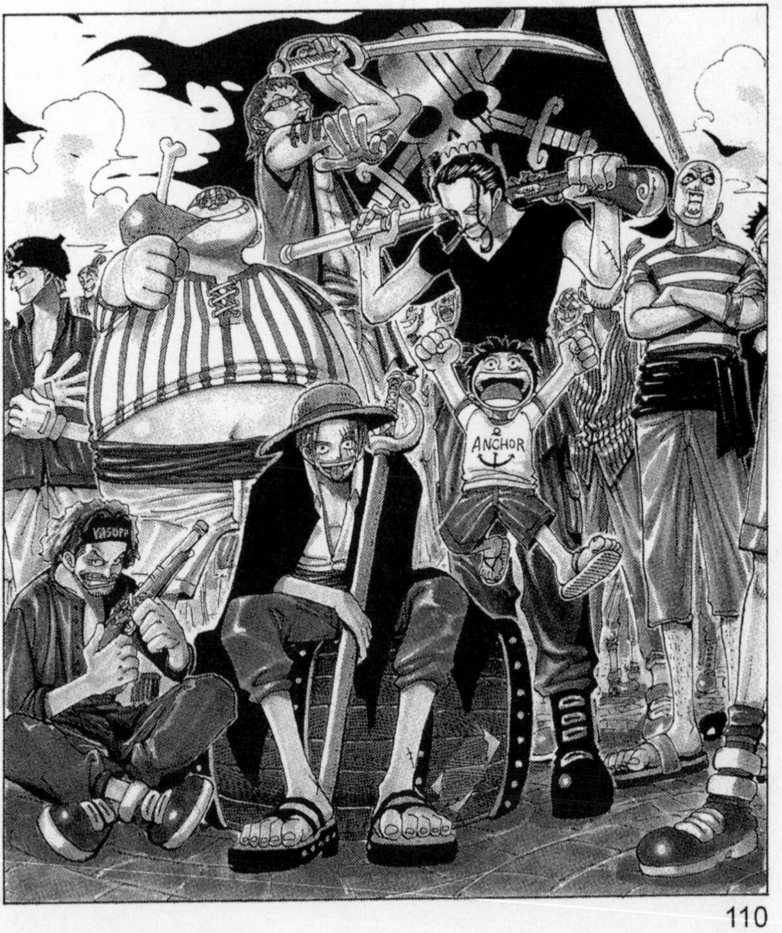
YASOPP
ANCHOR

READ THIS WAY

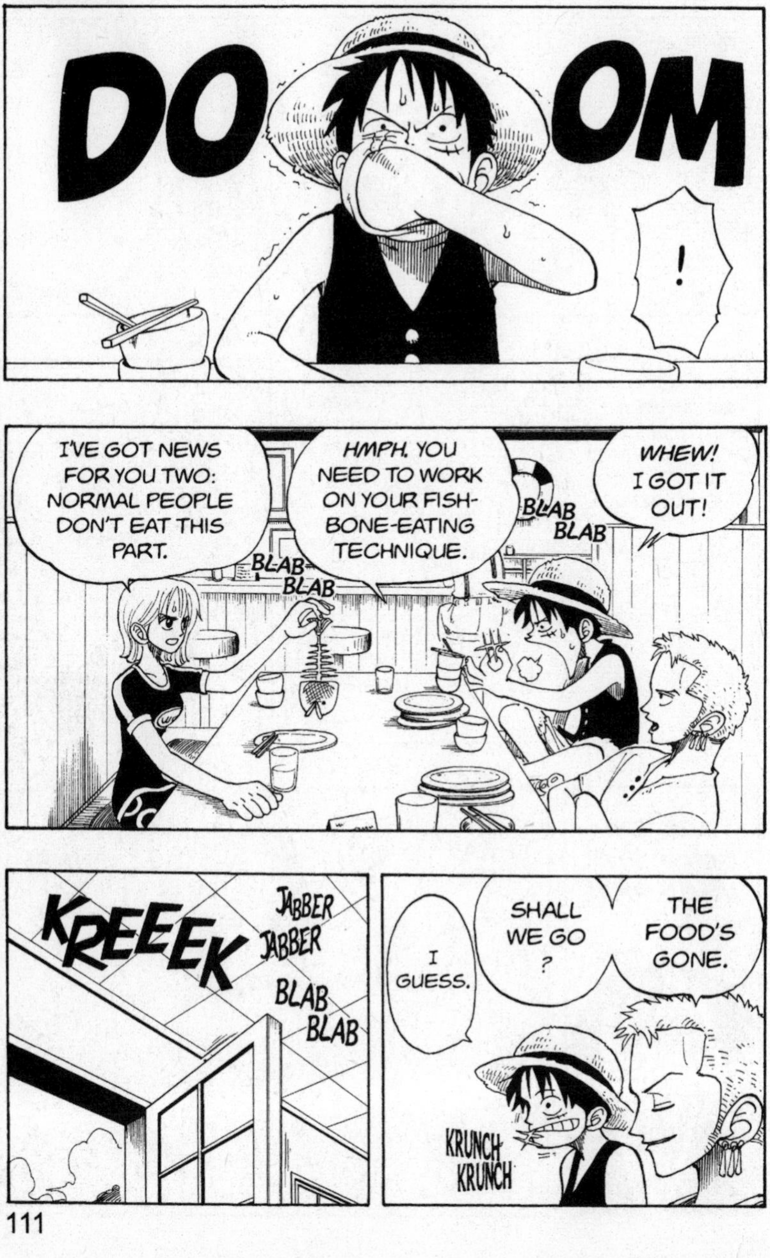
DO OM
!
WHEW! I GOT IT OUT!
BLAB BLAB
HMPH. YOU NEED TO WORK ON YOUR FISH-BONE-EATING TECHNIQUE.
BLAB-BLAB
I'VE GOT NEWS FOR YOU TWO: NORMAL PEOPLE DON'T EAT THIS PART.
THE FOOD'S GONE.
SHALL WE GO?
I GUESS.
KRUNCH KRUNCH
JABBER JABBER
BLAB BLAB
KREEEK

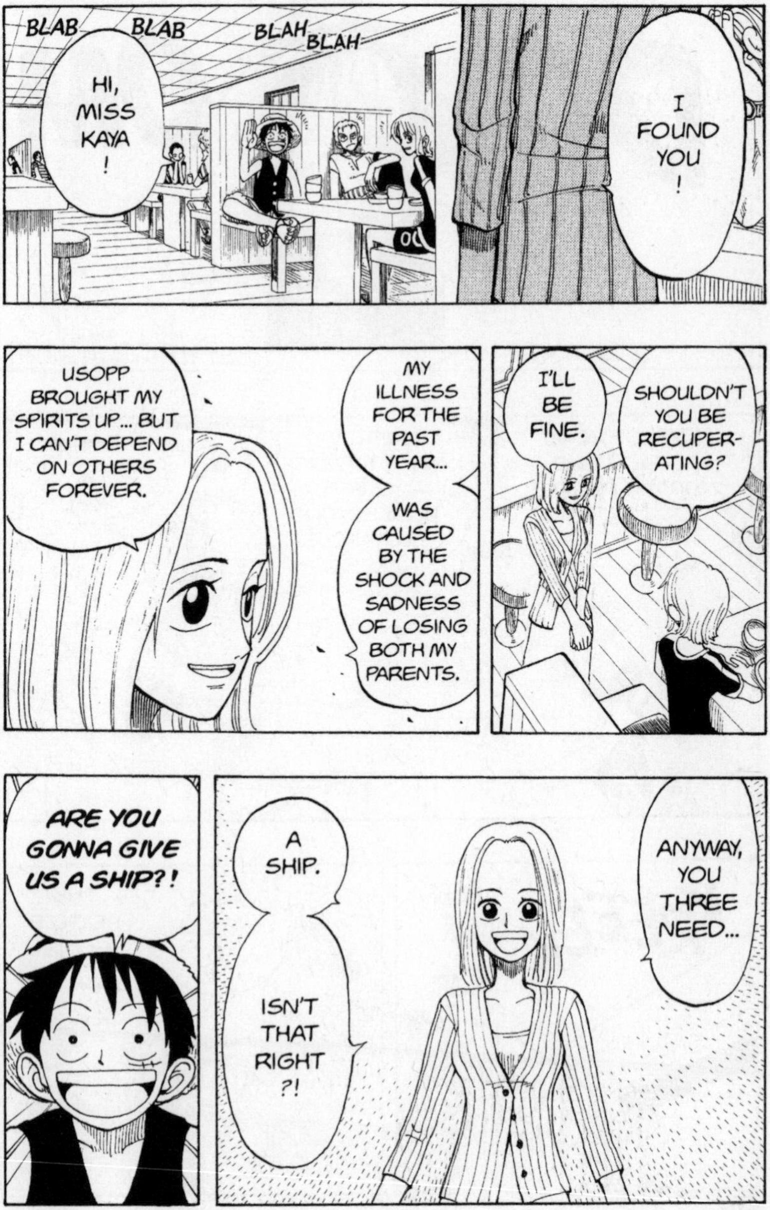
I FOUND YOU!
BLAH BLAH
BLAB
BLAB
HI, MISS KAYA!
SHOULDN'T YOU BE RECUPERATING?
I'LL BE FINE.
MY ILLNESS FOR THE PAST YEAR...
WAS CAUSED BY THE SHOCK AND SADNESS OF LOSING BOTH MY PARENTS.
USOPP BROUGHT MY SPIRITS UP... BUT I CAN'T DEPEND ON OTHERS FOREVER.
ANYWAY, YOU THREE NEED...
A SHIP.
ISN'T THAT RIGHT?!
ARE YOU GONNA GIVE US A SHIP?!

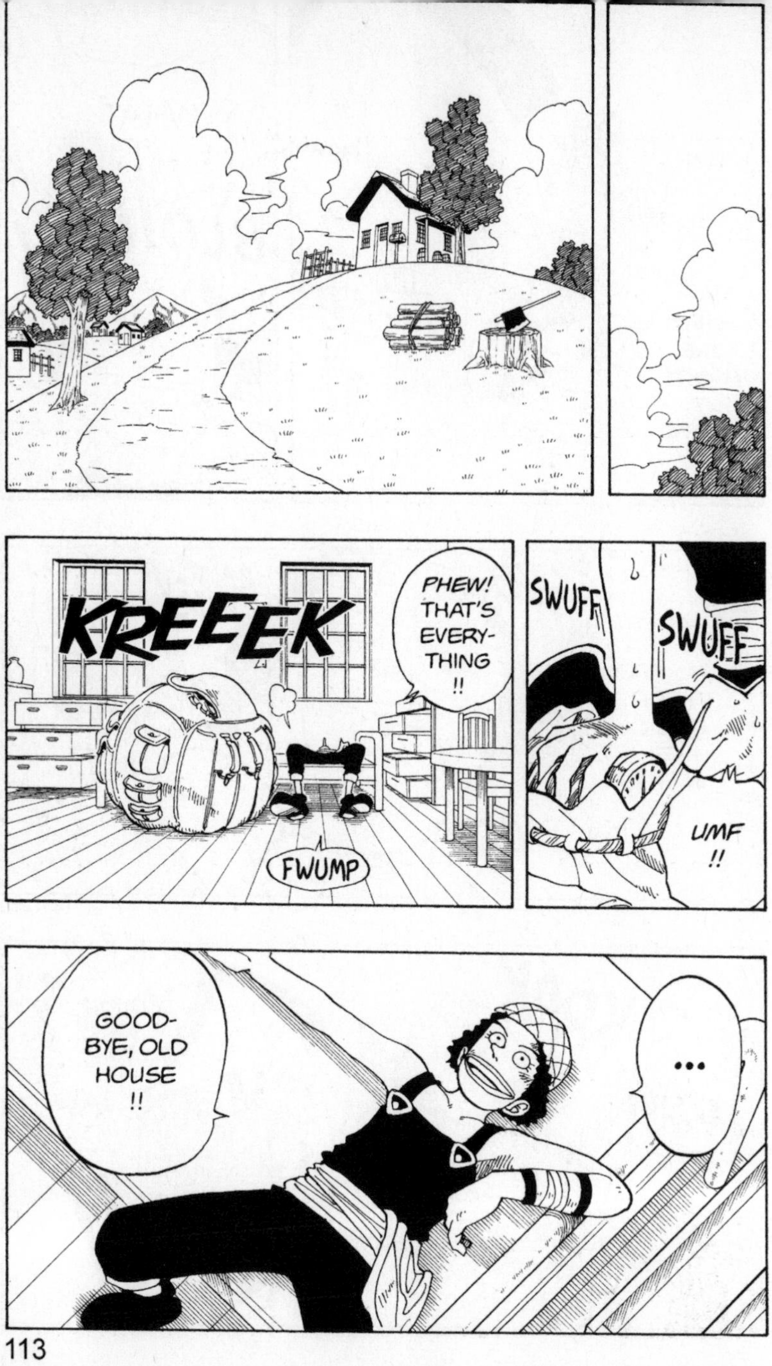
SWUFF
SWUFF
UMF !!
PHEW! THAT'S EVERY-THING !!
KREEEK
FWUMP
...
GOOD-BYE, OLD HOUSE !!

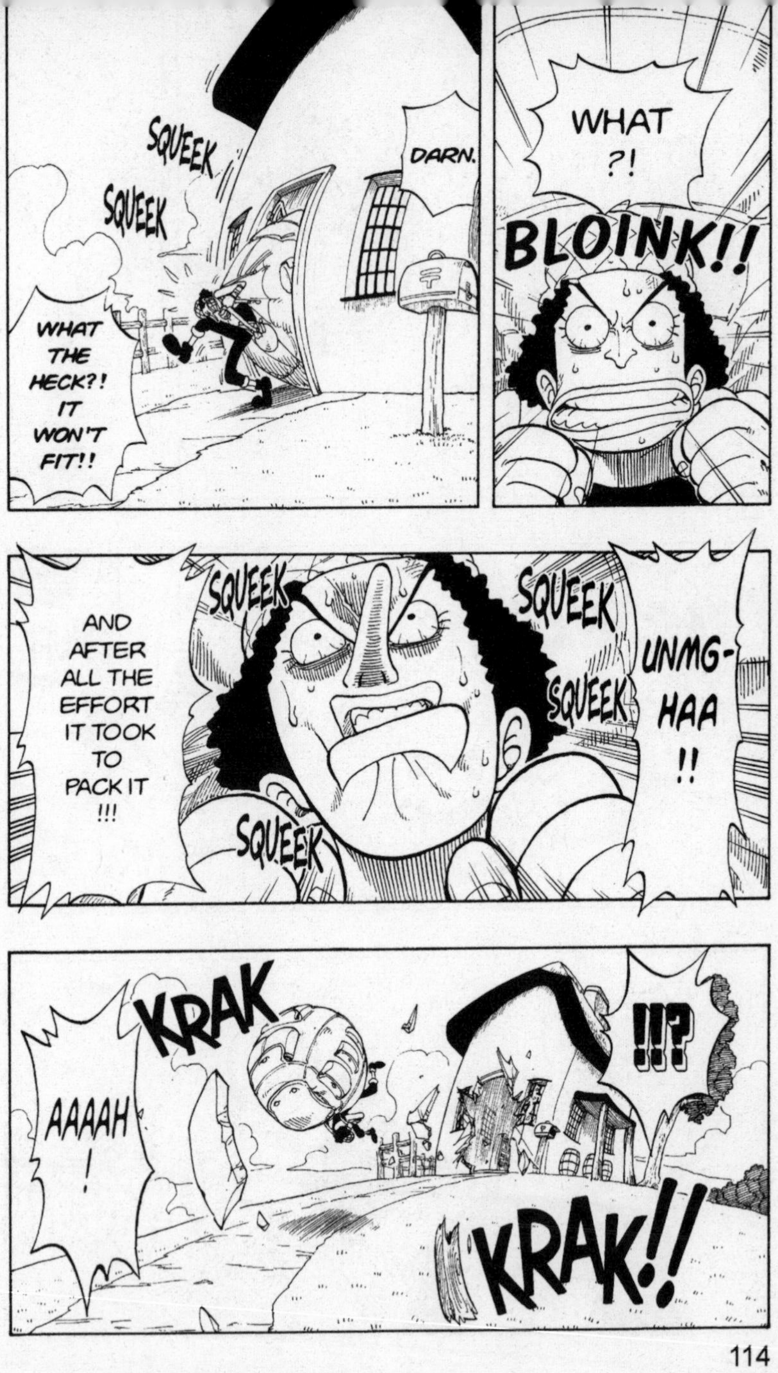
WHAT ?!
BLOINK!!
DARN.
SQUEEK
SQUEEK
WHAT THE HECK?! IT WON'T FIT!!
UNMG-HAA !!
SQUEEK
SQUEEK
SQUEEK
AND AFTER ALL THE EFFORT IT TOOK TO PACK IT !!!
SQUEEK
!!?
KRAK
AAAAH !
KRAK!!

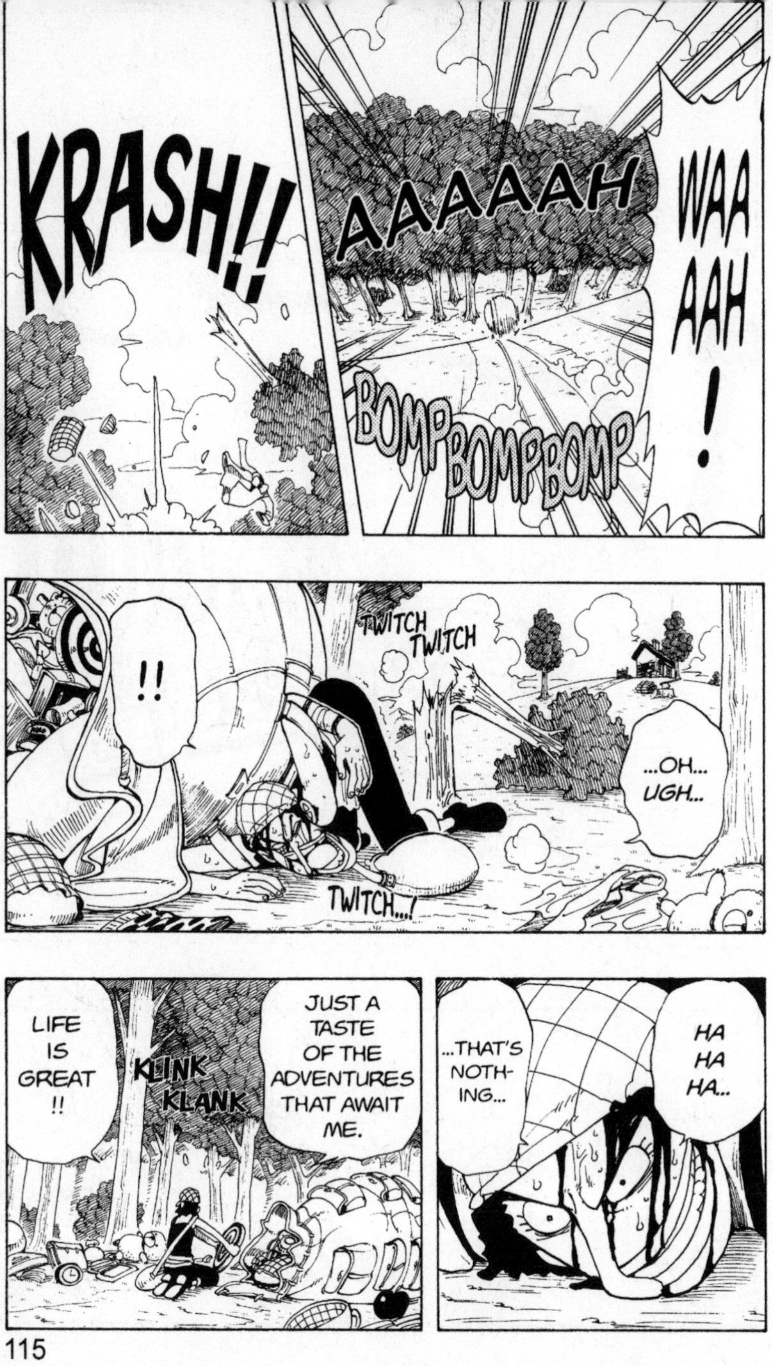
WAAAAH!
AAAAAH
BOMP BOMP BOMP
KRASH!!
...OH... UGH...
TWITCH TWITCH
!!
TWITCH...!
HA HA HA...
...THAT'S NOTHING...
JUST A TASTE OF THE ADVENTURES THAT AWAIT ME.
KLINK KLANK
LIFE IS GREAT!!

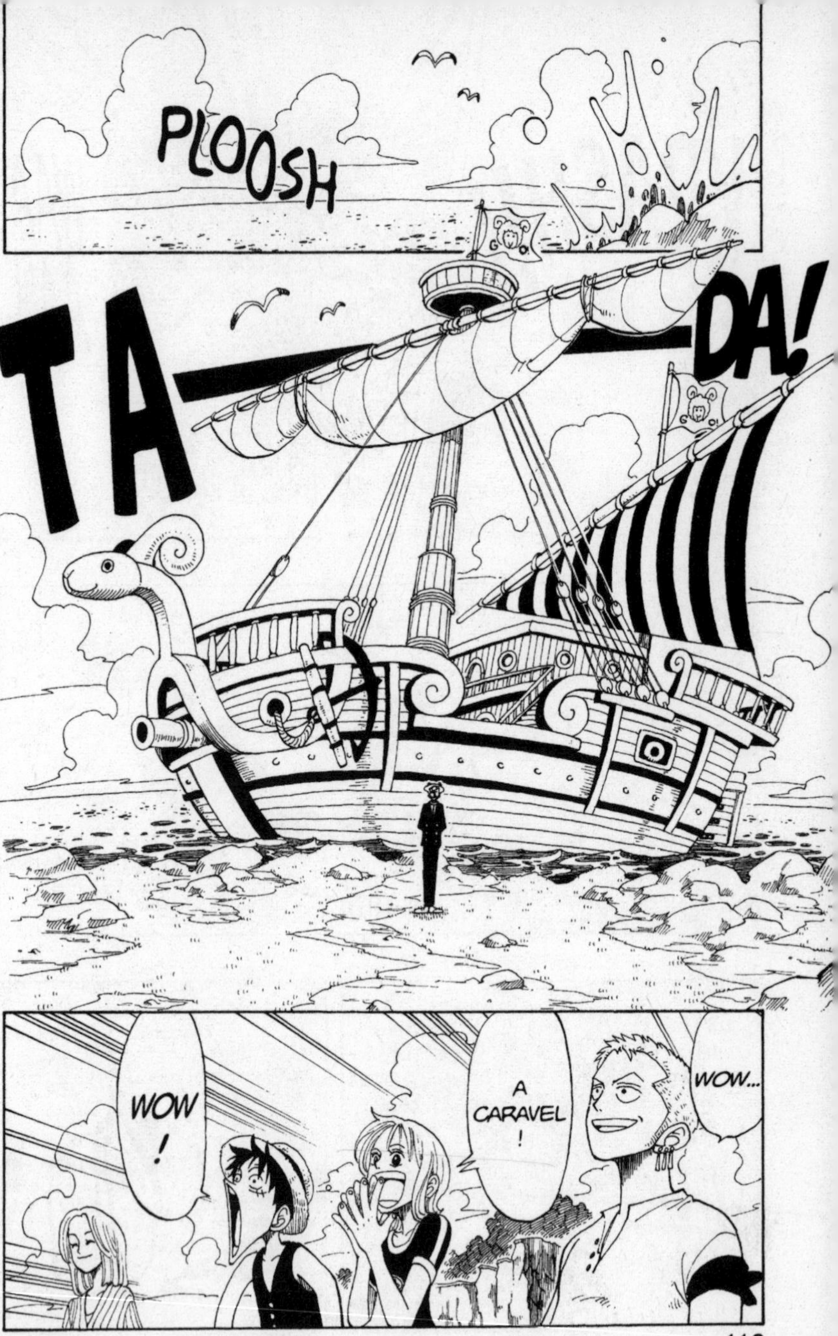
PLOOSH
TA—DA!
WOW...
A CARAVEL!
WOW!

READ THIS WAY

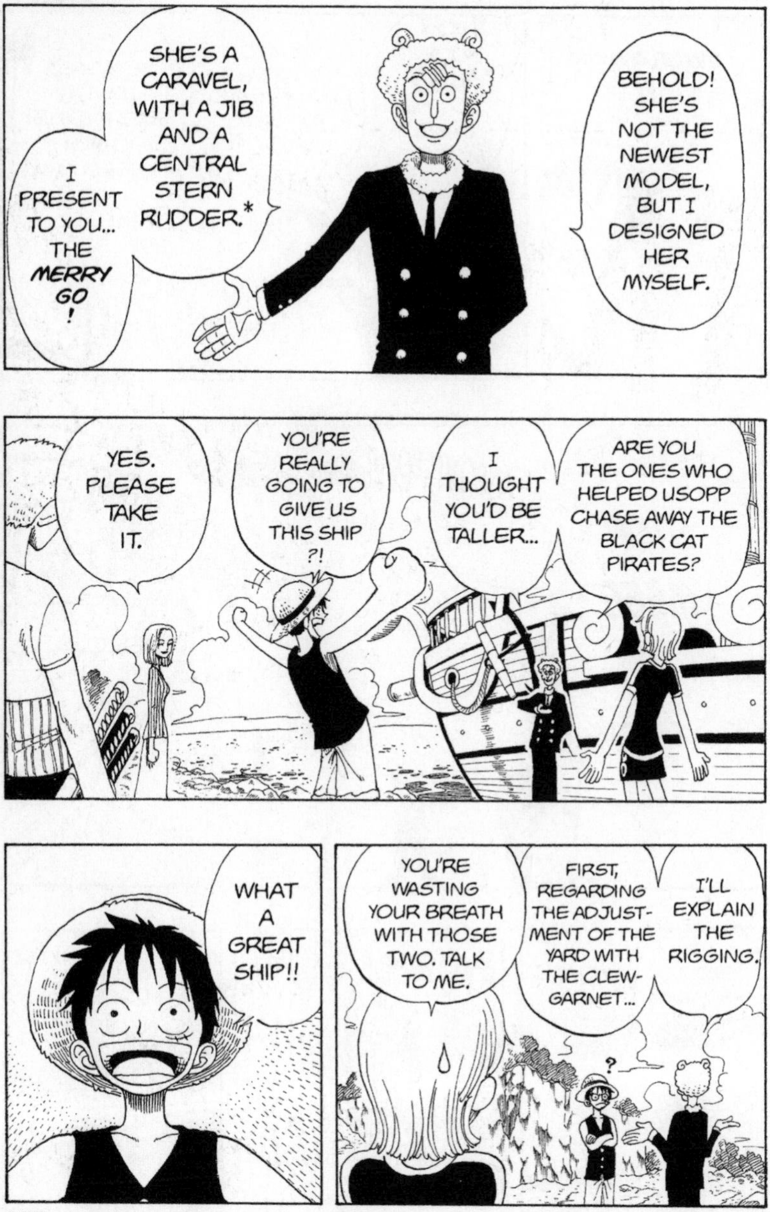
BEHOLD! SHE'S NOT THE NEWEST MODEL, BUT I DESIGNED HER MYSELF.
SHE'S A CARAVEL, WITH A JIB AND A CENTRAL STERN RUDDER.*
I PRESENT TO YOU... THE MERRY GO!
ARE YOU THE ONES WHO HELPED USOPP CHASE AWAY THE BLACK CAT PIRATES?
I THOUGHT YOU'D BE TALLER...
YOU'RE REALLY GOING TO GIVE US THIS SHIP?!
YES. PLEASE TAKE IT.
I'LL EXPLAIN THE RIGGING.
FIRST, REGARDING THE ADJUSTMENT OF THE YARD WITH THE CLEW-GARNET...
YOU'RE WASTING YOUR BREATH WITH THOSE TWO. TALK TO ME.
?
WHAT A GREAT SHIP!!

*CARAVEL: A KIND OF SAILING SHIP, COMMON IN OUR WORLD'S 15TH CENTURY.

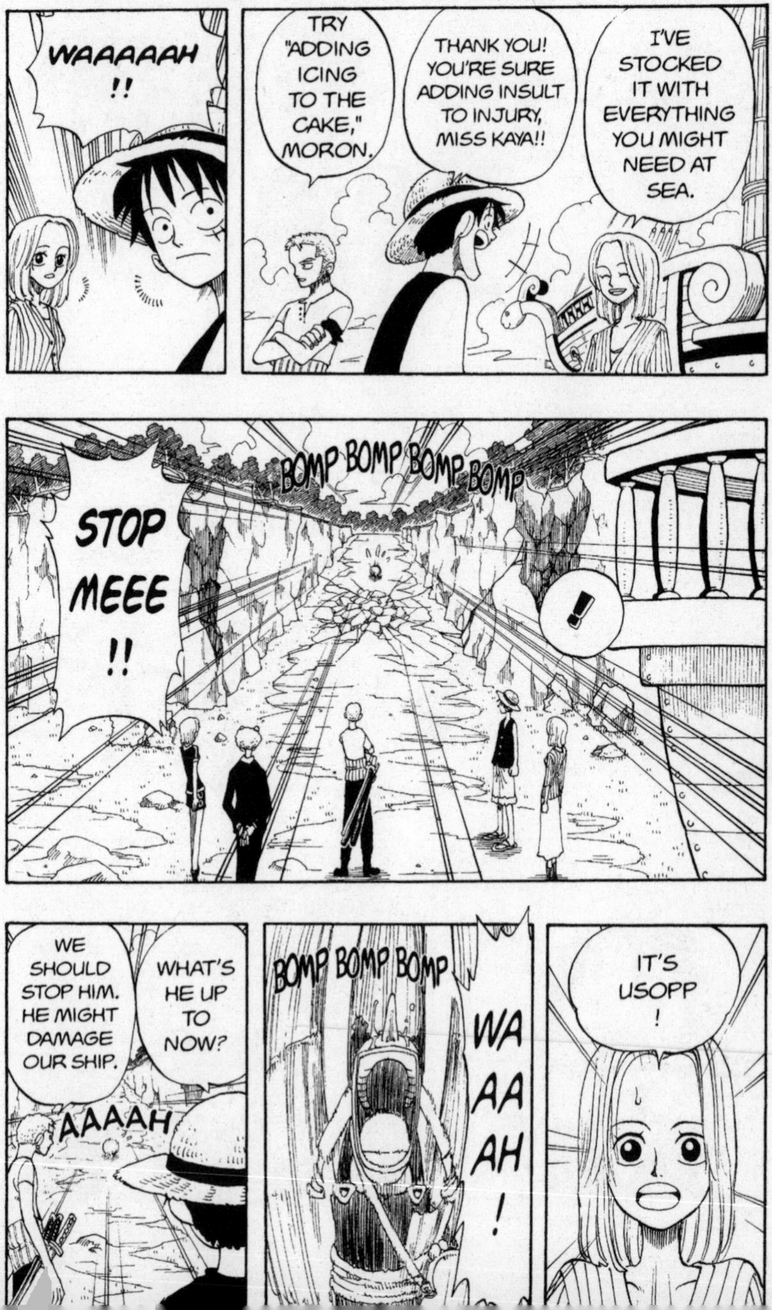
I'VE STOCKED IT WITH EVERYTHING YOU MIGHT NEED AT SEA.
THANK YOU! YOU'RE SURE ADDING INSULT TO INJURY, MISS KAYA!!
TRY "ADDING ICING TO THE CAKE," MORON.
WAAAAAH !!
BOMP BOMP BOMP BOMP
!
STOP MEEE !!
IT'S USOPP !
WAAAAAH !
BOMP BOMP BOMP
WHAT'S HE UP TO NOW?
WE SHOULD STOP HIM. HE MIGHT DAMAGE OUR SHIP.
AAAAH

READ THIS WAY

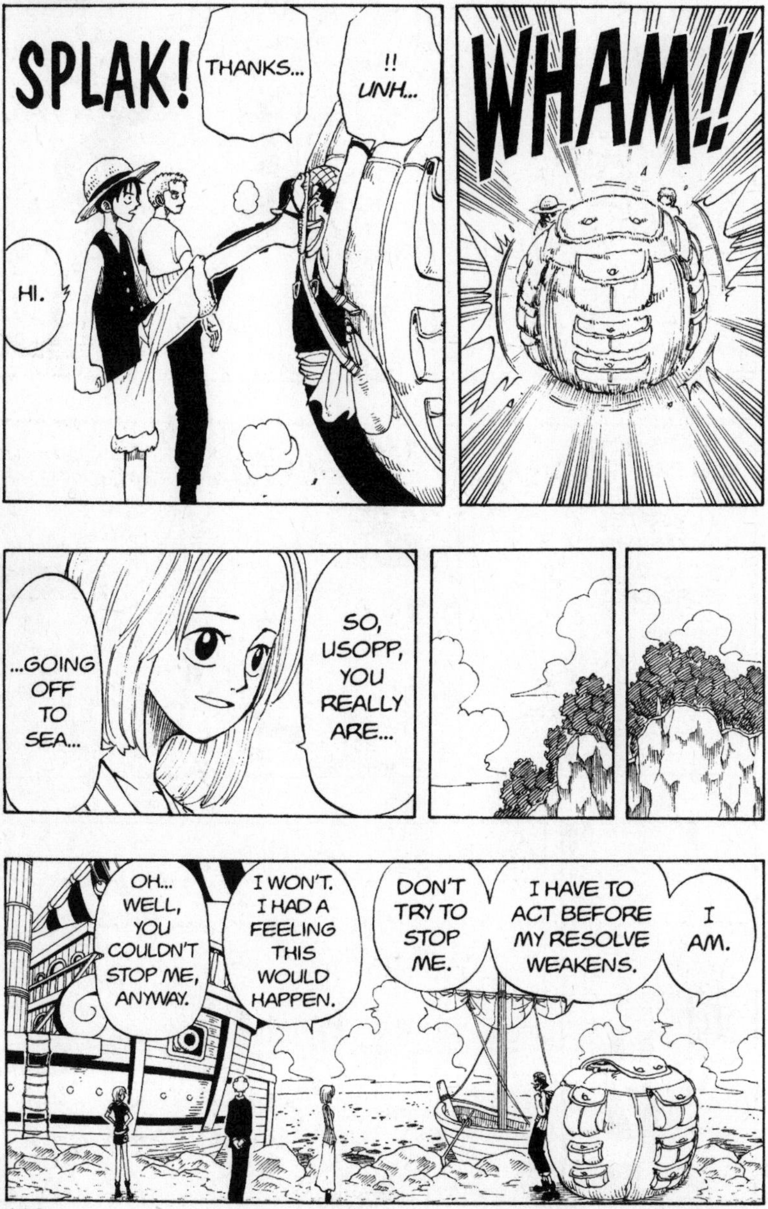
WHAM!!
!! UNH...
THANKS...
SPLAK!
HI.
SO, USOPP, YOU REALLY ARE...
...GOING OFF TO SEA...
I AM.
I HAVE TO ACT BEFORE MY RESOLVE WEAKENS.
DON'T TRY TO STOP ME.
I WON'T. I HAD A FEELING THIS WOULD HAPPEN.
OH... WELL, YOU COULDN'T STOP ME, ANYWAY.

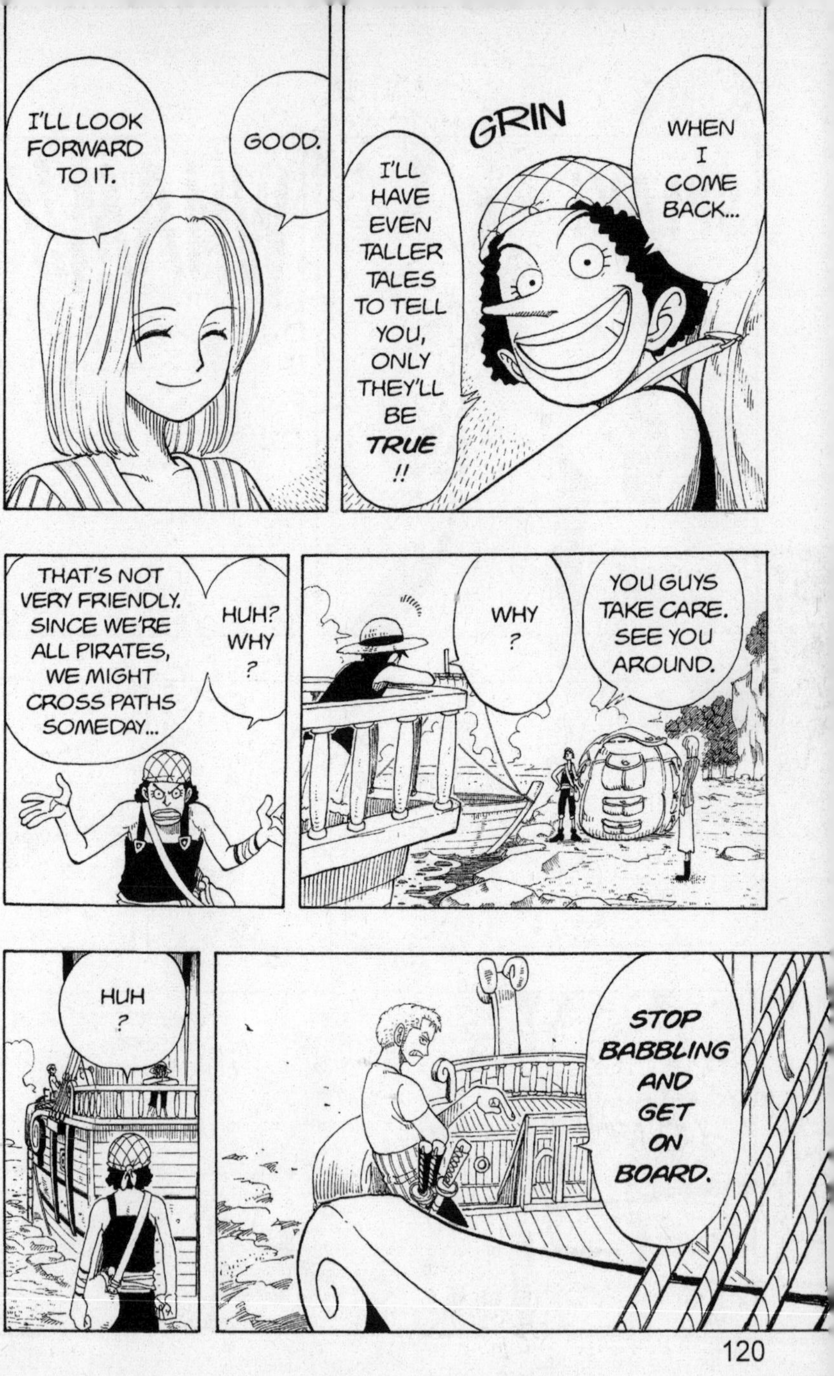
WHEN I COME BACK...
GRIN
I'LL HAVE EVEN TALLER TALES TO TELL YOU, ONLY THEY'LL BE TRUE!!
GOOD.
I'LL LOOK FORWARD TO IT.
YOU GUYS TAKE CARE. SEE YOU AROUND.
WHY?
HUH? WHY?
THAT'S NOT VERY FRIENDLY. SINCE WE'RE ALL PIRATES, WE MIGHT CROSS PATHS SOMEDAY...
STOP BABBLING AND GET ON BOARD.
HUH?

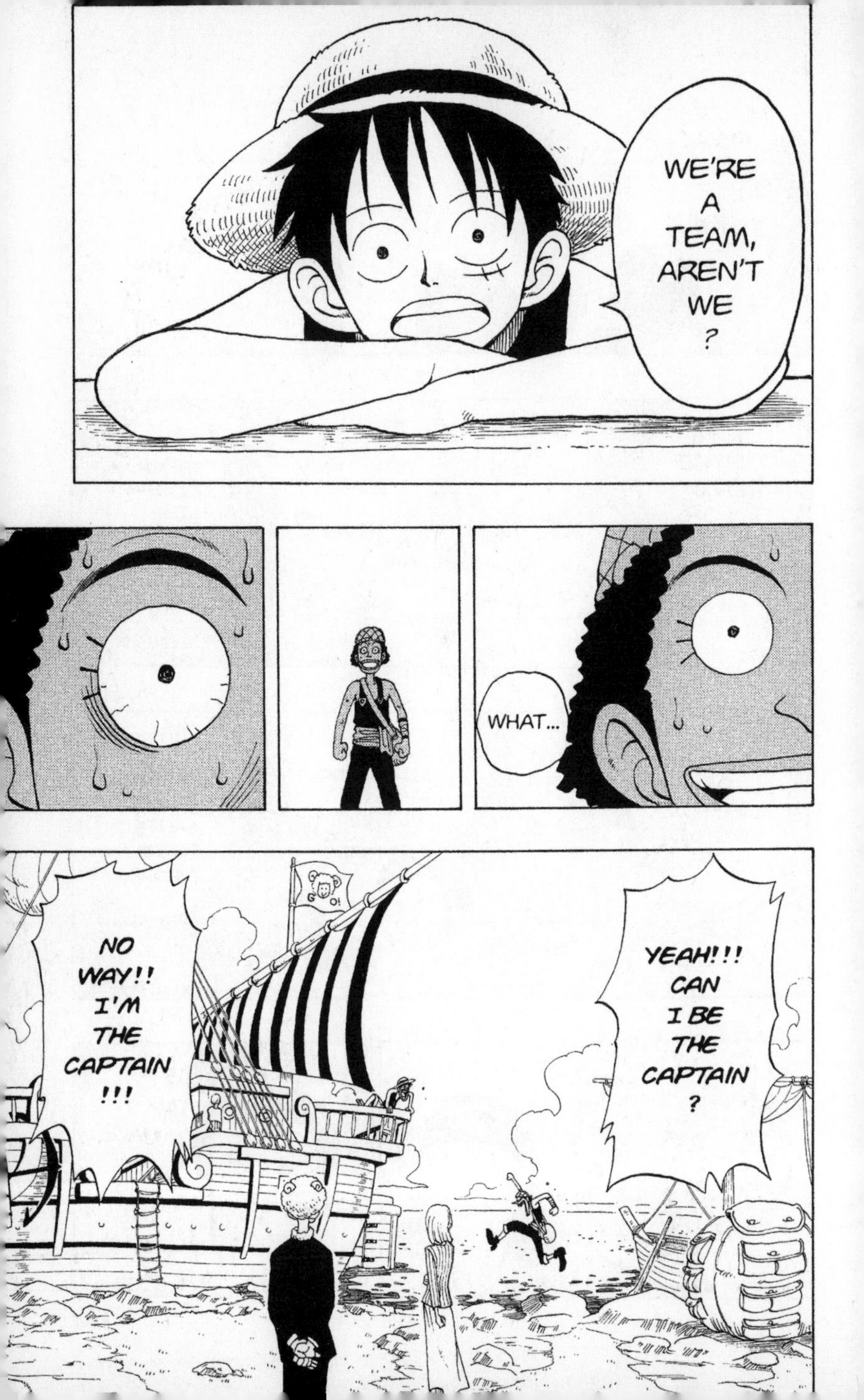
WE'RE A TEAM, AREN'T WE?
WHAT...
YEAH!!! CAN I BE THE CAPTAIN?
NO WAY!! I'M THE CAPTAIN!!!

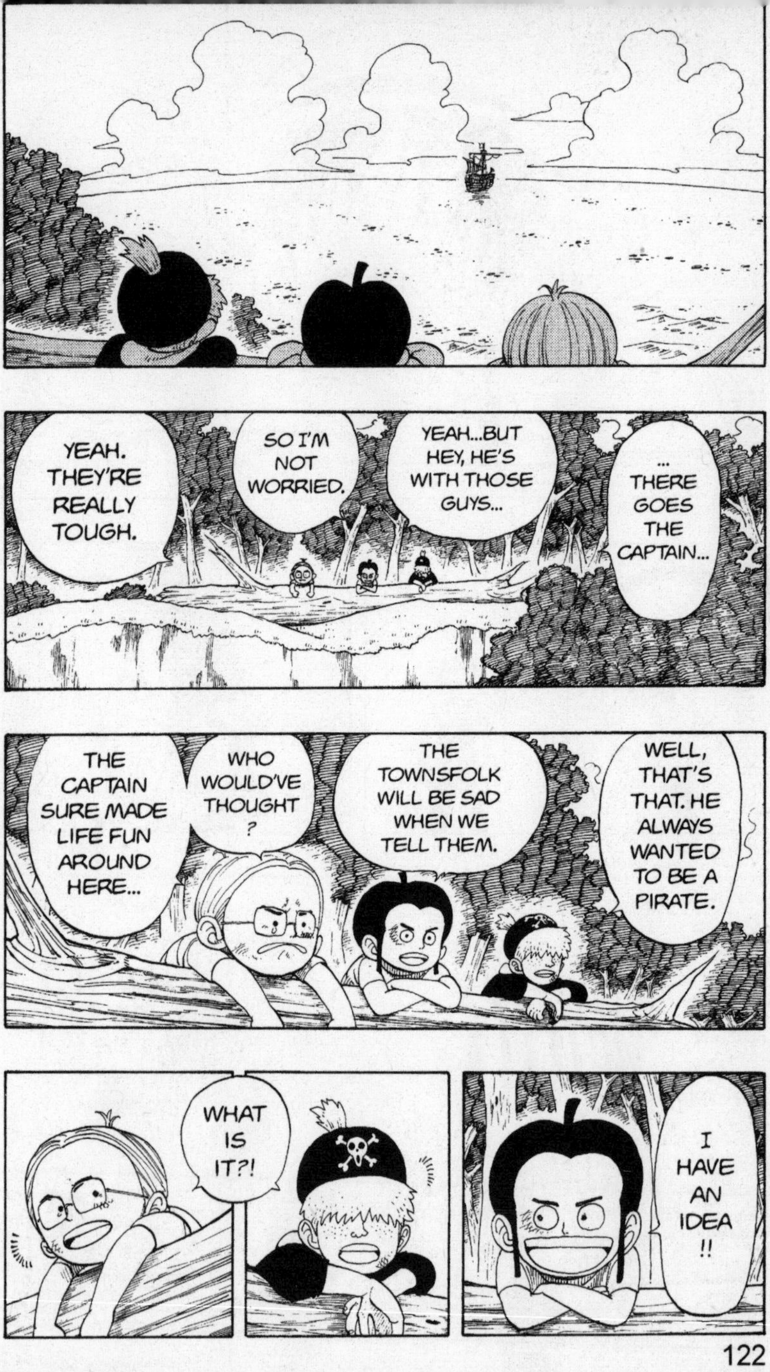
...THERE GOES THE CAPTAIN...
YEAH...BUT HEY, HE'S WITH THOSE GUYS...
SO I'M NOT WORRIED.
YEAH. THEY'RE REALLY TOUGH.
WELL, THAT'S THAT. HE ALWAYS WANTED TO BE A PIRATE.
THE TOWNSFOLK WILL BE SAD WHEN WE TELL THEM.
WHO WOULD'VE THOUGHT?
THE CAPTAIN SURE MADE LIFE FUN AROUND HERE...
I HAVE AN IDEA!!
WHAT IS IT?!

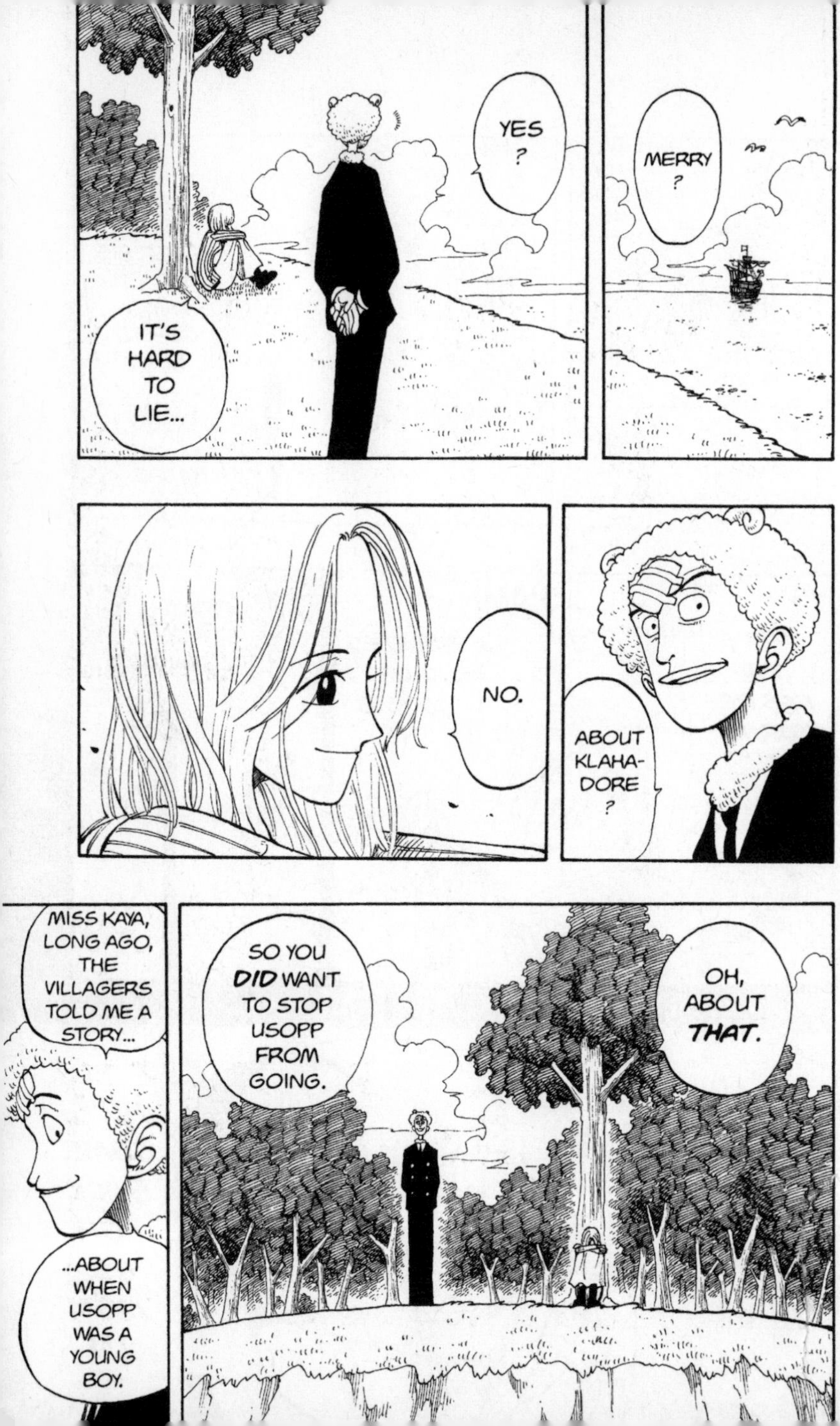
MERRY?
YES?
IT'S HARD TO LIE...
ABOUT KLAHA-DORE?
NO.
OH, ABOUT *THAT*.
SO YOU *DID* WANT TO STOP USOPP FROM GOING.
MISS KAYA, LONG AGO, THE VILLAGERS TOLD ME A STORY...
...ABOUT WHEN USOPP WAS A YOUNG BOY.

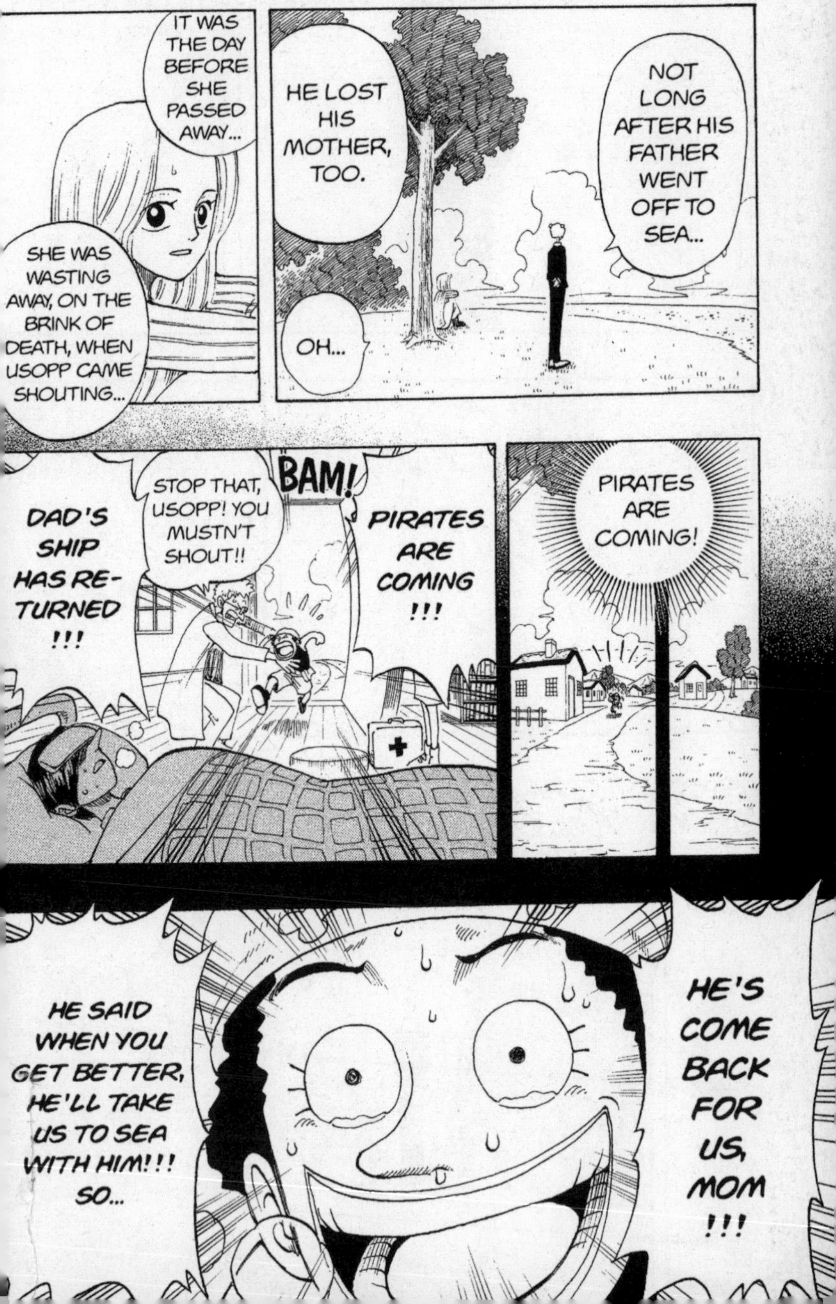
NOT LONG AFTER HIS FATHER WENT OFF TO SEA...
HE LOST HIS MOTHER, TOO.
OH...
IT WAS THE DAY BEFORE SHE PASSED AWAY...
SHE WAS WASTING AWAY, ON THE BRINK OF DEATH, WHEN USOPP CAME SHOUTING...
PIRATES ARE COMING!
PIRATES ARE COMING!!!
BAM!
STOP THAT, USOPP! YOU MUSTN'T SHOUT!!
DAD'S SHIP HAS RE-TURNED!!!
HE'S COME BACK FOR US, MOM!!!
HE SAID WHEN YOU GET BETTER, HE'LL TAKE US TO SEA WITH HIM!!! SO...

READ THIS WAY

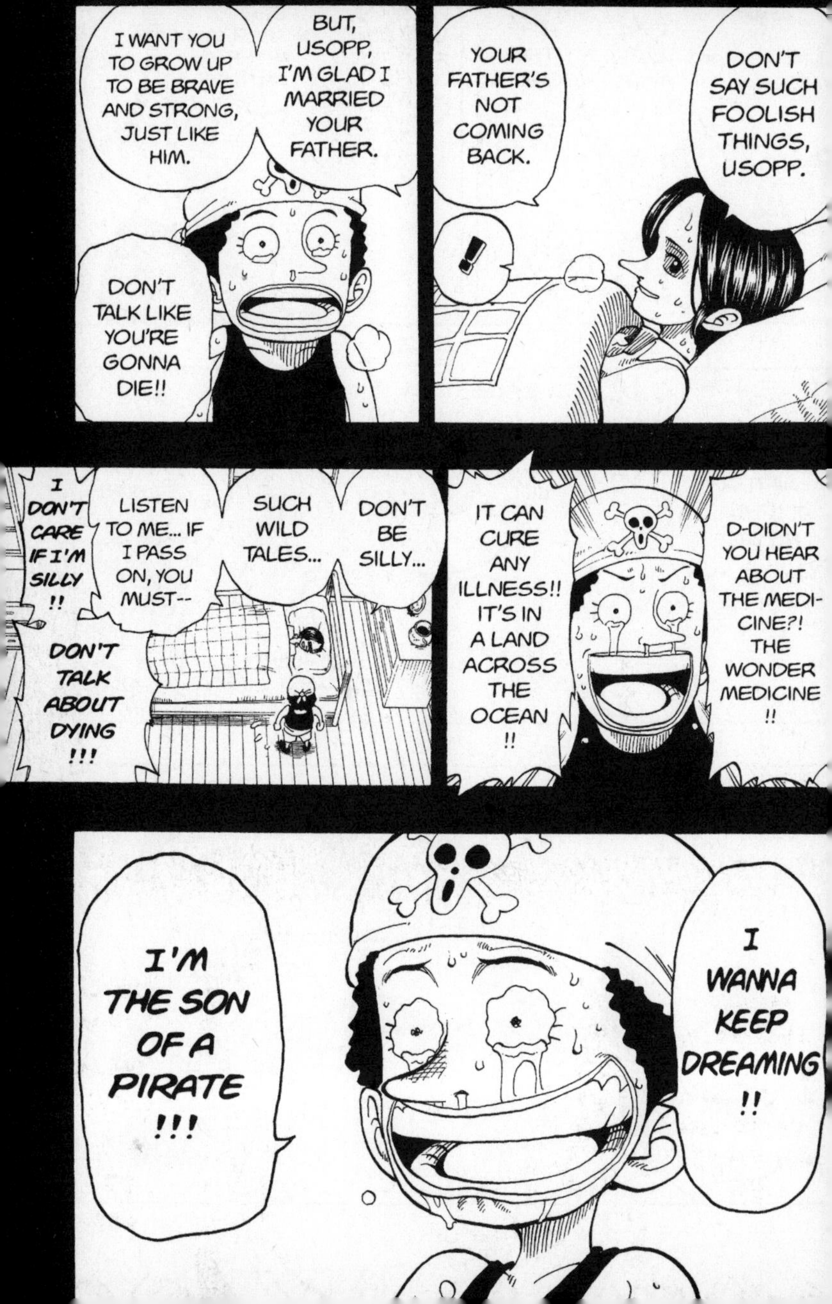
DON'T SAY SUCH FOOLISH THINGS, USOPP.
YOUR FATHER'S NOT COMING BACK.
!
BUT, USOPP, I'M GLAD I MARRIED YOUR FATHER.
I WANT YOU TO GROW UP TO BE BRAVE AND STRONG, JUST LIKE HIM.
DON'T TALK LIKE YOU'RE GONNA DIE!!
D-DIDN'T YOU HEAR ABOUT THE MEDICINE?! THE WONDER MEDICINE!!
IT CAN CURE ANY ILLNESS!! IT'S IN A LAND ACROSS THE OCEAN!!
DON'T BE SILLY...
SUCH WILD TALES...
LISTEN TO ME... IF I PASS ON, YOU MUST--
I DON'T CARE IF I'M SILLY!!
DON'T TALK ABOUT DYING!!!
I WANNA KEEP DREAMING!!
I'M THE SON OF A PIRATE!!!

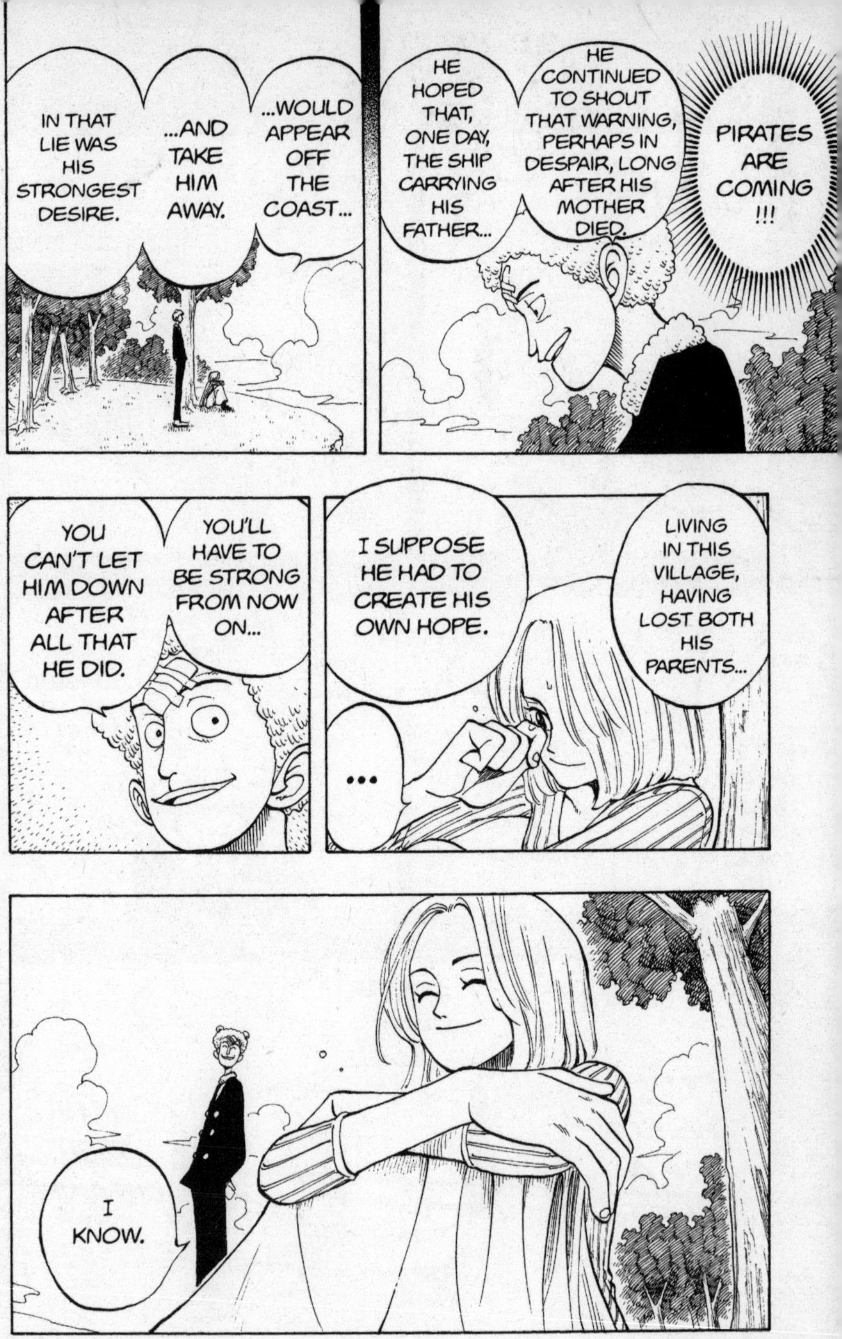
PIRATES ARE COMING!!!
HE CONTINUED TO SHOUT THAT WARNING, PERHAPS IN DESPAIR, LONG AFTER HIS MOTHER DIED.
HE HOPED THAT, ONE DAY, THE SHIP CARRYING HIS FATHER...
...WOULD APPEAR OFF THE COAST...
...AND TAKE HIM AWAY.
IN THAT LIE WAS HIS STRONGEST DESIRE.
LIVING IN THIS VILLAGE, HAVING LOST BOTH HIS PARENTS...
I SUPPOSE HE HAD TO CREATE HIS OWN HOPE.
...
YOU'LL HAVE TO BE STRONG FROM NOW ON...
YOU CAN'T LET HIM DOWN AFTER ALL THAT HE DID.
I KNOW.

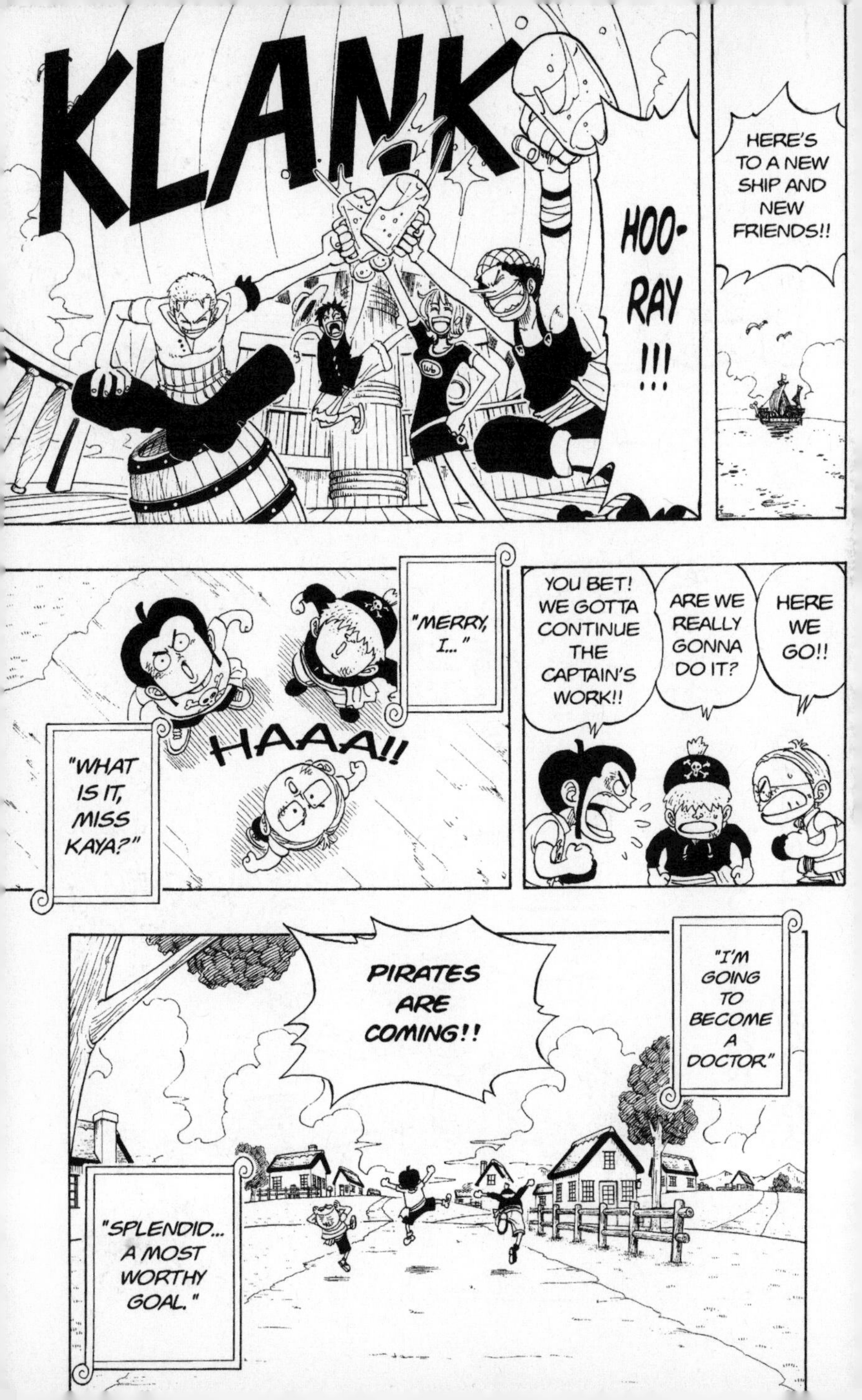
HERE'S TO A NEW SHIP AND NEW FRIENDS!!
KLANK
HOO-RAY!!!
HERE WE GO!!
ARE WE REALLY GONNA DO IT?
YOU BET! WE GOTTA CONTINUE THE CAPTAIN'S WORK!!
"MERRY, I..."
HAAAA!!
"WHAT IS IT, MISS KAYA?"
"I'M GOING TO BECOME A DOCTOR."
PIRATES ARE COMING!!
"SPLENDID... A MOST WORTHY GOAL."

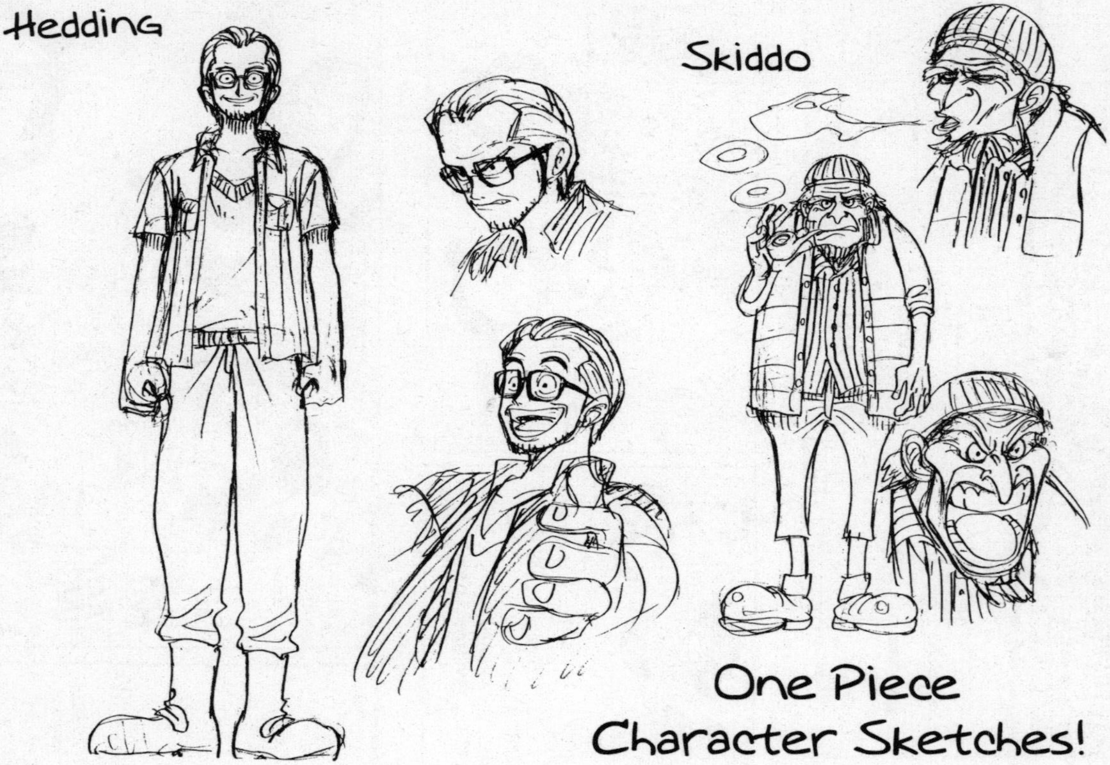
Hedding
Skiddo
One Piece
Character Sketches!

Chapter 42:
YOSAKU AND JOHNNY

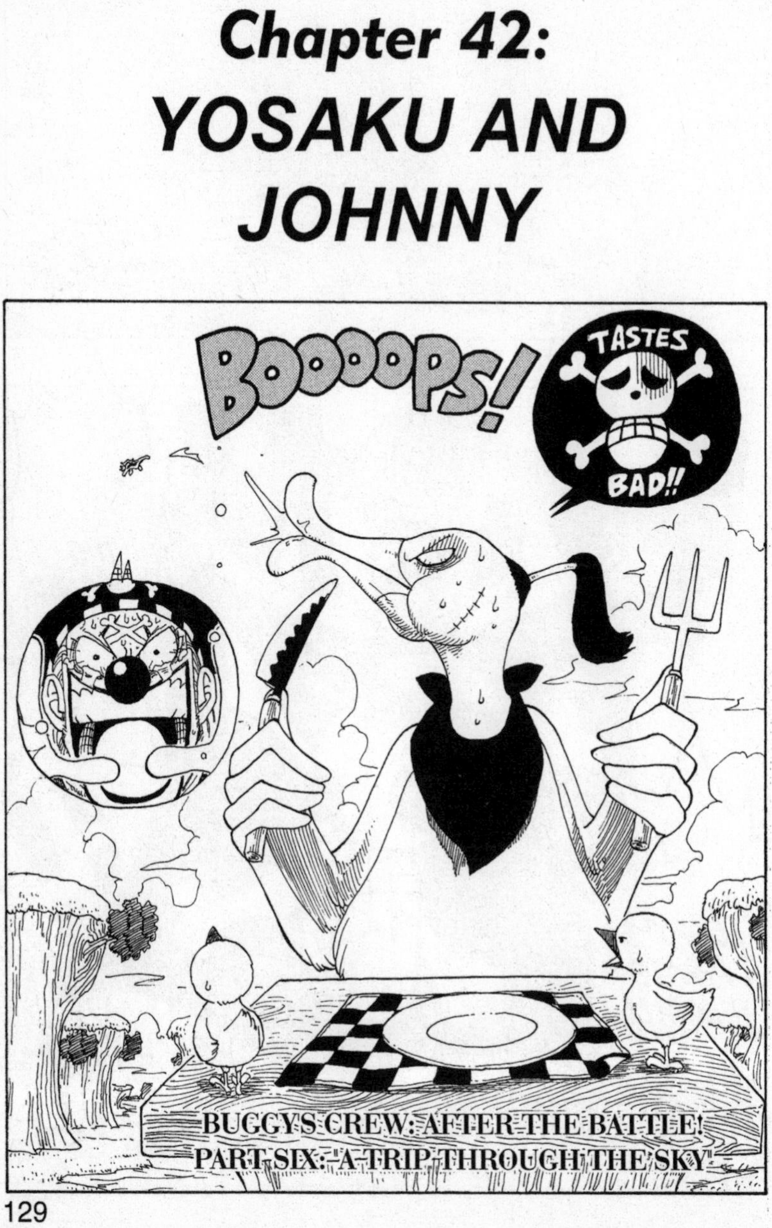
BOOOOPS!
TASTES BAD!!
BUGGY'S CREW: AFTER THE BATTLE!
PART SIX: A TRIP THROUGH THE SKY

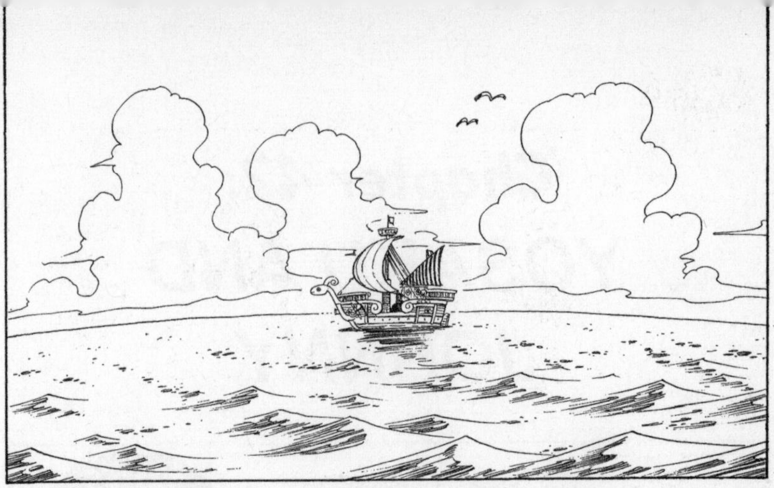

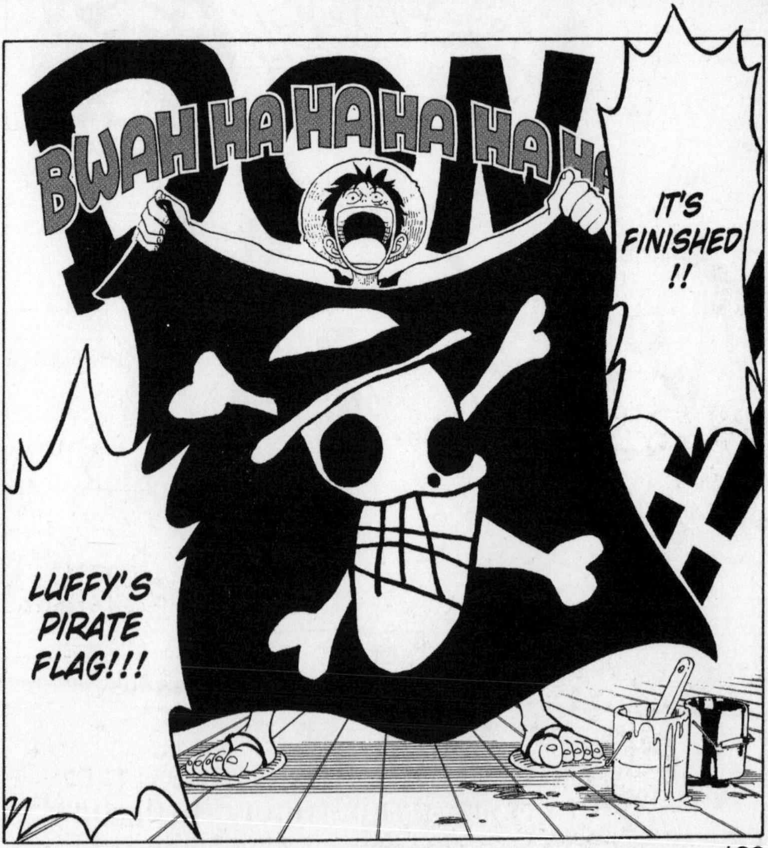
IT'S FINISHED!!
BWAH HA HA HA HA HA
LUFFY'S PIRATE FLAG!!!

READ THIS WAY

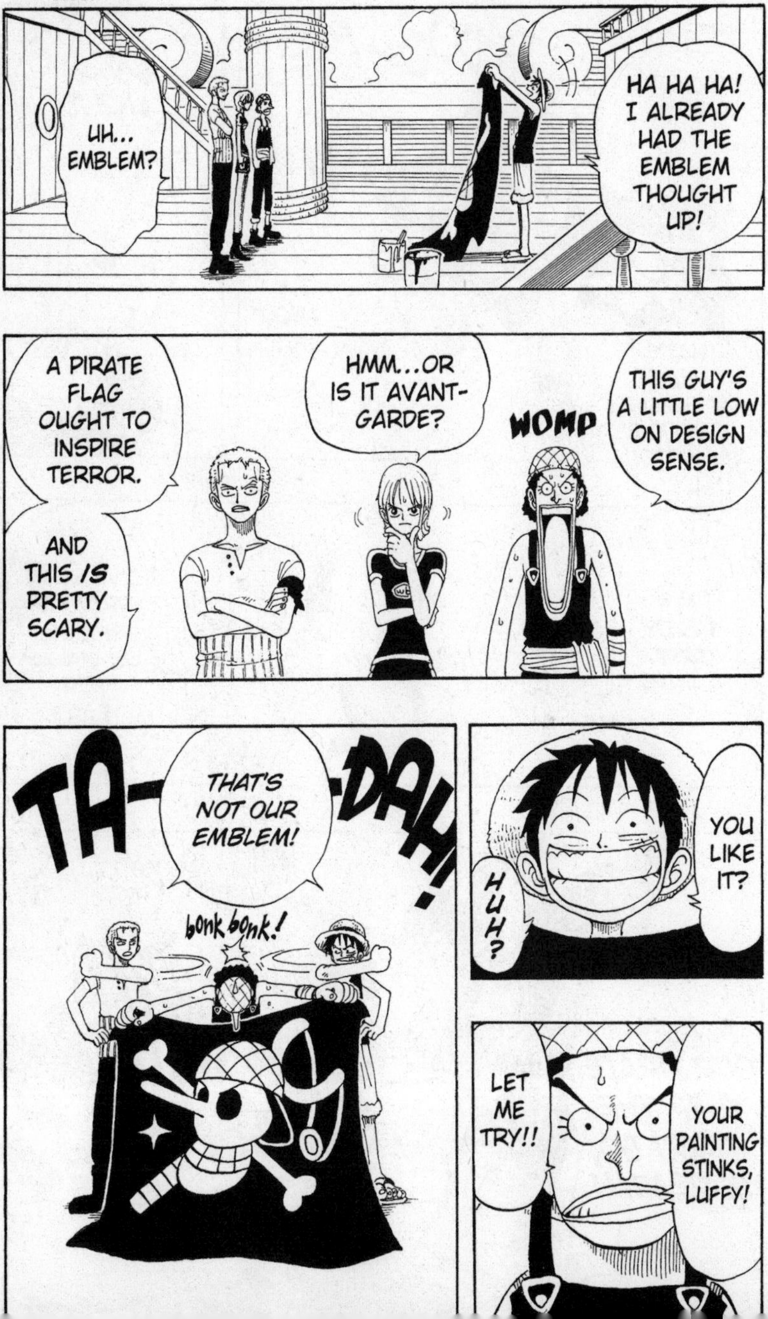
HA HA HA! I ALREADY HAD THE EMBLEM THOUGHT UP!
UH... EMBLEM?
THIS GUY'S A LITTLE LOW ON DESIGN SENSE.
WOMP
HMM...OR IS IT AVANT-GARDE?
A PIRATE FLAG OUGHT TO INSPIRE TERROR.
AND THIS IS PRETTY SCARY.
YOU LIKE IT?
HUH?
YOUR PAINTING STINKS, LUFFY!
LET ME TRY!!
TA-DAH!
THAT'S NOT OUR EMBLEM!
bonk bonk!

READ THIS WAY

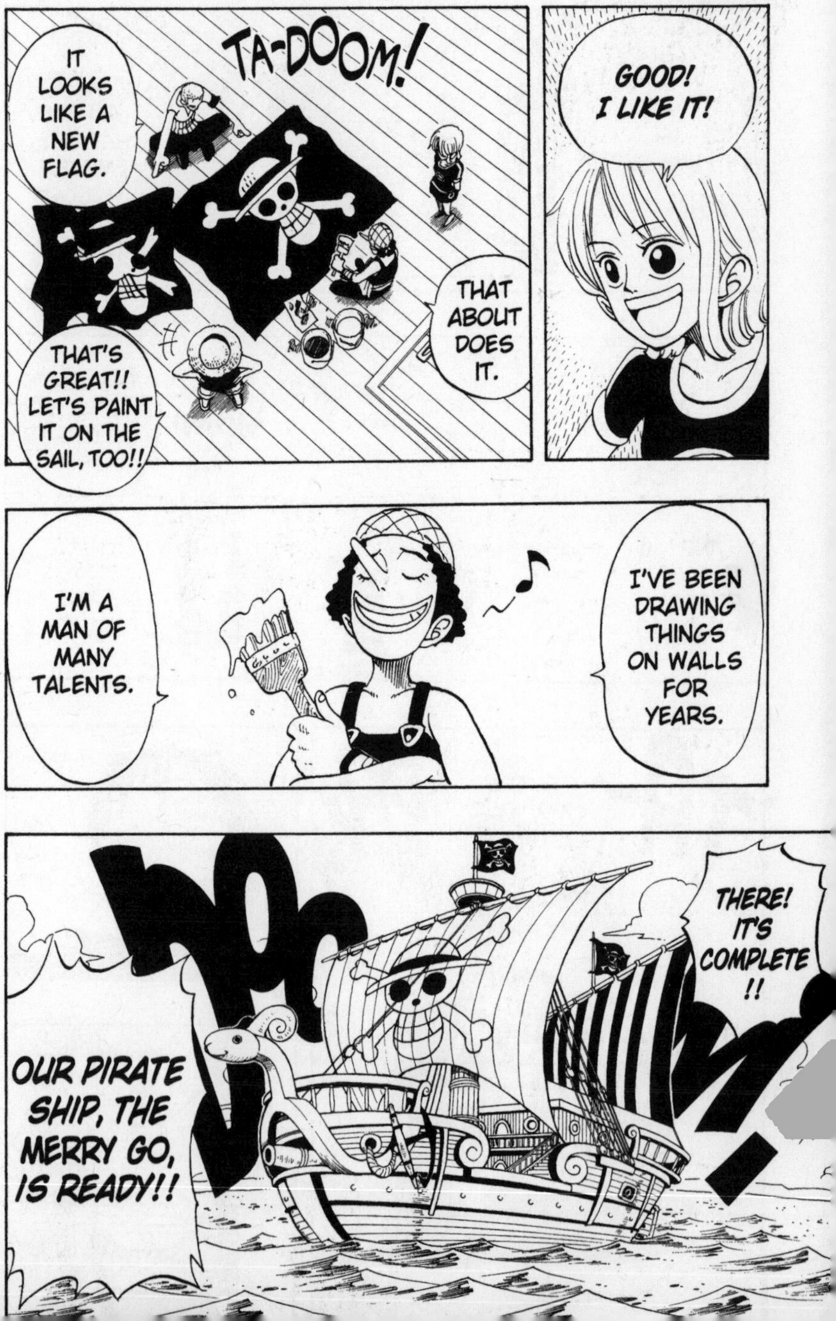
GOOD! I LIKE IT!
TA-DOOM!
IT LOOKS LIKE A NEW FLAG.
THAT ABOUT DOES IT.
THAT'S GREAT!! LET'S PAINT IT ON THE SAIL, TOO!!
I'VE BEEN DRAWING THINGS ON WALLS FOR YEARS.
I'M A MAN OF MANY TALENTS.
THERE! IT'S COMPLETE!!
OUR PIRATE SHIP, THE MERRY GO, IS READY!!

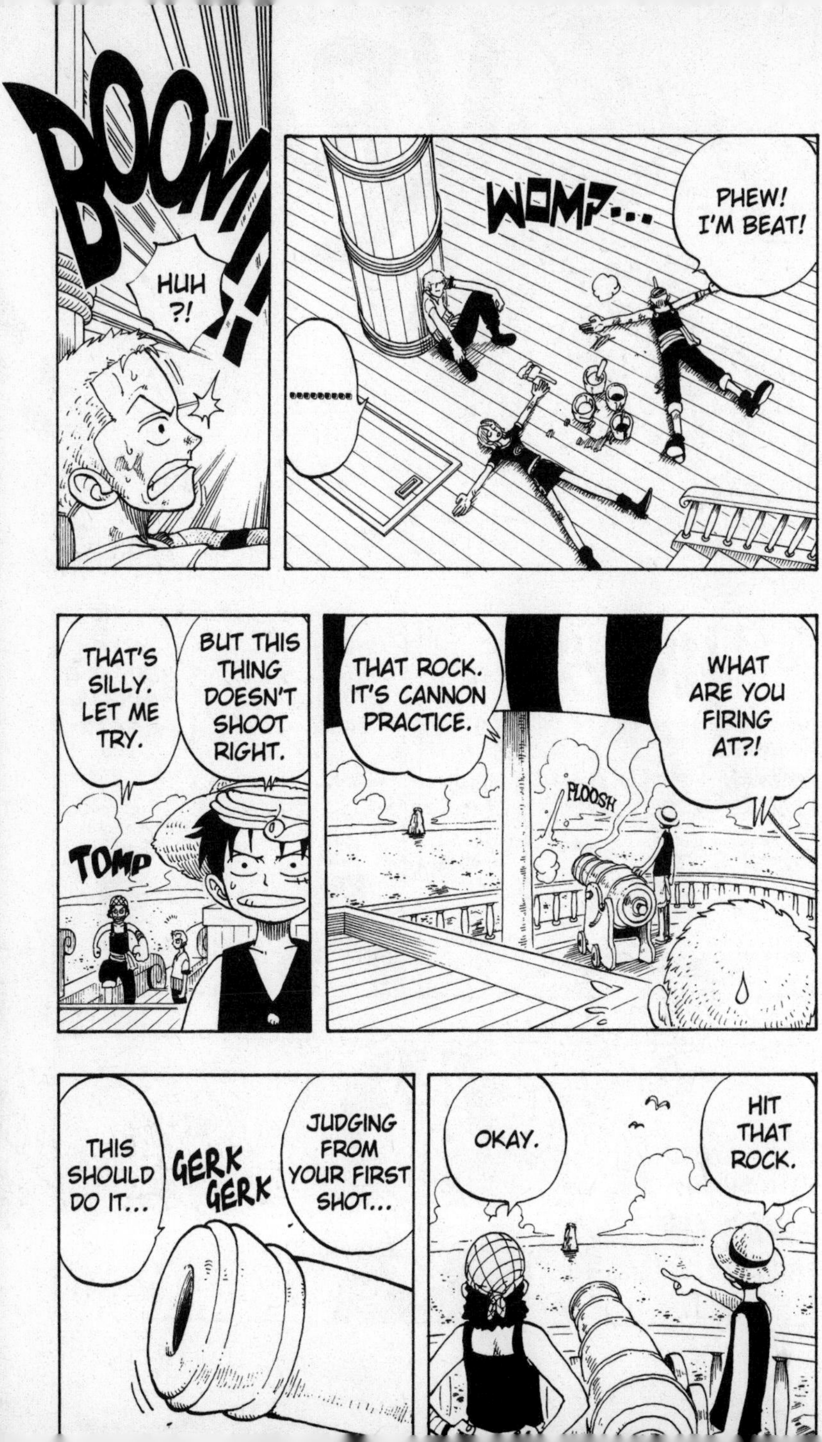
BOOM!!
HUH ?!
WOMP...
PHEW! I'M BEAT!
....
WHAT ARE YOU FIRING AT?!
THAT ROCK. IT'S CANNON PRACTICE.
PLOOSH
BUT THIS THING DOESN'T SHOOT RIGHT.
THAT'S SILLY. LET ME TRY.
TOMP
HIT THAT ROCK.
OKAY.
JUDGING FROM YOUR FIRST SHOT...
GERK GERK
THIS SHOULD DO IT...

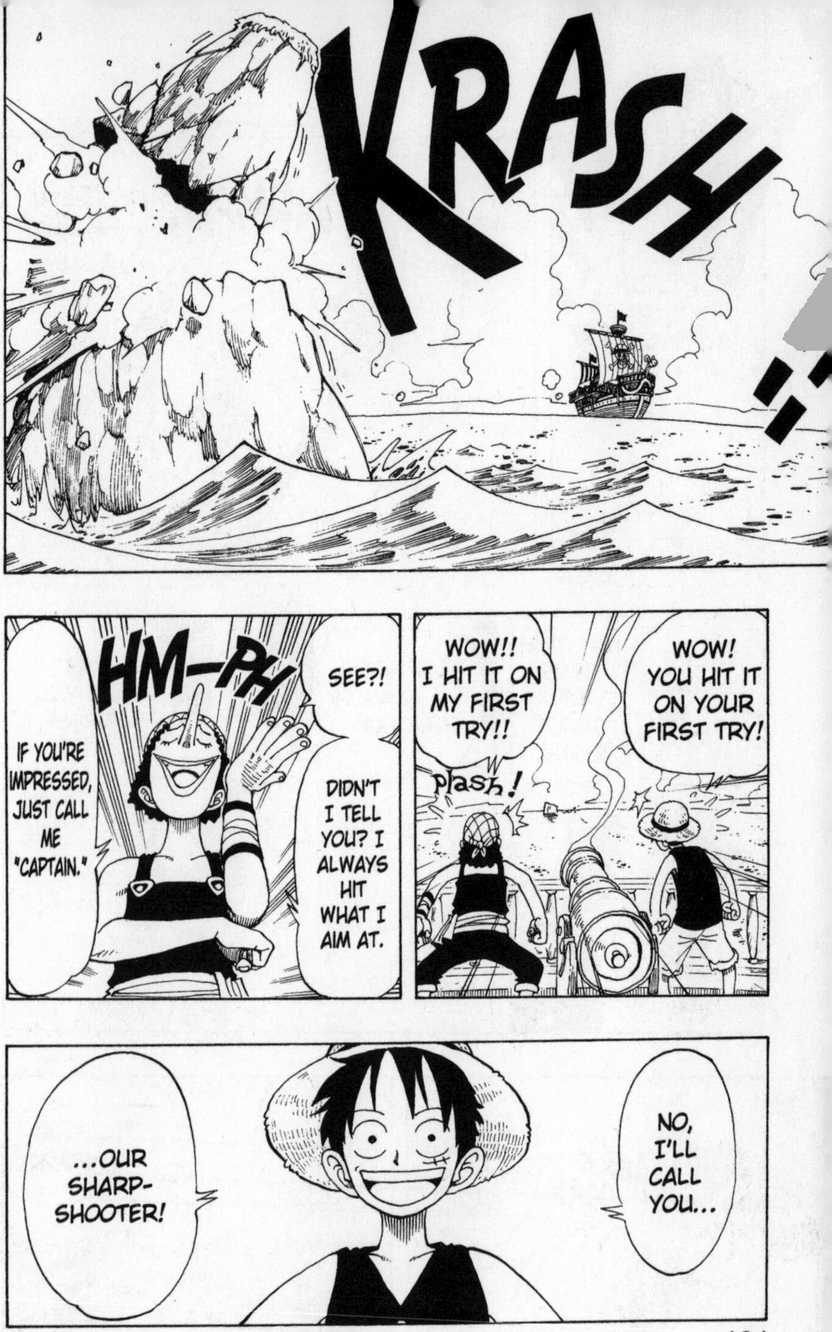
KRASH!!
WOW! YOU HIT IT ON YOUR FIRST TRY!
WOW!! I HIT IT ON MY FIRST TRY!!
plash!
SEE?!
DIDN'T I TELL YOU? I ALWAYS HIT WHAT I AIM AT.
HM-PH
IF YOU'RE IMPRESSED, JUST CALL ME "CAPTAIN."
NO, I'LL CALL YOU...
...OUR SHARP-SHOOTER!

READ THIS WAY

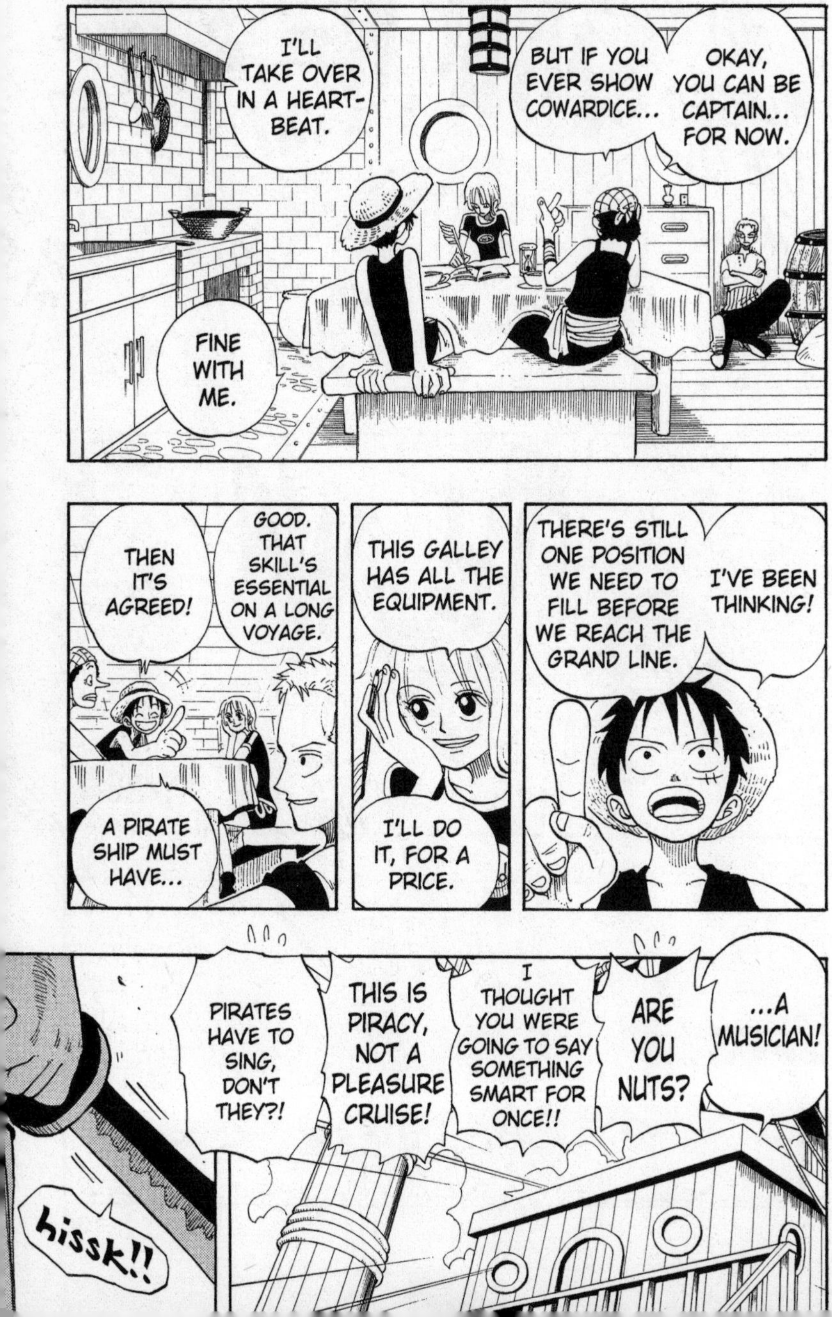
OKAY, YOU CAN BE CAPTAIN... FOR NOW.
BUT IF YOU EVER SHOW COWARDICE...
I'LL TAKE OVER IN A HEART-BEAT.
FINE WITH ME.
I'VE BEEN THINKING!
THERE'S STILL ONE POSITION WE NEED TO FILL BEFORE WE REACH THE GRAND LINE.
THIS GALLEY HAS ALL THE EQUIPMENT.
I'LL DO IT, FOR A PRICE.
GOOD. THAT SKILL'S ESSENTIAL ON A LONG VOYAGE.
THEN IT'S AGREED!
A PIRATE SHIP MUST HAVE...
...A MUSICIAN!
ARE YOU NUTS?
I THOUGHT YOU WERE GOING TO SAY SOMETHING SMART FOR ONCE!!
THIS IS PIRACY, NOT A PLEASURE CRUISE!
PIRATES HAVE TO SING, DON'T THEY?!
hissk!!

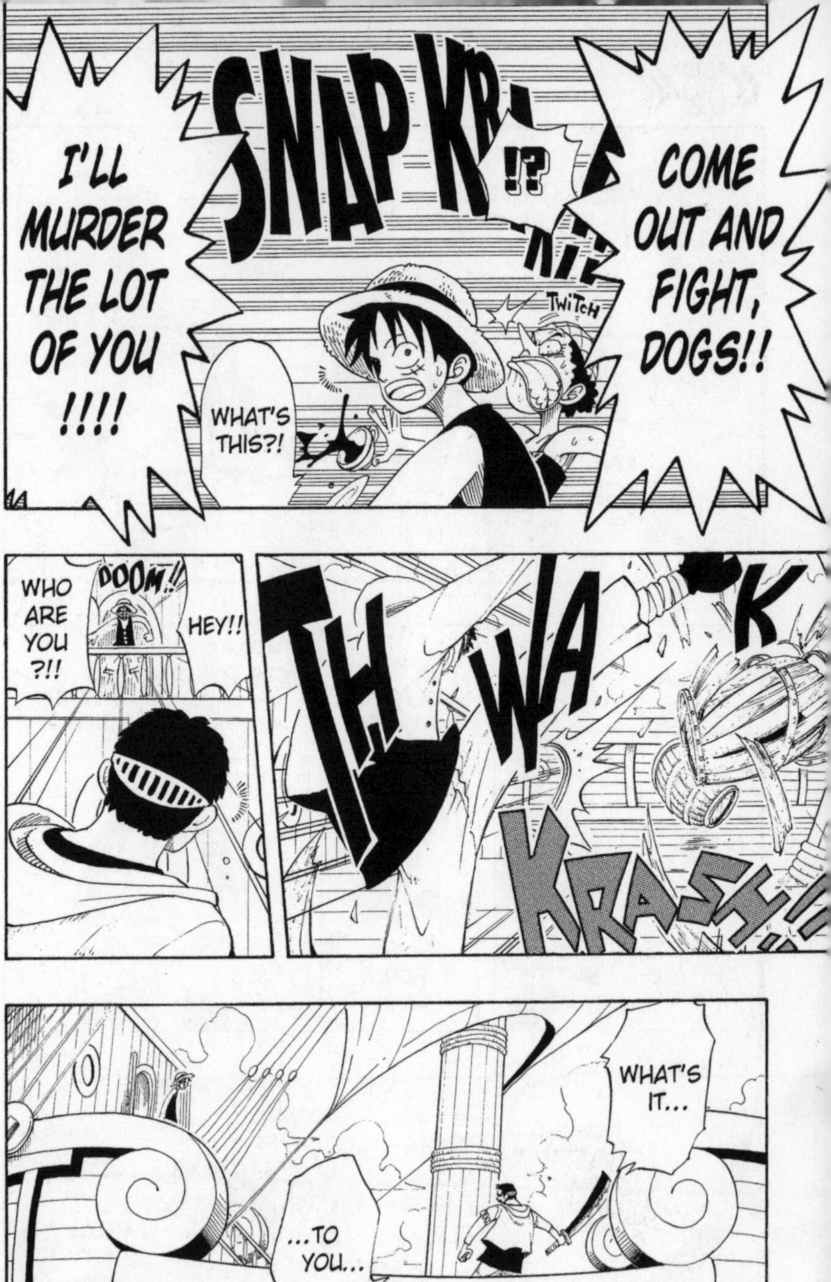
COME OUT AND FIGHT, DOGS!!
SNAP
!?
TWITCH
I'LL MURDER THE LOT OF YOU!!!!
WHAT'S THIS?!
THWAK
KRASH!!
HEY!!
DOOM!!
WHO ARE YOU?!!
WHAT'S IT...
...TO YOU...

READ THIS WAY

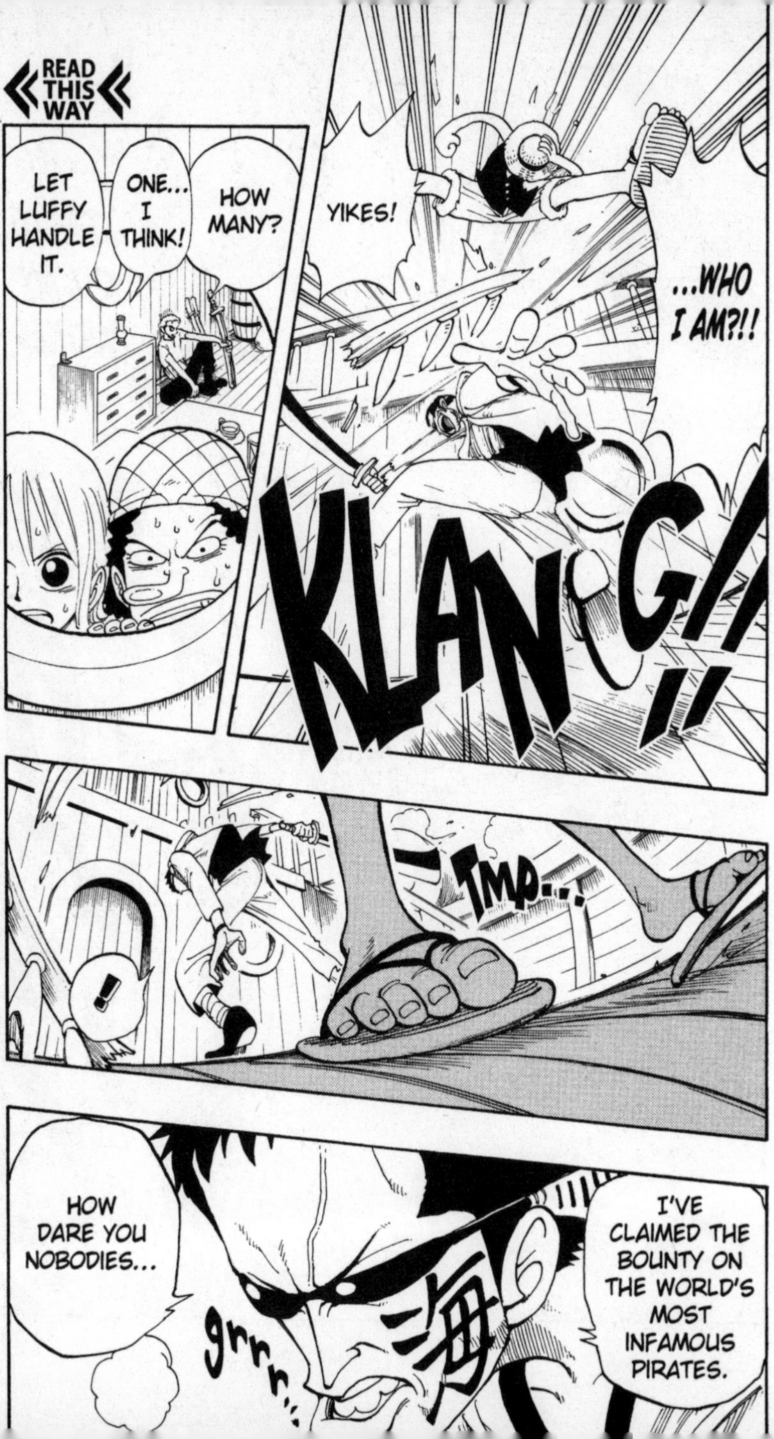
...WHO I AM?!!
YIKES!
KLANG!!
HOW MANY?
ONE... I THINK!
LET LUFFY HANDLE IT.
TMP...
!
I'VE CLAIMED THE BOUNTY ON THE WORLD'S MOST INFAMOUS PIRATES.
HOW DARE YOU NOBODIES...
grrr...

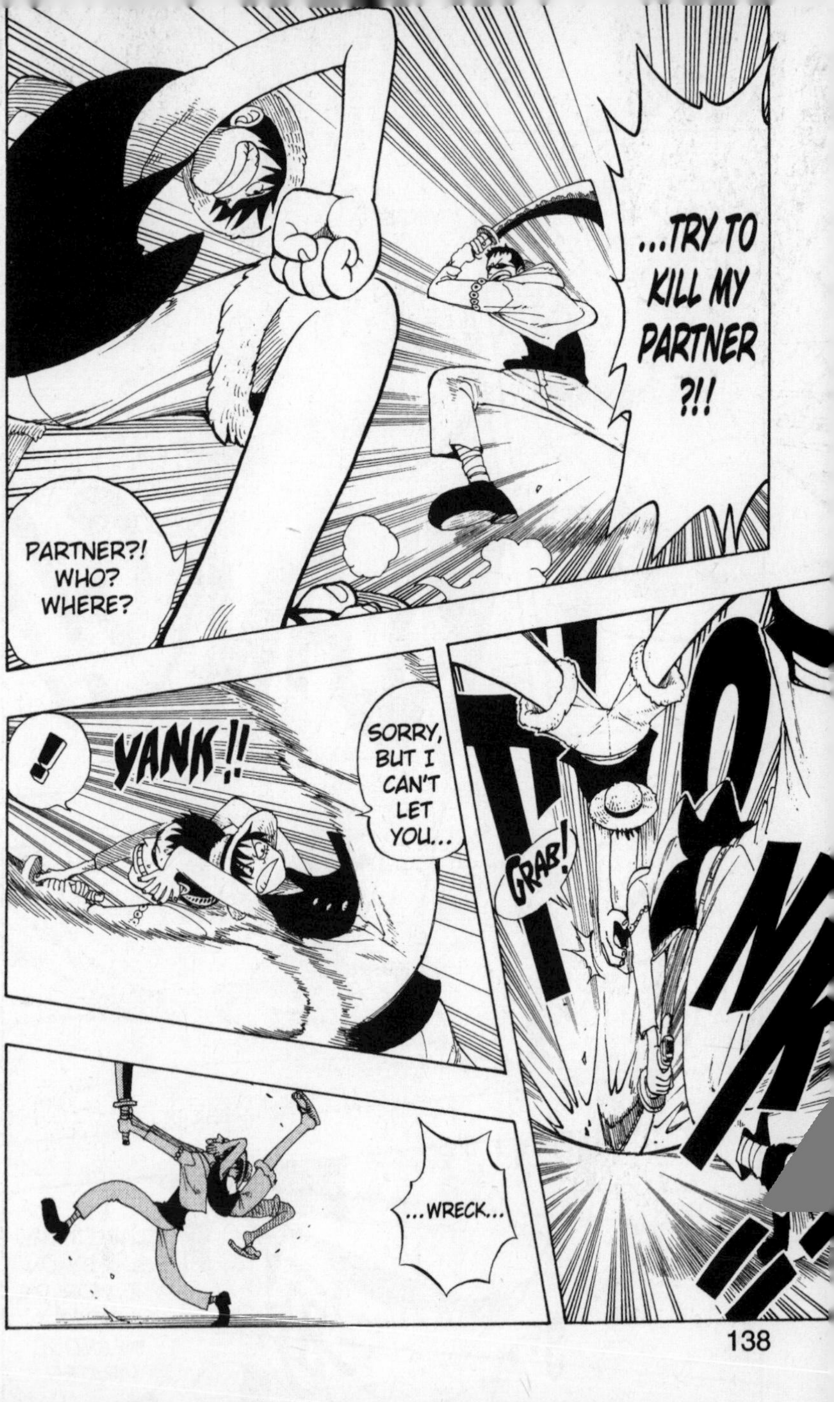
...TRY TO KILL MY PARTNER ?!!
PARTNER?! WHO? WHERE?
GRAB!
SORRY, BUT I CAN'T LET YOU...
!
YANK!!
...WRECK...

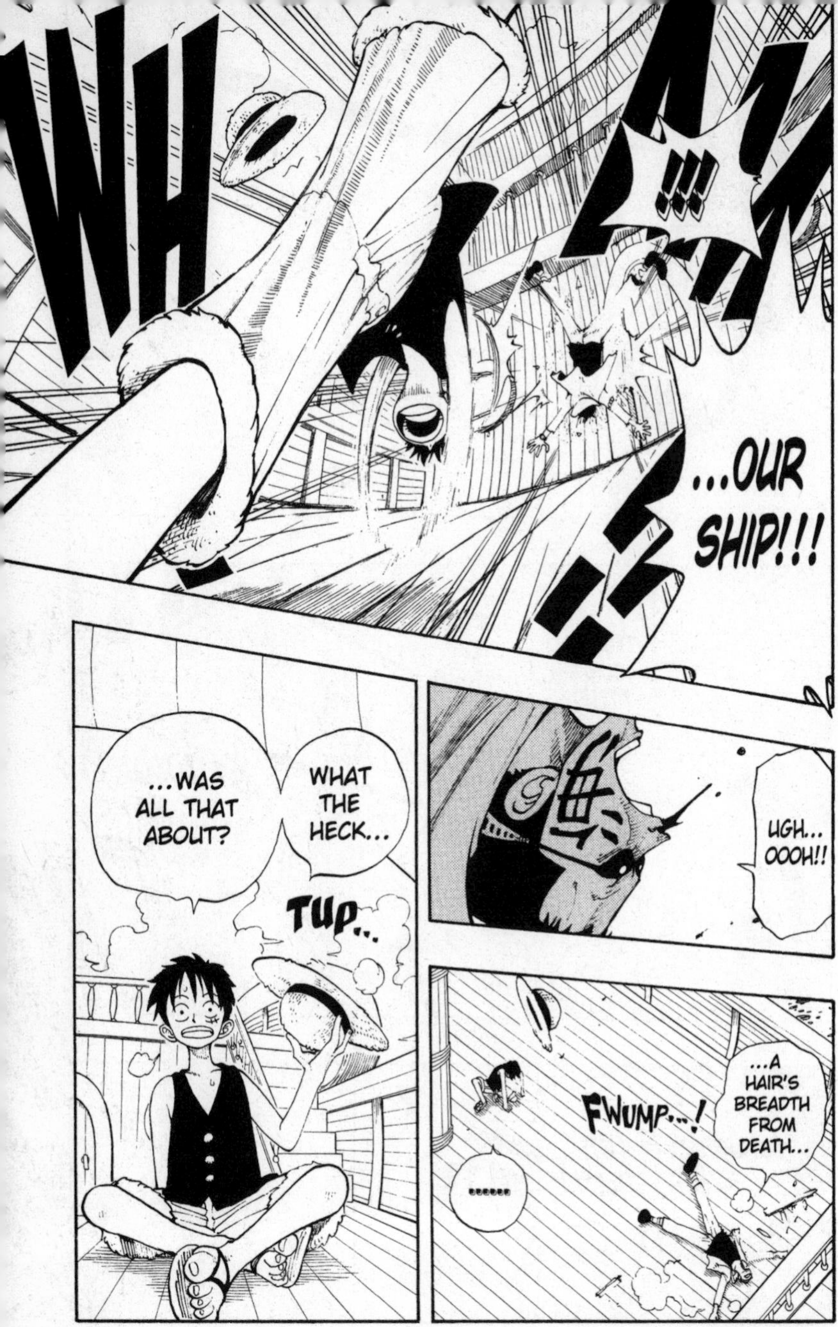

WH
AM!!!
...OUR SHIP!!!
UGH... OOOH!!
...A HAIR'S BREADTH FROM DEATH...
FWUMP...!
......
WHAT THE HECK...
...WAS ALL THAT ABOUT?
TUP...

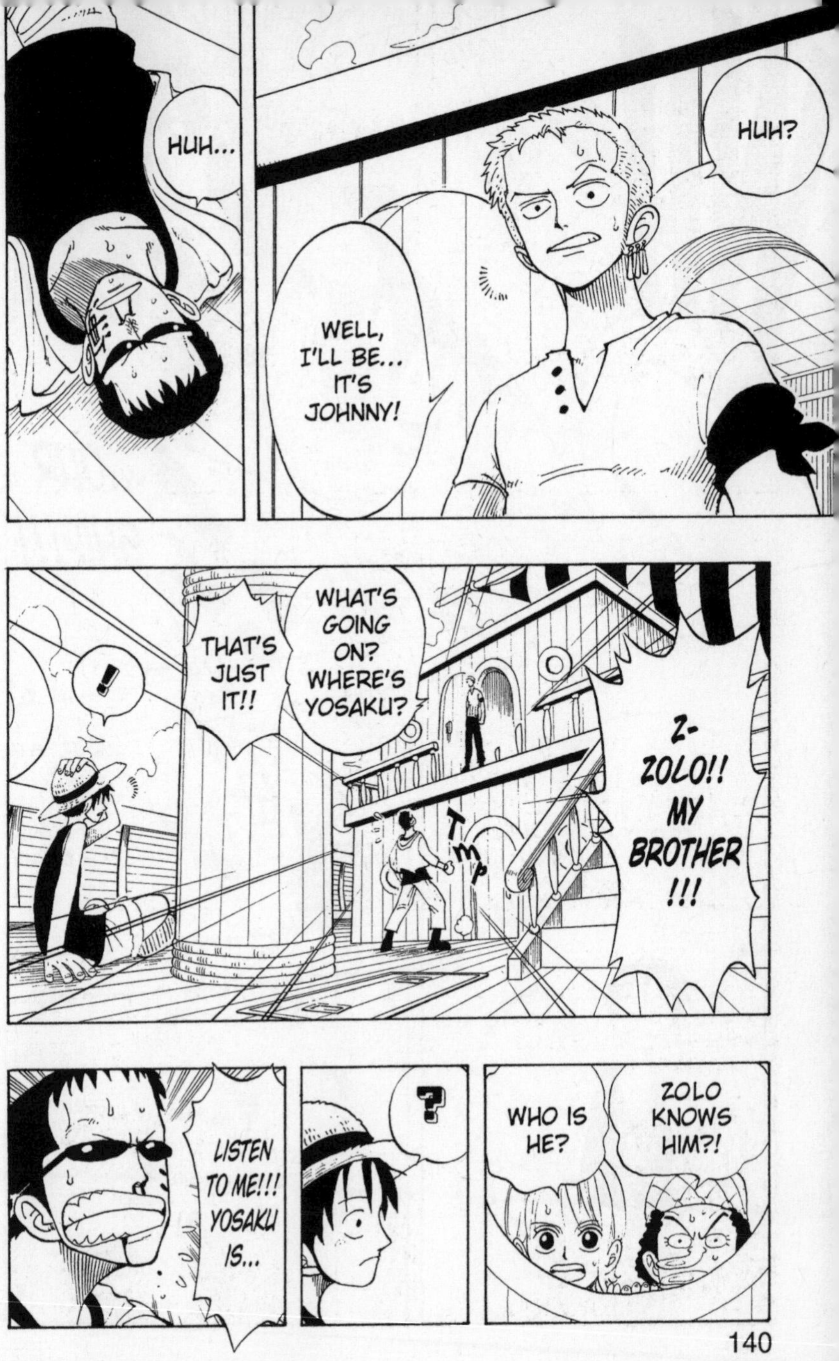
HUH?
WELL, I'LL BE... IT'S JOHNNY!
HUH...
Z-ZOLO!! MY BROTHER !!!
Tmp
WHAT'S GOING ON? WHERE'S YOSAKU?
THAT'S JUST IT!!
!
ZOLO KNOWS HIM?!
WHO IS HE?
?
LISTEN TO ME!!! YOSAKU IS...

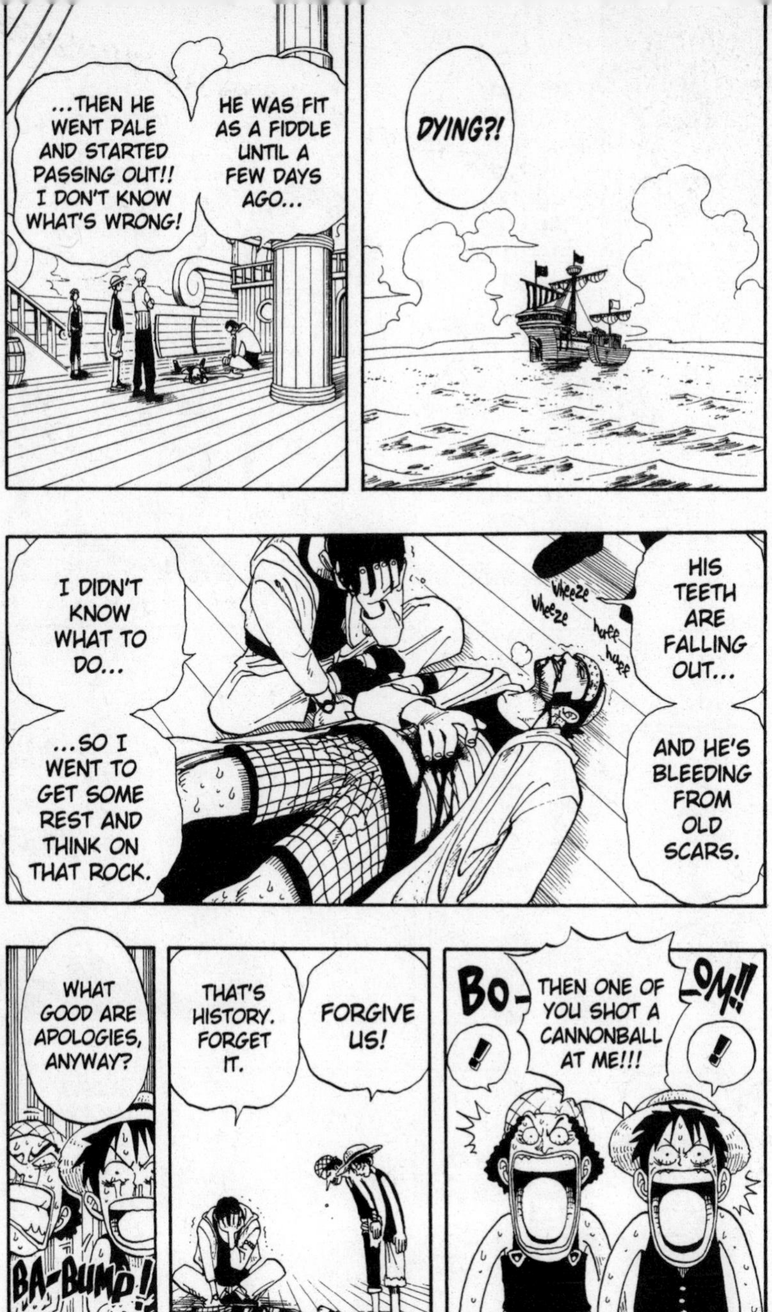
DYING?!
HE WAS FIT AS A FIDDLE UNTIL A FEW DAYS AGO...
...THEN HE WENT PALE AND STARTED PASSING OUT!! I DON'T KNOW WHAT'S WRONG!
HIS TEETH ARE FALLING OUT...
AND HE'S BLEEDING FROM OLD SCARS.
wheeze wheeze
huff huff
I DIDN'T KNOW WHAT TO DO...
...SO I WENT TO GET SOME REST AND THINK ON THAT ROCK.
BO-
-OM!!
THEN ONE OF YOU SHOT A CANNONBALL AT ME!!!
!
!
FORGIVE US!
THAT'S HISTORY. FORGET IT.
WHAT GOOD ARE APOLOGIES, ANYWAY?
BA-BUMP!

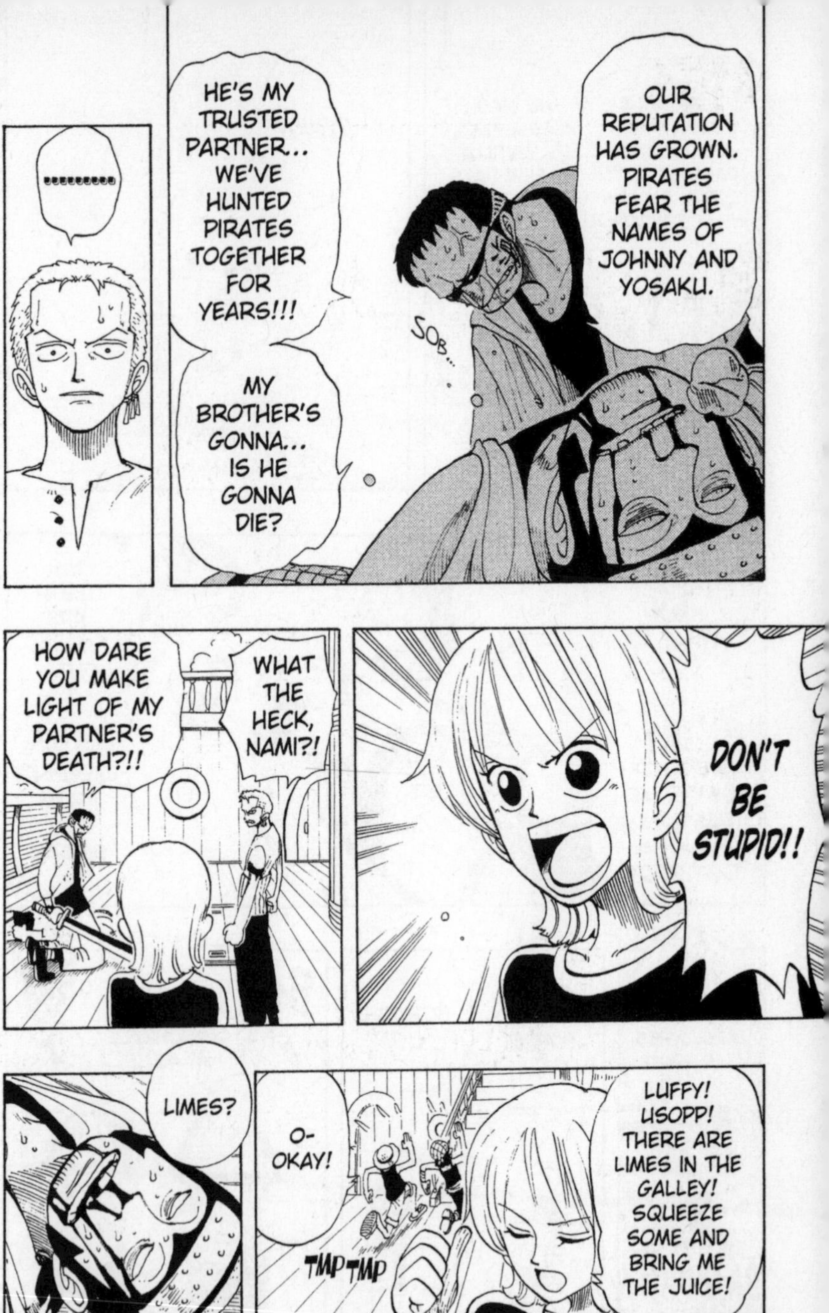
OUR REPUTATION HAS GROWN. PIRATES FEAR THE NAMES OF JOHNNY AND YOSAKU.
SOB...
HE'S MY TRUSTED PARTNER... WE'VE HUNTED PIRATES TOGETHER FOR YEARS!!!
MY BROTHER'S GONNA... IS HE GONNA DIE?
....
DON'T BE STUPID!!
WHAT THE HECK, NAMI?!
HOW DARE YOU MAKE LIGHT OF MY PARTNER'S DEATH?!!
LUFFY! USOPP! THERE ARE LIMES IN THE GALLEY! SQUEEZE SOME AND BRING ME THE JUICE!
O-OKAY!
TMP TMP
LIMES?

READ THIS WAY

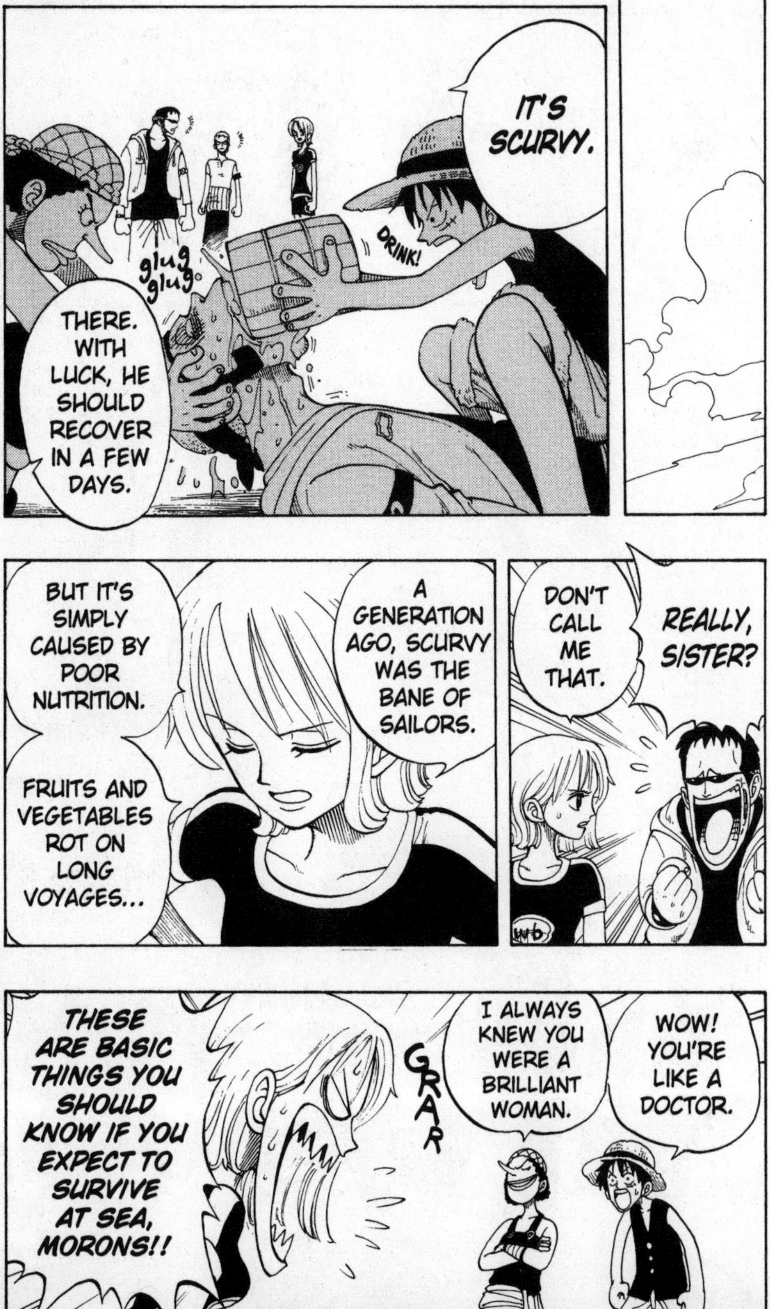
IT'S SCURVY.
DRINK!
glug glug
THERE. WITH LUCK, HE SHOULD RECOVER IN A FEW DAYS.
REALLY, SISTER?
DON'T CALL ME THAT.
A GENERATION AGO, SCURVY WAS THE BANE OF SAILORS.
BUT IT'S SIMPLY CAUSED BY POOR NUTRITION.
FRUITS AND VEGETABLES ROT ON LONG VOYAGES...
WOW! YOU'RE LIKE A DOCTOR.
I ALWAYS KNEW YOU WERE A BRILLIANT WOMAN.
GRAR
THESE ARE BASIC THINGS YOU SHOULD KNOW IF YOU EXPECT TO SURVIVE AT SEA, MORONS!!

READ THIS WAY

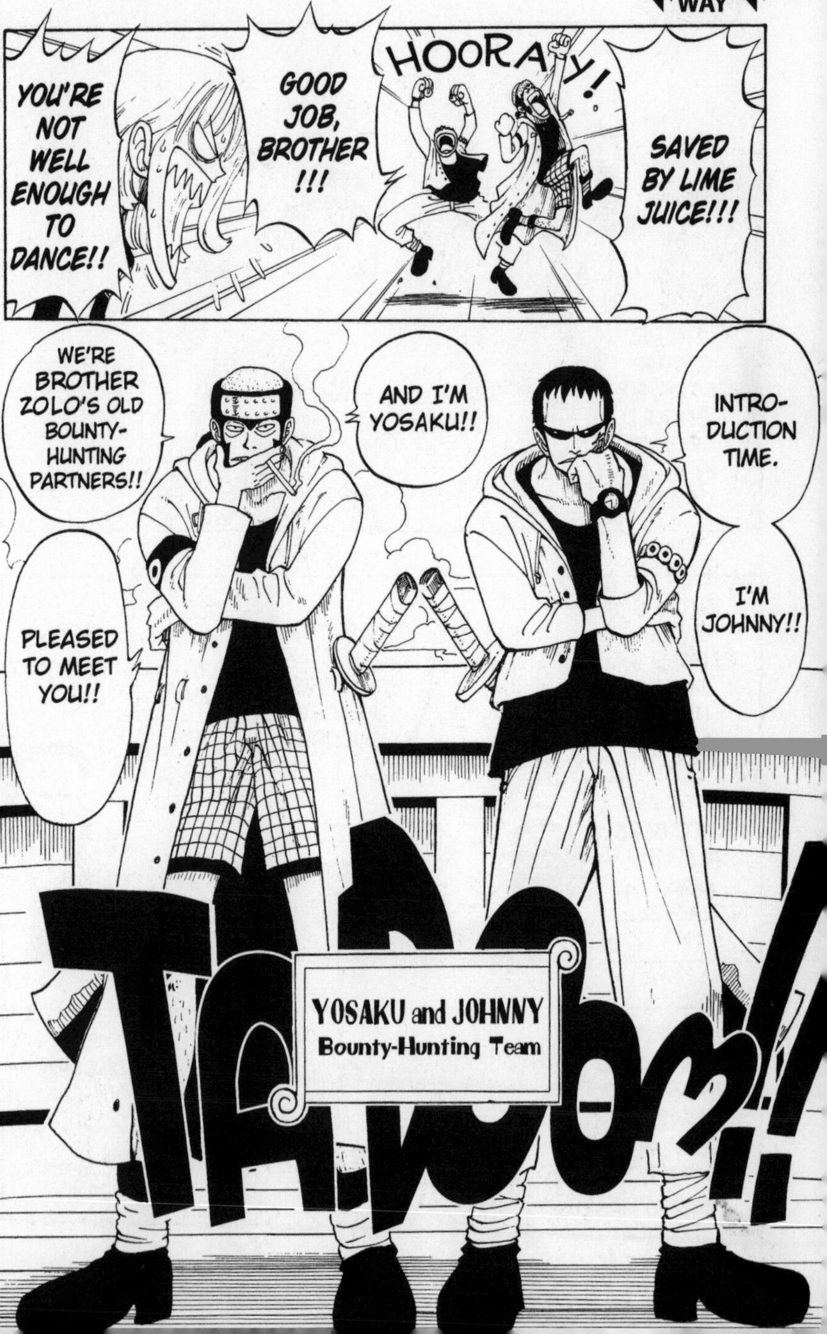
SAVED BY LIME JUICE!!!
HOORAY!
GOOD JOB, BROTHER!!!
YOU'RE NOT WELL ENOUGH TO DANCE!!
INTRO-DUCTION TIME.
I'M JOHNNY!!
AND I'M YOSAKU!!
WE'RE BROTHER ZOLO'S OLD BOUNTY-HUNTING PARTNERS!!
PLEASED TO MEET YOU!!
YOSAKU and JOHNNY
Bounty-Hunting Team
TA-DOOM!!

READ THIS WAY

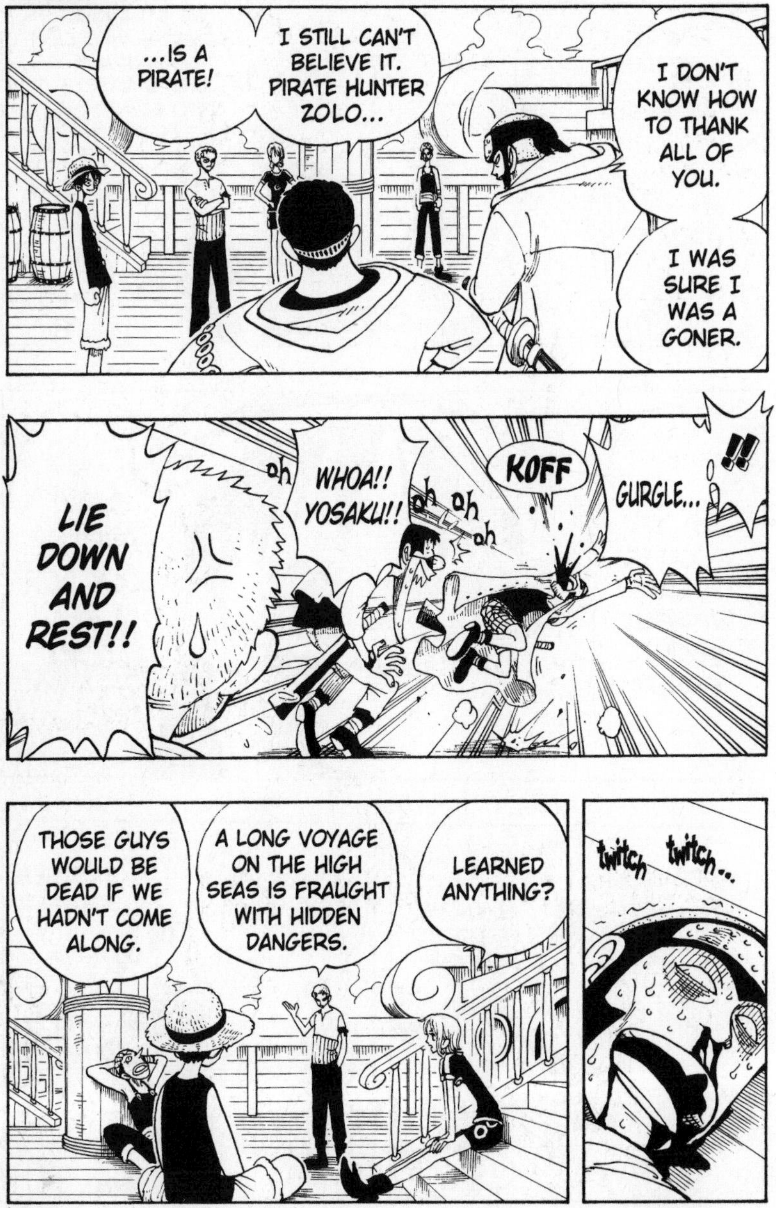

I DON'T KNOW HOW TO THANK ALL OF YOU.
I WAS SURE I WAS A GONER.
I STILL CAN'T BELIEVE IT. PIRATE HUNTER ZOLO...
...IS A PIRATE!
!!
GURGLE...
KOFF
oh oh oh
WHOA!! YOSAKU!!
oh
LIE DOWN AND REST!!
twitch twitch...
LEARNED ANYTHING?
A LONG VOYAGE ON THE HIGH SEAS IS FRAUGHT WITH HIDDEN DANGERS.
THOSE GUYS WOULD BE DEAD IF WE HADN'T COME ALONG.

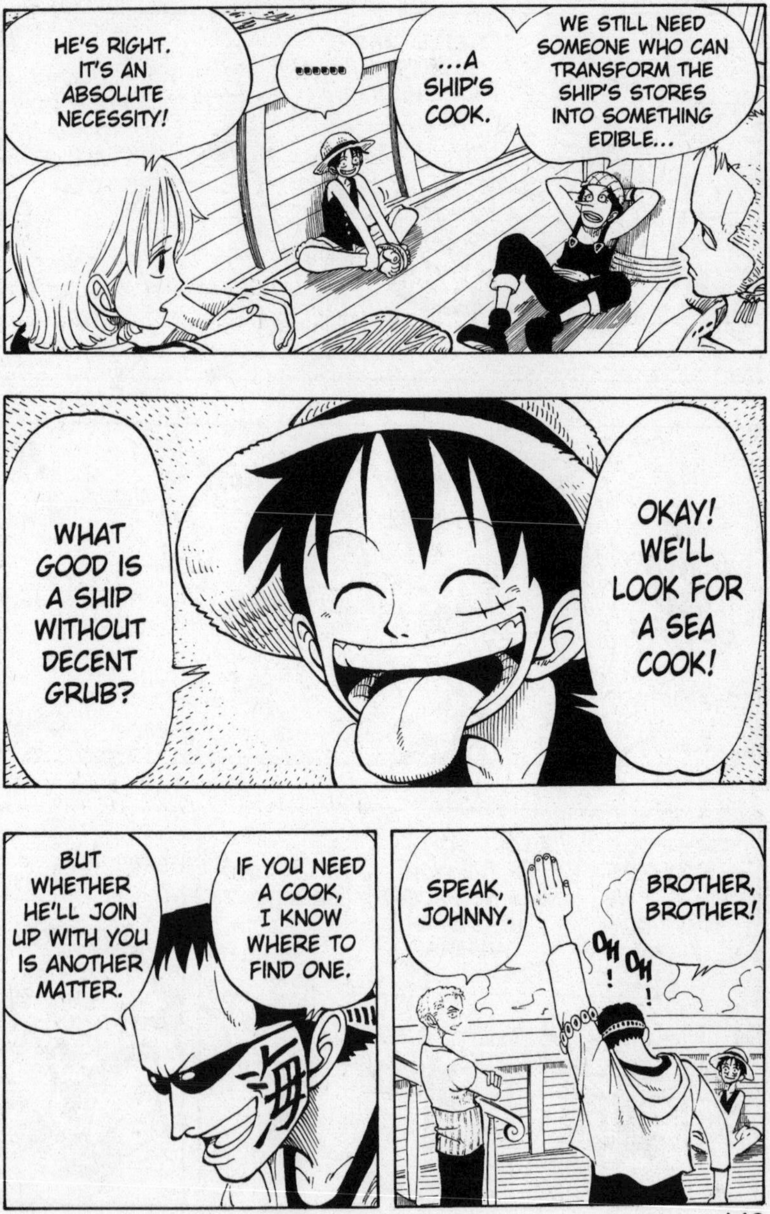
WE STILL NEED SOMEONE WHO CAN TRANSFORM THE SHIP'S STORES INTO SOMETHING EDIBLE...
...A SHIP'S COOK.
......
HE'S RIGHT. IT'S AN ABSOLUTE NECESSITY!
OKAY! WE'LL LOOK FOR A SEA COOK!
WHAT GOOD IS A SHIP WITHOUT DECENT GRUB?
BROTHER, BROTHER!
OH! OH!
SPEAK, JOHNNY.
IF YOU NEED A COOK, I KNOW WHERE TO FIND ONE.
BUT WHETHER HE'LL JOIN UP WITH YOU IS ANOTHER MATTER.

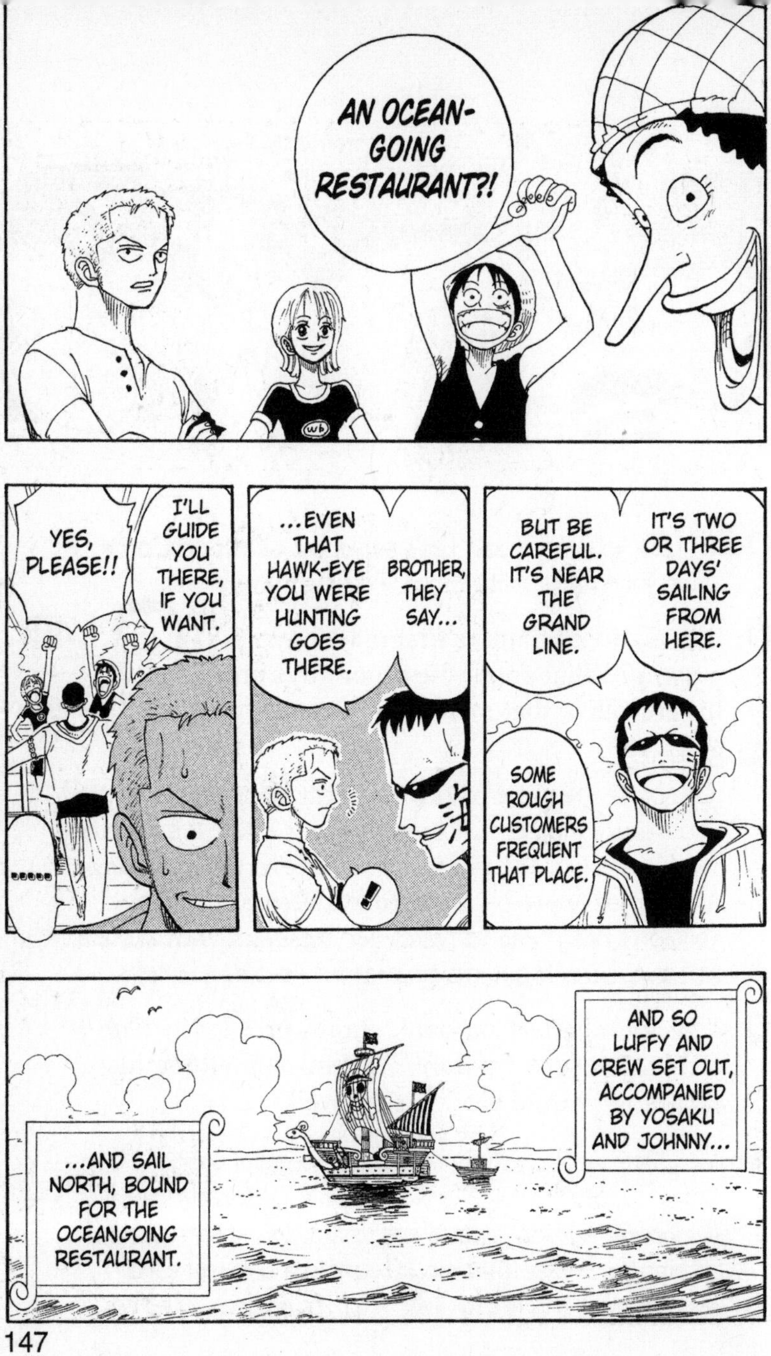
AN OCEAN-GOING RESTAURANT?!
IT'S TWO OR THREE DAYS' SAILING FROM HERE.
BUT BE CAREFUL. IT'S NEAR THE GRAND LINE.
SOME ROUGH CUSTOMERS FREQUENT THAT PLACE.
BROTHER, THEY SAY...
...EVEN THAT HAWK-EYE YOU WERE HUNTING GOES THERE.
!
I'LL GUIDE YOU THERE, IF YOU WANT.
YES, PLEASE!!
.....
AND SO LUFFY AND CREW SET OUT, ACCOMPANIED BY YOSAKU AND JOHNNY...
...AND SAIL NORTH, BOUND FOR THE OCEANGOING RESTAURANT.

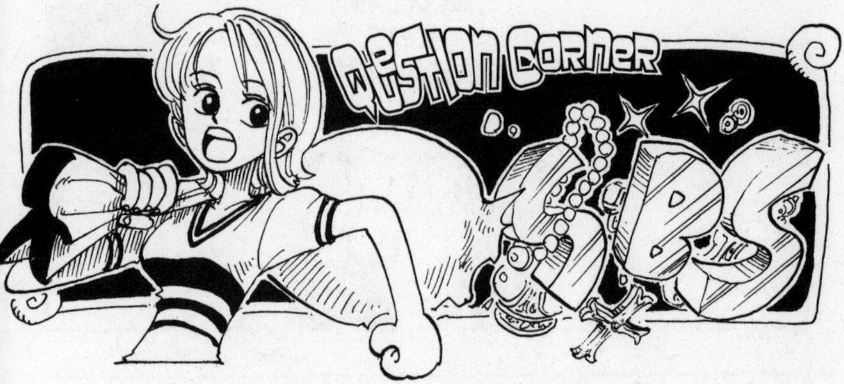
Question Corner
SBS

Oda: Thank you very much. Let's begin the Question Corner. On your feet! Attention!! Hold that pose!!

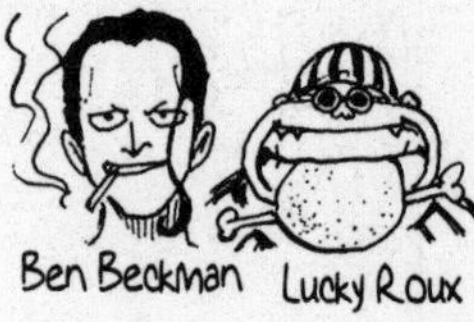
Ben Beckman
Lucky Roux

Q: Sensei, does Shanks's first mate have a name? What about the other guys on his crew, like that meat-eating man?

A: Be seated.
Of course they have names. The first mate's name is Shoofukutii Mouse. "Oh, because he has a face like a mouse," says Usopp. No, just kidding. His real name is Ben Beckman. And the fat guy who's always eating meat is Lucky Roux. You don't really need to remember these, but I got quite a few questions about their names, so I thought I'd reply.

Q: The sound effect "ta-dah!" shows up a lot in *One Piece.* But why "ta-dah!"? I think something like "ba-bing" would work just as well.

A: No. That wouldn't work. That just wouldn't work. When I write "ta-dah!," I draw with the feeling of "ta-dah!" If I wrote "ba-bing" I would end up drawing a "ba-bing" kind of picture. Maybe that would work in a gag scene. Or maybe something like "uh-huh." No, it's entirely different.

Chapter 43:
SANJI

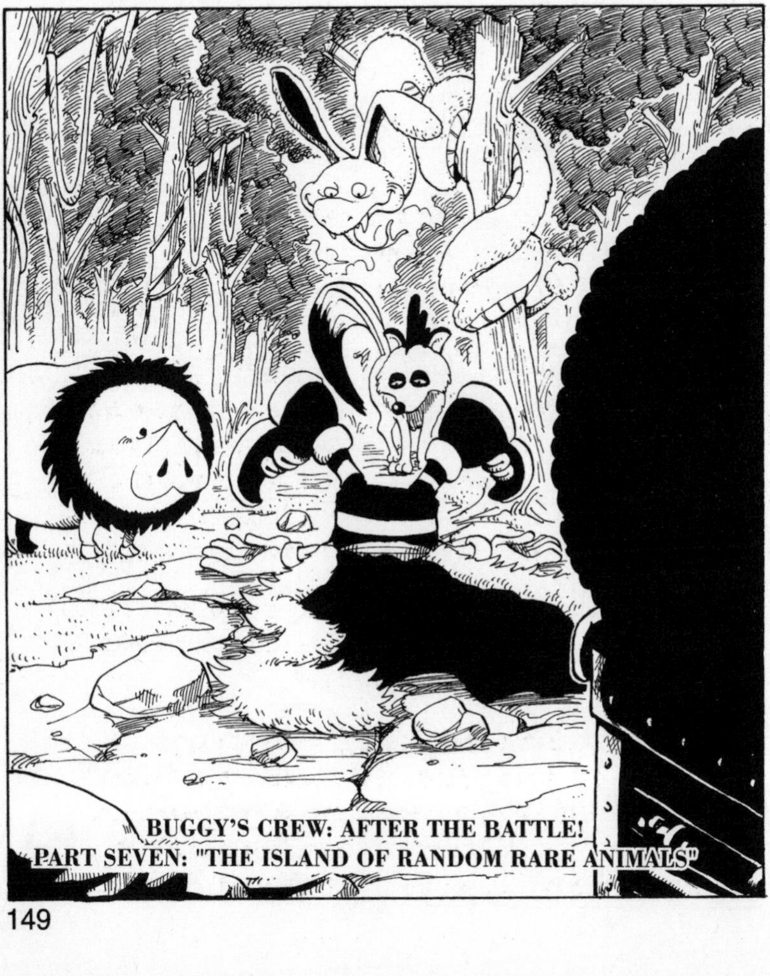
BUGGY'S CREW: AFTER THE BATTLE!
PART SEVEN: "THE ISLAND OF RANDOM RARE ANIMALS"

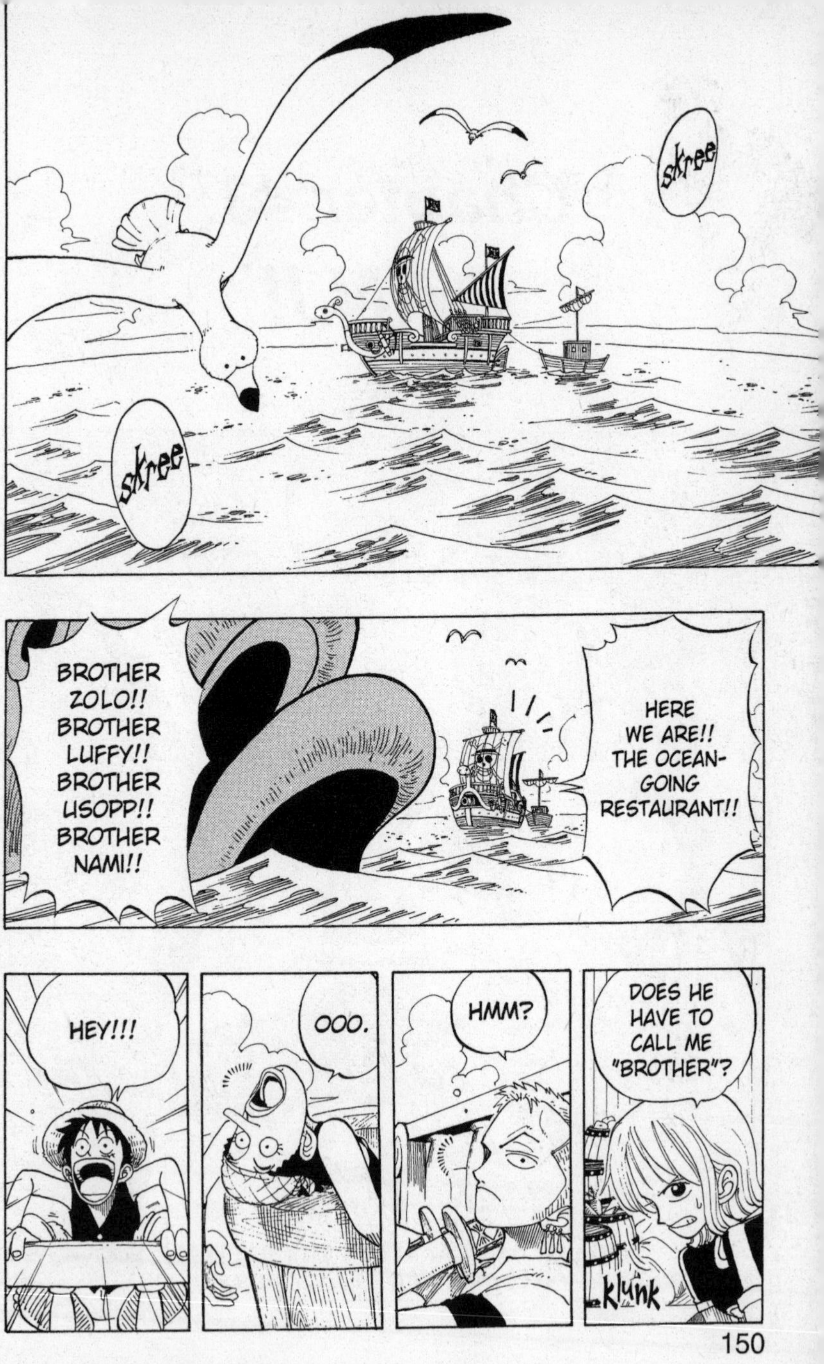
skree
skree
HERE WE ARE!! THE OCEAN-GOING RESTAURANT!!
BROTHER ZOLO!! BROTHER LUFFY!! BROTHER USOPP!! BROTHER NAMI!!
DOES HE HAVE TO CALL ME "BROTHER"?
klunk
HMM?
OOO.
HEY!!!

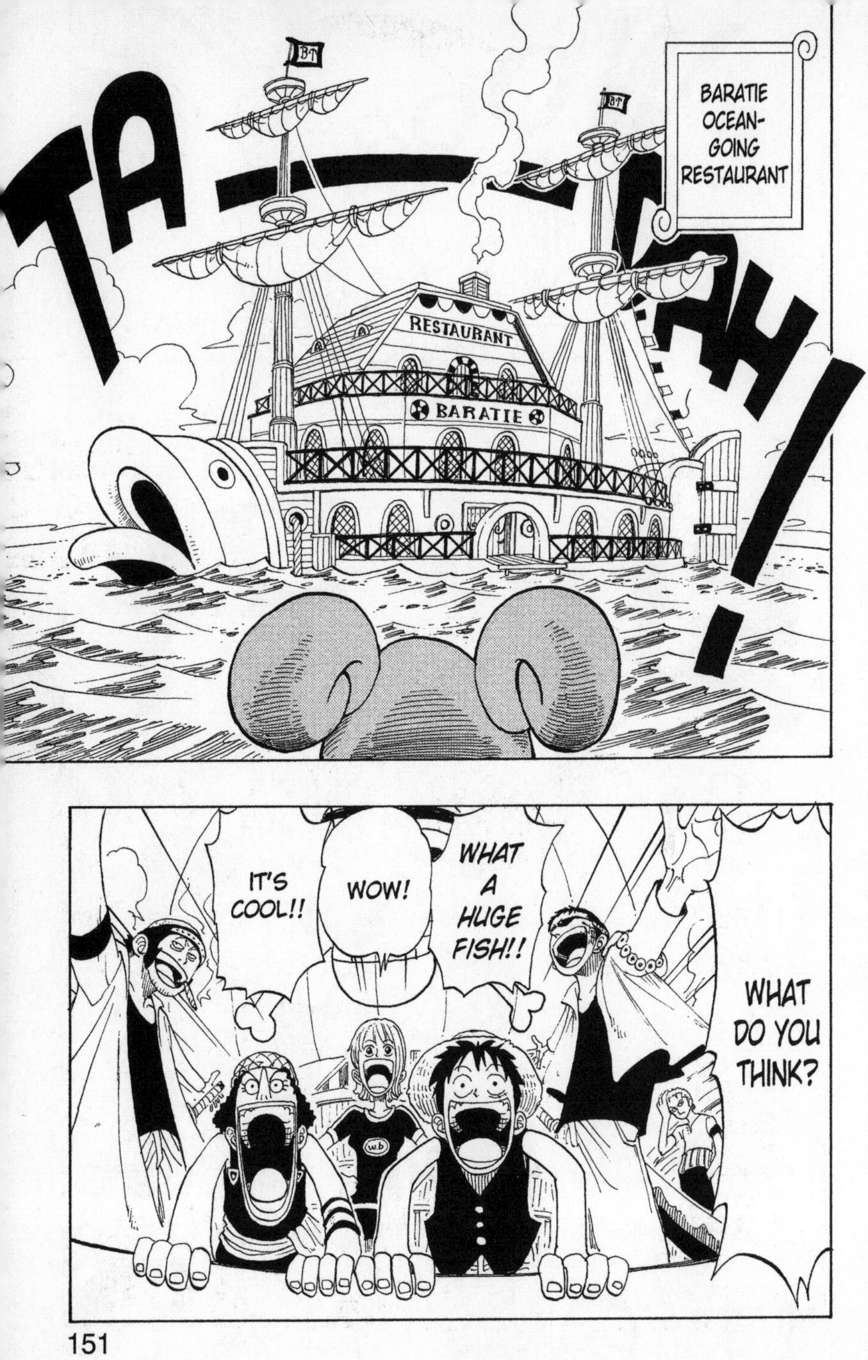
BARATIE OCEAN-GOING RESTAURANT
TA-DAH!!
RESTAURANT
BARATIE
WHAT DO YOU THINK?
WHAT A HUGE FISH!!
WOW!
IT'S COOL!!

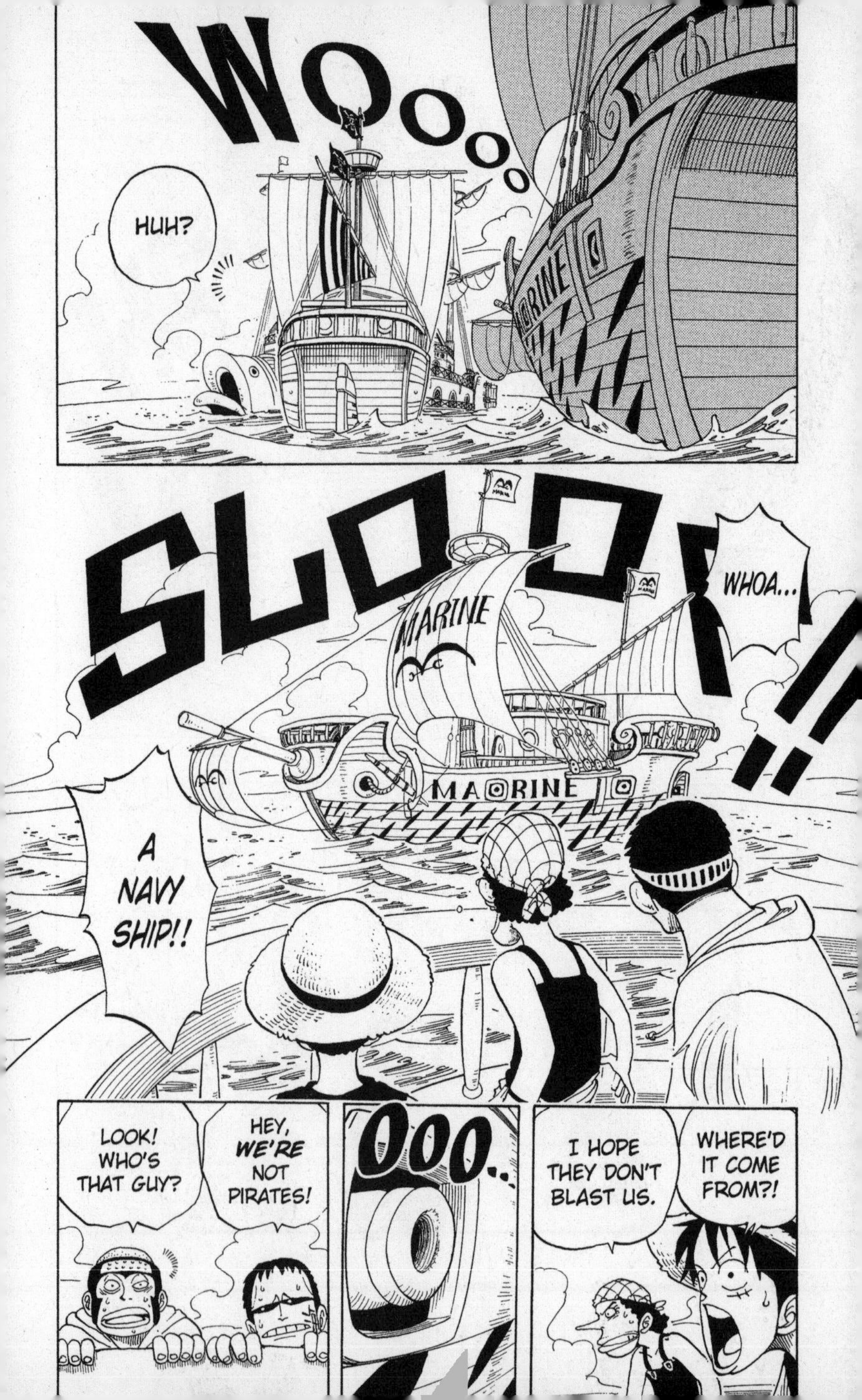
WOOOO
HUH?
WHOA...
SLOOP!!
A NAVY SHIP!!
WHERE'D IT COME FROM?!
I HOPE THEY DON'T BLAST US.
OOO...
HEY, *WE'RE* NOT PIRATES!
LOOK! WHO'S THAT GUY?

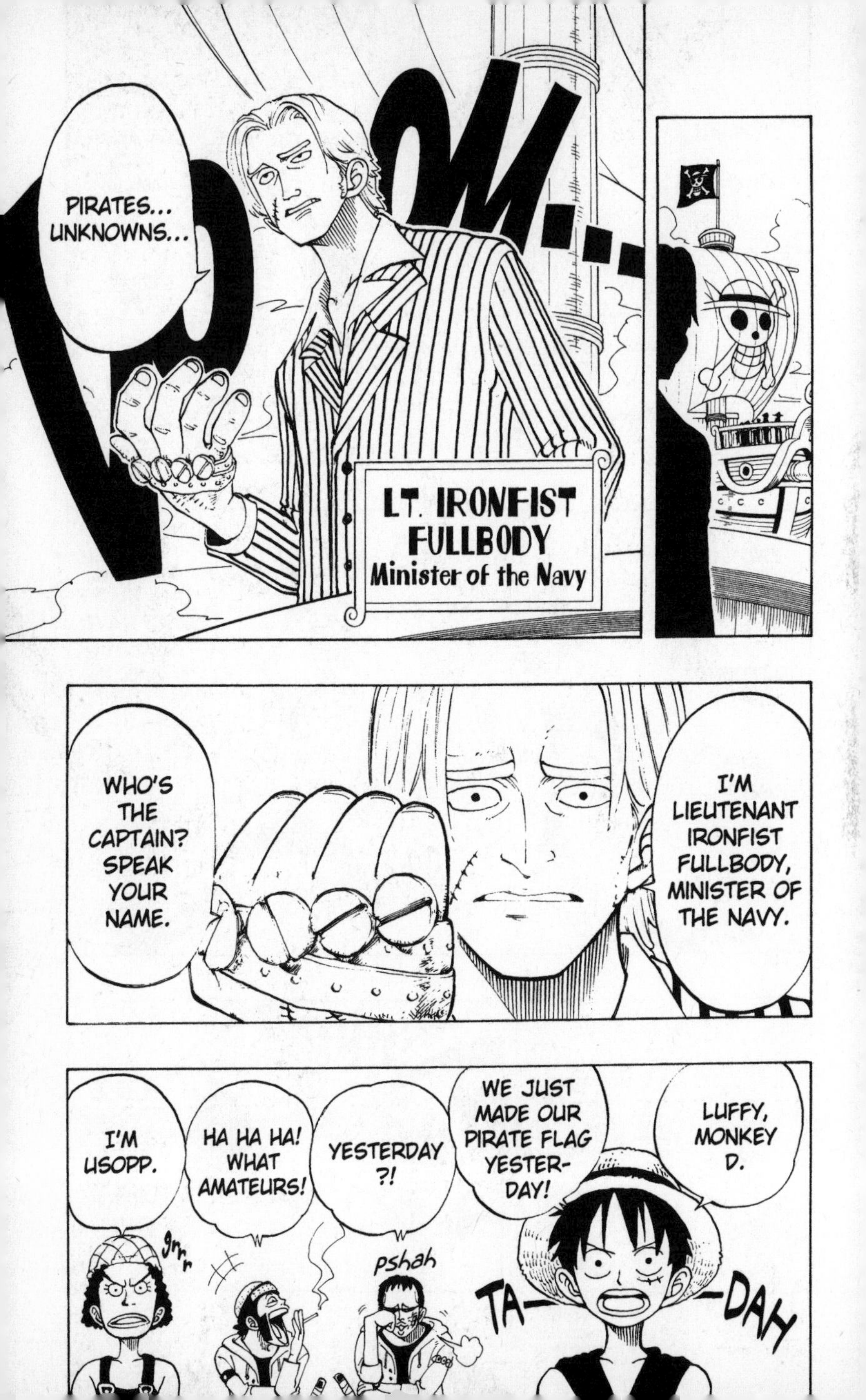
PIRATES... UNKNOWNS...
LT. IRONFIST FULLBODY Minister of the Navy
I'M LIEUTENANT IRONFIST FULLBODY, MINISTER OF THE NAVY.
WHO'S THE CAPTAIN? SPEAK YOUR NAME.
LUFFY, MONKEY D.
WE JUST MADE OUR PIRATE FLAG YESTER-DAY!
TA—
—DAH
YESTERDAY ?!
pshah
HA HA HA! WHAT AMATEURS!
I'M USOPP.
grrr

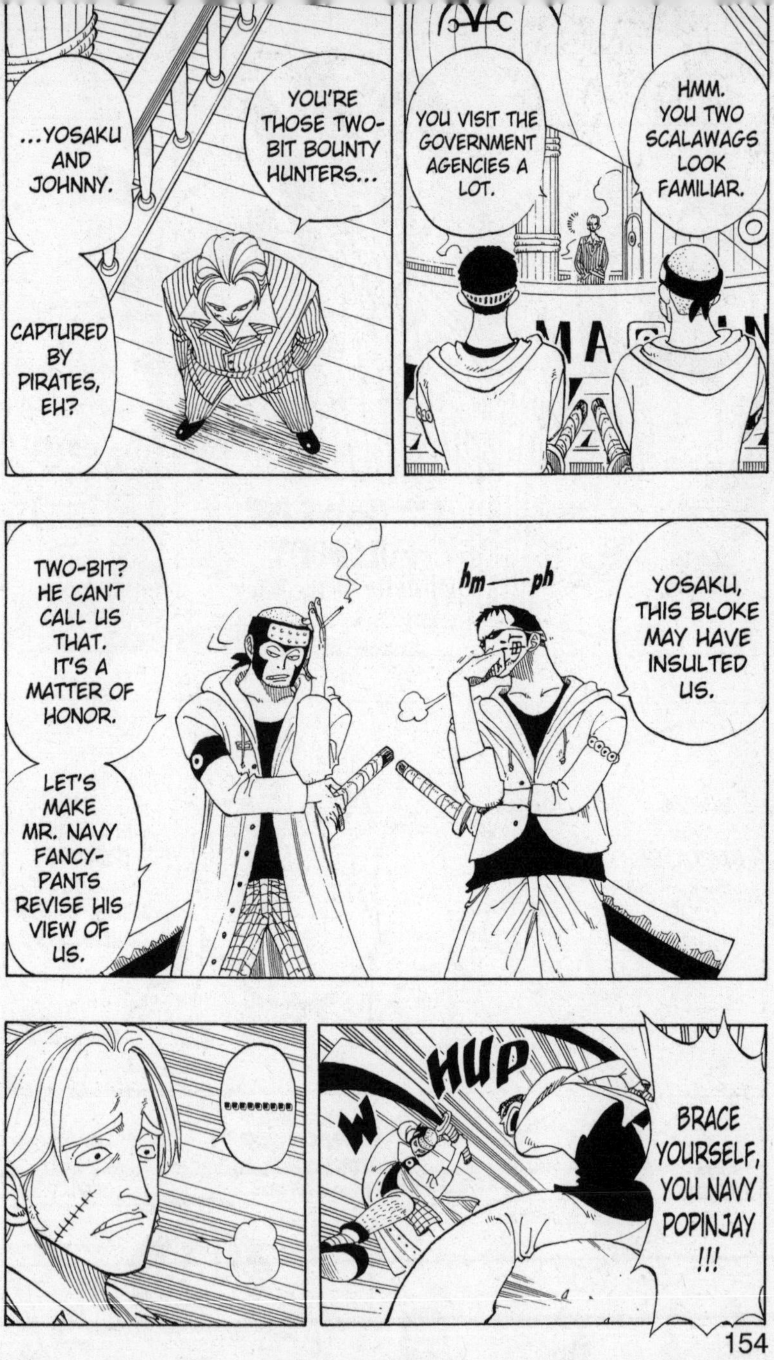
HMM. YOU TWO SCALAWAGS LOOK FAMILIAR.
YOU VISIT THE GOVERNMENT AGENCIES A LOT.
YOU'RE THOSE TWO-BIT BOUNTY HUNTERS...
...YOSAKU AND JOHNNY.
CAPTURED BY PIRATES, EH?
YOSAKU, THIS BLOKE MAY HAVE INSULTED US.
hm—ph
TWO-BIT? HE CAN'T CALL US THAT. IT'S A MATTER OF HONOR.
LET'S MAKE MR. NAVY FANCY-PANTS REVISE HIS VIEW OF US.
BRACE YOURSELF, YOU NAVY POPINJAY !!!
HUP
W
....

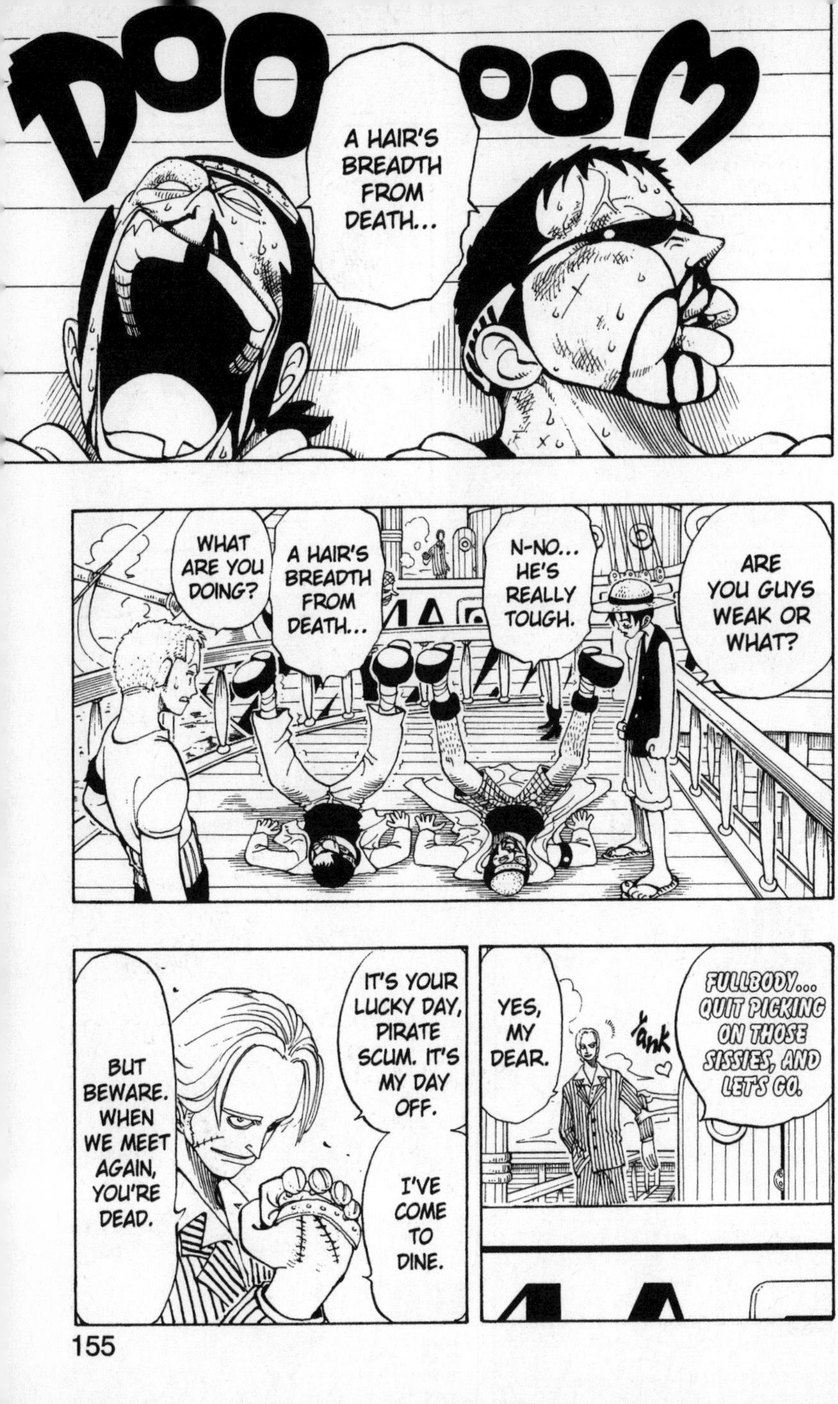
DOOOOM
A HAIR'S BREADTH FROM DEATH...
ARE YOU GUYS WEAK OR WHAT?
N-NO... HE'S REALLY TOUGH.
A HAIR'S BREADTH FROM DEATH...
WHAT ARE YOU DOING?
FULLBODY... QUIT PICKING ON THOSE SISSIES, AND LET'S GO.
Yank
YES, MY DEAR.
IT'S YOUR LUCKY DAY, PIRATE SCUM. IT'S MY DAY OFF.
I'VE COME TO DINE.
BUT BEWARE. WHEN WE MEET AGAIN, YOU'RE DEAD.

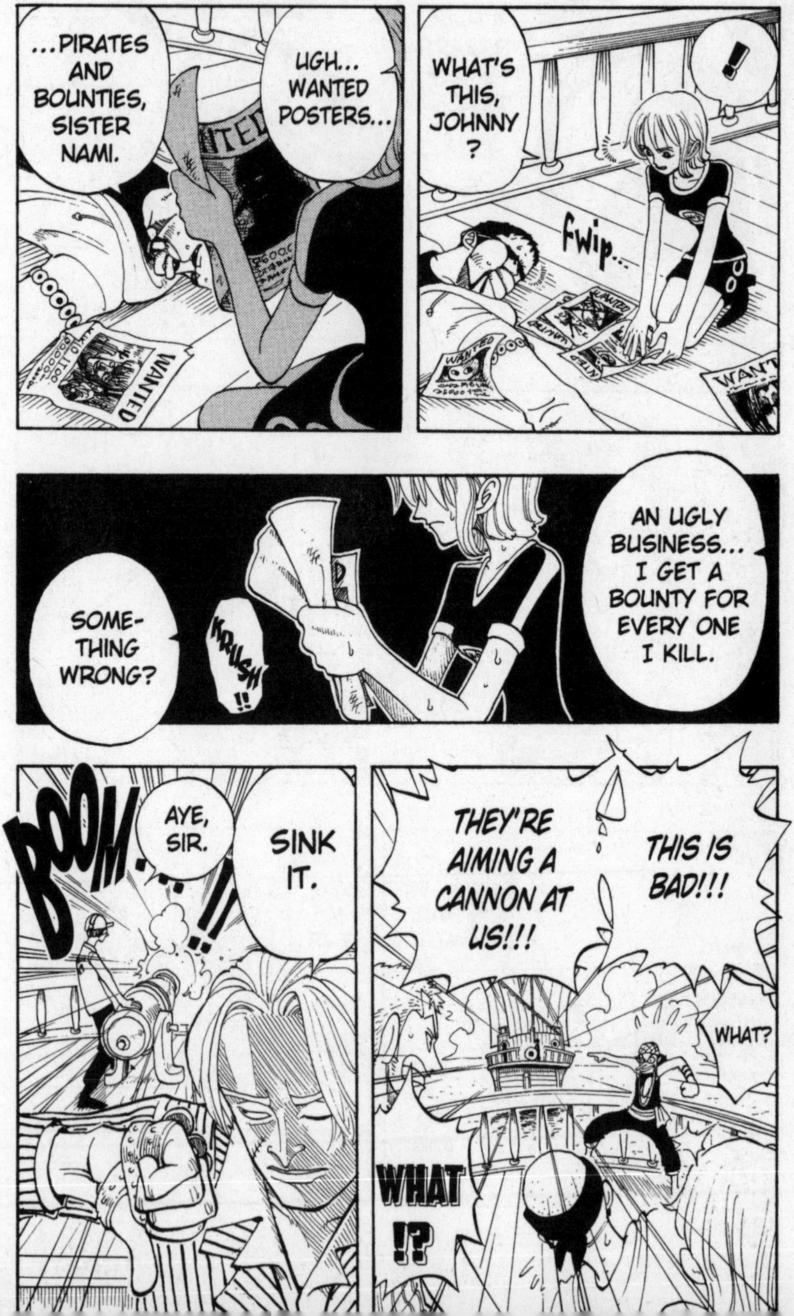
!
WHAT'S THIS, JOHNNY?
fwip...
UGH... WANTED POSTERS...
...PIRATES AND BOUNTIES, SISTER NAMI.
AN UGLY BUSINESS... I GET A BOUNTY FOR EVERY ONE I KILL.
KRUSH!!
SOME-THING WRONG?
THIS IS BAD!!!
THEY'RE AIMING A CANNON AT US!!!
WHAT?
WHAT!?
SINK IT.
AYE, SIR.
BOOM...!!

READ THIS WAY

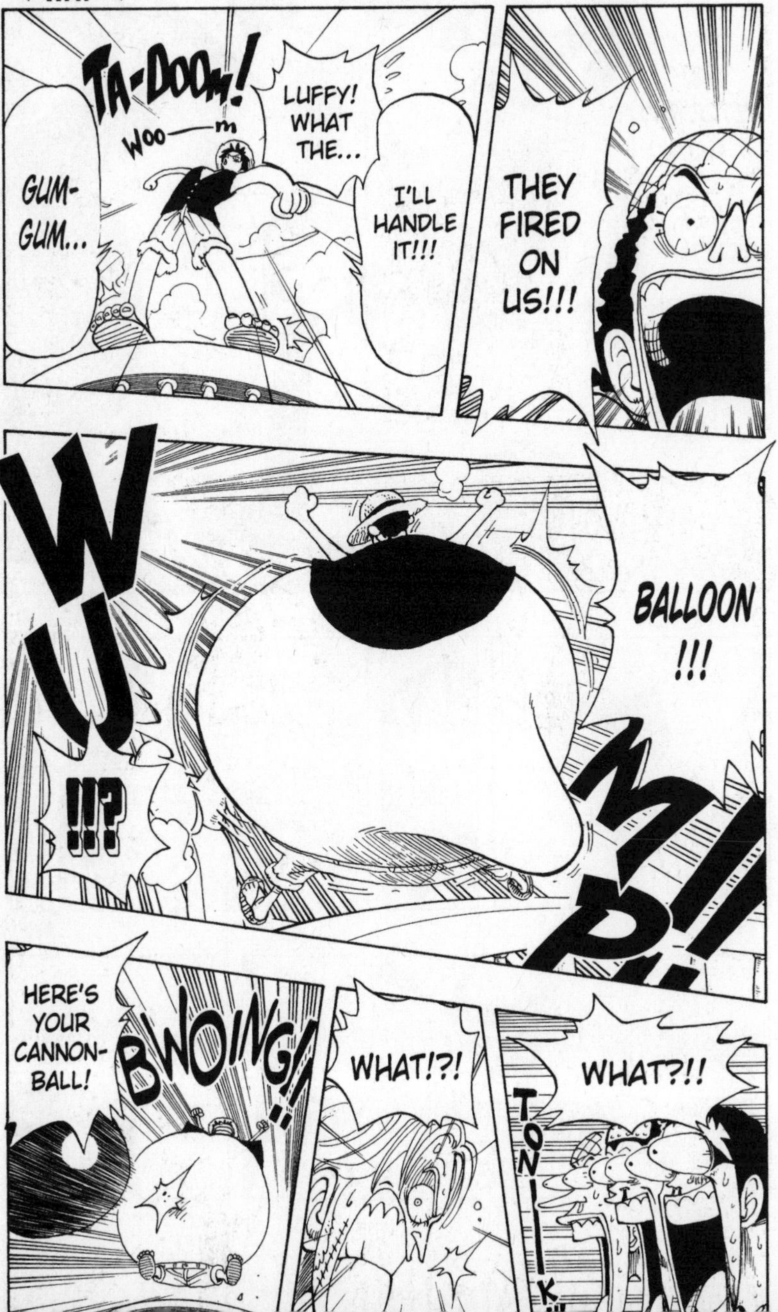
THEY FIRED ON US!!!
LUFFY! WHAT THE...
I'LL HANDLE IT!!!
TA-DOOM!
WOO—m
GUM-GUM...
BALLOON!!!
MIIP!!
WU
!!!?
WHAT?!!
TONK
WHAT!?!
HERE'S YOUR CANNON-BALL!
BWOING!!

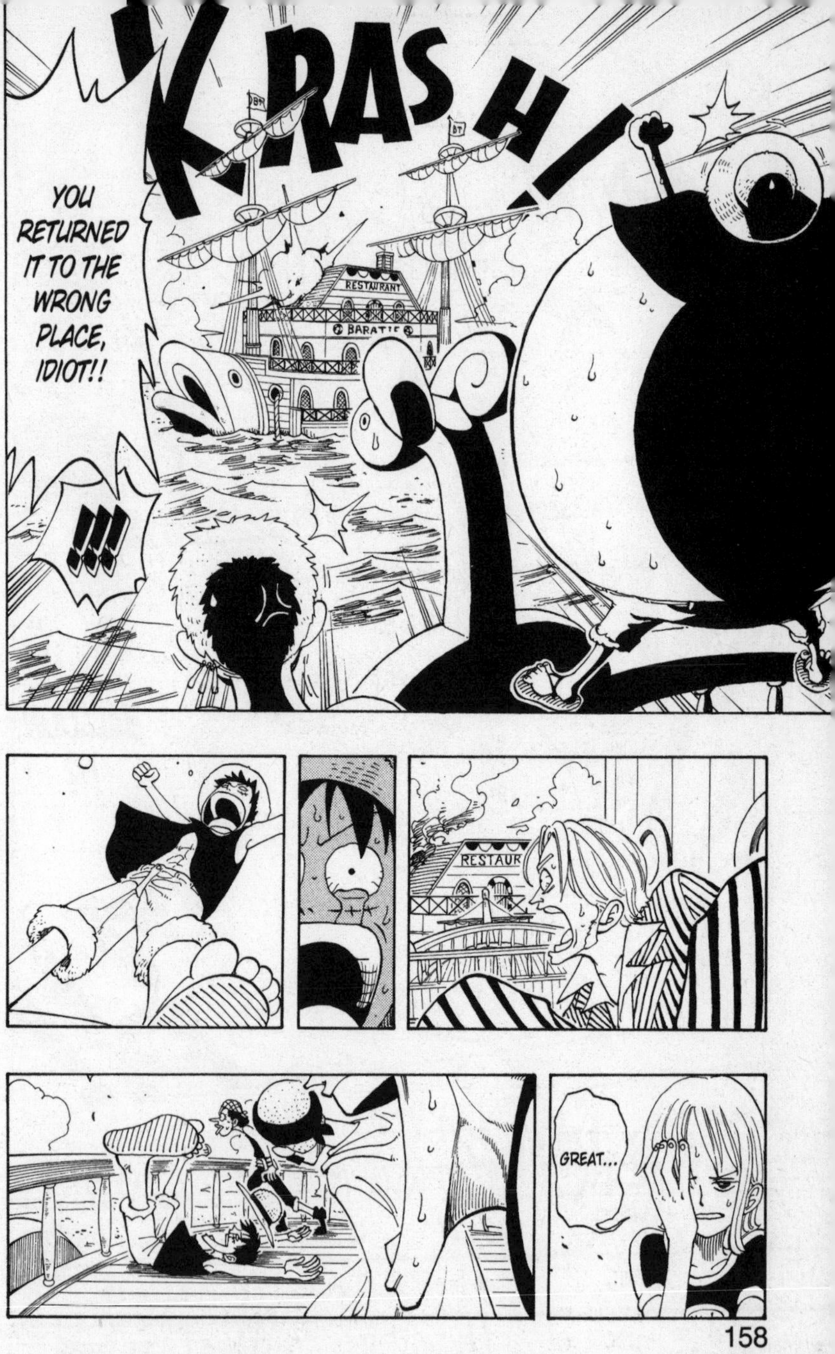
KRASH!
YOU RETURNED IT TO THE WRONG PLACE, IDIOT!!
!!!
GREAT...

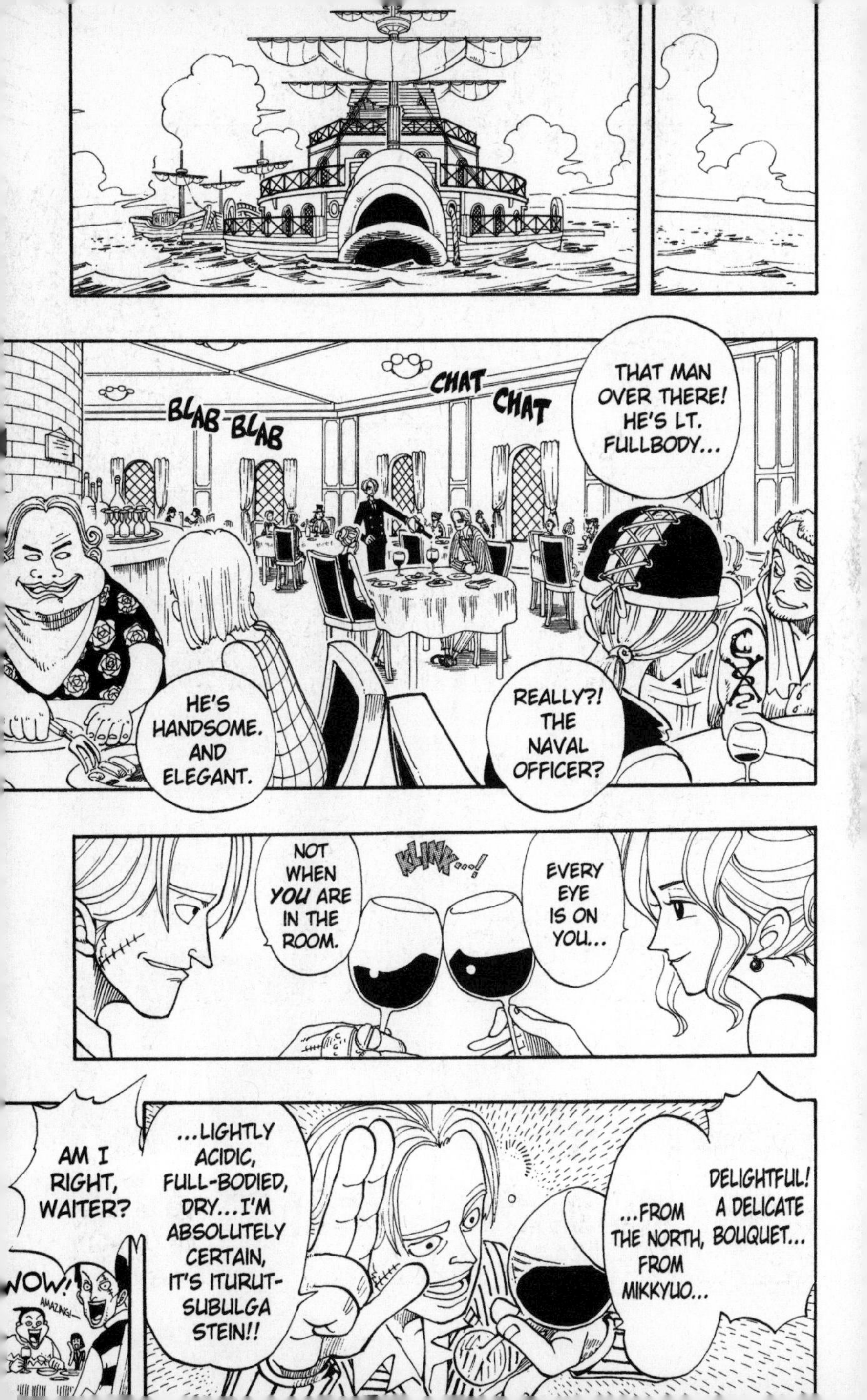
THAT MAN OVER THERE! HE'S LT. FULLBODY...
CHAT CHAT
BLAB BLAB
REALLY?! THE NAVAL OFFICER?
HE'S HANDSOME. AND ELEGANT.
EVERY EYE IS ON YOU...
KLINK...!
NOT WHEN YOU ARE IN THE ROOM.
DELIGHTFUL! A DELICATE BOUQUET...
...FROM THE NORTH, FROM MIKKYUO...
...LIGHTLY ACIDIC, FULL-BODIED, DRY... I'M ABSOLUTELY CERTAIN, IT'S ITURUT-SUBULGA STEIN!!
AM I RIGHT, WAITER?
WOW!
AMAZING!

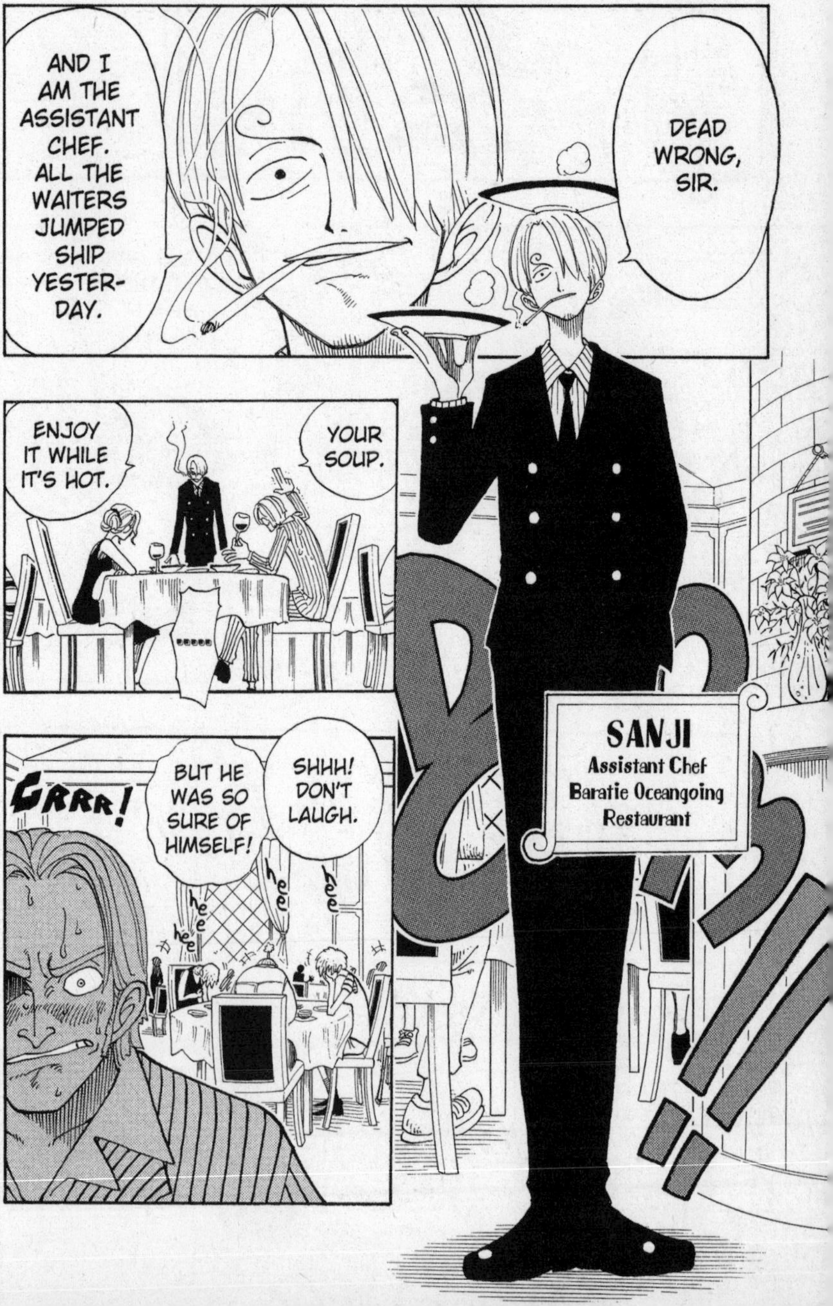
DEAD WRONG, SIR.
AND I AM THE ASSISTANT CHEF. ALL THE WAITERS JUMPED SHIP YESTER-DAY.
SANJI
Assistant Chef
Baratie Oceangoing Restaurant
YOUR SOUP.
ENJOY IT WHILE IT'S HOT.
SHHH! DON'T LAUGH.
BUT HE WAS SO SURE OF HIMSELF!
hee hee
hee hee
GRRR!

READ THIS WAY

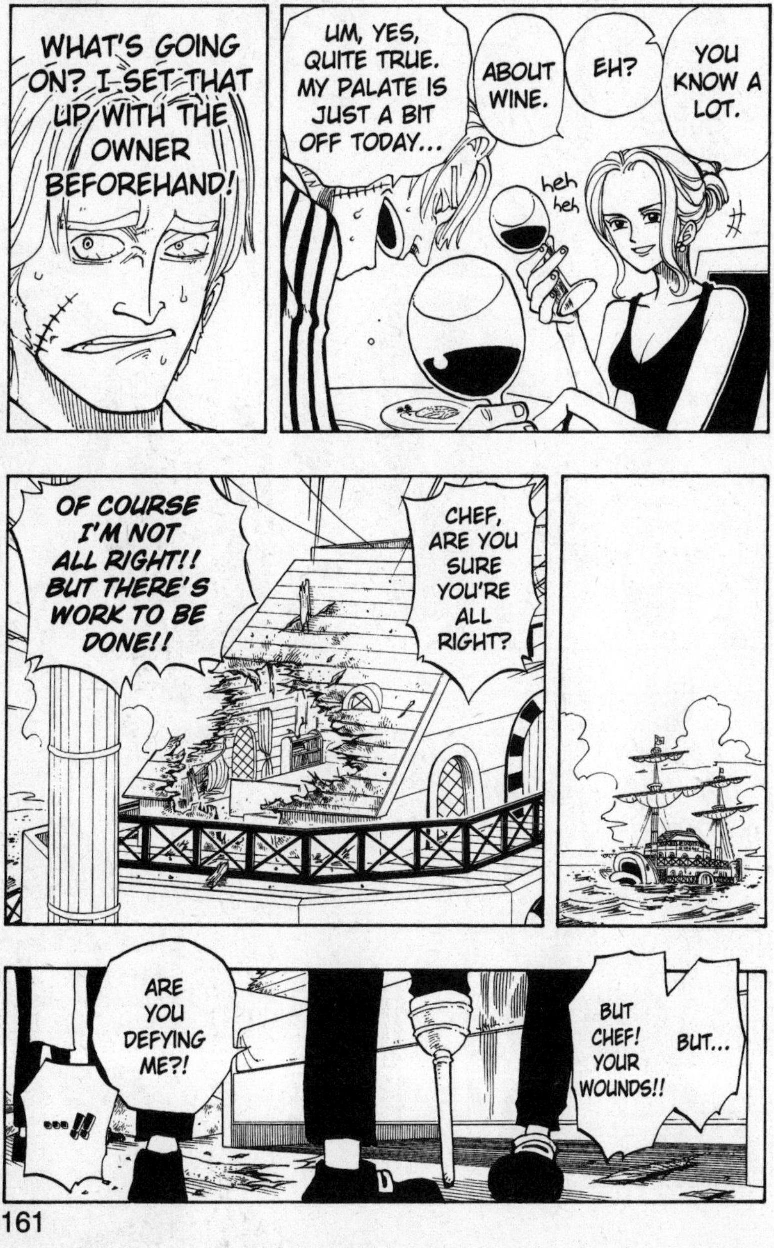
YOU KNOW A LOT.
EH?
ABOUT WINE.
heh heh
UM, YES, QUITE TRUE. MY PALATE IS JUST A BIT OFF TODAY...
WHAT'S GOING ON? I SET THAT UP WITH THE OWNER BEFOREHAND!
CHEF, ARE YOU SURE YOU'RE ALL RIGHT?
OF COURSE I'M NOT ALL RIGHT!! BUT THERE'S WORK TO BE DONE!!
BUT...
BUT CHEF! YOUR WOUNDS!!
ARE YOU DEFYING ME?!
...!!

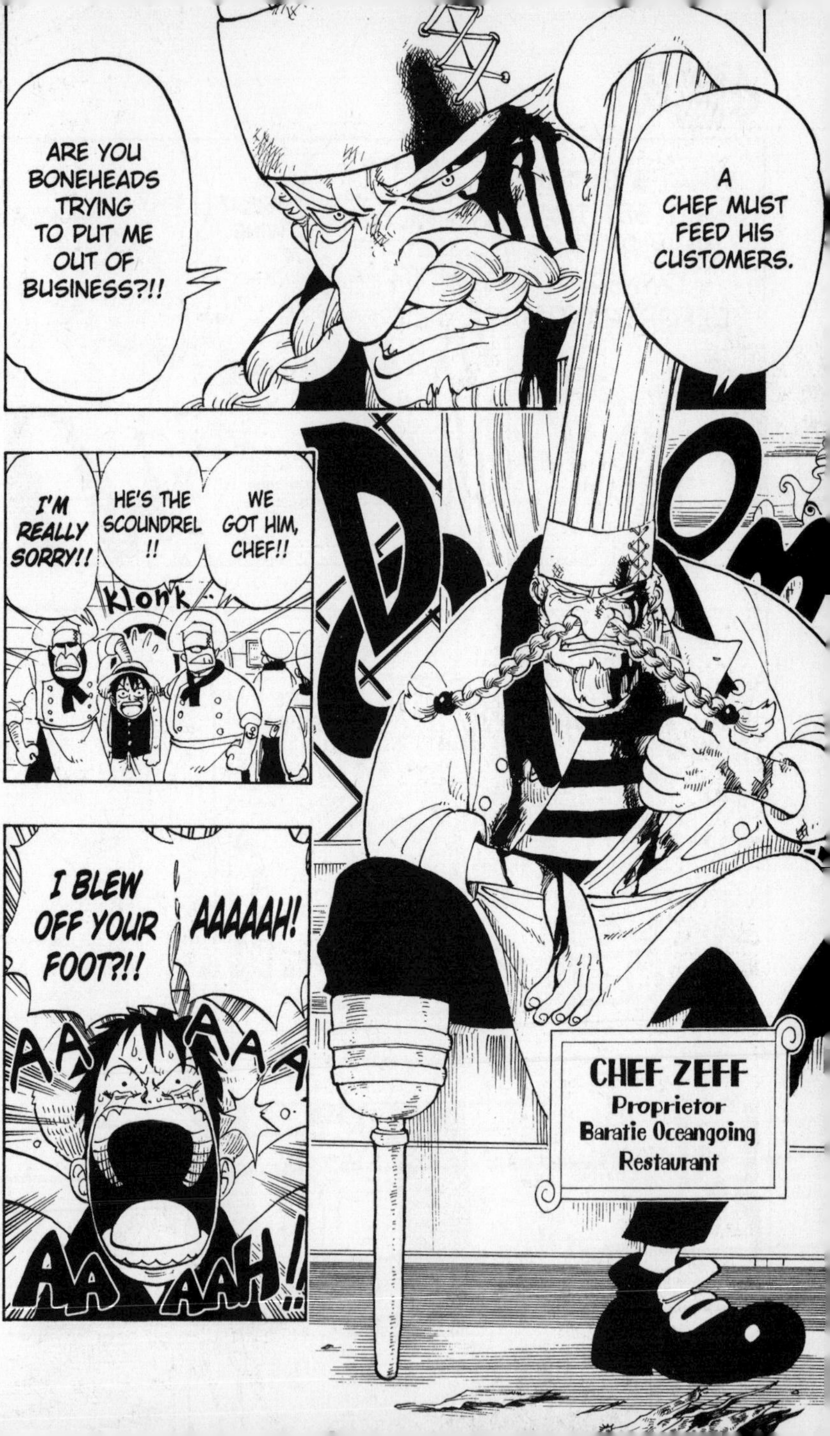
A CHEF MUST FEED HIS CUSTOMERS.
ARE YOU BONEHEADS TRYING TO PUT ME OUT OF BUSINESS?!!
DOOM
CHEF ZEFF
Proprietor
Baratie Oceangoing Restaurant
WE GOT HIM, CHEF!!
HE'S THE SCOUNDREL !!
I'M REALLY SORRY!!
Klonk
AAAAAH!
I BLEW OFF YOUR FOOT?!!
AAAAAAAAAH!!

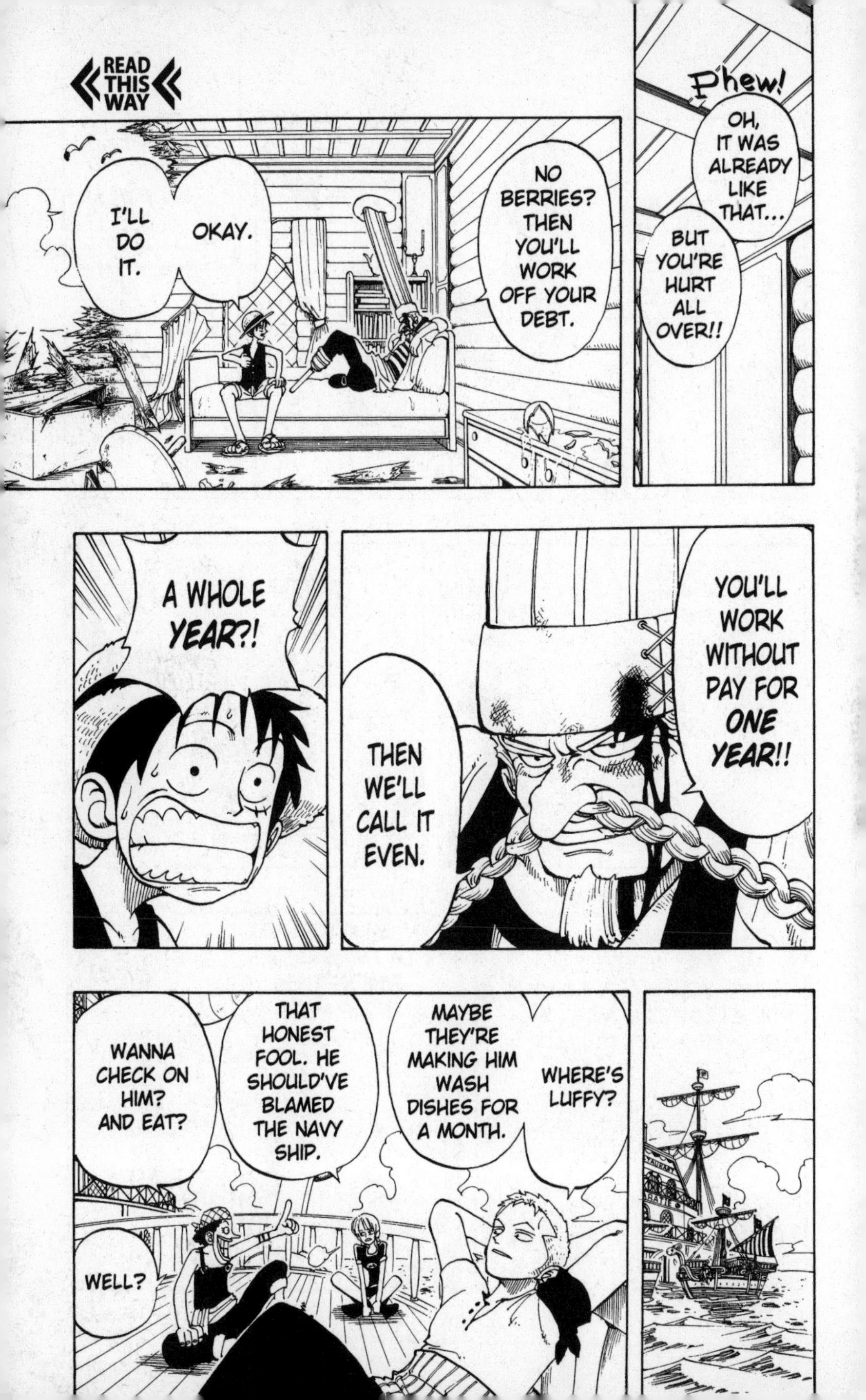
READ THIS WAY
Phew!
OH, IT WAS ALREADY LIKE THAT...
BUT YOU'RE HURT ALL OVER!!
NO BERRIES? THEN YOU'LL WORK OFF YOUR DEBT.
OKAY.
I'LL DO IT.
YOU'LL WORK WITHOUT PAY FOR ONE YEAR!!
THEN WE'LL CALL IT EVEN.
A WHOLE YEAR?!
WHERE'S LUFFY?
MAYBE THEY'RE MAKING HIM WASH DISHES FOR A MONTH.
THAT HONEST FOOL. HE SHOULD'VE BLAMED THE NAVY SHIP.
WANNA CHECK ON HIM? AND EAT?
WELL?

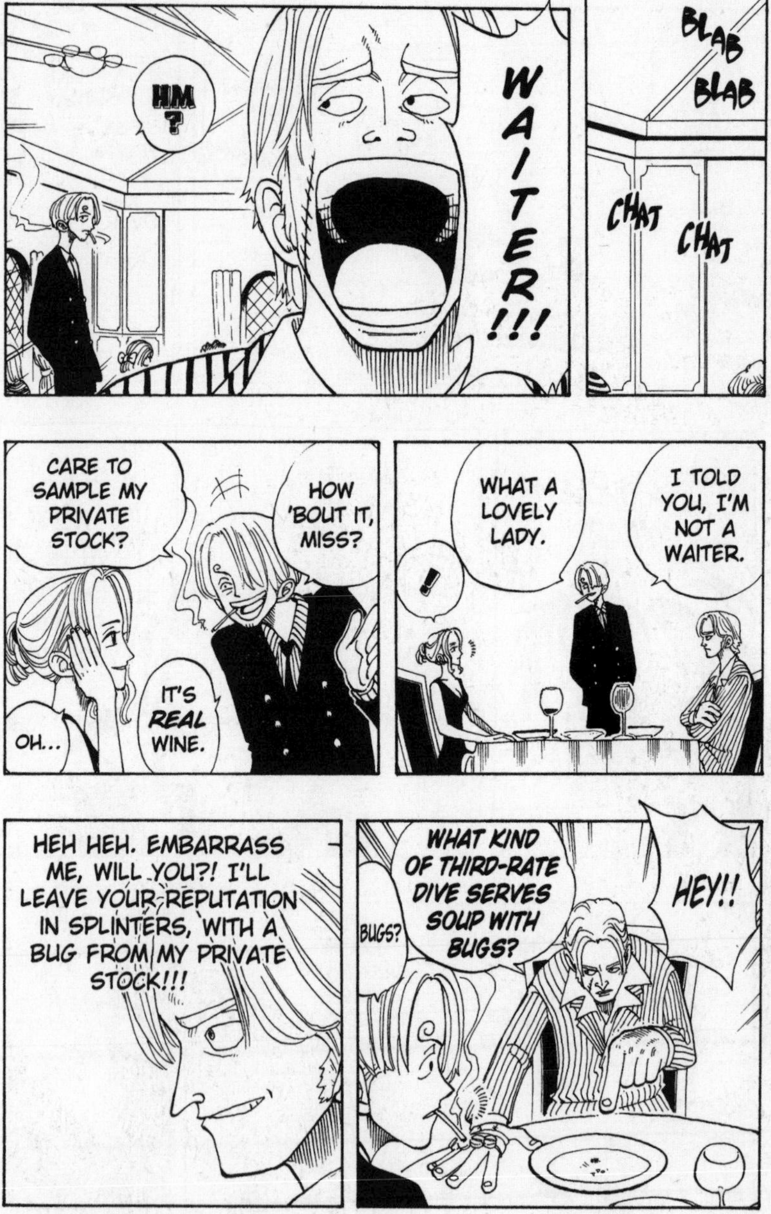
BLAB BLAB
CHAT CHAT
WAITER!!!
HM?
I TOLD YOU, I'M NOT A WAITER.
WHAT A LOVELY LADY.
!
HOW 'BOUT IT, MISS?
CARE TO SAMPLE MY PRIVATE STOCK?
IT'S REAL WINE.
OH...
HEY!!
WHAT KIND OF THIRD-RATE DIVE SERVES SOUP WITH BUGS?
BUGS?
HEH HEH. EMBARRASS ME, WILL YOU?! I'LL LEAVE YOUR REPUTATION IN SPLINTERS, WITH A BUG FROM MY PRIVATE STOCK!!!

READ THIS WAY

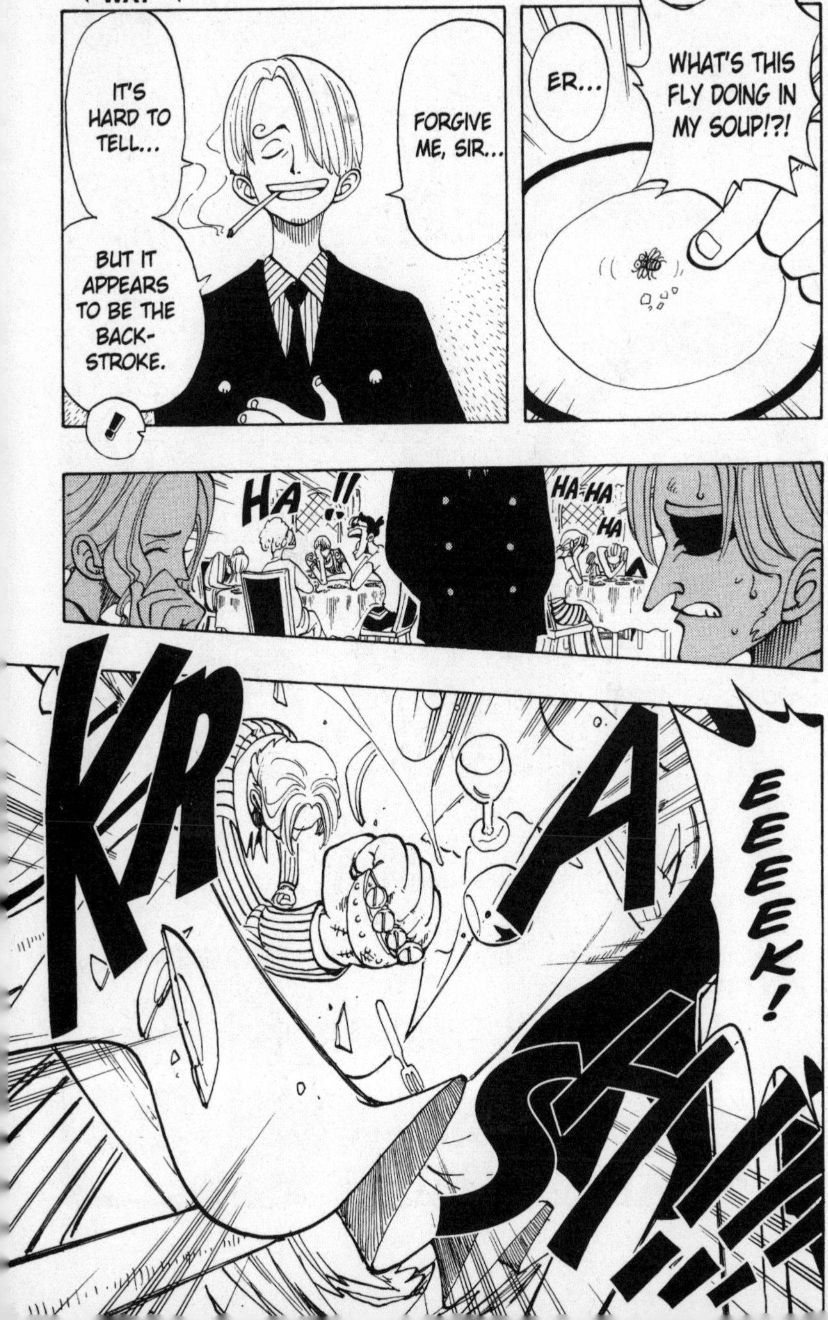
WHAT'S THIS FLY DOING IN MY SOUP!?!
ER...
FORGIVE ME, SIR...
IT'S HARD TO TELL...
BUT IT APPEARS TO BE THE BACK-STROKE.
!
HA HA HA
HA!!
KRASH!!!
EEEEEK!

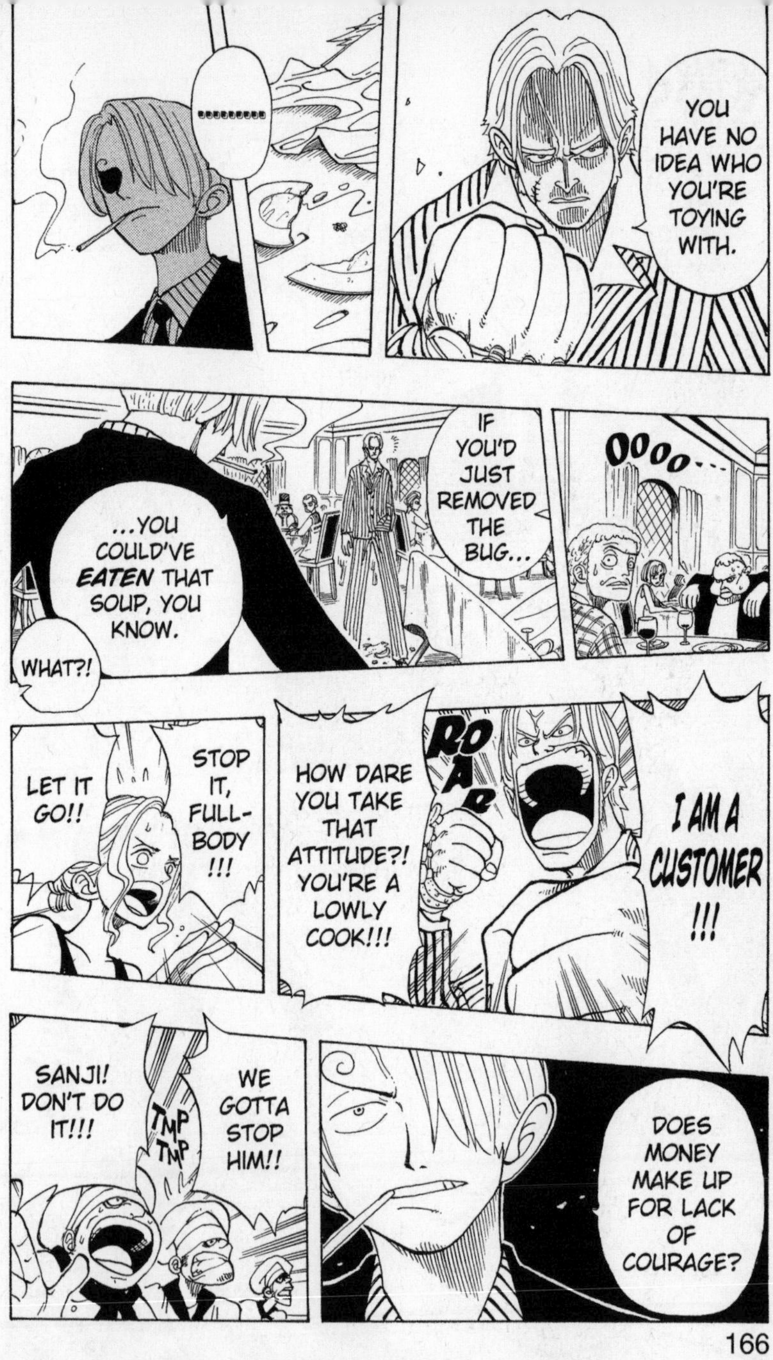
YOU HAVE NO IDEA WHO YOU'RE TOYING WITH.
....
OOOO---
IF YOU'D JUST REMOVED THE BUG...
...YOU COULD'VE EATEN THAT SOUP, YOU KNOW.
WHAT?!
I AM A CUSTOMER!!!
ROAR
HOW DARE YOU TAKE THAT ATTITUDE?! YOU'RE A LOWLY COOK!!!
STOP IT, FULL-BODY!!!
LET IT GO!!
DOES MONEY MAKE UP FOR LACK OF COURAGE?
WE GOTTA STOP HIM!!
TMP TMP
SANJI! DON'T DO IT!!!

READ THIS WAY

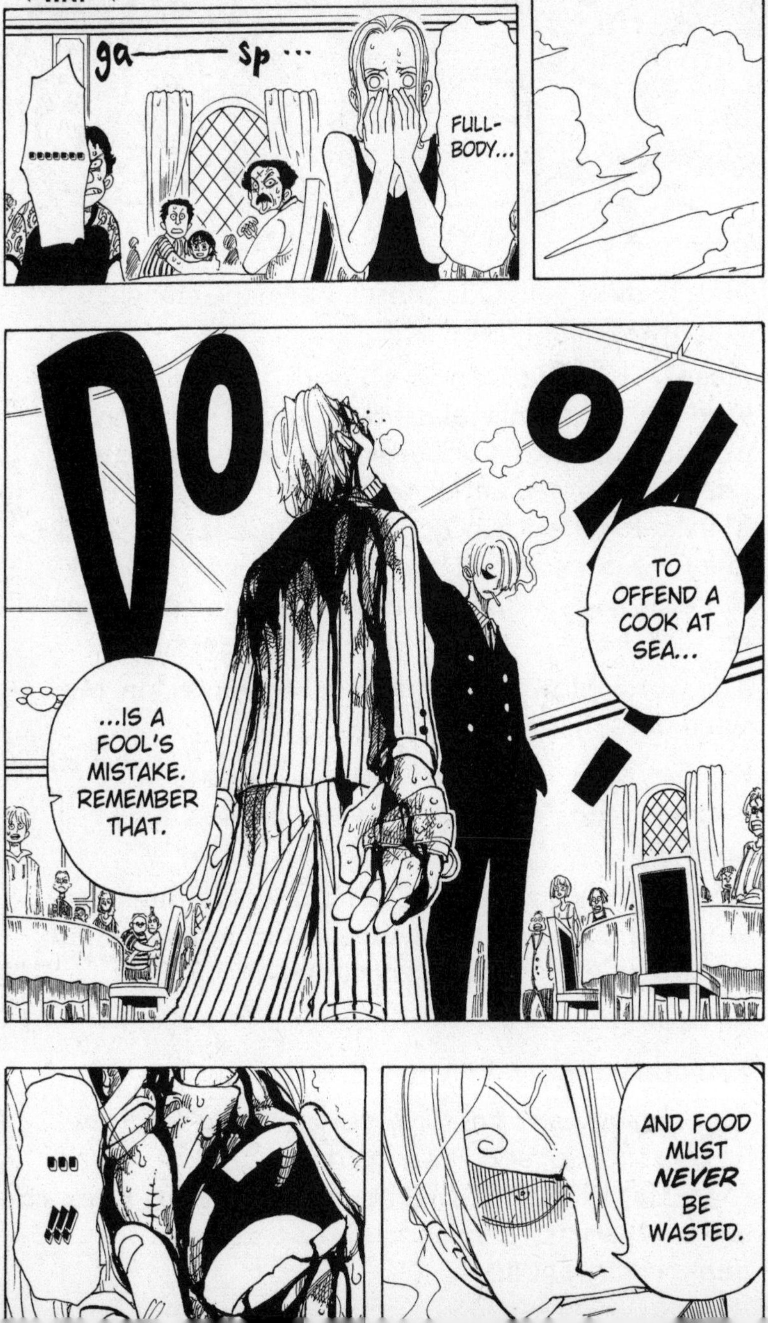
ga——sp ...
FULL-BODY...
......
DOOM!
TO OFFEND A COOK AT SEA...
...IS A FOOL'S MISTAKE. REMEMBER THAT.
AND FOOD MUST NEVER BE WASTED.
...
!!!

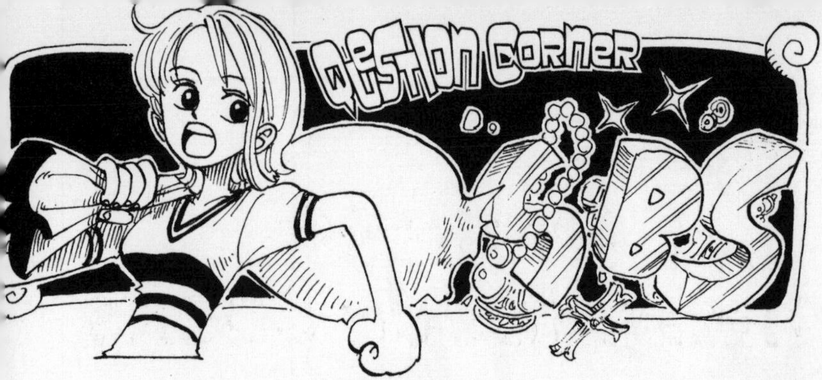
QUESTION CORNER
SBS

D: Nice to meet you, Oda Sensei. I love the manga you draw, called "NEP ECE."

O: Aaagh! It's been done to me!! I just love the kind of word mistakes that young girls and boys make. But I understand. How could you read such strange letters? The "O" and the "I" in the title logo don't look like letters, do they? Sorry about the funny design. What it really says is "ONE PIECE." You pronounce it "wan peesu." If you have time, learn it.

D: The word "Möwe" is printed on Morgan's chin, but what does that mean?

O: It's German. It means "Seagull" and is pronounced, "mee-be." After all, he's a seaman.

D: About Zolo's three sword style…I would think you wouldn't be able to talk with a sword in your mouth. By any chance…is he a ventriloquist?

O: Fine spirit.

D: You don't use Zipatone much. Is there some reason?

O: Once you start pasting tone, there's no end. It takes time, and it's a ~~pain in the~~…
My policy is that it's better to go with black and white than to just partially use tones.
Yeah, it's my policy.

Chapter 44:
THREE TOUGH COOKS

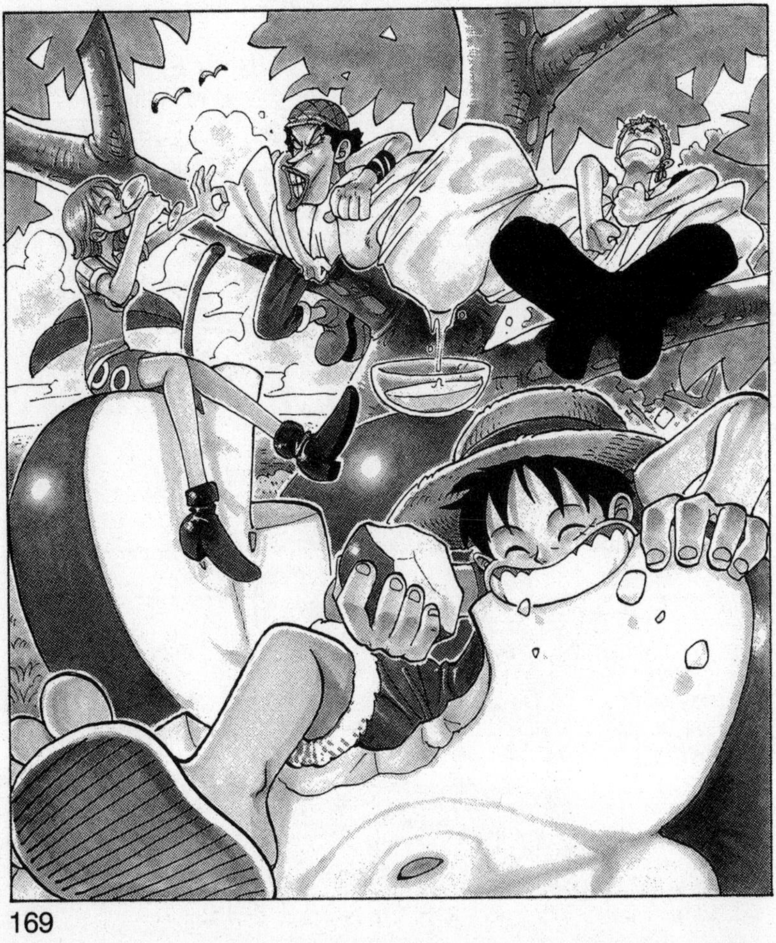

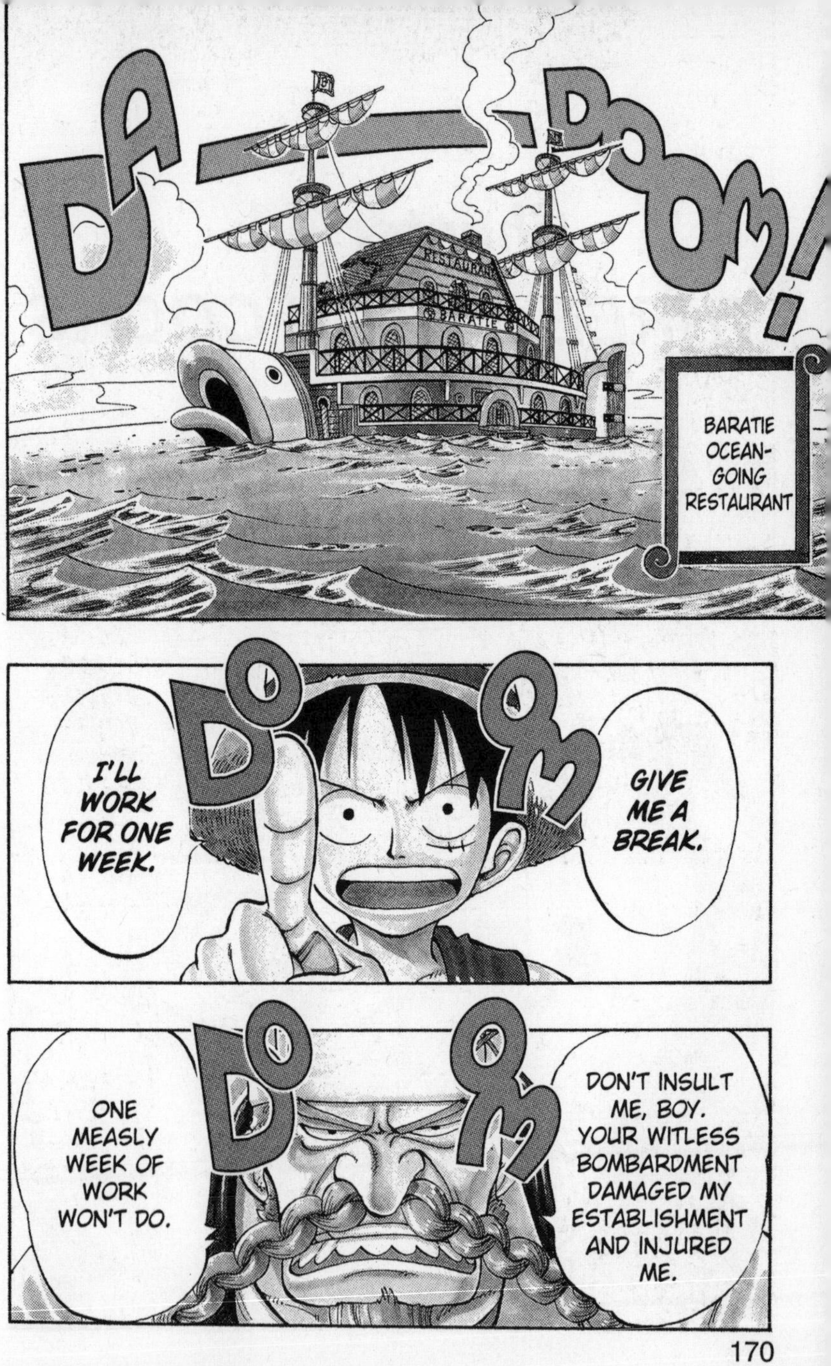
DA——DOOM!
BARATIE OCEAN-GOING RESTAURANT
DOOM
GIVE ME A BREAK.
I'LL WORK FOR ONE WEEK.
DOOM
DON'T INSULT ME, BOY. YOUR WITLESS BOMBARDMENT DAMAGED MY ESTABLISHMENT AND INJURED ME.
ONE MEASLY WEEK OF WORK WON'T DO.

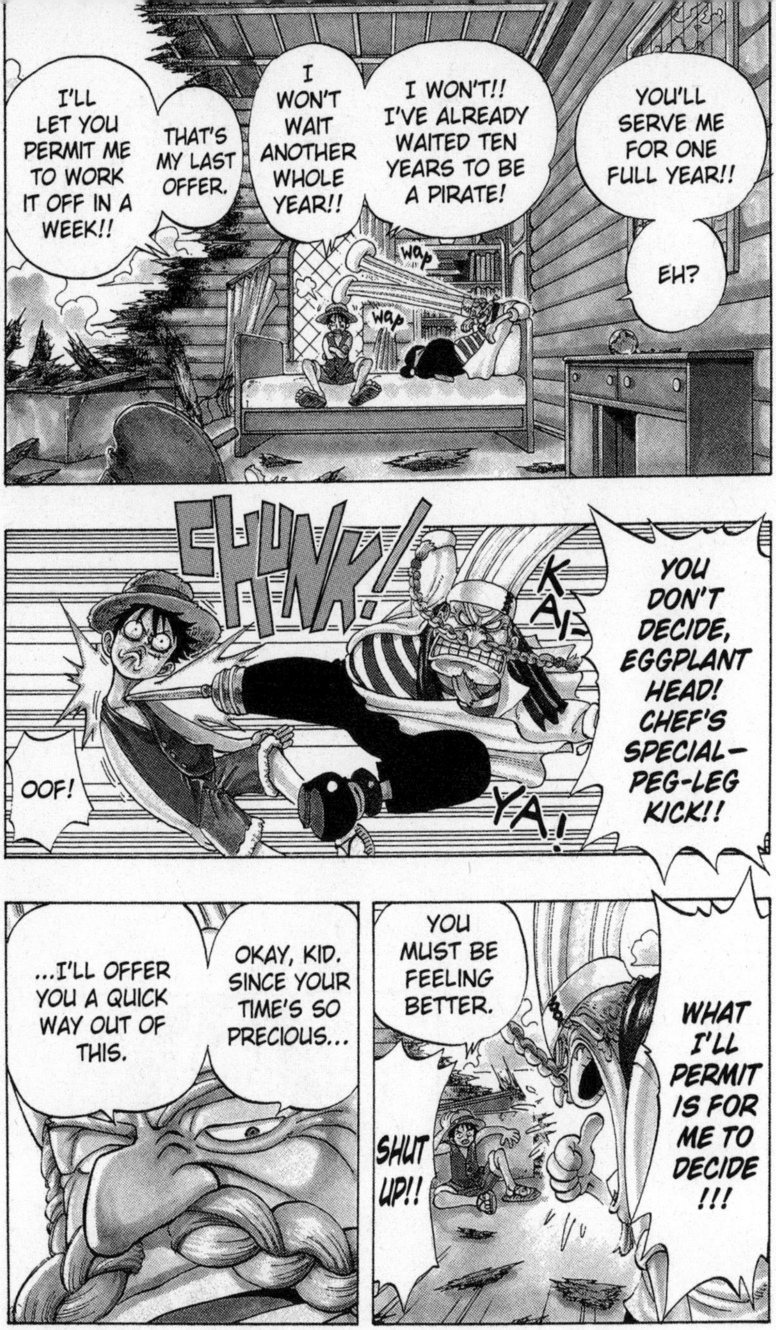
YOU'LL SERVE ME FOR ONE FULL YEAR!!
EH?
I WON'T!! I'VE ALREADY WAITED TEN YEARS TO BE A PIRATE!
I WON'T WAIT ANOTHER WHOLE YEAR!!
WAP
WAP
THAT'S MY LAST OFFER.
I'LL LET YOU PERMIT ME TO WORK IT OFF IN A WEEK!!
YOU DON'T DECIDE, EGGPLANT HEAD! CHEF'S SPECIAL—PEG-LEG KICK!!
KAI-
YA!
CHUNK!
OOF!
WHAT I'LL PERMIT IS FOR ME TO DECIDE!!!
SHUT UP!!
YOU MUST BE FEELING BETTER.
OKAY, KID. SINCE YOUR TIME'S SO PRECIOUS...
...I'LL OFFER YOU A QUICK WAY OUT OF THIS.

READ THIS WAY

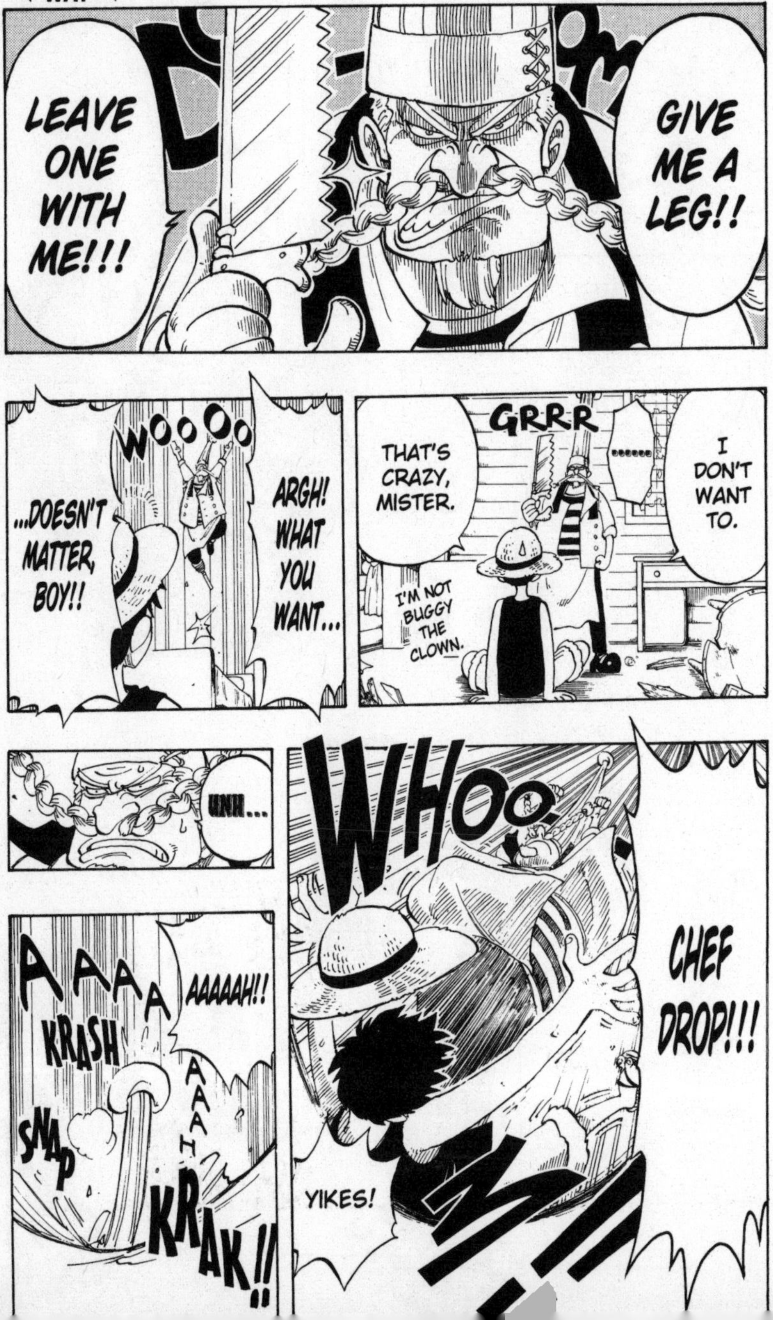
GIVE ME A LEG!!
LEAVE ONE WITH ME!!!
I DON'T WANT TO.
......
GRRR
THAT'S CRAZY, MISTER.
I'M NOT BUGGY THE CLOWN.
ARGH! WHAT YOU WANT...
WOOOO
...DOESN'T MATTER, BOY!!
WHOO-
CHEF DROP!!!
YIKES!
UNH...
AAAAAH!!
AAAA
KRASH
AAAH
SNAP
KRAK!!

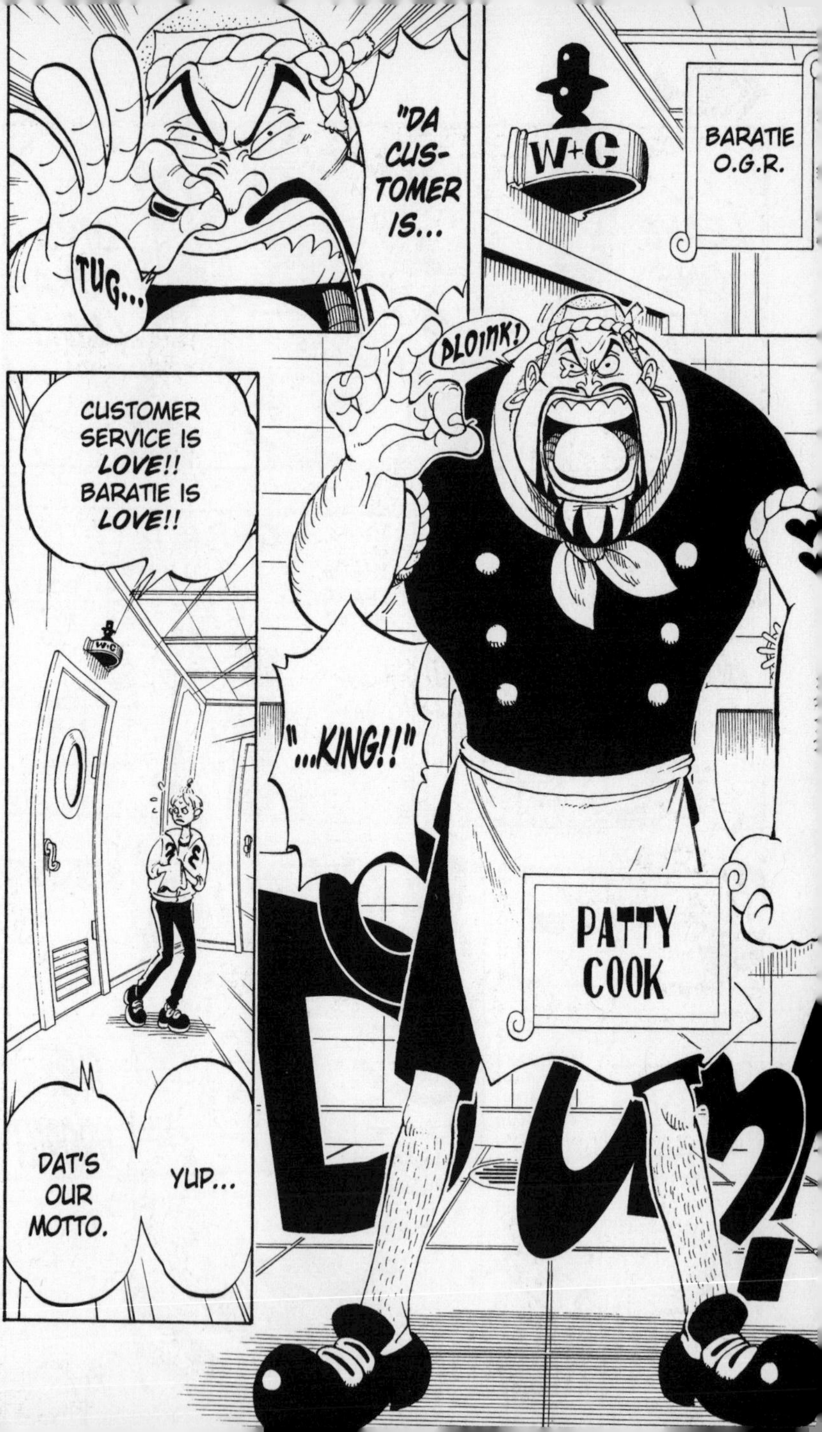
W+C
BARATIE O.G.R.
"DA CUSTOMER IS...
TUG...
PLOINK!
"...KING!!"
PATTY COOK
CUSTOMER SERVICE IS LOVE!! BARATIE IS LOVE!!
YUP...
DAT'S OUR MOTTO.

READ THIS WAY

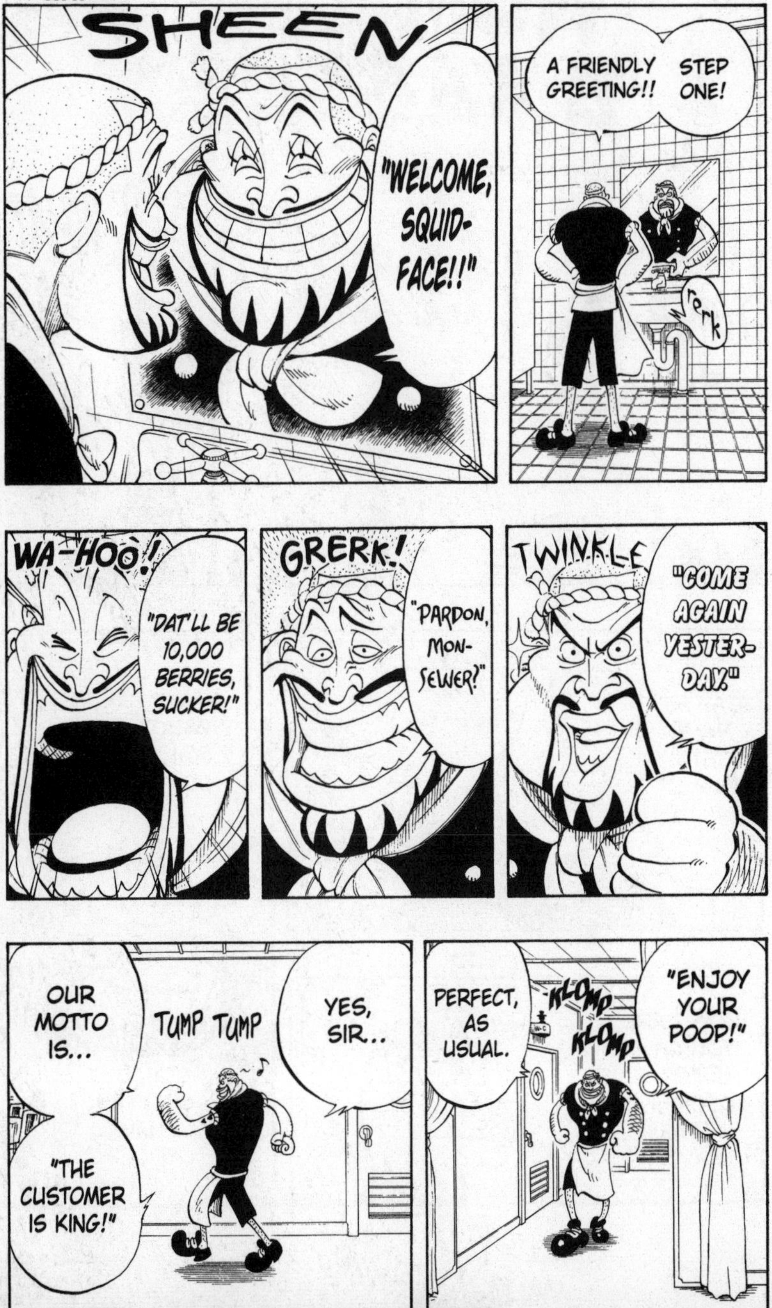
STEP ONE!
A FRIENDLY GREETING!!
rerk
SHEEN
"WELCOME, SQUID-FACE!!"
TWINKLE
"COME AGAIN YESTER-DAY."
GRERK!
"PARDON, MON-SEWER?"
WA-HOO!
"DAT'LL BE 10,000 BERRIES, SUCKER!"
"ENJOY YOUR POOP!"
KLOMP
KLOMP
PERFECT, AS USUAL.
YES, SIR...
TUMP TUMP
OUR MOTTO IS...
"THE CUSTOMER IS KING!"

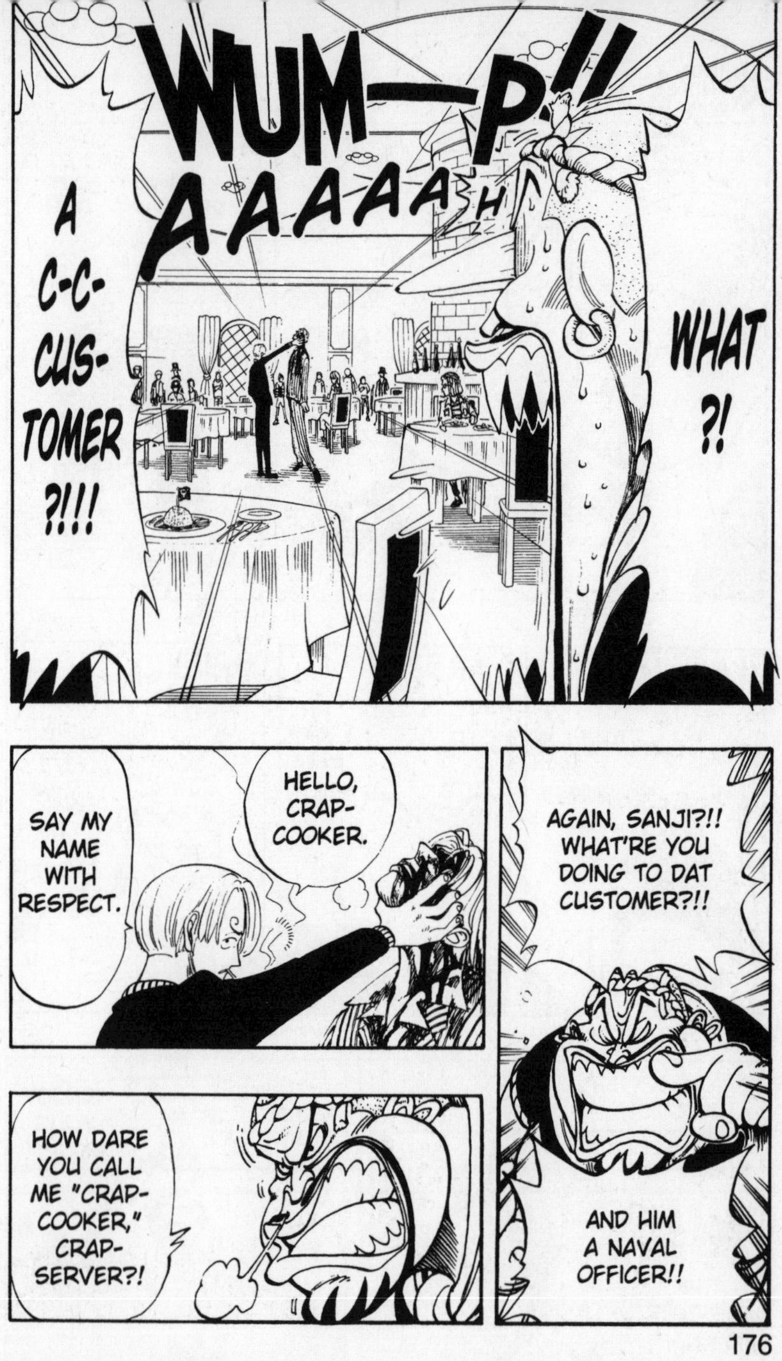
WUM-P!!
AAAAAH
WHAT?!
A C-C-CUSTOMER?!!!
AGAIN, SANJI?!! WHAT'RE YOU DOING TO DAT CUSTOMER?!!
AND HIM A NAVAL OFFICER!!
HELLO, CRAP-COOKER.
SAY MY NAME WITH RESPECT.
HOW DARE YOU CALL ME "CRAP-COOKER," CRAP-SERVER?!

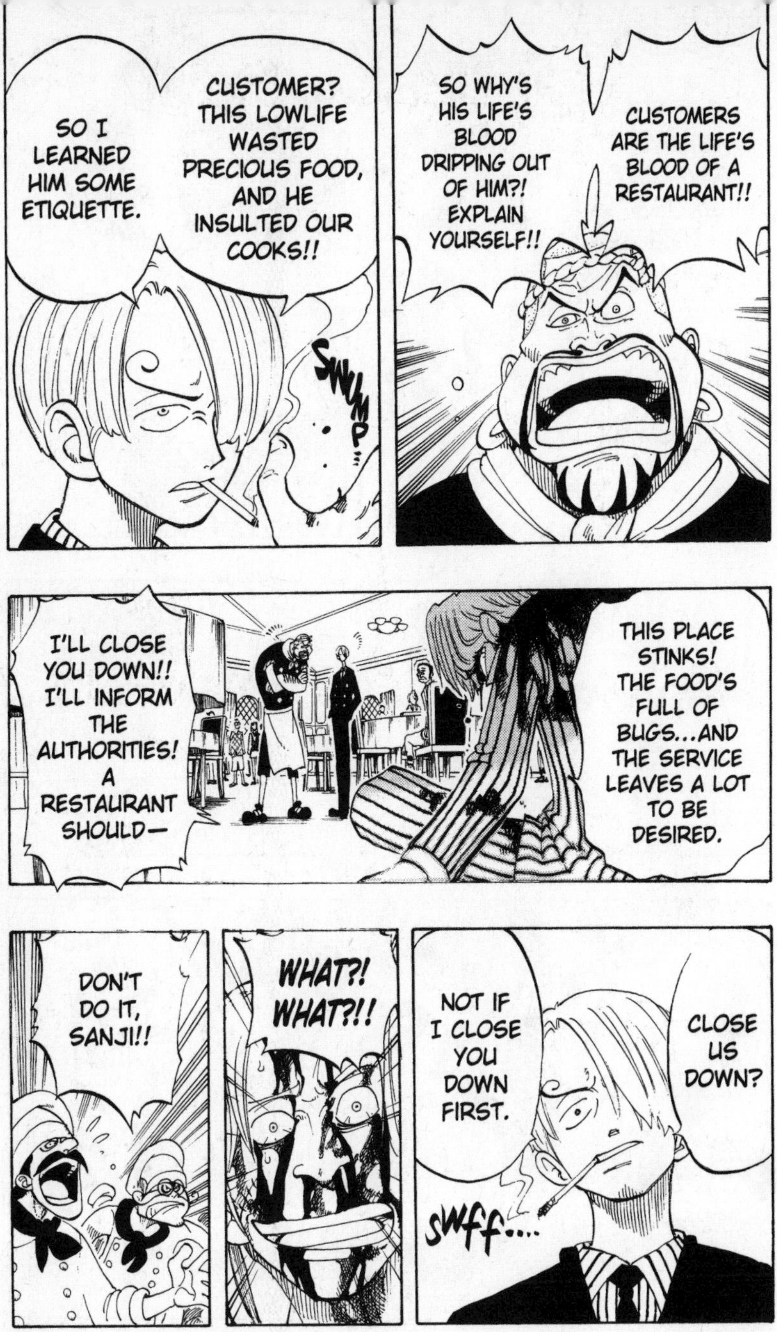
CUSTOMERS ARE THE LIFE'S BLOOD OF A RESTAURANT!!
SO WHY'S HIS LIFE'S BLOOD DRIPPING OUT OF HIM?! EXPLAIN YOURSELF!!
CUSTOMER? THIS LOWLIFE WASTED PRECIOUS FOOD, AND HE INSULTED OUR COOKS!!
SO I LEARNED HIM SOME ETIQUETTE.
SWUMP
THIS PLACE STINKS! THE FOOD'S FULL OF BUGS...AND THE SERVICE LEAVES A LOT TO BE DESIRED.
I'LL CLOSE YOU DOWN!! I'LL INFORM THE AUTHORITIES! A RESTAURANT SHOULD—
CLOSE US DOWN?
NOT IF I CLOSE YOU DOWN FIRST.
SWFF....
WHAT?! WHAT?!!
DON'T DO IT, SANJI!!

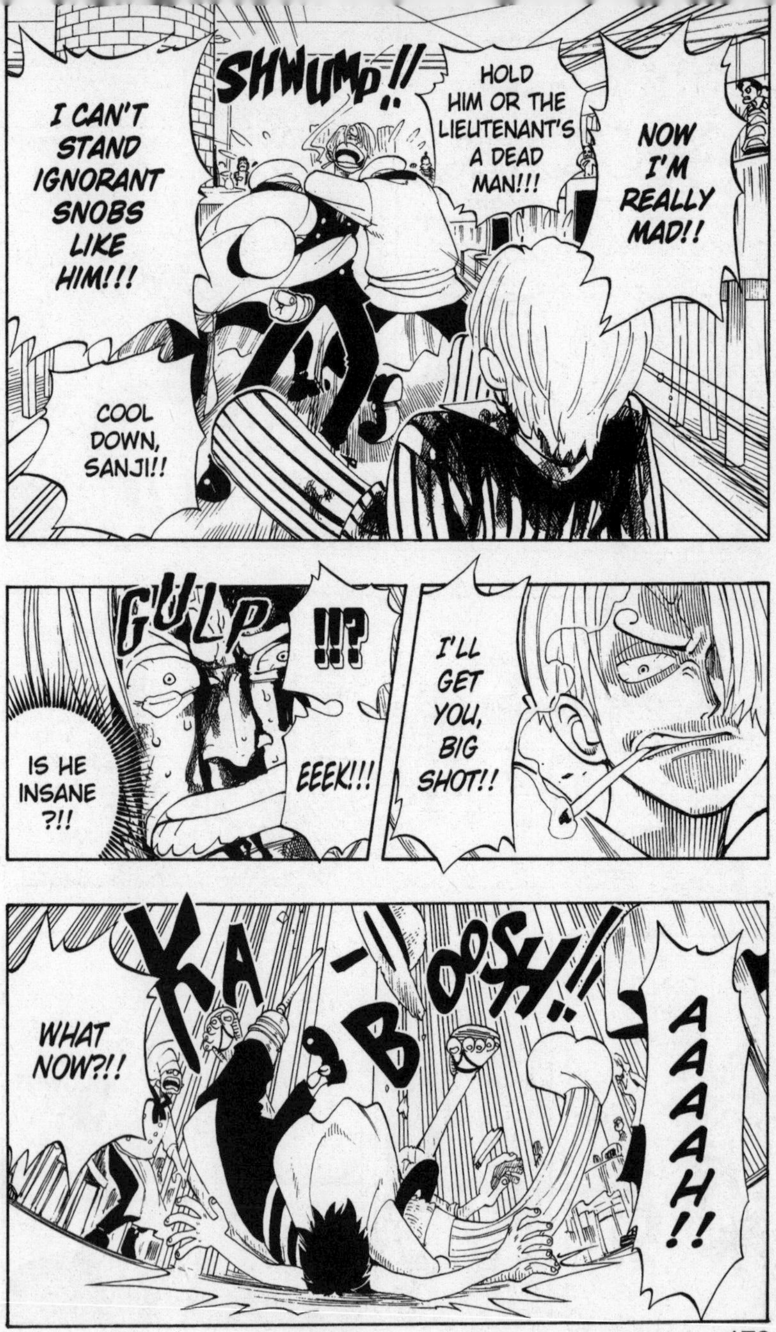
NOW I'M REALLY MAD!!
HOLD HIM OR THE LIEUTENANT'S A DEAD MAN!!!
SHWUMP!!
I CAN'T STAND IGNORANT SNOBS LIKE HIM!!!
COOL DOWN, SANJI!!
I'LL GET YOU, BIG SHOT!!
!!?
GULP
EEEK!!!
IS HE INSANE?!!
AAAAAH!!
KA-BOOSH!!
WHAT NOW?!!

READ THIS WAY

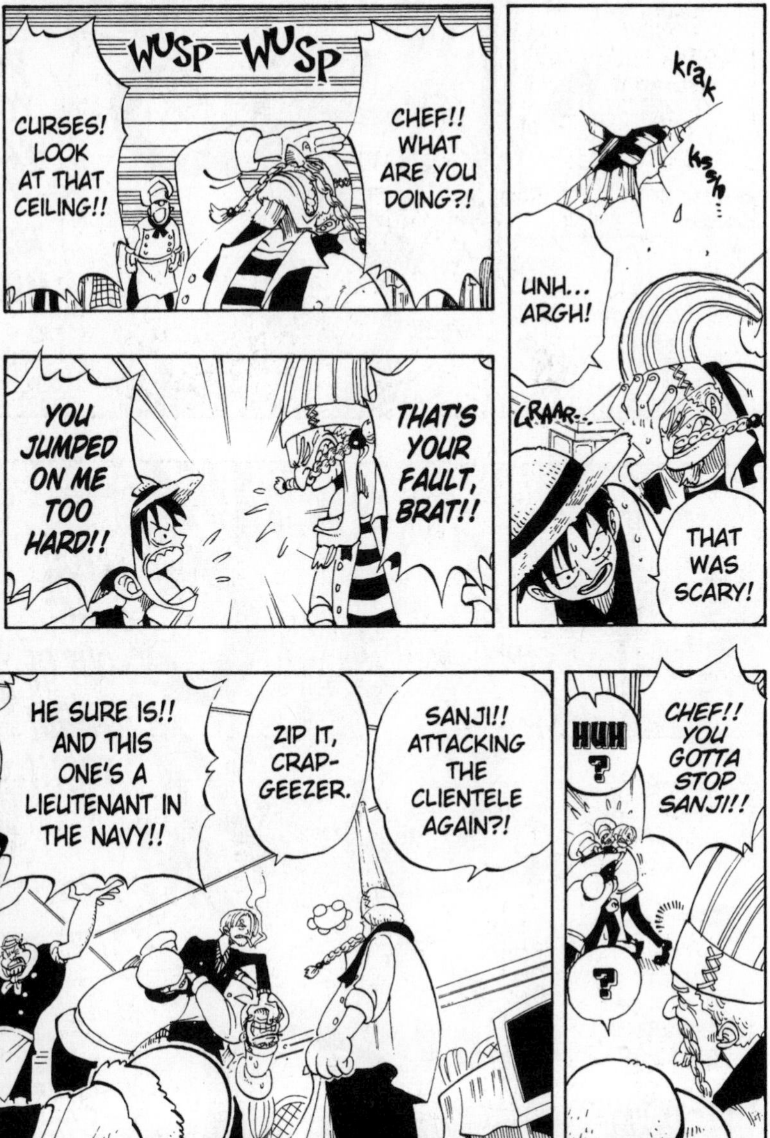
krak
kssh...
UNH... ARGH!
GRAAR...
THAT WAS SCARY!
WUSP WUSP
CHEF!! WHAT ARE YOU DOING?!
CURSES! LOOK AT THAT CEILING!!
THAT'S YOUR FAULT, BRAT!!
YOU JUMPED ON ME TOO HARD!!
CHEF!! YOU GOTTA STOP SANJI!!
HUH?
?
SANJI!! ATTACKING THE CLIENTELE AGAIN?!
ZIP IT, CRAP-GEEZER.
HE SURE IS!! AND THIS ONE'S A LIEUTENANT IN THE NAVY!!

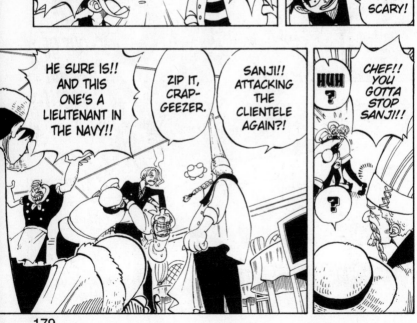

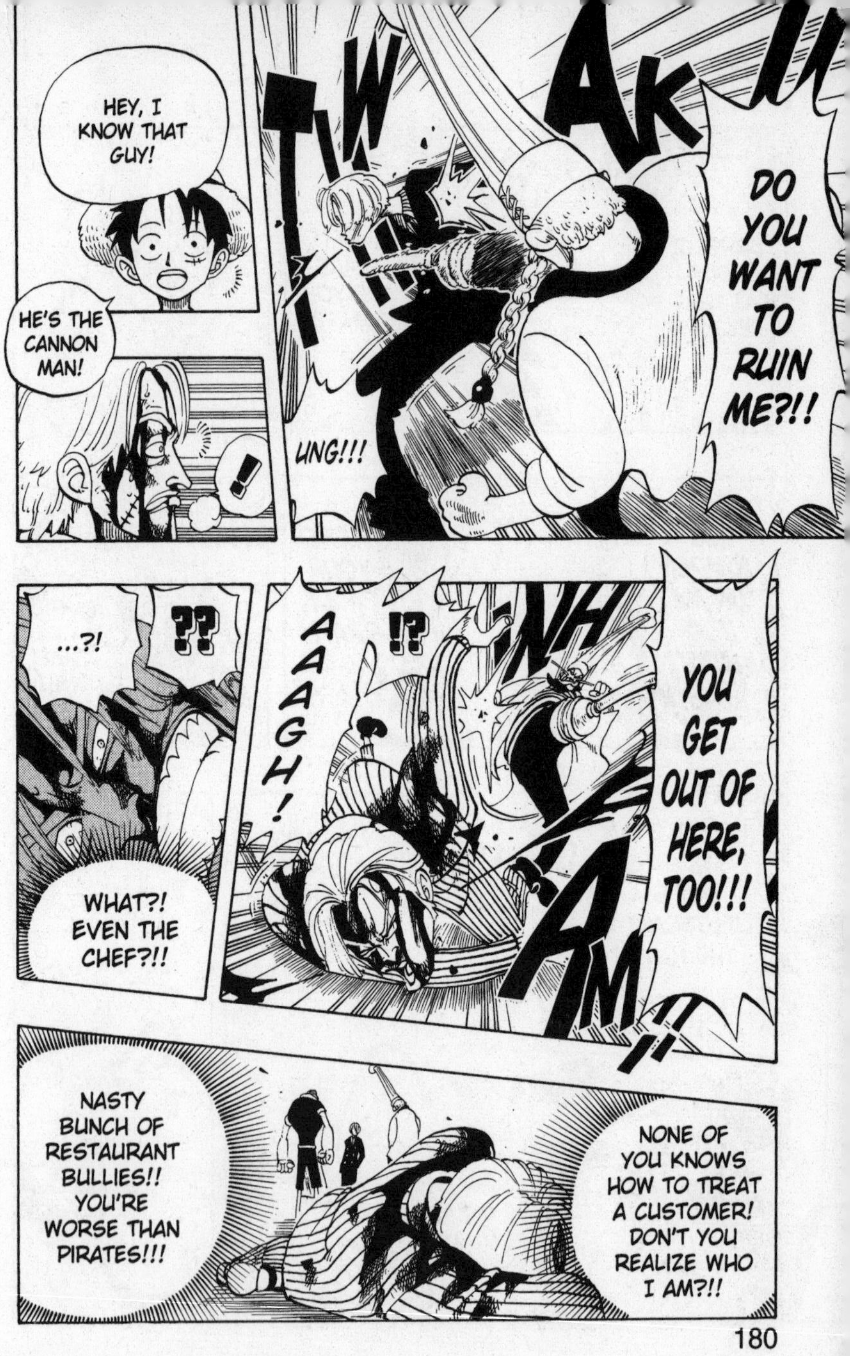
DO YOU WANT TO RUIN ME?!!
UNG!!!
HEY, I KNOW THAT GUY!
HE'S THE CANNON MAN!
!
YOU GET OUT OF HERE, TOO!!!
!?
AAAGH!
??
...?!
WHAT?! EVEN THE CHEF?!!
NONE OF YOU KNOWS HOW TO TREAT A CUSTOMER! DON'T YOU REALIZE WHO I AM?!!
NASTY BUNCH OF RESTAURANT BULLIES!! YOU'RE WORSE THAN PIRATES!!!

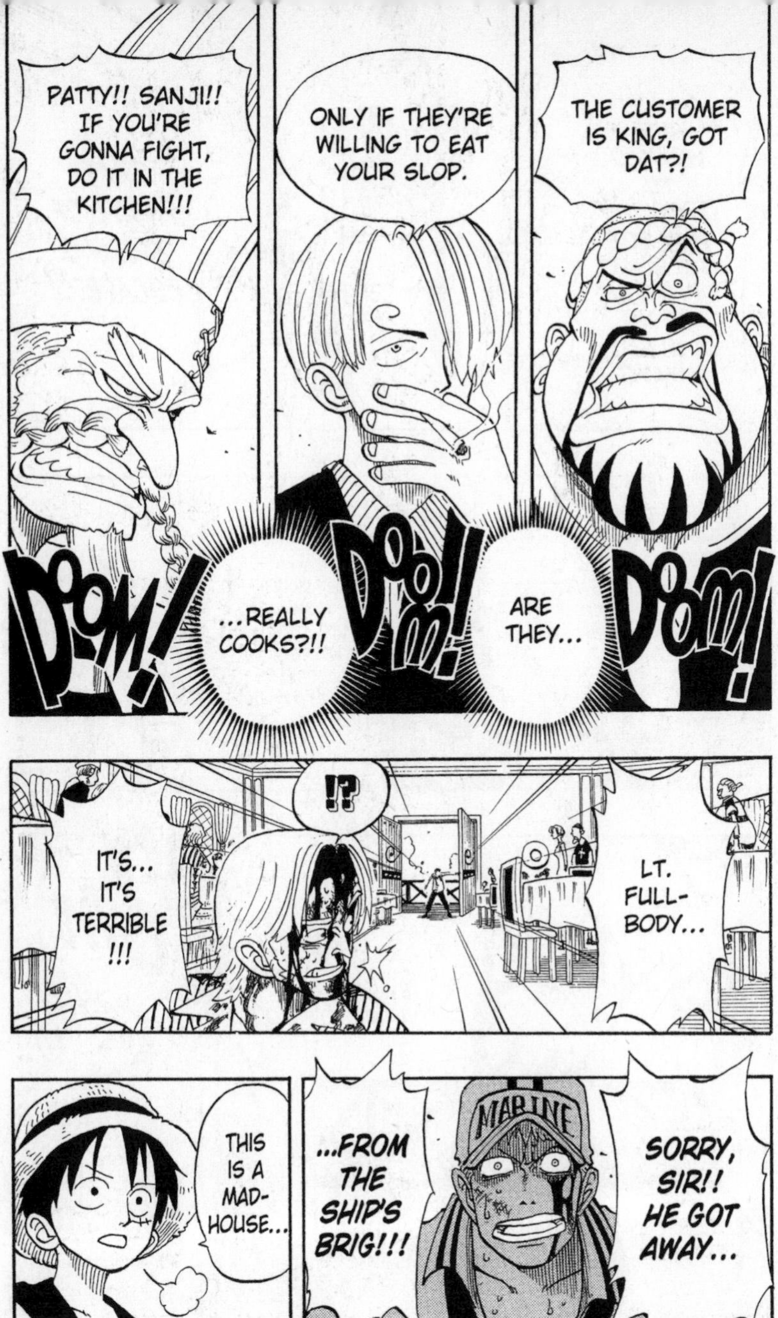
THE CUSTOMER IS KING, GOT DAT?!
ONLY IF THEY'RE WILLING TO EAT YOUR SLOP.
PATTY!! SANJI!! IF YOU'RE GONNA FIGHT, DO IT IN THE KITCHEN!!!
DOOM!
ARE THEY...
DOOM!
...REALLY COOKS?!!
DOOM!
LT. FULL-BODY...
!?
IT'S... IT'S TERRIBLE!!!
SORRY, SIR!! HE GOT AWAY...
...FROM THE SHIP'S BRIG!!!
MARINE
THIS IS A MAD-HOUSE...

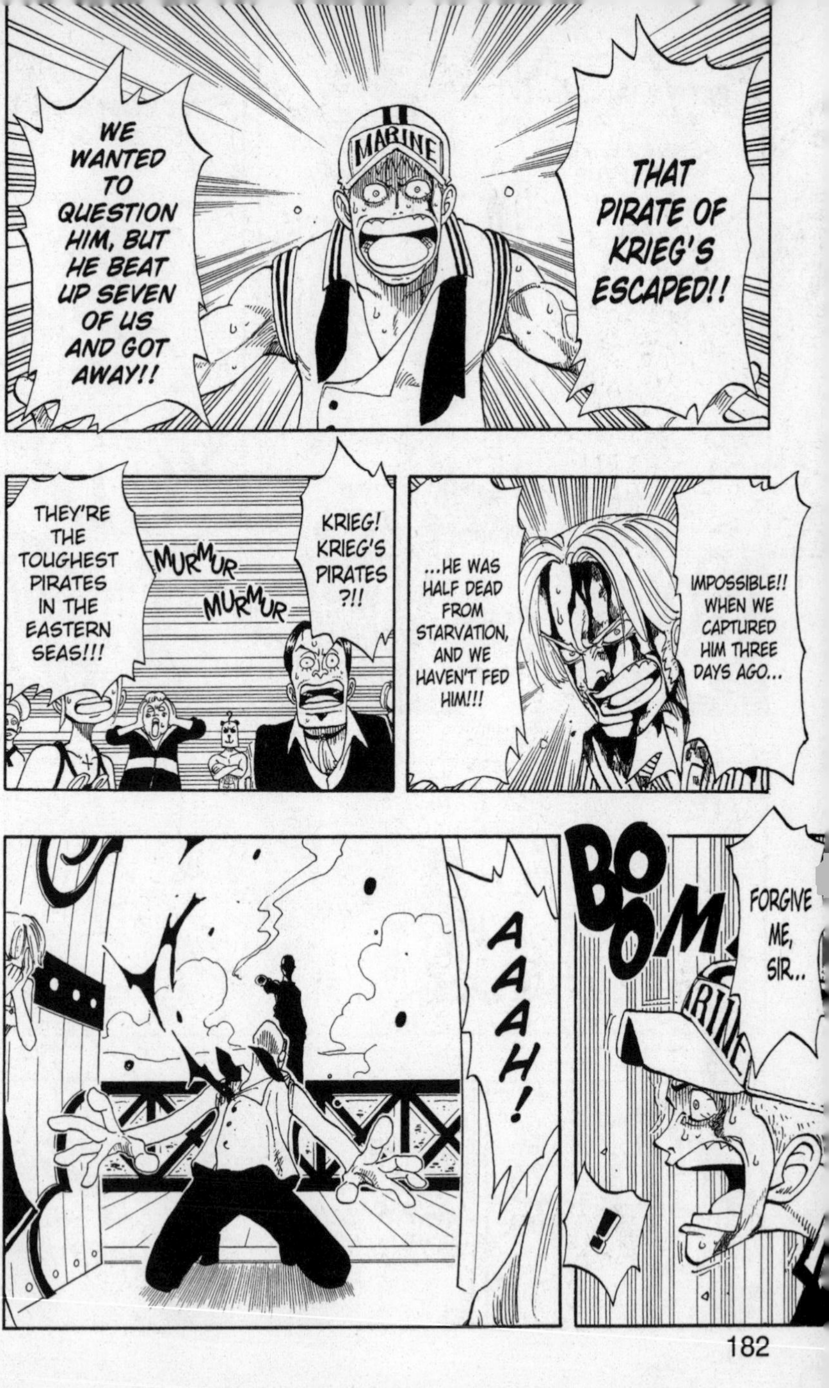
THAT PIRATE OF KRIEG'S ESCAPED!!
WE WANTED TO QUESTION HIM, BUT HE BEAT UP SEVEN OF US AND GOT AWAY!!
IMPOSSIBLE!! WHEN WE CAPTURED HIM THREE DAYS AGO...
...HE WAS HALF DEAD FROM STARVATION, AND WE HAVEN'T FED HIM!!!
KRIEG! KRIEG'S PIRATES?!!
MURMUR
MURMUR
THEY'RE THE TOUGHEST PIRATES IN THE EASTERN SEAS!!!
FORGIVE ME, SIR...
BOOOM
!
AAAAH!

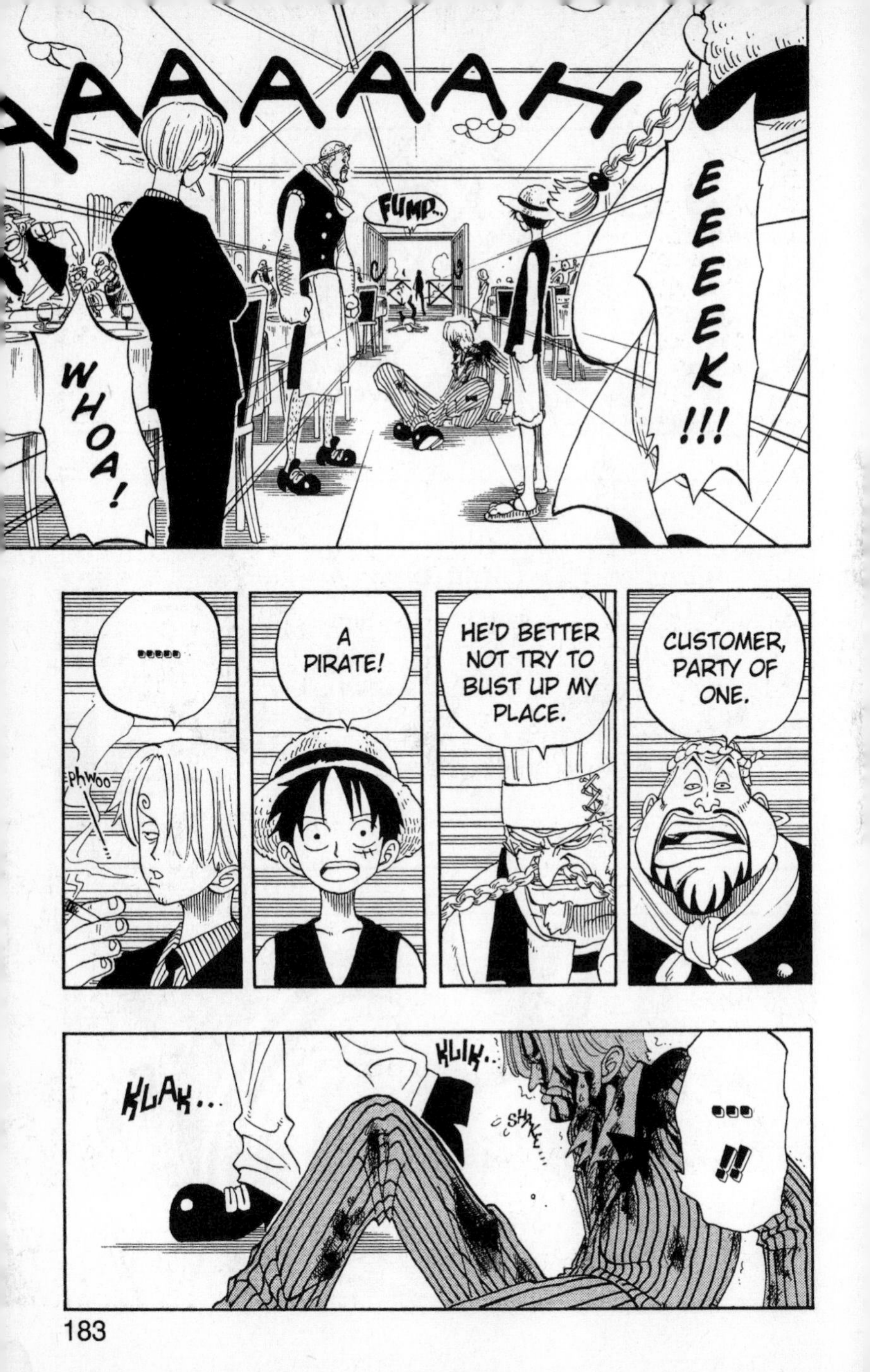
EEEEK!!!
FUMP..
AAAAAAH
WHOA!
CUSTOMER, PARTY OF ONE.
HE'D BETTER NOT TRY TO BUST UP MY PLACE.
A PIRATE!
.....
PHWOO
...!!
SHAKE...
KLIK..
KLAK...

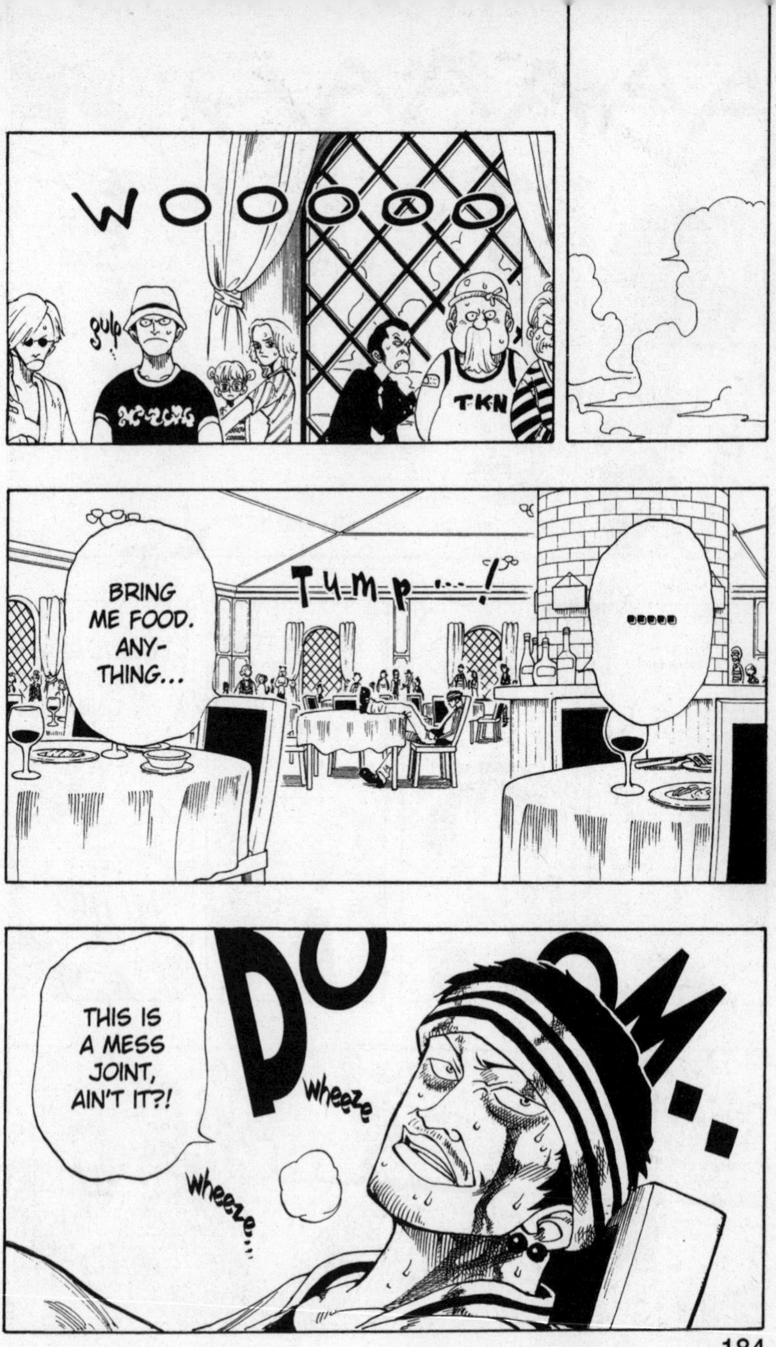
WOOOOO
gulp
TKN
.....
TUMP...!
BRING ME FOOD. ANY-THING...
DOOM..
wheeze
wheeze...
THIS IS A MESS JOINT, AIN'T IT?!

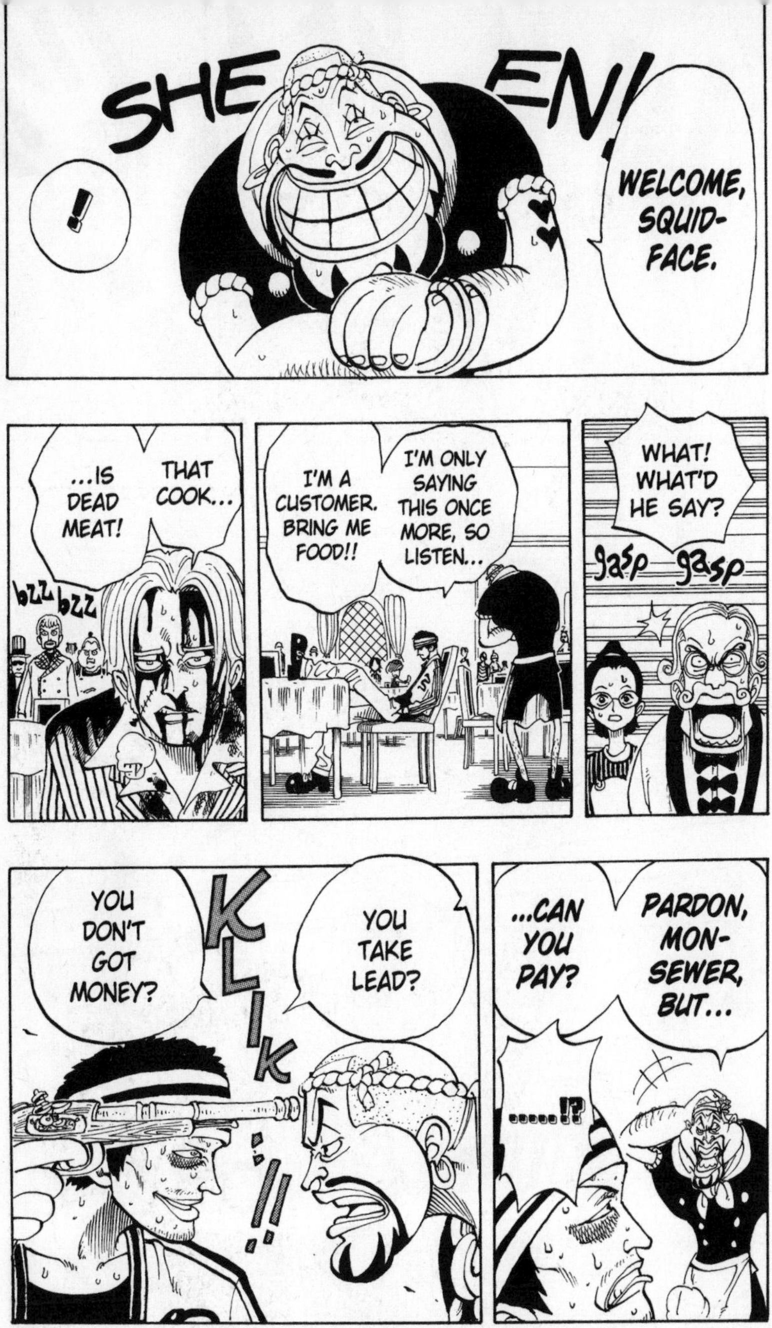
WELCOME, SQUID-FACE.
SHE
EN!
!
WHAT! WHAT'D HE SAY?
gasp gasp
I'M ONLY SAYING THIS ONCE MORE, SO LISTEN...
I'M A CUSTOMER. BRING ME FOOD!!
THAT COOK...
...IS DEAD MEAT!
bzz bzz
PARDON, MON-SEWER, BUT...
...CAN YOU PAY?
.....!?
YOU TAKE LEAD?
KLIK
!!
YOU DON'T GOT MONEY?

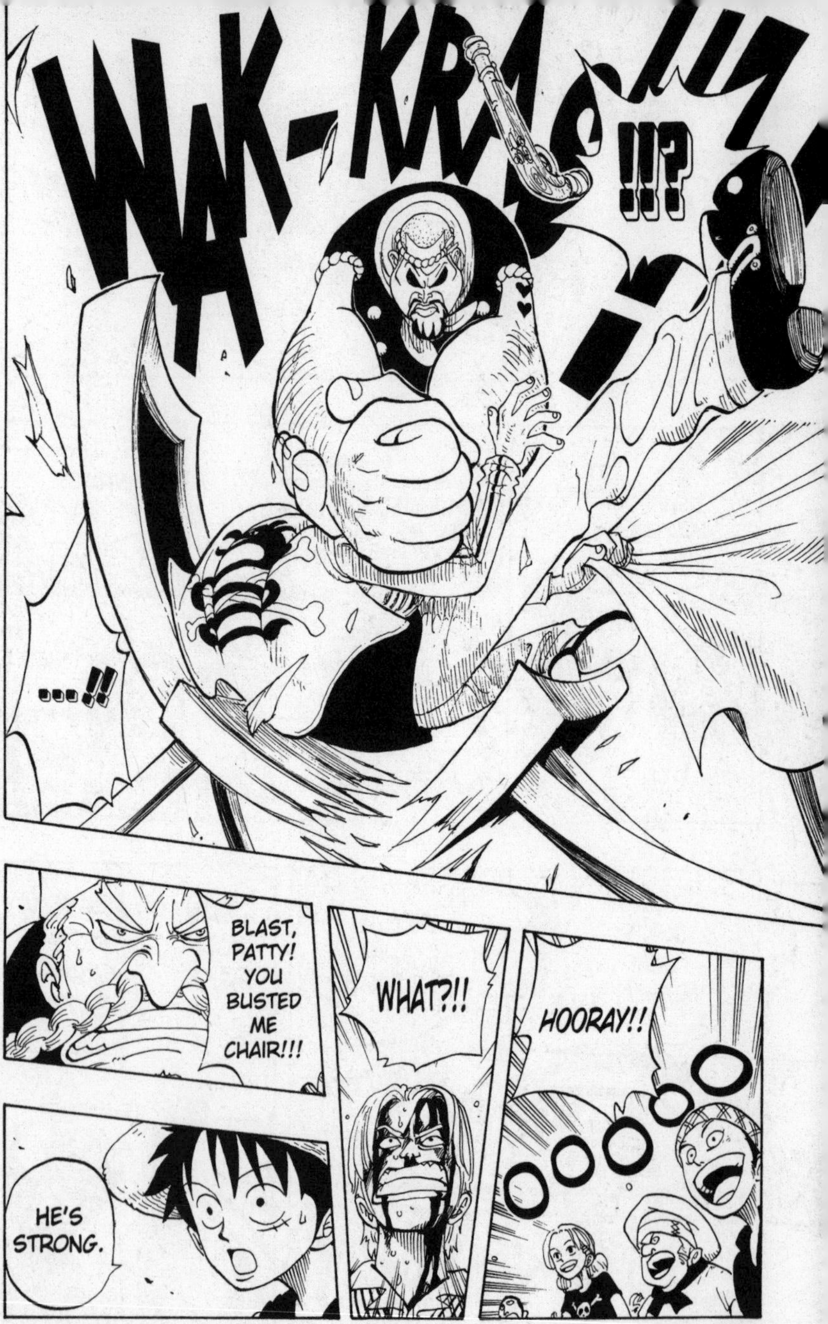
WAK-KRASH!!?
...!!
HOORAY!!
OOOOOO
WHAT?!!
BLAST, PATTY! YOU BUSTED ME CHAIR!!!
HE'S STRONG.

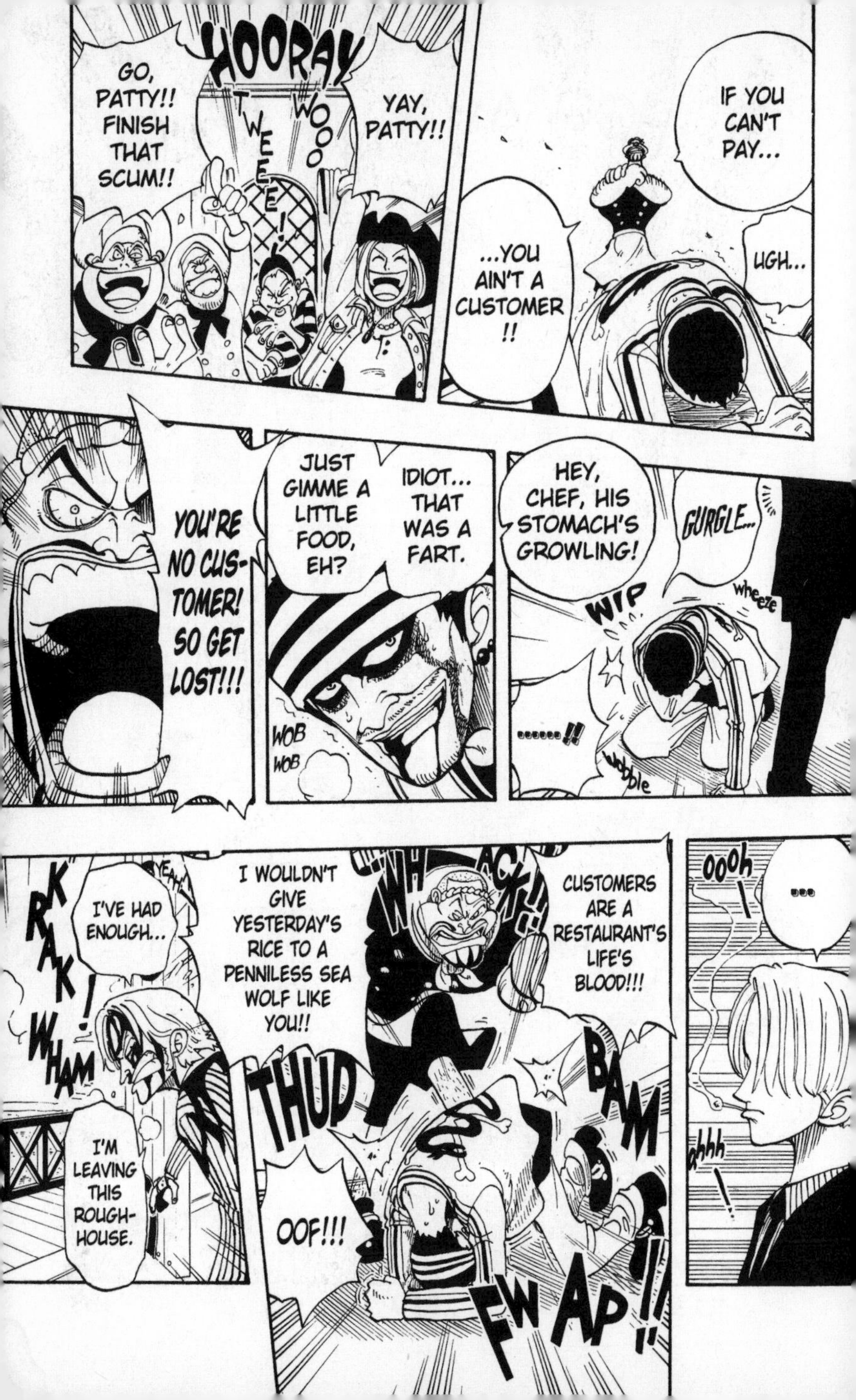
IF YOU CAN'T PAY...
UGH...
...YOU AIN'T A CUSTOMER!!
YAY, PATTY!!
WOOO
HOORAY
TWEEE!
GO, PATTY!! FINISH THAT SCUM!!
GURGLE...
HEY, CHEF, HIS STOMACH'S GROWLING!
WIP
wheeze
......!!
wobble
IDIOT... THAT WAS A FART.
JUST GIMME A LITTLE FOOD, EH?
WOB WOB
YOU'RE NO CUSTOMER! SO GET LOST!!!
...
oooh
ahhh
CUSTOMERS ARE A RESTAURANT'S LIFE'S BLOOD!!!
I WOULDN'T GIVE YESTERDAY'S RICE TO A PENNILESS SEA WOLF LIKE YOU!!
BAM
THUD
OOF!!!
FWAP!!
YEAH!
I'VE HAD ENOUGH...
KRAK!
WHAM
I'M LEAVING THIS ROUGH-HOUSE.

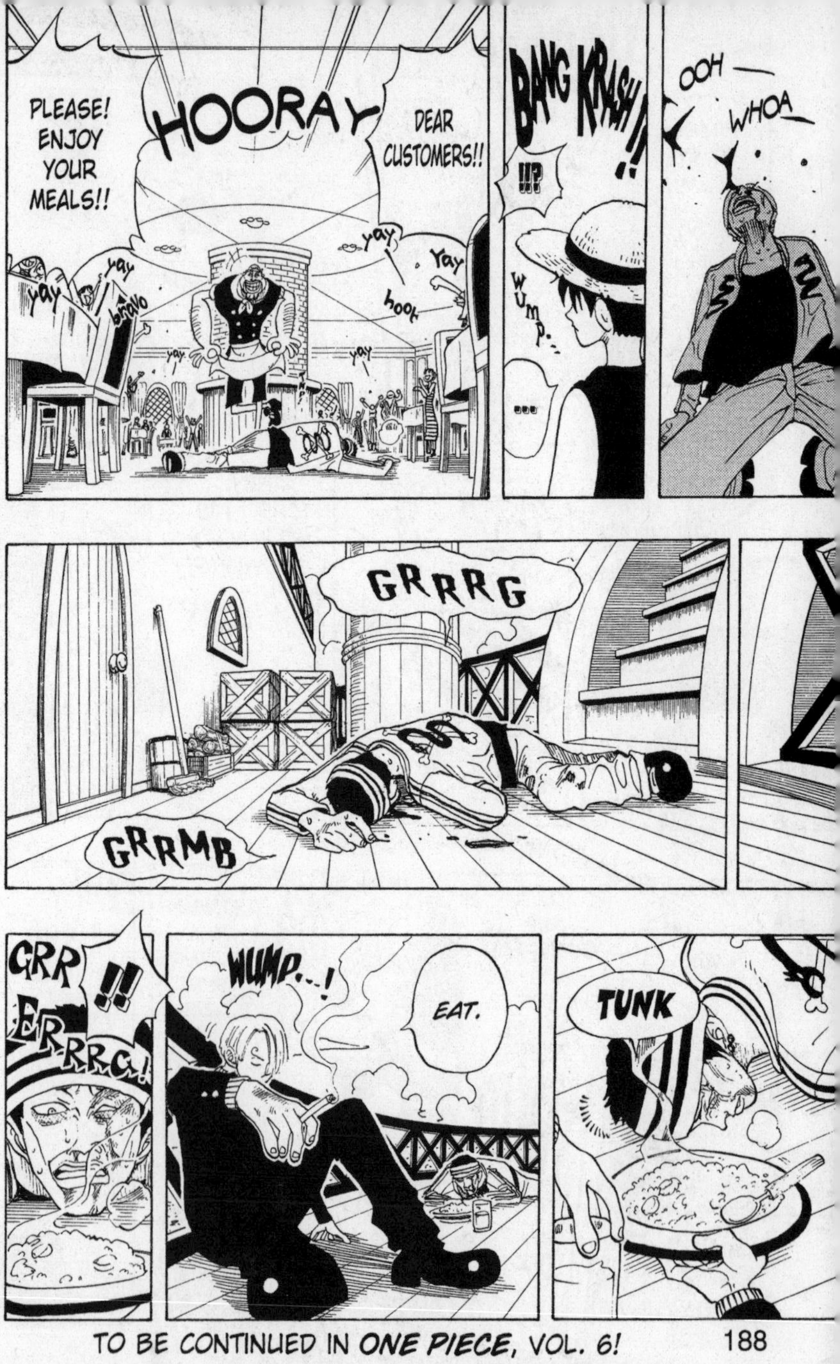
OOH —
WHOA —
BANG KRASH!!
!!?
WUMP...
...
DEAR CUSTOMERS!!
HOORAY
PLEASE! ENJOY YOUR MEALS!!
Yay
hoot
yay
yay
yay
yay
bravo
yay
GRRRG
GRRMB
TUNK
EAT.
WUMP...!
GRR!!
ERRRRG!

TO BE CONTINUED IN *ONE PIECE*, VOL. 6!

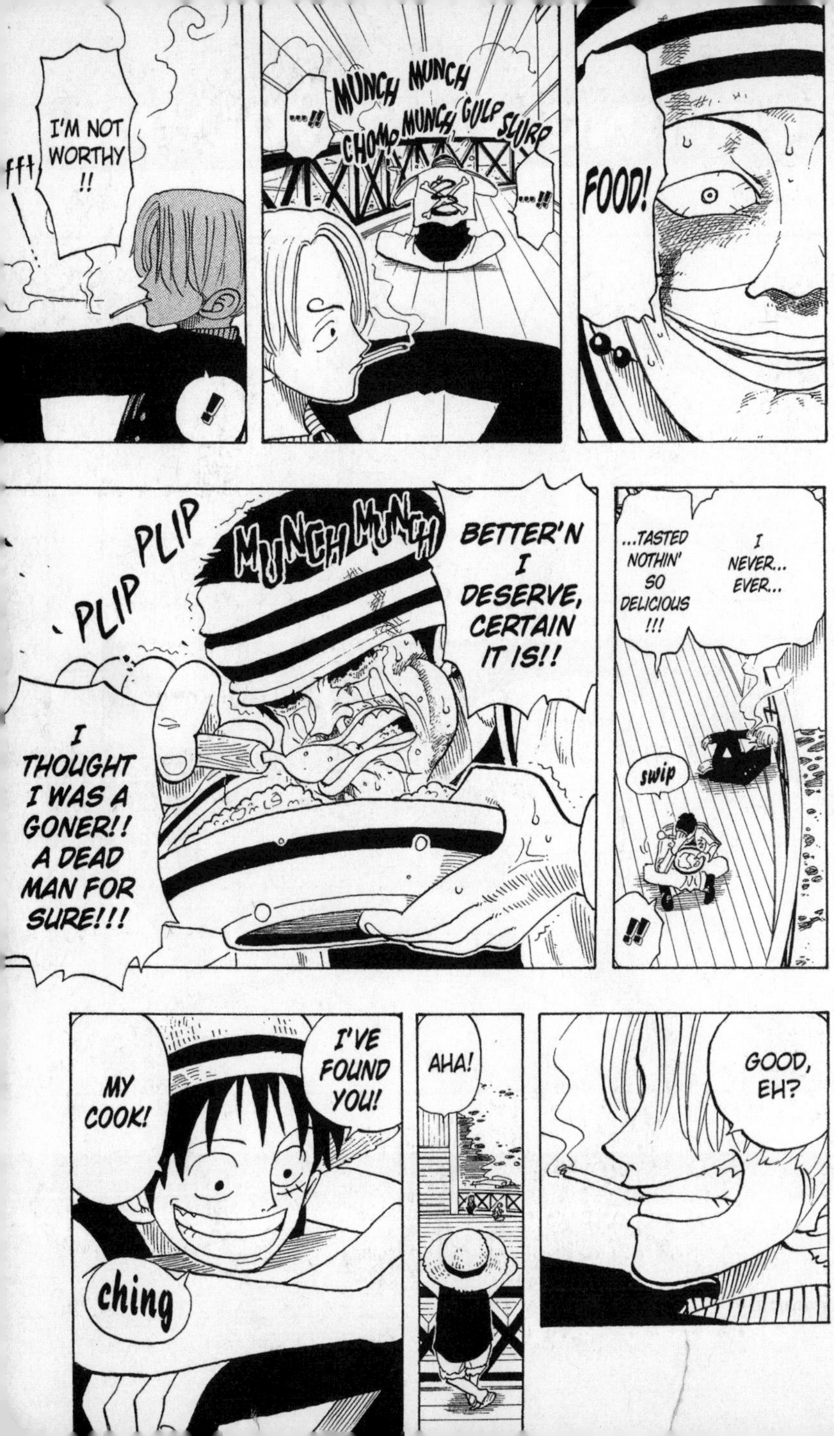
FOOD!
MUNCH MUNCH
CHOMP MUNCH GULP SLURP
...!!
...!!
I'M NOT WORTHY !!
fff
!
I NEVER... EVER...
...TASTED NOTHIN' SO DELICIOUS !!!
swip
!!
BETTER'N I DESERVE, CERTAIN IT IS!!
MUNCH MUNCH
PLIP PLIP PLIP
I THOUGHT I WAS A GONER!! A DEAD MAN FOR SURE!!!
GOOD, EH?
AHA!
I'VE FOUND YOU!
MY COOK!
ching

COMING NEXT VOLUME:

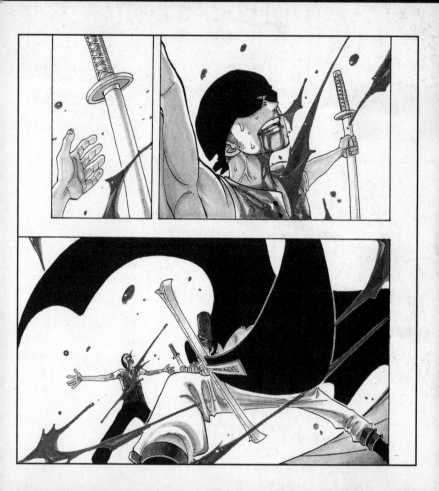

There's more trouble on the Baratie when Sanji meets up with the one member of Luffy's crew that he's interested in joining forces with… Nami! Meanwhile, Krieg's men battle the Baratie for a decent meal and Zolo encounters the challenge of a lifetime

You're Reading in the Wrong Direction!!

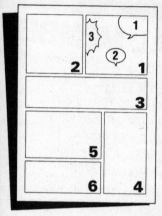

Whoops! Guess what? You're starting at the wrong end of the comic!

…It's true! In keeping with the original Japanese format, **One Piece** is meant to be read from right to left, starting in the upper-right corner.

Unlike English, which is read from left to right, Japanese is read from right to left, meaning that action, sound effects and word-balloon order are completely reversed… something which can make readers unfamiliar with Japanese feel pretty backwards themselves. For this reason, manga or Japanese comics published in the U.S. in English have sometimes been published "flopped"—that is, printed in exact reverse order, as though seen from the other side of a mirror.

By flopping pages, U.S. publishers can avoid confusing readers, but the compromise is not without its downside. For one thing, a character in a flopped manga series who once wore in the original Japanese version a T-shirt emblazoned with "M A Y" (as in "the merry month of") now wears one which reads "Y A M"! Additionally, many manga creators in Japan are themselves unhappy with the process, as some feel the mirror-imaging of their art skews their original intentions.

We are proud to bring you Eiichiro Oda's **One Piece** in the original unflopped format. For now, though, turn to the other side of the book and let the journey begin…!

—Editor